The Work of Democracy

The Work of Democracy

Ralph Bunche, Kenneth B. Clark,
Lorraine Hansberry, and the
Cultural Politics of Race

BEN KEPPEL

Harvard University Press   Cambridge, Massachusetts   London, England   1995

To my public school teachers, 1968–1992

Library of Congress Cataloging-in-Publication Data
Keppel, Ben.
    The work of democracy : Ralph Bunche, Kenneth B. Clark, Lorraine
Hansberry, and the cultural politics of race / Ben Keppel.
       p.   cm.
    Includes bibliographical references and index.
    ISBN 0-674-95843-8 (alk. paper)
    1. Afro-Americans—Civil rights.   2. Bunche, Ralph J. (Ralph
Johnson), 1904–1971.   3. Clark, Kenneth Bancroft, 1914–   .
4. Hansberry, Lorraine, 1930–1965.   5. Political culture—United
States—History—20th century.   6. United States—Race relations.
7. Civil rights movements—United States—History—20th century.
I. Title.
E185.61.K39   1995
305.8′00973—dc20

94-20606
     CIP

Contents

Representatives, Representations, and the Cultural Politics of Race   1

To paint the picture of how we live . . . is to compete with mighty artists:
the movies, the radio, the newspapers, the magazines, and even the Church.
They have painted one picture: charming, idyllic, romantic; but we live
another: full of the fear of the Lords of the Land, bowing and grinning
when we meet white faces, toiling from sun to sun, living in unpainted
wooden shacks that sit casually and insecurely upon the red clay.

    —Richard Wright (1941)

The process by which Americans have sought either to avoid or to come
to terms with the fact of racism in American life is the single most
important theme in the history of the United States. *The Work of Democracy* examines the chapter in this struggle that began during the Great
Depression and Franklin Delano Roosevelt's New Deal and ended at the
peak of American affluence with the demise of Lyndon Johnson's Great
Society.

    During these years, the symbolic significance of the African-American
was transformed. Before the Second World War, the "Negro" was largely
invisible in the nation's popular culture, except as a bulge-eyed and
stuttering fool, admired only for an alleged "simplicity." By the late
1940s the image of the African-American was being gradually recast
into a more positive stereotype, embodied in the poised and dignified
celluloid image of Sidney Poitier, as the quintessential American, whose
struggle for freedom is the essence of the nation's destiny and higher
purpose.

    Underlying this revolution in image and sensibility was an equally
important assumption: that the economic, social, and political status of
African-Americans was the most accurate reflection, at any given time,
of the condition of American democracy. The emergence of this belief
is as significant as the legal and legislative achievements of the postwar
civil rights movement, and deserves closer scrutiny.

This cultural transformation is both the essence of the postwar civil rights movement and its most profound legacy. It is what Martin Luther King, Jr., meant when he argued in 1963 that the achievement of racial equality was but one aspect of a larger enterprise that he called "the work of democracy."[1] Once civil rights had been won, King argued, the final stage of the work of democracy would be to unite all Americans, regardless of race, in the reconstruction of American society into a truly social, economic, and political democracy.[2] Such a revolution as King envisioned requires a cultural mobilization to both achieve and legitimate desired changes.

In this book, I examine the public lives of United Nations diplomat Ralph Bunche, social scientist Kenneth Clark, and playwright Lorraine Hansberry to reflect upon this watershed period in American cultural politics. By the phrase "cultural politics," I am referring to the processes of public contest and debate by which the members of a culture rearrange and reconstruct the key words, symbols, and icons that constitute its brick and mortar. This process of representational transformation embodies two separate, but intertwined, goals: the collective attempt to gain coherence in the midst of rapidly changing historical realities, and the attempt by shifting combinations of individuals and groups to impose a direction on how these changing historical realities will play out.[3]

My first concern is with the way in which each of my subjects worked creatively with the active themes and symbols of the existing political culture to enlarge the application and significance of certain common meanings, while simultaneously forging new ones. My second aim is to illuminate how, over time, each of these individuals themselves became symbols: shorthand representations of the integrationist solution to American race relations.

While Bunche, Clark, and Hansberry served as public faces of "the Negro experience" to white America, their representative status also symbolized more than this: as the emphasis of racial discourse and the backdrop against which it was projected changed, their images came also to evoke the varying ideological contexts within which "enlightened" Americans came to think about American race relations. Bunche, Clark, and Hansberry were each skilled in making use of finite—and perishable—resources of cultural contestation, and realized that their voices gained power at particular moments in the national discourse over racial injustice. In turn, it was out of these cultural convergences that they found themselves being cast by the mainstream media into icons of the American struggle to achieve racial equality. As participant-symbols in the cultural politics of this era, Bunche, Clark, and Hansberry each entered what their colleague Ralph Ellison described as "that area of the national life where political power is institutionalized and translated into democratic ritual and national style."[4]

Historically, the black American had been fated to exist in the public imagination chiefly as a crudely drawn symbol of social pathology. "This is why," James Baldwin argues,

> his progress, his relationship to all other Americans has been kept in the social arena. He is a social and not a personal or a human problem; to think of him is to think of statistics, slums, rapes, injustices, remote violence; it is to be confronted with an endless cataloguing of losses, gains, skirmishes; it is to feel virtuous, outraged, helpless, as though his continuing status among us were somehow analogous to disease— cancer, perhaps, or tuberculosis—which must be checked, even though it cannot be cured. In this arena the black acquires quite another aspect from that which he has in life. We do not know what to do with him in life; if he breaks our sociological and sentimental image of him we are panic-stricken and we feel ourselves betrayed.[5]

In the early 1930s, James Weldon Johnson, former executive secretary of the National Association for the Advancement of Colored People (NAACP), called upon African-Americans to "rear a group of Negro American writers and artists who can smash the old stereotypes, and replace them with newer and truer ones."[6] The emergence of Richard Wright, Chester Himes, and Gwendolyn Brooks in the thirties and forties and, among others, Ann Petry, Ralph Ellison, Margaret Walker, James Baldwin, and Lorraine Hansberry in the fifties and sixties constituted the rich fulfillment of this hope.

Indeed, the cultural politics that surrounded, mediated, interpreted, and broadcast these and other developments did produce new stereotypes of African-Americans. The Sambo image would be replaced by representations that, while affirmative, were often as one-dimensional—and as confining and obscuring of individuality, complexity, and genuine dignity—as had been their malevolent predecessor.[7] This is the territory I explore in the pages that follow.

The Social Foundations of a Cultural Politics

A cultural politics requires a social base to give it life. In the case at hand, several key ideological, demographic, economic, and intellectual developments during the first third of the twentieth century shook loose certain stabilizing elements of the cultural status quo. Chief among these changes were the Great Migration, the demolition of social scientific support for racist doctrines, and the election of a federal government that was receptive to, if not directly supportive of, significant social reform. In addition, the rise of the mass media produced new forms of public discourse.

The cultural politics that eventually brought forward Ralph Bunche, Kenneth Clark, and Lorraine Hansberry as participant-symbols of racial equality began to take form during the Great Depression, with its final shape cast from the ideological terms of the Second World War and the Cold War that followed. The accelerating industrialization of the North to meet the demands of two world wars, as well as the continuing economic and social stagnation of the South, sparked a "great migration" of 6.5 million African-Americans northward between 1910 and 1970. As Nicholas Lemann observes, "the great black migration made race a national issue in the second half of the [twentieth] century—an integral part of the politics, the social thought, and the organization of ordinary life in the United States."[8]

The Great Migration was not merely a reflexive abandonment of Southern poverty and racism in favor of greater income and the hope (although not the realization) that greater tolerance would be found in the North; it also bespoke the emergence of a more pointedly assertive and visible "New Negro" who would no longer be content to accept a historically predetermined place at the bottom of American society. Alain Locke, the tribune of the New Negro and of the Harlem Renaissance, wrote with characteristic prescience in 1933:

Large masses of the Negro population have been subjected to the galvanizing shocks of change and have thus been stimulated to rapid progress. Because of the new concentrations in city areas, there has been a marked heightening of the sense of group solidarity and common interests. This will prove to be the most powerful factor in the whole situation, if ever the exigencies of Negro life should demand large-scale mass action. And if the present heavy social and economic pressure on the Negro should increase, or even be maintained, such demands will undoubtedly arise.[9]

These crosscurrents of possibility and repression sharpened the face that African-Americans showed to the white "mainstream." One of the most important signs of this change was the emergence of the prizefighter Joe Louis as an African-American icon of power and resistance, especially among working class youth. As one Washington, DC, high school senior told the sociologist E. Franklin Frazier in 1940, "For years whites have kicked Negroes about and I'm happy somebody came along who could kick the stuffing out of the toughest 'hombres' the whites could put up against him . . . I think he's [sic] important for Negroes to feel that one of their kind . . . could excel . . . against the best white competition . . . Despite all the odds, he succeeded. That's the test of a man's ability and courage." Or, as another boy succinctly put it: "That's one Negro white men respect." The success of the Brown Bomber, Frazier wrote, enabled working class youth to "inflict vicariously the aggressions which they would like to carry out against whites for the discrimination and insults which they have suffered."[10] A generation later, Lawrence Levine reminded us of how Joe Louis symbolized the demand of African-Americans that "they be accepted in American society not merely as Americans but as black Americans, not merely as individuals but as a people."[11]

The intellectual consensus on race was also moving in a new direction. During the 1920s and 1930s, social scientists—many of whom were themselves European immigrants—had largely destroyed the intellectual and scientific basis for racism.[12] The New Deal allied itself with these efforts; as Richard Weiss has argued, the federal government actively participated in promoting the idea that America was a "nation of nations" rather than an Anglo-Saxon enclave.[13] A world war against an explicitly race-conscious fascism finally transformed the toleration of racism as an indelible feature of American life into a national disgrace. It followed that the responsibility of every American was to eradicate racism in favor of democracy and social justice.

The Second World War obliterated distances between continents and peoples. The world was now an ideologically divided and economically polarized global village, with the United States its most powerful member. It was also a community in which human rights and self-determination would become paramount concerns. The Cold War between the United States and the Soviet Union would serve as the most sustained context in which the persistence of American racism was broadcast instantly to every corner of the world—as evidence of hypocrisy in the "land of the free." As Americans stepped forward to offer lessons in democracy to the rest of the world, the attendant global scrutiny raised uncomfortable questions about how well Americans had learned those lessons themselves.

The mass media broadcast and magnified this social, cultural, and political revolution across the nation. During the opening decades of the twentieth century, the popular press was joined by other communication forms—radio, motion pictures, newsreels, and photo magazines such as *Life* and *Look.* The most powerful and ubiquitous of all these instruments was television, which entered popular culture in 1948. These mass media were prerequisites for the emergence of modern participant-symbols and the attendant cultural politics discussed in this book.[14] To an extent unprecedented in history, these media had the capacity to create instant icons and cultural heroes, though these figures' time in the spotlight was often fleeting.[15]

This communications revolution was by no means limited to the white media. As Theodore G. Vincent notes, one of the consequences of the Great Migration was that the black press was transformed "from an institution for the cultured elite into a mass media organ for all black people."[16] "Hundreds of thousands who formerly read nothing," James Weldon Johnson declared in 1934, "today read the Negro periodicals." As a result, Johnson concluded, "the Negro press as a racial agency is today second only to the Negro church in the number of people reached and influenced."[17]

As we shall see, the black press played an important role in creating the public arena into which Bunche, Clark, and Hansberry would enter as symbols of a "new Americanism." Bunche's scholarly triumphs, for instance, were announced to African-Americans around the nation long before he became a household name in white America. As with Bunche, Clark's academic accomplishments, his research into the origins of racial stereotyping, and the pioneering community work he undertook with his wife, Mamie Phipps Clark, at the Northside Center for Child Development were picked up first by the black press. African-American publications also played a vocal and important part in transforming Lorraine Hansberry into the "civil rights playwright."

In addition to being subjects of the black press, both Clark and Hansberry began their careers by helping to shape this new and vital medium. As the student editor of the Howard *Hilltop,* Clark refashioned a previously staid organ of college social life and athletic exploits into a controversial voice that participated in the political and economic debates of the 1930s. As a writer for Paul Robeson's *Freedom* in the early 1950s, Hansberry fought to keep African-American political discussions from narrowing too quickly into conversations about achieving empty paper concessions and mere "civil rights."

The strategic importance of American race relations led to the discovery of Bunche, Clark, and Hansberry by the white press. These formative participant-symbols of a new Americanism that held diversity and pluralism at its center were held up as proof to the world that the American change of heart on race was indeed genuine and permanent. That Bunche, Clark, and Hansberry were situated within the parameters of a redefined Americanism did not mean that they surrendered their differences in order to become submerged within an already constituted mainstream. On the contrary, these three individuals meant to take the nation at its word when it talked of Americanism, and, by appropriating the symbolic phrases of this discourse, they intended to carry the statement "all men are created equal and are endowed by their Creator with certain inalienable rights" to its full democratic and egalitarian conclusion.

In the world challenged by Joe Louis, to be American required that one deny the racism at the nation's core. Bunche, Clark, and Hansberry did not merely wish to append that fact to the national memory: they meant to redefine Americanism according to the implications of this sad history and thereby redraw the boundaries of political possibility.

In so doing, they hoped that the foundation for a solidarity beyond race would be laid down, and that the need to differentiate between being merely American and being African-American would be obliterated. They hoped that American culture would be inclusive enough—and honest enough—about the undemocratic and racist chapters in its past to create an Americanism capable of honoring in full measure the "American Negro." The pursuit of such goals would be a formidable challenge at any time. To take on this task in the midst of a politically and culturally restrictive Cold War, as these three did, was especially audacious.

The Stereotyping of Racial Equality

We are indebted to a whole generation of historians—from George Fredrickson and Winthrop Jordan to Alexander Saxton and Gary Nash—for a comprehensive understanding of the ways in which racism has been variously constituted in American popular culture.[18] However, we have yet to explore systematically what might well be thought of as the stereotypes of popular postwar racial liberalism. Examining the public lives of Bunche, Clark, and Hansberry allows us to examine the cultural politics by which the achievement of racial equality was transformed into a transcendentally American objective. The vehicle for achieving this change in public sympathies was that of the role model, or participant-symbol. Such participant-symbols were living, tangible—albeit at times ambivalent—monuments to the possibility that the nation could attain racial equality.

The clearest way of understanding the role that Bunche, Clark, and Hansberry played in this complex cultural process is to consider their public lives in relation to an earlier historical case, namely the cultural role that Henry Louis Gates, Jr., ascribes to Frederick Douglass in the racial discourse of the nineteenth century: that of serving as the "representative colored man of the United States." Douglass, Gates argues, was representative not in the sense that he depicted "the mean, the mode or the median of the Afro-American community of the nineteenth century"; rather, "Douglass was the representative colored man in the United States because he was the most presentable. When Douglass spoke, when Douglass wrote, he did so 'for' the Negro, in relation of part for whole. He spoke to recreate the face of the race, its public face." In Gates's view, Douglass was "the most representative colored man . . . because he was the race's great opportunity to re-present itself in the court of racist public opinion."[19] In the prime of their public lives, Bunche, Clark, and Hansberry (like Jackie Robinson, Ralph Ellison, James Baldwin, and Gwendolyn Brooks) would each perform a role similar to that performed by Douglass: acting, albeit in more hospitable times, as updated versions of the presentable face of a people whom the dominant cultural imagination had, for centuries, quite literally defaced.

Bunche, Clark, and Hansberry became symbols as the result of the cultural politics that had been created by two world wars and the Great Migration. The substance and boundaries of this cultural politics were publicly announced by Gunnar Myrdal in *An American Dilemma,* his two-volume indictment of racial injustice in the United States sponsored by the Carnegie Foundation. Myrdal presented what was rapidly crystallizing as the official explanation of the impact of World War II on American life: "What has actually happened within the last few years is not only that the Negro problem has become national in scope . . . It has also acquired tremendous international implications . . . The situation is actually such that any and all concessions to Negro rights in this phase of the history of the world will repay the nation many times, while any and all injustices inflicted upon him will be extremely costly."[20] Myrdal's book served as an intellectual marker of the conventional wisdom concerning where Americans had been and where they must now go, and the public lives of Bunche, Clark, and Hansberry were understood by the postwar media as falling within the intellectual outlines of Myrdal's famous primer.[21]

Bunche, for example, not only articulated, but eventually came to personify, a nation newly sensitized to its world-historical mission to resolve the "American dilemma" and thus to truly earn its position as the exemplar of democratic pluralism. Myrdal's advocacy of a comprehensive role for social science in the repair of American democracy was taken over by Clark in the years after *Brown v. Board of Education,* the decision that officially banished "separate but equal" schooling from

American public life. Myrdal's belief in the pull of the individualistic "American creed" was embedded in the foundation of Hansberry's *A Raisin in the Sun,* one of the boldest critiques of what Hansberry called the "American Way" to appear in the Cold War era.

Although the social and cultural roles performed by a participant-symbol readily confer an unusual degree of influence, it is a position more accurately defined by the limits it imposes. The experiences of Bunche, Clark, and Hansberry illustrate the point. While Bunche certainly interpreted his life story as powerful confirmation of the Alger ethic, he did not intend that this should be the *only* lesson that the public should draw from it. At the height of the post–World War II Red Scare, for example, Bunche was more concerned with exemplifying and articulating an Americanism that was unashamedly inclusive and accepting of difference. This aspect of Bunche's public life was, however, overwhelmed by the image of Bunche as a latter-day Horatio Alger promoted in the press.

A similar fate met Hansberry ten years later. While her leftist political ideology kept her from being transformed into an icon by the mainstream media of 1959, her much-heralded play, *A Raisin in the Sun,* was another matter: Hansberry was believed to have penned a universal evocation of the American dream. What the critics missed was Hansberry's fidelity to the difficulty and the tragedy of recent African-American experience. *Raisin* was, among other things, an impressive historical document of the Great Migration and how it had quite literally moved every aspect of African-American life.

Though Clark's words as a social science expert were not as often filtered through as distorted an interpretive screen as were Bunche's and Hansberry's, he nonetheless came to doubt the efficacy of his chosen public role as "psychologist to society." In the turbulent decade and a half following *Brown v. Board,* Clark came to believe that, in the final analysis, most white Americans were insincere in their professed allegiance to racial equality, and that no authoritative disclosure about the rampant violence and want existing within the American "dark ghetto" could alter this mind-set.

The experiences of these three figures differ in specific detail, but they speak with an unmistakable unanimity about how the underlying cultural politics of the Cold War, though strategically helpful to the advancement of civil rights in some ways, operated in others to limit the work of democracy.

In studying these three individuals, I intend first to locate the impetus each felt toward public life and to identify the cultural categories within which they came to place their own life stories and from which they constructed public programs. My second goal is to examine how each individual felt about the most important representations of them put forward by others.

Individuals and societies engage in the search for usable pasts because identifying such pasts is essential to the renewal of the individual and the collective sense of self. To fully understand their public lives, we must try first to identify the key events and interpretations of events from which Bunche, Clark, and Hansberry drew the social significance of their experiences as African-Americans. What events served as the interpretive basis for the texts that they would create about themselves, and about society? Which events became stories chosen by the media to explain their lives to others?

Ralph Bunche: The Local Training of a Goodwill Ambassador

Out of the anti-colonialist and anti-Nazi thrust of the Allied war effort— and the memory of the failed peace that had followed World War I— the United Nations emerged as the symbol and guarantor of a world order based on equality and self-determination. Ralph Bunche's successful negotiation of an end to the first Arab-Israeli war in 1949 was widely interpreted as a vindication of the United Nations as an institution, and of the hopes that had brought it into being. Bunche's feat proved that the United Nations could fulfill its peacekeeping mandate; indeed, the very fact of a "Negro-American" as a high-ranking diplomat and troubleshooter at the UN confirmed for many that a new era in human history was indeed under way.

That the new postwar order came to be represented through the experiences and biography of Bunche was the work of both the UN public relations operation and sympathetic journalists in America and abroad. This process of personalization was most extensive in the United States.

The Ralph Bunche story, as told in magazine feature stories and a 1954 teleplay, was a composite of some of the most powerful aspirations in postwar popular culture: an appetite for models of African-American achievement, American internationalism, and the universal application of the Horatio Alger myth. The single blemish on Bunche's ideological record—a vocal flirtation with Marxism in the mid-1930s—was one that he shared with many others who would occupy the "vital center" in the forties and fifties.

In Bunche, both the mainstream white and the African-American press also had an ideal embodiment of Cold War liberalism. During the late 1940s—years when significant dissent against the postwar Red Scare could still be heard—Bunche was often called upon to confirm that Paul Robeson and W. E. B. Du Bois represented "the attitudes of very few Negroes indeed" and to affirm that "Negroes" harbored "no . . . nationalist or separatist ambitions."[22] Bunche's humble origins also earned him official recognition as the winner of the American Schools and Colleges Association's Horatio Alger Award for 1952. Norman Vincent Peale, who chaired the awards committee, wrote that Bunche's "advance in the Horatio Alger tradition is indicative both of his personal greatness and [of] American opportunity that is always present here."[23]

What melded the biographical details of the Ralph Bunche story into a compelling and resonant cultural myth was its conformation to the American pattern of a rise from rags to riches. "I was born very much east of the railroad tracks in industrial Detroit," Ralph Bunche told an audience of the League for Industrial Democracy in 1951, "not only in and of the working class but in and of a racially disadvantaged American group as well."[24] Bunche's childhood—his family's migration to California as well his upbringing by his maternal grandmother Lucy Johnson—reached a wide audience through an admiring teleplay broadcast in prime time in 1954.

The narrative of Bunche's early years is but one piece of a far larger story of African-Americans on the move—culturally, intellectually, and physically—in determined pursuit of lives free of the marks of American oppression: slavery, sharecropping, and Jim Crow. Ralph Bunche (originally spelled Bunch) was born in Detroit, Michigan, on August 7, 1903.[25] Spurred by illness, personal tragedy, and the desire to secure an economic foothold in a region of the country not so bound to the dictates of Jim Crow, the family was on the move for much of the next several years, not settling down permanently until they reached Los Angeles in early 1917. As if to mark the close of this difficult and turbulent period in his early life—which had included the death of his mother and the disappearance of his father—and the beginning of a more hopeful chapter in the family's history, Bunch followed his grandmother's advice and marked the family's arrival in California by adding an "e" to his surname.[26]

In later life, after Bunche had become an icon of racial equality, these years would also provide the raw material for hagiographic celebrations of Bunche as an exemplar of a reinterpreted American experience. Journalists from the leading feature magazines of postwar America took great pleasure in repeating the story of Bunche's tragic early years as an orphan, and of his youth in Los Angeles as a star pupil who succeeded despite the fact that he was forced by harsh economic circumstances to work outside of school to support his family.[27] Bunche's public career began well before his graduation from UCLA in the spring of 1927. As one local booster wrote in a letter introducing Bunche to African-American leaders in the East: "He is a leader of young people in Los Angeles . . . [and] was one of the most popular of the undergraduates at the university this year, and has already made a definite contribution toward racial understanding by his scientific and friendly approach."[28]

As a leader of African-American youth whose academic exploits were occasionally mentioned in the pages of the NAACP journal *The Crisis,* Bunche received his first experience at diplomacy as a kind of goodwill ambassador to the older generation. "It occurs to me," the young Bunche told an assemblage of leaders of the Los Angeles African-American community in 1926 or 1927, "that the older and the younger generations are quite estranged. They live . . . in worlds apart."[29] Bunche approached this audience in the same way as he would so many others in his later public life: as a witness to, as well as a product of, a life lived in search of the fundamental, unifying values and experiences that underlay difference. As such, he was an ideal conduit for the "exchange of ideas."[30] The range of topics that this generational diplomat was willing to tackle is surprising indeed—world government, the psychology of human relations, the role of youth in arresting the subtle encroachments of Jim Crow in the public pools of his beloved Los Angeles ("Must we go on passively like lambs to the fold and accept such conditions . . . or should we rise up in a body to fight such an absurd action in a state which guarantees freedom and equality to all?"), and Bunche's favorite topic of the early years, the need for African-Americans to break loose from the "rut of single-track Republicanism or anything-else-ism."[31]

It is certainly no coincidence that Bunche's program as a goodwill ambassador bears a close resemblance to that presented in the pages of the *California Eagle*. The *Eagle,* as the primary vehicle for mobilizing the area's black community, would later play a key role in the local fund-raising campaign to send Ralph Bunche to Harvard. In its pages, the *Eagle* urged black citizens to adopt an attitude of political independence in a "Golden State [that] remains . . . the only state . . . where no recognition is accorded [Negroes]." The *Eagle* similarly advised its readers to maintain a vigilant outlook for slanders against the community or any other overtures to the enactment of Jim Crow "in this western country where . . . the sun shines three quarters of the year, where flowers bloom the whole year round."[32]

An equally important source of cultural resonance that had its origins in these years was Bunche's devout, pragmatic, and reformist internationalism, a cast of mind no doubt strengthened by the many undergraduate courses in foreign relations and international law that Bunche took as a scholarship student at UCLA.[33] Like many of the intellectuals of his generation, Bunche believed that the unfinished business of world affairs lay in the elaboration of the Wilsonian world order, a task to which he would devote most of his professional life.

One year before graduation, in the winning entry to a UCLA oratorical contest, Bunche submitted an uncompromising brief in favor of Wilsonian internationalism. Bunche saw Wilson's League of Nations and the World Court as "quite indispensable as initial steps in the inevitable banding together of all entities into an international body politic."[34] In response to doubters, Bunche, in language very close to that of the "cultural democracy" movement of the thirties and the Roosevelt-Willkie brand of progressive internationalism ascendant during the 1940s, submitted American federalism as exhibit A:

Right here on our own threshold we have developed a form of government which may well be adaptable to . . . international difficulties. Our original thirteen colonies were rent by social and economic rivalries, dislikes, distrusts and sectional jealousies, comparable in many respects to those prevalent among the nations of the world today. Nevertheless, common bonds of human interest drew them into a single political union in which their differences were dissolved, and from which there emerged our present great American commonwealth.[35]

As Bunche saw it, the great task of the next generation would not lie in institution-building, but rather on the infinitely more challenging plane of refashioning the human spirit. Exuding the Progressives' confidence in the capacity of trained and purposeful intelligence to perfect human arrangements, Bunche ventured that "we are but human vessels into which society pours the ingredients which make us character-possessing . . . individuals." This being the case, Bunche asks, "why . . . is it not possible for us to accomplish with human beings what Luther Burbank has done with horticultural specimens?"[36]

One year later, the valedictory address before the UCLA graduating class of 1927 provided Bunche with yet another occasion to elaborate upon what would become a lifelong theme: the imperative need for humanity's individual members to "become more *altruistic* and less selfish . . . *love* more and hate less [and] become more *internationally-minded*" (emphasis in the original). In a speech that would serve as the basis for his many public addresses from the 1940s through the early 1960s, Bunche called upon his classmates to cultivate the "fourth dimension of personality": the ability to "expand up and out from our narrow immediate world."[37]

To his family, and to the professional community that celebrated his accomplishments and backed his graduate career with its fund-raising drive to send Ralph Bunche to Harvard, Bunche was already a sort of local institution. As such, the young Bunche's future success would not only serve the broader interests of "the race," but would also symbolize the bright possibilities for African-Americans promised in the Golden West, a region where, though ethnic and racial tensions were high, Jim

Crow had not yet been systematically institutionalized.[38] Even in this early phase of his public life, Bunche demonstrated his ease in the role of goodwill diplomat and his fluency in the language of intercultural understanding—a language that would become ubiquitous in American political culture with the coming of the Second World War and the decades that followed.

Kenneth Clark: Apprenticeship of an Immigrant Integrationist

In the late 1930s the anthropologist Ruth Benedict, on the advice of her mentor, Franz Boas, took on his role as "social scientist to the public." The prime task entailed in this activist role was the refutation of racist social ideas, a task made more urgent by the fact that Hitler was marshaling state power in Europe's most "advanced" culture to exterminate the world's "inferior races." Provoked by this international threat, as well as by the fragile state of American democracy, Benedict and academic psychologists like Otto Klineberg, ably abetted by his fellow members of the Society for the Psychological Study of Social Issues (SPSSI), undertook a similar mobilization. The culmination of this campaign was the publication in 1944 of Gunnar Myrdal's instant classic, *An American Dilemma*. Like Ralph Bunche, his closest colleague in the preparation of *Dilemma*, Myrdal became affiliated with the United Nations, which, in Myrdal's case, removed him as an active participant in the domestic discourse on race and democracy that his book had done so much to codify and legitimate.

With the reintensification of racial protest in the early 1960s, psychologist Kenneth B. Clark became a "New Myrdal," achieving widespread recognition as one of the nation's leading authorities on race relations. Clark's analyses of the civil rights movement as it evolved from the Negro Revolt of the early sixties to the Black Power movement of the middle and late sixties were featured in a wide range of popular periodicals, including *Ebony, Esquire,* and *Psychology Today.* It was because of his status as an African-American "expert" that Clark emerged as a collective representative of black America.

Clark's work as the principal social science advisor to the NAACP Legal Defense and Education Fund, as well as his role in founding one of the nation's first and largest community action programs, established him as a prominent symbol of the pragmatic, activist social science of the Kennedy-Johnson years. *Life* magazine, for example, in a photo essay on the "action-intellectuals" of the Great Society, included a portrait of a bespectacled, pipe-smoking Clark. His iconic image was further enhanced when *Dark Ghetto,* his widely read 1965 study of his experiences as a community activist in Harlem, became an essential text in the first generation of Afro-American Studies courses.[39]

Embedded in Clark's early years are the origins of a social agenda that counted the public education system as a major force in the remaking of American society. For Clark, the New York City public schools introduced him, as a six-year-old immigrant from the Canal Zone, to both the possibilities promised by American democracy and the sharp boundaries that were part of its daily operation.

The Clarks, like the Johnsons, were a family on the move in an explicit search for greater vocational opportunity for the parents and better life opportunities for the children. The family of Miriam Hanson, Clark's mother, had moved from Kingston, Jamaica, to the Panama Canal Zone to open a dry goods store, which served the laborers building the canal.[40] Some years later, Miriam Hanson, now married to another transplanted Jamaican, Arthur Bancroft Clark, a cargo superintendent for the United Fruit Company, began looking toward another move, this time to the United States. Arthur Clark rejected the move after being warned by United Fruit that it would be unable to keep him in a job of comparable pay and status. This proved to be the last and most decisive of many disagreements between the two, and Miriam Hanson Clark, her two children in hand, left for New York City.[41]

Any discussion of the origins of Kenneth Clark's public life must begin with his arrival in a Harlem that was in demographic transition. The lessons that Clark drew from those years form the intuitive core of his social philosophy. Clark was five years old when he arrived at Harlem's P. S. 5 at 140th Street and Edgecombe Avenue. Although some of his early classmates and neighbors were African-Americans, most were the children of Jewish and Irish immigrants.

Miriam Hanson Clark provided another indispensable ingredient to her son's success. Like Bunche's "Nana," Miriam Clark encouraged in her son the belief that, with effort and education, a better life was attainable. In this, Miriam Clark had an ally in Marcus Garvey's Universal Negro Improvement Association, of which she was an active member for many years. At first glance, it might seem ironic that the mother of a man known as a leading integrationist might find solace in an organization whose program contained prominent elements of racialist thinking. However, as historian Robert A. Hill has argued, the rituals and rhetoric of racial pride of the Garvey movement were joined to a strong emphasis on economic striving, general self-improvement, and political engagement.[42] Upon their arrival in the United States, West Indian immigrants such as Miriam Clark entered a society that, unlike their own, was acutely race-conscious.[43] Not only did these new arrivals face a hostile majority white culture, but they encountered deep suspicion from native-born African-Americans as well.[44] In such a forbidding cultural environment, one in which the doctrines of Anglo-Saxon racial superiority were at least as inextricably American as the Horatio Alger myth, Miriam Clark, like other West Indian immigrants, saw Garvey as the "avangel of black success," a spiritual ally in the struggle upward.[45]

As a seamstress in New York's garment district, Miriam Clark's activism extended to her workplace, where she served as an organizer and shop steward for the International Ladies' Garment Workers Union. Her activism also directly served the advancement of her children. When she learned that her son, in spite of an excellent academic record, had been tracked to attend a vocational school instead of the excellently regarded George Washington High School, she personally and quite bluntly intervened.[46]

By the time of Clark's graduation from George Washington High School, the surrounding community had become predominantly African-American. The irony of living in an increasingly segregated community in which few if any of the positions of intellectual authority—such as teaching—were held by African-Americans convinced young Clark to forgo both the tuition-free City College of New York and the prestigious Columbia University (where he would, in fact, conclude his graduate work) in favor of Howard University, which was under the leadership of its first African-American president, Mordecai Johnson. At age seventeen, Kenneth Clark headed to the South, the historical home of African America, which he viewed as "an unknown, foreign land."[47] Clark's choice of Howard would prove to be rewarding for him, providing as it did an ideal staging ground for rehearsing the role of public activist.

Almost immediately upon his arrival on campus Clark met the professors who were "teaching a perspective on life and race" that would convince him that "disciplined intelligence could be an instrument for racial justice [and] social and economic justice." Meeting late at night over beer with his tutors—political scientist Ralph Bunche, economist Abram Harris, philosopher Alain Locke, and psychologist Francis C. Sumner—Clark became both a witness to, and a participant in, debates that held center stage among African-American intellectuals from the era of the Great Depression through the Second World War: Did the liberation of African America lie in class-based coalitions with white sharecroppers, day laborers, and industrial workers? Was such a coalition possible? Was the New Deal equal to the challenge? Or were the legal and otherwise reformist and racial strategies of the NAACP and the National Urban League still the most practical and effective vehicle toward equality?[48]

As a student leader widely recognized as "outspoken and democratic," Clark took the leading role in bringing these debates to the student body.[49] In the spring of 1933, the Howard student body elected Clark editor-in-chief of the student newspaper, the *Howard Hilltop*.[50] In addition to championing such traditional student issues as the need to allow press coverage of student government, and dispensing advice to incoming freshmen, Clark also argued for a franker discussion of current events and a more active assault on the social crisis of the Great Depression. In an editorial that reflected not only his mentor Bunche's dissatisfaction with the political economy of the New Deal but also the political scientist's fear that the economic crisis would be solved by rearmament and military adventurism, Clark attacked Roosevelt's program as consisting of little more than "presidential hypodermics" that might induce a "temporary positive reaction." Clark's real fear was the "scramble of war preparations indulged in by our ruthless . . . European and Asiatic neighbors." Clark predicted that such an arms race might well goad Roosevelt into increasing military spending, thus creating a deficit whose cost "will be borne by the same patient little taxpayer who will [also] be used as . . . fodder in the war toward which . . . the big-shots are so rapidly coasting."[51]

Such overtly political editorials had repercussions on campus, especially given that the university received a significant annual appropriation from Congress. Mordecai Johnson, a former Baptist minister whose considerable political skills had wrested a much-increased level of funding from a Depression-era Congress obsessed with austerity, was especially vigilant against campus activities that might undermine federal support.[52] The roles that Bunche and Harris allegedly played in promoting radicals on campus (they had been leading sponsors of a conference at Howard entitled "The Status of the Negro in the Economic Crisis," at which the New Deal was criticized by them and others) had already been scrutinized by congressional investigators.[53] It was testimony to Johnson's political resourcefulness that the university had so far escaped congressional retribution.

Clark's activism was not confined to the pages of the *Hilltop*. In his senior year he barely escaped expulsion for his role in leading the Howard Twenty, a group of students who staged a sit-in on Capitol Hill to protest Jim Crow in the eateries there. After reading extensive newspaper coverage in the *Washington Post* as well as the *New York Times,* Johnson moved again to forestall congressional opponents. He offered to expel Clark and to deny him a degree. After a lengthy secret disciplinary hearing, the threatened expulsion was dropped. Clark credited Bunche with saving his diploma.[54]

An education at Howard University in the 1930s offered Clark a broad intellectual framework. It would be a collaboration with another Howard undergraduate, however—Mamie Phipps of Hot Springs, Arkansas—that would provide him with a practical vehicle for translating this framework into specific social action. Equally important, Mamie Phipps became Clark's most direct connection to the experience of southern African-Americans.

Phipps was the daughter of Harold H. Phipps, a physician, and Katy Florence Phipps. As a medical doctor, Harold Phipps was an esteemed member of the community; despite her father's respected class position, however, Mamie Phipps was still forced to attend the town's vastly inferior "colored" school. Nor did her social position protect Phipps from an early exposure to the violence underlying such racist social arrangements. Among her most deeply etched memories, from age six, was that of a mob of Klansmen from Little Rock who brought their victim to the edge of Hot Springs and lynched him. Eleven years later, in the fall of 1934, Phipps, unlike the self-confident New Yorker she would soon meet and marry, was forced to travel to college in the dark of a railway car with drawn curtains. At Howard, Phipps found herself consistently being bested by the better educated and intellectually assertive students from northern schools; as a result, she spent the following summer at Howard making up academic deficiencies. Phipps's later decision to stay on for a master's degree at Howard to study the origins and consolidation of racial consciousness came directly from these experiences—experiences far different from the formative training that had allowed Kenneth Clark to join the staff of the *Hilltop* in his first semester.[55]

In his excellent popular history of the *Brown* decision, *Simple Justice,* Richard Kluger refers to Kenneth Clark as the "doll man," the psychological expert whose experiments using dolls to test the level of racial self-awareness in African-American children were perhaps the most important nonlegal testimony presented to the Supreme Court. It was Mamie Clark, however, a daughter of the South and a witness to its caste system, rather than Kenneth Clark, socialized in the more subtle, if no less brutal, racial etiquette of Harlem, who designed them. Mamie Clark would be the influential if publicly silent partner in Kenneth Clark's effort in the early 1960s to act as the public interpreter of a new chapter in the American racial crisis: one that was predominantly urban and Northern.

Lorraine Hansberry:
Early Lessons of the Civil Rights Playwright

Lorraine Hansberry's *A Raisin in the Sun* was embraced as a social watershed and a dramatic classic when it debuted on Broadway on March 11, 1959. Entering the national consciousness less than two years after the heroic stand of the Little Rock Nine and less than one year before the Southern sit-ins sponsored by the Student Nonviolent Coordinating Committee launched a decade of political activism and social reform, *A*

Raisin in the Sun was christened as the quintessential "civil rights play." As the story of an African-American family's struggle against the ghetto and the numerous ways in which a check for $10,000 complicates and intensifies, rather than resolves, these struggles, *Raisin* was as misinterpreted as it was praised. As the critical mainstream interpreted the play, the decision of the family matriarch to use a large portion of this money (the benefits from her late husband's life insurance policy) to buy a house in a white neighborhood represented an appealing and reassuring sense of what integration would entail.

Raisin quickly transformed Hansberry into a leading cultural figure. At twenty-eight years of age, Hansberry had already served nearly a decade in the battle against McCarthyism as a close ally of actor-activist Paul Robeson, the best-known African-American victim of the Red Scare. With the financial and critical success of her first play serving as a legitimating platform, Hansberry endeavored to continue the political work that Robeson had begun, but that had become severely impeded by the United States government's harassment of him. In the end, however, *Raisin* was all that most Americans would ever know about Hansberry, who died of cancer in January of 1965 at the age of thirty-four. Within a very few years, as intellectuals sought to incorporate the lessons of the antiwar and civil rights movements into their teaching about the American experience, *Raisin*'s historical reputation would fall. Rather than being perceived as a radical in the Du Bois–Robeson tradition, Hansberry was written off as the creator of a politically retrograde and aesthetically derivative sop that made the civil rights movement seem unthreatening to middle-class whites.

This interpretation of Hansberry was a profound disservice to her, and an equally unfortunate oversimplification of the content of her best-known drama. Far from being a celebration of assimilationism, *Raisin* reflects Hansberry's deep awareness of the conflicts within the African-American community that, in a few years, would burst out into the open. For an avowedly political drama, *Raisin* is notable for the subtleties it portrays and the ambivalences to which it gives expression. For instance, Hansberry did not pretend that the Younger family's ultimate decision to move to Clayborn Park solved anything beyond proving the great courage of her characters. The story line gives every indication that the resistance of their would-be neighbors looms large in the near future. The oft-repeated claim (more fully explored in Chapter 6) that *Raisin* is a happy-ending, Horatio Alger story of ethnic arrival tells more about the blinders worn by American critics in the late 1950s than it does about the subject of *A Raisin in the Sun.*

To fully understand *Raisin* and its author requires an understanding of the connection that Hansberry drew between her life and her art and politics. She was the last of four children born to Carl A. and Nantille L. Hansberry of Chicago's Southside on May 19, 1930. Originally from Mississippi and Tennessee, respectively, the elder Hansberrys had settled in Chicago as part of the Great Migration.

Carl A. Hansberry was a key figure in the founding of one of Chicago's first black banks and, in 1936, established Hansberry Enterprises, a real estate syndicate that, by 1941, controlled property housing four thousand families and was worth in excess of $250,000.[56] An unfinished autobiographical essay by Lorraine Hansberry included in *To Be Young, Gifted, and Black* (a posthumous collage of her work) leaves the strong impression that she was ambivalent about the fact that she came from the black bourgeoisie, outside the "Rooseveltian atmosphere of the thirties." Hansberry was moved, for instance, to follow the statement that her father had "amassed a fortune" with the parenthetical qualification that "he had done nothing of the kind . . . [He] had simply become a reasonably successful businessman of the middle class."[57]

Carl Hansberry was the dominant figure in the Hansberry household, "a man who seemed always to be doing something so brilliant and/or unusual that to be doing something brilliant and/or unusual was the way I assumed fathers behaved," Lorraine Hansberry later reflected. Carl Hansberry's activities extended well beyond entrepreneurial pursuits. As one who "believed that the 'American Way' could be made to work," Hansberry pursued political reform as one of the few remaining black Republican candidates for Congress in an era that found African-Americans turning to the Democratic Party; he also sought legal redress under the auspices of the Hansberry Foundation.[58] At its helm, Hansberry invested much of his wealth in a campaign to "encourage and promote respect for all laws, especially those as related to the civil rights of American citizens."[59]

It was in this capacity that Carl Hansberry mounted a challenge to the racially exclusionary housing covenants that had prevented the family's move from the Southside to the Hyde Park section of Chicago. Hansberry won what amounted to merely a symbolic victory from the Supreme Court in the 1943 case of *Hansberry v. Lee,* for enforcement of the decision proved to be impossible. Hansberry's victory, however, did bring results of a different kind: it brought him to the attention of the Federal Bureau of Investigation. In a memo written for J. Edgar Hoover, Hansberry's work as a successful businessman and as an "ardent supporter" of the NAACP was noted.[60] In 1945, Carl Hansberry, who by then had moved to Mexico, died of a cerebral hemorrhage; his youngest daughter later concluded that "American racism helped kill him."[61] Such elements as these in Lorraine Hansberry's early life provided some of the animating tensions of *Raisin.*

Carl Hansberry's entrepreneurial drive, as well as his willingness to contest the barriers preventing the full enjoyment of American democracy by blacks, forms the template for the character of Walter Lee in *Raisin.* The play was dedicated, however, not to Carl Hansberry, but "to Mama: in gratitude for the dream." Perhaps this was a tribute to Nantille Hansberry for her heroic effort to keep the family together during the legal fight over *Hansberry v. Lee.* As Lorraine Hansberry told the *New Yorker* in the spring of 1959, "My mother is a remarkable woman, with great courage. She sat with us in that house [that her father had bought in a white neighborhood] for eight months—while Daddy spent most of his time in Washington fighting his case—in what was, to put it mildly, a very hostile neighborhood." Recalling the traumatic events of her life that became the basis for *Raisin,* Hansberry continued, "I was on the porch one day with my sister, when a mob gathered. We went inside, and while we were in our living room, a brick came crashing through the window with such force that it embedded itself in the opposite wall. I was the one the brick almost hit."[62]

To say that Hansberry drew on these early experiences in her later life is not to say that she followed in the steps of her parents; in many respects the journey she charted for herself took quite a different course. Hansberry dramatized her realization of the need to construct an understanding of life at odds with that of her parents by casting a particular moment of her childhood as marking the crucial divide: her first day of kindergarten, when she was sent to school in a mink coat. As Hansberry recounted the episode, she was promptly roughed up by a group of class-mates, the offending coat stained with ink. Writing with third-person detachment, Hansberry recalled: "Ever since then she had been antago-nistic to symbols of affluence. In fact, from that day she had chosen her friends from among her assailants."[63]

In a sense, her eventual acceptance by these children marked the be-ginning of her long journey away from the comforts of class offered by her family. Neither her parents' decision to leave the South nor their wealth, social prominence, and political activism were sufficient to in-sulate Hansberry from the experience of the ghetto. In an account of her years at Betsy Ross Elementary School, Hansberry writes:

It was *not* an old building but, on the contrary, a relatively new and modern one. Its substandard quality had been planned from the drawing board. From its inception Betsy Ross had been earmarked as a ghetto school, a school for black children, and, therefore, one in which as many things as possible might be safely thought of as "ex-pendable." That, after all, was why it existed: not to give education but to withhold as much as possible, just as the ghetto itself exists not to give people homes but to cheat them out of as much decent housing as possible.

I was given . . . one-half the amount of education prescribed by the Board of Education. This was so because the children of the Chicago ghetto were jammed into a segregated school system. I am a product of that system and one result is that—to this day—I cannot count properly. I cannot add, subtract or multiply with ease. Our teachers, devoted and indifferent alike, had to sacrifice something to make the system work at all—and in my case it was arithmetic that got put aside most often. Thus, the mind which was able to grasp university-level reading materials in the sixth and seventh grades had not been sufficiently exposed to elementary arithmetic to make even simple change in a grocery store.

This is what is meant when we speak of the scars, the marks that the ghettoized child carries through life. To be imprisoned in the

ghetto is to be forgotten—or deliberately cheated of one's birthright—
at best.[64]

Immediately upon her graduation from Chicago's Englewood High
School (from which the Pulitzer Prize–winning poet Gwendolyn Brooks
had graduated fourteen years earlier) in January 1948, Hansberry continued her education at the University of Wisconsin. In a lightly novel-
ized account of her experiences in college, Hansberry recalled that her
academic career in Madison "had begun awkwardly and it had stayed
that way." Two years later, Hansberry left the University of Wisconsin
to pursue a career on the staff of Paul Robeson and W. E. B. Du Bois's
Harlem newspaper, *Freedom.* The move was facilitated by the Hansberry
family's long acquaintance with the renowned singer and actor.[65] Hansberry's decision was, however, fraught with considerable risk since, by
1950, the federal government's harassment of Robeson, Du Bois, and
other African-American leftists with affinities with Communism (real
and imagined) had reached its height.[66] Nevertheless, at age twenty,
Hansberry left Madison for New York, shedding the life of the middle-
class public university student for that of the economically marginal
bohemian. Hansberry sustained herself in spirit by occasional writing for
Freedom and other journals on the left, and supported herself financially
by jobs as a secretary and as a waitress. In the years following Carl
Hansberry's solitary exile in Mexico, Lorraine Hansberry moved deter-
minedly away from the classical American liberal individualism of her
father and toward the historical materialism of Robeson and Du Bois.[67]

Lorraine Hansberry's life history makes sadly ironic the misrepresen-
tation of *Raisin* and its author, first by a mainstream press insistent that
its own expectations be projected onto Hansberry's vision, making the
latter invisible, and second—and with equal unfairness—by arbiters of
blackness equally insistent that *Raisin* be remembered dismissively as a
kitchen melodrama from an era whose ideas and struggles were best
forgotten. What has been lost in these critiques is an insight into the
commitments that shaped *A Raisin in the Sun* into a vivid social and
political document. Hansberry's play, in fact, portrayed the American
Way to which her parents had given proud allegiance, and, at the same
time, incisively critiqued the ways in which racism prevented its full
realization.

Representation and Reevaluation

The iconic representations of Bunche, Clark, and Hansberry came under attack in the 1960s and 1970s, and the earlier oversimplified, if positive, stories of their accomplishments were replaced with equally inaccurate and clumsily conceived explanations of the purportedly illusory and fallacious nature of their contributions. Each of the three, in different ways, came to be interpreted as a token from an ideologically disreputable era. This era was presumed to be one in which such tokens joined a putatively acquiescent mainstream in naively trusting that American democracy could be redeemed: that democratic capitalism, in its American design, could be reconstructed and rationalized to correct its most fundamental inequities; that the popularization of "brotherhood" through the United Nations might eradicate racism; that the Youngers' steadfast labors might actually be rewarded—someday.

By the early seventies, Bunche was widely dismissed as one "who served in white society rather than fighting for black needs"; Harold Cruse looked upon Clark as representative of an ideology that had left the NAACP "hopelessly trapped"; and Amiri Baraka, one of Hansberry's staunchest defenders today, recalls that, in the late sixties, "young militants like myself . . . thought Hansberry's play was part of the 'passive resistance' phase of the movement . . . We thought her play was 'middle-class' in that its focus seemed to be [as many white critics had said] on 'moving into white folks' neighborhoods,' when most blacks were just trying to pay their rent in ghetto shacks."[68] While revivals of *A Raisin in the Sun* in the seventies and eighties—which include scenes cut by Hansberry from the original—have done much to undermine this reading of the play, there still remain those who categorize it as nothing more than a "kitchen melodrama."[69]

Virtually no participant-symbol was immune from retrospective demotion from the pantheon of heroes in the postwar struggle for equality. This was even true of perhaps the most revered participant-symbol of them all: Jackie Robinson. Hank Aaron, who became a participant-symbol in his own right when he toppled Babe Ruth's home-run record in 1974, has written that many of the black players of the early 1970s seemed to forget their debt to Jackie Robinson all too easily. In his autobiography, Aaron states that this attitude among his peers "hardened my resolve" to challenge still-prevalent stereotypes of African-American inferiority by becoming the "all-time home run champion in the history of the game that had kept black people out for more than sixty years."[70]

The retrospective demotion of these formative participant-symbols, either through explicit attacks or equally cutting silences, was part and parcel of the cultural politics that have come to be remembered in short-hand as "the sixties." That era, Audre Lorde wrote some years ago:

> [was] characterized by a heady belief in instantaneous solutions. They were vital years of awakening, of pride, and of error. The civil rights and Black power movements rekindled possibilities for disenfran-chised groups within this nation. Even though we fought common enemies, at times the lure of individual solutions made us careless of each other. Sometimes we could not bear the face of each other's differences because of what we feared those differences might say about ourselves . . . But any vision which can encompass all of us, by definition, must be complex and expanding, not easy to achieve . . . There is no monolithic solution to racism, to sexism, to homo-phobia. There is only the conscious focusing within each of my days to move against them, wherever I come up against these particular manifestations of the same disease. By seeing who the *we* is we learn to use our energies with greater precision against our enemies rather than against ourselves.[71]

In assessing these great struggles, we would do well to heed George Lipsitz's cautionary admonition about declaring historical winners and losers, for, as he points out, "victory and defeat are not mutually exclu-sive categories." As modest as the reformist achievements of the civil rights movement may appear when measured against its own greater goals, it is necessary to recall that Bunche, Clark, and Hansberry were among the early symbols of a movement that "reverberated to every corner of the world in subsequent years and served as the impetus for oppositional action on innumerable fronts."[72]

In the end, the focus of this study is centered on recovering the ways in which Bunche, Clark, and Hansberry, along with the other participant-symbols of the postwar years, were the architects of the postwar rerepresentation of African-Americans in American culture. As the words of Lorde and Lipsitz make clear, this movement and this era have provided a clear road map that has been used by other excluded Americans in their subsequent struggles to gain political and cultural legitimacy.[73] Collective memory is the best guarantee that American culture can never be completely reorganized to forget the lessons learned in the midst of performing the work of democracy.

Ralph Bunche
Photo by Carl Van Vechten (Library of Congress)

Ralph Bunche and American Racial Discourse

2

Dear Dr. Du Bois:

   . . . Since I have been sufficiently old to think rationally and to appreciate that there was a "race problem" in America, in which I was necessarily involved, I have set the goal of my ambition service to my group . . . I would like to inquire if there is any way that I can be of service to my group this coming summer . . . I am willing to tackle any problem or proposition which will give sufficient return for bare living expenses. I feel that there must be some opportunity connected with the N.A.A.C.P. or as a teacher. I have had a liberal education, extensive experience in journalism, forensics, and dramatics, as well as athletics, and I am young and healthy. I can furnish the best of recommendations, both from the faculty of the University [of California] and from the Race leaders of the Pacific Coast.

   Trusting that I may hear some word of encouragement from you in the near future, I am

Sincerely yours . . .

     —Ralph Bunche (May 11, 1927)

My dear Mr. Bunche:

   I do not know of any opening for you just now, but I shall keep your case in mind. I would be very glad to help you in any way if I see a chance.

Very sincerely yours . . .

     —W. E. B. Du Bois (June 7, 1927)

Ralph Bunche's work as a goodwill ambassador began well before his appointment to the United Nations secretariat, and even before his graduation from UCLA in June 1927. As he wrote in his letter to W. E. B. Du Bois early the month before, "I have been very active in Cosmopolitan clubs, and inter-racial discussion groups, and have often been sent from this University . . . to lead discussion groups, and I feel that a great deal of good has been done thereby." As he prepared to depart UCLA for Harvard, the west coast for the east, and adolescence for young adulthood, Bunche consciously opened the next chapter in his life by seeking the advice of the greatest living icon of learning and leadership among African-Americans. Bunche's letter to the greatest "race leader" of the age yielded little encouragement. In any case, armed with an MA in government from Harvard, Bunche's teaching career would formally begin one year later, in July 1928, when he joined the faculty of Howard University as an instructor in political science.

The Great Depression brought Du Bois and Bunche into further contact, but as combatants on opposing sides of the central debate among black intellectuals during the Depression years: whether to build an independent African-American "nation within a nation" or instead to pursue an alliance with white labor for a class-based program of economic and social reform. Du Bois, disillusioned by years of trying to build such a unified proletarian alliance, favored the concept of a self-sufficient African-American economy, at least until the leaders of white labor could prove their willingness to work with African-Americans; Bunche and his colleagues rejected this advice as backward-looking and impractical. In the new political alliances provoked by the Great Depression, Bunche saw the possibility of a biracial workers' movement.

After the war, Bunche and Du Bois would again be at odds, when Du Bois argued that a close identity of interest existed between African-Americans, oppressed people throughout the world, and the Soviet Union. Remembering all too well the peace that was lost after World War I, Du Bois saw in the United Nations a vehicle through which the imperialism of the Great Powers would be perpetuated. Bunche, by contrast, was an architect and advocate of the UN, and emerged from the war deeply mistrustful of former colleagues on the left who had repeatedly tailored their views to conform to Soviet foreign policy.

Whatever goodwill may have developed between the two men after their initial round of correspondence in 1927 had certainly disappeared by 1948, when Du Bois, in the midst of being marginalized for his avowed Marxism, attacked Bunche, then the acting mediator of the first Arab-Israeli Peace, for allegedly undermining Israeli interests in accord with "a dominant group of Americans" whose sole desire was to "rule the world as heir to British imperialism."[1] Little more than two years later, Bunche, now a Nobel Peace Laureate—and an icon in his own right—pointedly refused to attend a testimonial dinner for Du Bois. Although Bunche still admired Du Bois for "his great work, for his eminence, and for his invaluable contributions to the progress of the American Negro," Bunche was angered that Du Bois's attack had been tendered in the form of an "apology" to the Jewish community "in the name of the American Negro."[2]

While the lives of these two influential intellectuals both spanned the Depression years and the Cold War, the conclusions that each drew from this era were very different. Du Bois represented an elder statesman's disillusionment with America and with the democratic capitalist order that it advocated by its very existence. Bunche, on the other hand, spoke as one keenly aware of how worldwide revolutionary changes had created new cultural and political imperatives that weakened previous barriers to world order and social justice. The new situation created by these changes strengthened the hand of those who were advocating a social revolution.

Bunche and Du Bois came to signify two opposing poles of opinion among African-American intellectuals. During the 1950s, the African-American left, for whom Du Bois and Paul Robeson spoke, was systematically persecuted by the federal government; Bunche, however, was a favored symbol for the American political mainstream of supposed progress on race. By the middle 1960s, Bunche would come under attack as a mere token, while Du Bois and Robeson would begin to assume respectability in the eyes of the Black Power movement as prescient critics of American capitalism.

This chapter explores the formative years of Bunche's ideological development. The conclusions Bunche had arrived at by 1940, while not responsible for his emergence ten years later as an icon, strongly informed how Bunche sought to use his later celebrity to legitimate the striving of American society toward racial equality as a national priority. How the icon—which was the work of others—obscured Bunche's own intentions as a public figure is the subject of Chapter 3.

From his academic post at Howard, Bunche chose an activist role, developing into a leading critic of the New Deal and experimenting briefly with constructing an alternative to the NAACP, the National Negro Congress (NNC). Bunche and his NNC cofounders, Abram Harris, A. Philip Randolph, and John P. Davis, envisioned the Congress as a third force between the NAACP and the insurgent industrial labor movement led by the CIO; the founders intended the NNC to be an organization capable of mounting a challenge to American capitalism that reached across ethnic and racial lines. Bunche and his colleagues were impatient not only with Du Bois's seeming retreat into the dream world of a racialist socialism, but also with the world-weary realism of James Weldon Johnson, the former Executive Secretary of the NAACP. Typical of the attitude that so unnerved Bunche (but one he would embrace in later years as an icon and elder statesman of the postwar mobilization for racial equality) was Johnson's apparent willingness to split the difference between the two camps—to argue that a little of each prescription, if taken in moderation, would lead to victory.

To the partisans of Du Bois, Johnson counseled against economic separatism while at the same time arguing that "common sense compels us to get whatever and all the good we can out of the system of imposed segregation . . . but that we should use that experience . . . steadily and as rapidly as possible to destroy the system. The seeming advantages of imposed segregation are too costly to keep." To the young rebels, who foresaw wider horizons of political possibility in an alliance with militant labor, and to those still further estranged from his "middle way"—those who saw a new dawn in an alliance between African-Americans and the Communist party—Johnson put the matter more simply still: his opposition to these programs was "not because I am unconscious of the need of fundamental social change, but because I am considering the realities of the situation. Conservatism and radicalism are relative terms. It is as radical for a black American in Mississippi to claim his full rights under the constitution . . . as it is for a white American in any state to advocate the overthrow of the existing national government. The black American in many instances puts his life in jeopardy, and anything more radical than that cannot reasonably be required."[3] Participating in this debate would be Bunche's initiation into public life.

In addition to serving as an intellectual base from which to argue the nation's future with some of the brightest intellectuals of the era, Howard University also served as a jumping-off point for Bunche into a wider world beyond the United States. Since his undergraduate years at UCLA,

Bunche had been a devout Wilsonian internationalist, envisioning a world federation along the American model. Twice during the 1930s Bunche took leaves from Howard to spend extended periods studying the political structure of European colonialism and apartheid from vantage points in London, Paris, southwest Africa, and Capetown, as well as examining the outlines of international cooperation at the headquarters of the League of Nations in Geneva. The itinerant international scholar developed close working relationships with the leading intellectuals of his generation. A partial list of Bunche's extended intellectual network during the Howard years includes the immigrant writer Louis Adamic, anthropologists Melville Herskovits and Franz Boas, founder of the *Journal of Negro History* Carter G. Woodson (Bunche was a member of its initial editorial board), preeminent 1930s historian of Southern Reconstruction Howard Beale, scholar-activists C. L. R. James and W. E. B. Du Bois, and father of Kenyan independence Jomo Kenyatta.

The international events of the late 1930s and early 1940s opened yet another phase in Bunche's professional life. Disillusioned by the American Communist Party's infiltration of the NNC, Bunche, Harris, and Randolph resigned, thus leaving the Congress an organization existing only on paper. Like many of his intellectual cohorts, Bunche was moved by the menacing prospect of a world war provoked by the successes of an imperialistic and explicitly race-conscious fascism to reconsider his early criticism of Franklin Roosevelt's catch-as-catch-can version of social democracy; he came to see in it a hopeful—if manifestly imperfect—alternative to the dark blueprint being followed by the Axis powers. As one of the few American academic specialists on African affairs (and on what were then known as "dependent areas") Bunche left Howard and moved across town, first to the Office of Strategic Services and then, in 1944, to the State Department. By war's end, Bunche's résumé displayed the professional landmarks of a consummate bureaucrat and liberal internationalist, and Bunche was recruited to serve in a high office within the citadel of that rejuvenated faith, the United Nations.

The Education of a Liberal Internationalist

During his first five years at Howard, Bunche was, as always, frenetically busy. In addition to his teaching responsibilities, Bunche also served as administrative assistant to Mordecai Johnson, Howard's first African-

American president, a man intent on building the institution into a major university, competitive with the nationally known centers of learning on the other side of the color line.

Johnson's most important early accomplishment was to substantially enlarge the faculty and physical plant, and to stabilize congressional appropriations for the university with the enactment by Congress of Public Law 634 in 1928, which authorized an annual appropriation "to aid in the construction, development, improvement and maintenance of the university."[4] The significance of this achievement, as Vincent J. Browne explains, is that "prior to this time . . . Congress had simply voted 'gratuities.' However, from 1928 to the present Howard has been able to depend on Federal appropriations amounting to about 60% of operating costs."[5]

Over the next four years, Johnson commanded the necessary resources to begin moving Howard into the front rank of American higher education. Central to this effort was his recruitment of several young and intellectually gifted professors, including Bunche in political science, Abram Harris in economics, E. Franklin Frazier in sociology, poet Sterling Brown in English, and the return, after a brief absence, of Alain Locke to the senior faculty in philosophy. "We are trying to build up at Howard," Locke wrote to the Julius Rosenwald Foundation, "a group of younger students of the race problem competent to discuss it from the international as well as the national angle." Bunche, in Locke's evaluation, was "the keystone for this group."[6]

Uppermost in Bunche's mind during these years was the completion of his doctoral studies. As Locke's endorsement suggests, the focus of Bunche's work was to be an exploration of the subject on which he had written and spoken about extensively as an undergraduate at UCLA: the need to build an international community in which racism and the competition for empire would have no place. Such an endeavor followed upon Du Bois's 1903 analysis, expressed in the phrase that would become most closely associated with him: "The problem of the twentieth century," Du Bois declared in *The Souls of Black Folk*, "is the problem of the color line—the relation of the darker to the lighter races of men in Asia and Africa, in America and the islands of the sea."[7] During his first years at Howard, Bunche strove to construct a dissertation topic that would permit him to examine American race relations as part of this international "color line." Bunche's commitment to such intellectual internationalism also reflected his pragmatic assessment that "the Negro of all scholars . . . must develop a broad and international background if his own contribution to our own peculiar domestic problem are to have much impress."[8]

Bunche first chose as his subject an examination of race relations in Brazil, with an eye toward what such relations might suggest about the American experience. Although such a project would be pursued ten years later by no less a figure than E. Franklin Frazier, backed by a grant from the Guggenheim Foundation, Bunche's own proposal was rejected by the Julius Rosenwald Foundation. According to Bunche's dissertation advisor, Arthur N. Holcombe, Foundation director Edwin Embree feared that "there might be some danger that an American student would be led astray by the position of Negroes . . . in Brazil. Indiscreet utterances and reports on the basis of the Brazilian experience might really do more harm than good in this country."[9] This unfavorable decision moved Bunche toward an alternate topic, one more explicitly emphasizing his own long-standing interest in the development of a system of world government: an examination of the fate of former European colonies placed in the care of the League of Nations by the Versailles Treaty. Arguing that "European withdrawal from Africa is neither possible nor desirable within a long period of years," Bunche proposed to examine "the best possible system of administration" for insuring the "fair and proper use of Africa's vast resources."[10] This subsequent proposal met with success, and Bunche received a $2,000 grant from the Rosenwald Foundation.[11]

In Geneva, the young African-American scholar enthusiastically took the opportunity "to observe the League [of Nations] machinery in action." "It is quite thrilling," Bunche wrote to George Arthur of the Rosenwald Foundation, "to see the delegations from Liberia, Haiti, and Abyssinia in their proper places on the [Assembly] floor. I have been hoping that some of them would do a bit of speaking before I leave in the next few days."[12] Bunche was so inspired by these scenes of a new world government in the making—a government in which racism and segregation would have no place—that he extended his stay in Geneva in order to observe "an important commission of the League considering the slavery question" and to witness "the ultimate emancipation of Irak [*sic*] from the mandatory status into a full-fledged independent state and League member."[13]

Aimed at specialists in public administration and international relations, Bunche's dissertation, "French Administration in Togoland and Dahomey," was an exhaustively researched document drawing from the holdings of the French colonial administration, the British Museum, and the League of Nations.[14] Bunche compared the style of French administration in two adjacent areas in West Africa: Togoland, a former French colony now administered by its former colonial rulers as a mandate of the League of Nations, and Dahomey, a region still under French colonial administration.[15] Bunche concluded that in neither case was the "native" population being prepared for "an ultimate and specific political status," and he expressed the hope that the French would be wise enough to "prepare the African for membership in the civilized world."[16] Even if the French should not choose such an enlightened path, Bunche observed, "the very forces exploiting much of [the African's] human and material wealth also open to him the white man's storehouse of knowledge, experience and technique." As Bunche assessed the situation, "it is too much to assume that the natives of Dahomey, with their background of powerful ancestral rulers and independence, or the natives of Togo, whose country does not belong to France . . . will accept the virtual tyranny of French administrative bureaucracy."[17]

For the student of Bunche's role in American discourse, his dissertation is important for the degree to which it expresses, in language that was carefully modulated to fit within the intellectual conventions of its era, his belief that a postcolonial era would soon arrive, the ideological infrastructure for this transformation having been laid by European colonialism itself. In Africa, Bunche discerned a people "being pulled unwittingly . . . into the mainstream of the political, social and economic life of the civilized world . . . The African," charged Bunche, "is being pushed out of his old collectivism into individualism by Europeans who cannot understand or tolerate his uniform and communal life . . . The demands of modern industry require the breaking up of his quiet village life." Deploying the metaphors of an industrial capitalist world, Bunche charged that "the African is not only being changed; he is being cast in new moulds [*sic*]," being, in essence, " 'manufactured' on a large scale."[18] Bunche's field notes suggest his strong interest in the interaction—and the clash—between traditional African culture and industrialized, individualistic, and capitalistic western culture. Bunche, for instance, carefully described the responses of Africans to Joe Louis fight films, as well as to more traditional Hollywood fare. In pursuing this line of analysis, Bunche was trying to answer for himself whether such American commodities, like the import of French education into Togoland and Dahomey, would eventually stimulate a greater political consciousness in Africans.[19]

Two years after receiving his doctorate in 1934, Bunche left Howard again, this time on a two-year sabbatical funded by a fellowship from the Social Science Research Council. Bunche looked upon this sabbatical as an opportunity to "broaden my research, training and [intellectual] equipment" in order that he might be competent to study "the *effect* [emphasis in the original] of imperial rule on retarded peoples."[20] As a result of his previous research forays abroad, Bunche returned home ready to undertake an ambitious interdisciplinary and comparative study of race relations, to be focused on South Africa and the southern United States; Bunche's intent was to "indicate the general pattern of racial attitudes, the cliches, the racial stereotypes, the rationalizations for racial policies, and the true historical causes for racial prejudice, as discovered in South Africa and which are especially familiar to the American South."[21] The Second World War and Bunche's decision to leave the academy for a career at the State Department and the United Nations prevented the completion of this project.

"An Attitude of Intense and Courageous Criticism"

With the award of his doctorate in January 1934, Bunche entered the public debate on the relationship of racial problems to the other crises afflicting Depression-era America. For the remainder of the thirties, even when traveling in Africa and Europe, Bunche campaigned relentlessly for a social movement equal to the international economic crisis and the growing specter of fascism. Between 1935 and 1941, Bunche addressed diverse audiences, ranging from the "unemployed men and women, students and graduates" of the Citywide Forum and a group of "Fort Hare [sic] students" in Basutoland during one his fieldwork trips in Africa to members of the Princeton University School of Public and International

Affairs.[22] What Bunche argued for is described easily enough: "a constructive, humane American political program"—a Second Reconstruction—guaranteeing African-Americans "employment, land, housing, relief, health protection, unemployment and old-age insurance, enjoyment of civil rights—all that a twentieth-century American citizen is entitled to."[23]

The capital city to which Bunche returned in 1933 after his first research expedition to Europe and Africa was consumed with the excitement of Franklin Roosevelt's New Deal. As Richard Weiss has argued, the signal contribution of the New Deal to American political culture is not so much the extent to which the administration's policies adhered to a rigorous and coherent program of social democracy as in its attitude of experimentation, and in its fostering of an ambiance of genuine empathy for the plight of minority groups, no matter their race or country of origin. The social workers and activists who came to Washington as New Dealers—foremost among them Harry Hopkins and Frances Perkins—and others, such as the writer Louis Adamic, propagated what Weiss describes as a "new orthodoxy" that not only celebrated minority contributions to American life, but identified America's first and second generation immigrants as the *"real* Americans:" "real" because the ultimate test of the nation's legitimacy as a political, cultural, and social democracy lay in the consequences of these immigrants' encounters with American society.[24]

Another factor directing scholarly attention toward minority groups in the thirties was the revolutionary use being made of mass technology in the political realm; geographical distances were being rendered insignificant, and it was believed that, as a result, new social and political solidarities were becoming possible.[25] "Now that the aeroplane has . . . abolished the distances that once separated the nations and peoples and the radio has converted the world into one great whispering gallery," sociologist Robert Park suggested, "the great world—intertribal, interracial, and international—the world of business and politics—has grown at the expense of the little world, the world of intimate, personal loyalties in which men were bound together by tradition, custom, and natural piety."[26] As one commentator suggested in 1937, the "modern world of economic competition and shifting social relations" had created a "marginal man," an individual forced to reconcile life in two worlds, the disappearing "little world" of his past in a "primitive" society—more and more preserved only in memory—and the "great world" created by the "expansion of Western civilization over the globe." American cities had been transformed into "mosaics" of diversity, "the real melting pots of culture."[27] In this changed atmosphere, to which both a sensitivity to the social and cultural implications of modern technologies and new attitudes within social science on the significance of racial and ethnic differences contributed, new cultural spaces were created in which to rework the meaning of national identity.

The discussions surrounding these demographic and technological changes also made new cultural resources available to those—such as the Howard intellectuals—who were engaged in establishing the legitimacy of Negroes as full American citizens. The most suggestive of these new perspectives was the immigrant analogue, the idea that African-Americans shared an experience and a destiny with other excluded Americans. For some, the analogue was given credence by the fact that, in a period of immigration restrictions, African-Americans occupied the cultural and social space that, twenty years earlier, had been claimed by the immigrant. Charles S. Johnson of Fisk University, for example, explicitly tied his optimism about the African-American future in the United States to the fact that blacks, thanks to new immigration restrictions, now found themselves "occupying many of the same positions as the immigrant." This development, in Johnson's view, meant that "both the theory and the machinery which has been developed for dealing with the immigrant are being transferred to the Negro."[28] With the accomplishments of the Harlem Renaissance freshly in mind, Johnson believed African-Americans to be in the process of acquiring a sense of "group self-respect" that, in their struggles, had been achieved in years past by "Jews, Poles and other oppressed groups":

> The Negro is going through the same process. It always means a tremendous acceleration of activity. The best parallel to the Negro is the Jew, who has experienced most of the same handicaps. It seems to be an eternal paradox that the best way to make people go ahead is to try to hold them back. If the Jew had suffered no limitation, the world would be much poorer, for the drive of his reaction has given us eminent contributions. In the same way I venture to prophesy that

in the next generation or two the group that will make far and away the most progress will be the Negroes.[29]

Langston Hughes, one of the best-remembered voices of the thirties, offered his own interpretation of blacks as part of the immigrant mosaic in his 1938 poem "Let America Be America Again," which read in part:

> Yet I'm the one who dreamt our basic dream
> In that Old World while a serf of kings,
> Who dreamt a dream so strong, so brave, so true,
> That even yet its mighty daring sings
> In every brick and stone, in every furrow turned
> That's made America the land it has become.
> O, I'm the man who sailed the early seas
> In search of what I mean to be my home—
> For I'm the one who left dark Ireland's shore,
> And Poland's plain, and England's grassy lea,
> And torn from Black Africa's Strand, I came
> To build a "homeland of the free."[30]

In the discourse on racial difference that was emerging during the thirties, blacks and immigrants were understood to be indispensable actors in the continual re-creation of American culture.[31] Alain Locke, in an argument heard increasingly during the decade, and that eventually became a mainstay of postwar American political culture, held that African-Americans, as the closest American equivalent to a peasant class, were the defining influence in the creation of a genuinely American culture. Referring to the Negro spirituals, Locke writes, "As we approach the peasant stock of the Irish, Italian, German and Russian nations, we see that they all have their well-spring. It has simply been the lot of the Negro in America to be the peasant class, and thus to furnish the musical sub-soil of our national music." Elaborating on this theme further, Locke predicts that, "developed along the lines of its own originality, we may expect a development of the Negro folk song that may equal or even outstrip the phenomenal choral music of Russia."[32]

The immigrant analogue for comprehending the place of blacks in American democracy also framed Melville Herskovits's early efforts to reconceive of the "Negro" as an "African-American." Taking his case to the readers of *American Scholar* in the late thirties, Herskovits reports that "the further we can carry this investigation and the more we can learn about the African background the better the understanding we shall have of these aspects of the ancestral culture that, in the case of the Negro as of all our other minority folk, has not been entirely lost but continues in some measure to function significantly."[33]

The most striking consequence of the focus on blacks as distinctive cultural contributors with similarities to "other immigrant groups . . . whose histories have more than their share of persecution and abuse" was the creation of a distinction between culture and race.[34] Culture was understood to be the intergenerationally shared memory of a distinctive collective history and experience, while race, previously an elastic term describing distinct cultural groups, was, under the pressure of Boasian anthropology, coming to mean a biologically insignificant but politically powerful social construction used by economic and political elites to distinguish a "socially submerged class . . . from the dominant."[35] No less an expert on race relations than Robert Park predicted in the thirties that "race conflicts . . . in the modern world will be more and more in the future confused with, and eventually superceded by the conflicts of classes."[36] According to historian Nancy J. Weiss, this attitude was widely shared by the stewards of New Deal domestic policy.[37]

Sterling Brown, who served as the National Editor for Negro Affairs in the WPA Writers' Project between 1936 and 1939, captured well the sense that Negroes possessed significance not so much because of their race, but as one of many cultural minority groups.[38] Brown introduced and justified his ground-breaking anthology of African-American cultural creations, *The Negro Caravan,* as bringing together the most comprehensive "literary record of America's largest minority group, and in so doing, it sheds light upon American culture and minority problems." Invoking language commonly associated with the advocates of ethnic pluralism and cultural democracy in the thirties, Brown remarks of his anthology that "it pieces out a mosaic more representative than is to be found in any other volume."[39]

"Negro culture" was certainly to be uncovered, studied, indeed created, but such an undertaking was to be free of an attitude of racial boosterism or "racialism." Such work was charged with examining the Negro in relation to other minorities in America. Locke, certainly one of the leading advocates for African-American culture of his generation, warned his students away from racialism because "it leads to an intellectual narrowness and provincialism which I call Ghetto-mindedness." Speaking to freshman students enrolled in his course "Negro Thought and Leadership" in the early 1940s, Locke warned:

> Too many of you have it, too many of our leaders have it . . . It is the psychological stigma of inferiority, the backfire of prejudice . . . Among whites, this false way of looking at the Negro and his situation leads to equally unfortunate and unintellectual results: Nordist racialism, the rationalization of the false doctrine of Negro inferiority in terms of "fundamental and inescapable differences" between human racial groups . . . All racial chauvinism or racial pipe-dreaming are products of a false notion of the true situation, which is one of inescapable interpenetration of all elements of a given society living . . . in a common culture and framework of institutions.[40]

According to Locke, the New Negro movement of the 1920s in which he had played a significant part had been "much misunderstood" as a racialist project. Rather, Locke argues, the New Negro movement, like the Irish Renaissance, was a "revival of very admirable folk values" and "folk-culture." Locke attributed the failure of the movement to receive greater "internal racial support" to a lack of fidelity among its artists to African-American folk-cultural values: "Had they been truer to their materials and more devoted to the folk they were portraying . . . they would have been greater artists, and in the end, they would have achieved greater artistic stature."[41]

Locke posed the challenge facing his students as the need to avoid "racial isolationism." The "shackling of the mind [with] the sense of inferiority and helplessness," was, Locke maintained, an essential "part of the strategy of Negro domination and exploitation [by whites]." Locke held that the study of African-American culture was the most powerful antidote available for the feelings of isolation and marginality endured by blacks, because it confirmed the undeniable—although deliberately obscured—reality that "Negro thought, expression and group action have always been integral parts of the movements and ideas of the general American culture." Locke advised his listeners that "I want you at least to learn . . . early in your intellectual careers to see yourselves, both as individuals and as a racial group, in terms of [a] national and world perspective . . . For only as you do . . . will you have any scientific or effective comprehension of your interests, problems or plans of action."[42]

Although it would be several years before the word "integration" would come to signify the aspiration of African-Americans, Locke's injunctions suggest some of the meanings held by that term. Certainly (as Kenneth Clark would later argue with respect to American education) integration was a necessity that had yet to be achieved. In another sense, however—one strongly expressed in the work of Langston Hughes, Lorraine Hansberry, and many others—integration was also seen as an inevitable and auspicious fact of American culture to which every American must bear witness. From this perspective, blacks, like other minorities, were minorities primarily in terms of their collective lack of status and power; blacks, like poor whites, were the victims of "disabilities" resulting from political and economic "disorganization."[43] In essence, Locke contended, African-Americans needed what the Irish had also lacked for so meany years: "healthy solidarity and intelligent leadership."[44]

The immigrant analogue served American racial discourse in two ways. First, it persuasively exemplified the cultural legitimacy—indeed the indispensability—of African-Americans to American life, for they were its genuine peasantry, the bearers of its greatest burdens, and the creators of its most resilient cultural characteristics. Second, African-Americans, as the nation's closest approximation of a peasant class, were also therefore integral members of America's proletariat. The great migration of blacks from the rural South to the industrializing urban North during the teens and twenties had thus, it was believed, fulfilled an important precondition for the integration of African-Americans into American society on an equal footing with white Americans. As E. Franklin Frazier wrote in 1939: "These industrial workers are acquiring a new outlook on life and are dominated less by the ideals and standards of the brown middle class or workers in domestic and personal services. It appears that, as the Negro becomes an industrial worker, he assumes responsibility for the support of his family and acquires new authority in family relations. Moreover, as the isolation of the black worker is broken down, his ideals and patterns of family life approximate those of the great body of industrial workers."[45] The arrival of African-Americans into the industrial economy of the urban North was, Frazier believed, removing the final barriers to a grand transracial alliance encompassing the entire American working class. Locke's injunctions to his students to abandon "ghetto-mindedness" and to develop a wider-lensed and more sophisticated worldview was another such effort to contribute to the creation of such an alliance.

Bunche himself never invoked the immigrant analogue. Fresh from studies at Northwestern University with Melville Herskovits, at the London School of Economics, and at the British Museum, Bunche's postdoctoral work is notable for its class consciousness and its engagement with Marxism. According to Bunche, race, as a social influence, acts as a relatively minor force, one that only magnifies and compounds for African-Americans the injuries of class that they suffer with the rest of the "largely inert and inarticulate American masses." Southern blacks, Bunche believed, shared with their poor white brethren "the mentality and psychology of peasant people."[46] The extracultural burden borne by African-Americans—the mark, Bunche asserted, that set them decisively apart in American democracy—was the psychological mark left upon white Americans by the African-American's legacy of slavery: "The majority of Americans have absorbed the slave heritage of the Negro, the racial stereotypes that derive from it, and find it difficult to accept him on terms other than those implicit in a lower color caste within society."[47]

Bunche contended that this cultural baggage was, however, relatively trivial when set against the problems of the African-American as a member of the working class. Blacks, according to Bunche, received their primary identity not as members of a race, but as members of the "peasant proletariat class."[48] When arguing in this vein, for example, Bunche denied that there existed a uniquely "Negro feeling," stating that "the nearest I come to getting the *real* [emphasis in the original] Negro feeling is when I stick my hands in my pockets. But the feeling I get is not a Negro feeling but one of poverty, and tho [sic] it is well-nigh universal among Negroes, it is shared by millions of folks who don't happen to have black, brown or yellow skins."[49]

Race, Bunche claims, is a social construction "readily used" by "certain basic economic and political forces" to "rouse and rationalize emotional reactions"; economic and political elites "found in the theoretical characteristics of the Negro a very useful ally."[50] Race, in Bunche's opinion, stood as "one of the most serious obstructions in the alignment of the [American] population along lines of normal class interests." In his 1936 book *A World View of Race,* Bunche went still further when he argued that, "if we can remedy the fundamental economic dilemmas of our social structure . . . the race problem will take care of itself."[51]

Bunche shared this view of the economic crisis with his closest colleague at Howard, the economist Abram Harris. Writing in *The Crisis* of March 1930, Harris called for the creation of "a labor movement which would connect the Negro's special racial demands with its broader economic and social reforms . . . Progressives must show the Negro masses that their problem, like that of the white masses, is inevitably that of work and wages." As for the role of race, Harris was emphatic that it represented a kind of false consciousness imposed from above: "The antipathy between white and black bears all of the earmarks of class prejudice which has been rationalized in justification of the exploitation and subjugation of the Negro."[52] Harris opposed not only what he believed to be an overemphasis on narrowly racial problems by established civil rights leaders, but also selective buying campaigns meant to punish local merchants who refused to honor African-American patronage by offering them employment.[53] Such narrow "racialism," Harris argued, blinded its partisans to deeper social consequences: "This campaign would merely meet the unemployment of Negroes with the displacement of whites. But in the final analysis it would be the hundreds of thousands of black workers in white industry who would have to bear the cost of the movement's success in obtaining a few thousand jobs for Negro clerks, salesmen and managers."[54]

In addition, Harris and Bunche had no sympathy whatsoever for the notion advanced by Hughes and Du Bois that Africa remained in some way an important aspect of the cultural identity of the Negro. Echoing his Howard colleague Frazier, Bunche told an audience in London during his stay at the London School of Economics in 1937 that the Negro was "a 'minority' only in [the] strictly racial sense, but not culturally, economically or politically."[55] Continuing his reformulation of Frazier's views, Bunche argued that the black American "has been torn away from his [African] origins and dumped into an entirely new milieu . . . in which he finds himself [to be] a racial minority group."[56]

Bunche rejected as futile "frantic efforts being made to claim and preserve" whatever remained—or was imagined to remain—of the black American's distant African past. He insisted that the cultural tools for the liberation of American blacks were exactly those available to other Americans: the explicit and implicit promises of egalitarian democracy embedded in the founding documents of the American political tradition. The most appropriate goal, therefore, of minority politics was for such groups, immigrant or racial, to "ally themselves with those progressive groups who are aiming not at the solution of race problems alone, but at developing American society into a lush economic and political democracy in which there will be real opportunity . . . for all citizens."[57]

The most compelling intellectual challenge to this class-based analysis came from Du Bois, the elder statesman of African-American scholarship.[58] Though he shared Harris and Bunche's opinion that an interracial coalition held together by powerful, inclusive, and democratic industrial unions was a worthy ideal, he believed that it was beyond reach in the foreseeable future. "I am convinced," Du Bois wrote to George Streator, a mercurial ally of Bunche and Harris, "from wide contact with the working people of the United States . . . that the great majority of them are thoroughly capitalistic . . . and the last thing that they would want to do would be to unite in any movement whose object was the uplift of the masses of Negroes to essential equality with them." Recalling his own unhappy experience with rabidly exclusionary craft unions, Du Bois was willing to "keep in close touch" with the rising industrial unions, but held that they represented "a . . . small minority of the labor movement of the United States"—a circumstance he believed was unlikely to change.[59]

Du Bois advocated his own bracingly radical plan, one that was as sketchily defined as anything put forward by Bunche and Harris. Du Bois advocated the creation by African-Americans of an economic "nation within a nation," a vision based on gaining control of the vast economic power of twelve million African-Americans so as "to secure wide economic independence through the exchange of services and the exchange and manufacture of goods." With their consumer and productive power under their own control, African-Americans could then direct their own economic and social development toward the creation of a socialist model to "which the whole world is bound to come to some day." In addition, Du Bois maintained that following a strategy of protecting African-Americans by utilizing the "very segregation of which they are victims" would have tremendous benefits far beyond economic renewal. The success of this experiment would "stop this great people from being ashamed of itself, of its color and history; of living together and working together and to realize that race segregation is the white man's loss and not the black man's damnation."[60]

If Bunche and Harris disagreed with Du Bois as to strategy, they were in complete accord with him as to the inadequacy of the New Deal. In a series of criticisms that would inspire a loyalty investigation of him in the early 1950s, Bunche placed little hope in the New Deal as an agent of significant change, charging that it was "merely an effort to refurbish the old individualistic-capitalistic system and to entrust it again with the . . . welfare of the American people." That the New Deal should be "inconsistent, vague and confused . . . a mass of self-contradictory experimentation" reflected not the undisciplined intellect of Franklin Roosevelt, but rather, Bunche thought, a basic contradiction between the problem—capitalism—and the imperative solution—wise social planning: "The dilemma of the New Deal . . . merely reflects the basic dilemma of capitalism. Either capitalism must surrender itself to intelligent and scientific social planning (and this it cannot do, for such planning involves a single ownership of the means of production for use rather than for profit) or else it must blunder on, repeating and perpetuating the errors which inevitably lead a poorly planned industrial society into periodic depression."[61]

The exact character of Bunche's alternative to the New Deal was unclear, but, like Locke and Harris, he believed that it required a new cadre of leadership—one more forward thinking and less racialist. The established leaders were, in Bunche's analysis, creatures of their bourgeois class allegiances, "allergic to democracy," hobbled by a misplaced "respect for established boundaries of conduct," and content to confine their activities and concern to "the very narrow world" to which they happily belonged.[62] Bunche contended that the established leadership of the NAACP and the National Urban League was "tied to the apron-strings of white bourgeois philanthropists and its goal [is] the attainment of bourgeois status for a small and insignificant portion of the race."[63]

In searching for a remedy to this situation, Bunche joined with John

P. Davis, Abram Harris, and A. Philip Randolph in 1935 to form the National Negro Congress (NNC), an organization dedicated to bringing together the "collective wisdom of all freedom-loving sections of our population" and "creating a public opinion which will force real consideration from public officials." Students of the NNC have rightly focused on its pursuit of a radical alternative to the New Deal, but the call to the first meeting of the Congress also reflected a deep concern for the connection between foreign and domestic affairs, a theme favored by Bunche throughout his public life:

> Negroes observe with deep indignation the war on Ethiopia by fascist Italy ... The memory of the human slaughter of the last war, of Jim Crow stevedore battalions for Negroes, of Gold Star Mothers forced into Jim Crow ships to visit the graves of their dead sons overseas, makes Negroes oppose war. The full knowledge of the impoverishment which war and fascism bring to the entire nation make them strong in their desire for peace, resolute in their fight against war and fascism.[64]

The NNC fell far short of achieving the grand vision of its founders. By 1940, Randolph and Bunche had exited, citing the infiltration of the NNC by the Communist Party, an outcome accomplished with the active cooperation of Davis.[65]

Bunche was also convinced that part of the mission of the African-American university, especially in such times of crisis, was to provide a necessary counterleadership, to offer "the Negro community ... a sound and reasoned interpretation of the relation of present-day conflicts and forces to the welfare of the Negro people."[66] African-American colleges and universities must contribute students schooled in an "attitude of intense and courageous criticism," Bunche counseled, trained to "understand clearly the operation of the society in which they live," for "never has the race been in greater need of courageous, independent and trained thinkers, and our schools must provide them."[67]

Debating the Dilemma

The coming of the Second World War brought subtle changes in Bunche's outlook. Faced with the "immediate choice between imperfect, buffetted democracy on the one hand and totalitarianism on the other," as he put it, Bunche chose a path taken by other independent leftists who, as Judy A. Kutulas points out, "continued to advocate collective solutions to America's economic problems, but . . . tempered their socialism with a new respect for American society and a stronger antipathy toward anything that might concentrate power too narrowly."[68] Events abroad led Bunche to the conclusion that "Marxist, Liberal and radical thinkers . . . are confronted with the collapse of their dreams with respect to collectivism."[69]

Still, the excesses of the fascist right and the communist left abroad did not call forth in Bunche an immediate rejection of a Marxist framework. Marxism, Bunche believed, remained "fundamental and strong," even as it needed to be reworked: "Marx was not a prophet who could foresee all through eternity. Marxism must be applied today in light of the capitalistic world in the thirties." Bunche held that "the vital question is whether it is possible to conduct industrial states, whether they be totalitarian or capitalist-democratic, without a progressively developing bureaucracy." He suggested that questions could no longer be framed in sweeping terms, but that "it may well be that we have to make our choices of the future in terms of rather narrower alternatives; i.e., whether we have more or less bureaucracy, more or less collectivism."[70]

Bunche's own blueprint for the future placed great faith in democratic unionism. His most sustained opportunity to develop these ideas came when he collaborated with Gunnar Myrdal on the research that led to *An American Dilemma.* In the lengthy essays that Bunche composed for Myrdal between 1939 and 1941, he advocated, in very general and abstract terms, that the key to achieving the necessary transformation of American society lay in the creation of one all-encompassing and democratically organized union that would unite all races by uniting all workers.[71] Bunche expressed the hope that this democratic all-workers union could act as a monitor of, and a counterforce against, the further accretion of power by a centralized government. Bunche anticipated that industrial democracy could function if the power over its direction was wielded by worker-managers operating within this as-yet unformed union. As for the examples before him of a mass union movement, Bunche considered both the A.F. of L. and the C.I.O. to be too "inept" to handle the job.[72]

The arrival of war in Europe put an end to Bunche's theorizing about the future design of American industrial democracy. The fascist crisis abroad underlined for Bunche the urgent need to preserve and defend the existing American structure. In a passionate address before the Association of Negro Colleges and Secondary Schools in December 1940, one of his last during this chapter of his public life, Bunche proclaimed that "a . . . world revolution is now in progress," one that held an especially chilling significance for American blacks; as Bunche phrased his warning, "Never since the Civil War has a conflict meant so much to the Negro and his future as the one which now engulfs the world."[73] As Bunche wrote in a memorandum to Myrdal in the spring of 1940, "These are perilous times for the Negro. It is not at all beyond the realm of possibility that the Negro could find himself marooned in a fascist world."[74] Bunche was less fearful of a German invasion of the United States than that continued Nazi military successes might stimulate a homegrown fascist movement. "There is in America," Bunche reminded Myrdal, "an abundance of raw material from which fascism is woven."[75] The still-bleeding wounds of the Great Depression had, Bunche presumed, lowered the nation's collective immunity against fascism: "We have more than our share of hoodlums . . . We have huge stores of frustrated youth . . . and thousands of [them] throughout the nation [are] eager to hop on any bandwagon that offers the prospect of escape from unemployment and an empty future."[76]

Under a thoroughgoing American version of National Socialism, Bunche prophesied that "what happened to the Jew in Germany would . . . be child's play compared to what would happen to the Negro, the Jew and other minority groups here." While it was imperative that the domestic struggle against Jim Crow not be abandoned, Bunche, who only a few years before had been a severe critic of capitalism and of the New Deal program to rescue it, admitted that "the emphasis in our democratic thinking must be shifted . . . Of what avail is it to concentrate on the fight for rights when the democratic structure itself is threatened with destruction?"[77] "The fight now," Bunche challenged the students of Lincoln University in Jefferson City, Missouri, "is not to save democracy, for that cannot be saved which is not possessed. But black and white Americans alike must fight to maintain those conditions under which they may continue to strive for the realization of democratic ideals."[78]

By the spring of 1941, the shift in Bunche's thinking away from the Marxian model was complete. In a submission to an essay contest on the next decade of american foreign policy sponsored by the College of William and Mary, Bunche argued that the future of American democracy relied not on the creation of new institutions led by the worker-managers of a democratic union movement, but on the "enlightened leadership of labor and business management."[79] The stark ideological terms of the Second World War caused Bunche to reassess his political philosophy. The choice between fascism and communism made the New Deal now seem a more attractive social program—a genuine middle way between these extremes.

The rise of Nazism, while it turned Bunche into a mainstream social democrat, also led him to perceive African-Americans as having a crucial symbolic significance to American society; for Bunche, these crisis years made African-Americans the most recognizable symbol simultaneously of American democratic achievement and of its still long-unfulfilled promise. During the early 1930s, such an emphasis would have been anathema to Bunche, incompatible as it was with his primary political project of building alliances between African-Americans and other minorities who together formed the majority of the American proletariat. The shift in democratic thinking that the war caused in Bunche resulted in a shift in his thinking about race: "Today, for all thinking people, the Negro is a shining symbol of the true significance of democracy. He has demonstrated what can be achieved with democratic liberties even when grudgingly and incompletely bestowed. But the most vital significance of the Negro . . . to American society . . . is the fact that democracy which is not extended to all of the nation's citizens is a democracy that is mortally wounded."[80] This role as symbol, Bunche argued, implied a weighty responsibility for the black community. Bunche implored African-Americans to reject the racialist interpretations of the war that were pressed by some quarters of the African-American press—that it was a "white man's war" or an "imperialist's war."[81] He said that such conclusions represented a tendency on the part of some to "think Negro," and reflected the "curse of minority status" imposed on the African-American by the "hard-bitten prejudice" of the white majority.[82]

Bunche's speeches to educational and political groups between 1935 and 1941 were his most significant writings as an academic. His role as the principal advisor and "coordinator of information" to Myrdal on the Carnegie Foundation Study "The Negro in America" (published as *An American Dilemma: The Negro Problem and American Democracy*) offered Bunche the opportunity to set these ideas down in a more permanent form—preparatory, perhaps, to their presentation to a larger and more general audience.[83] Bunche produced four book-length interpretive essays for Myrdal: "Conceptions and Ideologies of the Negro Problem," "The Programs, Ideologies and Tactics of Negro Betterment and Interracial Organizations," "Brief and Tentative Analysis of Negro Leadership," and "The Political Status of the Negro." Bunche prefaced each one with a general analysis usually drawn directly from his speeches.

Bunche hoped that Myrdal would use the generous resources provided to him by the Carnegie Foundation to ask hard questions about the American experience and to explore its central contradictions, such as Bunche's thesis that "there has never been in democratic America, a real movement embracing and representative of the masses of the population":[84]

> The study of the political status of the Negro is, in itself, a partial record of the short-comings of American democracy. I think that at least we should raise some questions concerning the seeming inability of American democracy to 'democ' and the essential reasons for it in a period when there are already too many people who are . . . lukewarm toward democracy . . . There are too many people who will say . . . if democracy cannot quickly correct its short-comings, it does not deserve to survive . . . Among those who take such views are many Negroes despite the fact that it is obviously suicidal for the Negro if totalitarianism in any form should be substituted for our present democratic concepts.[85]

Bunche encouraged Myrdal to "probe deeper into [American] social thinking" and to put before a national audience the questions that Bunche had been posing for several years to his own audiences: "Is there more admiration for the Nazi way of life than we think, because it works so well and Americans like things that work well? What is there for an American brand of fascism . . . to fasten itself upon the country? Are we further along the road to fascism than we think? . . . Are we developing an American gestapo? Finally, what steps can we take to safeguard our democratic institutions and move toward the realization of our democratic ideals?"[86] Bunche, in essence, was calling into question whether there really existed, in the minds of most Americans, an "American dilemma"—a tension between a professed belief in equality and the routine toleration of antiegalitarian behavior, such as Jim Crow laws—that nagged insistently at the conscience. Bunche himself was clearly skeptical.[87]

Bunche's collaborative work with Myrdal was not restricted to writing. Bunche accompanied Myrdal, for example, on the Swede's field research in the South, where they observed the "American dilemma" firsthand. Especially memorable to Myrdal was a visit to a Southern jail where, while Myrdal lunched with the warden, Bunche was sent to eat with the members of a black chain gang.[88]

One can search Myrdal's text in vain for traces of either Bunche's questions or his outspoken analysis of the American scene. In volume 1 of *An American Dilemma* Bunche is briefly quoted by Myrdal to substantiate an important aspect of his argument: the pervasiveness among Americans, whether "white, black, red or yellow," of what Myrdal calls the American Creed. In volume 2, Bunche is cited again, this time as an example of a social type: "Marxian-influenced Negro intellectuals."[89]

Bunche could not have been taken entirely by surprise at Myrdal's authorial decision, as the affiliation with Myrdal had been difficult for Bunche. In a memo written to Myrdal in the early morning hours of August 31, 1941, Bunche blasted Myrdal for the way in which the research had been handled: "To speak quite frankly . . . I think our procedure on the study has been quite mad . . . In our worship of deadlines . . . we have converted the work on the study into work on a plantation level. We have had to have 'overseers' who would spur us on to greater effort, who would pep us up and encourage us in an attempt to do the humanly impossible, and even . . . to crack the whip over us in good old Simon Legree fashion."[90] But as much as Bunche detested these conditions, he worked unrelentingly. "Myrdal was adept at pushing the little button that made you keep at it," Donald Young remembered. "This didn't work well on the [other] Negro members of the staff who," Young theorized, "had not been as thoroughly socialized to respond to the academic buttons . . . It worked on Ralph. Ralph would work nights, Saturdays and Sundays."[91]

Writing to Bunche in early 1942, Myrdal confessed that "I will only be able to skim the cream of the cream of your bulky knowledge."[92] Myrdal seems to have regarded Bunche's ideologically assertive introductory essays, however, less as cream, and more as expendable husks that stood between Myrdal and what he considered to be the most relevant kernels of fact collected by Bunche. That Myrdal should choose not to associate himself or the Carnegie Foundation with Bunche's controversial analyses and prescriptions for change is hardly surprising, given that Myrdal's goal as well as his mandate was to produce a document that was, as much as possible, politically and ideologically unassailable.[93] Myrdal also received blunt criticism of Bunche's analysis from the NAACP and the National Urban League. Roy Wilkins, for example, dismissed Bunche as an armchair thinker who "is able to theorize on social movements. He can do this without any great danger to himself, and without . . . having to produce results in any program of social action."[94]

Myrdal's personal opinion of Bunche's analysis of the place of African-Americans in national politics seems to have been quite favorable. He encouraged Bunche to publish his work on "the conceptions and ideologies of the Negro problem," saying, "I think that such a book would be extremely useful, and I know that it wouldn't take much time to do it. It will not overlap my work at all as I am building my chapter in a different way."[95] Whatever the case, given the more conservative direction in which American political culture was about to move, Bunche had ample reason later to be grateful for Myrdal's reticence in using his work. As it was, Bunche was subjected to a loyalty investigation nearly twenty years later on the basis of his writings from the 1930s.

An American Dilemma would achieve its reputation as "the most powerful instrument of action in the field of race relations since Harriet Beecher Stowe's *Uncle Tom's Cabin*" because Myrdal was brilliantly attentive to the cultural politics of wartime America.[96] Myrdal was, by no means, the originator of the argument that there existed an "American dilemma," for this thought developed into a signal theme of wartime political culture. Alain Locke, for example, writing as the guest editor for a *Survey Graphic* "special number on color," called attention to the " 'paradox of race' [which] has become our democracy's greatest dilemma."[97]

An earlier and far more broadly popular best-seller of the wartime period, Wendell Willkie's *One World,* urged Americans to fight our "imperialisms [of race] at home."[98] As Carey McWilliams noted in 1951, "it would be impossible to exaggerate the importance of the role that Wendell Willkie played in the war years in forcing an honest approach to the problem of discrimination in American life. [His writings] represented the most statesmanlike approach to the problem of discrimination to be voiced by an American politician in our time. In large part, moreover, Willkie was a symbol of the way in which a large element of the white majority was responding to the challenge of the times."[99] Hollywood producer Darryl F. Zanuck, in fact, was so impressed with the popularity of *One World* that he briefly considered producing a movie version of it. Those plans were aborted, however, after Twentieth Century–Fox failed to turn a profit on an expensive and hagiographic biography of Woodrow Wilson, whom Zanuck had held up as "an early-day Willkie."[100]

Civil rights leaders Walter White, James Weldon Johnson's successor as Executive Secretary of the NAACP, and A. Philip Randolph, President of the Brotherhood of Sleeping Car Porters of America, were equally vocal in their pursuit of a "Double V," a victory against both fascism and racism at home and abroad. With the efforts of these two activists, the organized campaign for civil rights reached more deeply than ever before into the African-American community. Although Randolph's threatened march on Washington never took place, his tactical maneuvers resulted in the establishment, by the executive order of President Roosevelt, of the Fair Employment Practices Commission and, more important, the ideological mobilization of the entire African-American community around the idea of achieving a Double V. White's visible part in the campaign for a "Double Victory" changed the status of the NAACP in the African-American community. Prior to the war, the organization had been a white, middle-class organ. By the war's end, the membership had grown tenfold and was now drawn most heavily from the ranks of the African-American working class.[101]

An American Dilemma therefore gave official and scientific sanction to a position already being articulated by large segments of the American public.[102] It was this imprimatur of scientific objectivity that separated Myrdal's *Dilemma* from Willkie's *One World,* making one the classic text of a generation, and leaving the other a curiosity of wartime popular culture. Myrdal's great public triumph was the last scene of the first act in the so-called Americanization of the Negro, summarizing a generation of change in American social thought. The "true import" of the "Negro problem" transcended its social, economic, and political dimensions and was isolated as "the moral dilemma of the American—the conflict between his moral valuations ... on the general plane, which we call the 'American Creed' ... and ... the valuations on specific planes of individual and group living." Myrdal's testimony identified "the American Negro problem [as] a problem in the heart of every American."[103]

The "Negro problem" was now front and center on the national stage. A succession of public vignettes—the entry of Jackie Robinson into major league baseball, the integration of the armed forces, the celebration of Ralph Bunche as a representative of a "more vital Americanism," the arguing of the case *Brown v. Topeka,* and the March on Washington (the first officially sanctioned protest march)—affirmed the commitment of America and its citizens to resolve the "American dilemma."

Between 1942 and 1944 Bunche served as the Director of the Africa Section of the Research Analysis Branch of the Office of Strategic Services (the predecessor to the Central Intelligence Agency); for the remainder of the war he was a member of the postwar planning staff of the State Department. At the OSS Bunche's primary mandate was to gather the most accurate information possible on the political situation and strategic resources of the African continent. To accomplish this mission, Bunche relied on his contacts within the Phelpes-Stokes Foundation to interview African students studying in the United States. Bunche also strove, with little success, to argue against "inept American approaches" to the politics of Africa, while advocating that "a special effort should be made to preserve ... the native legend of America as a liberalizing force in the world."[104]

While the freewheeling atmosphere of the OSS was more to Bunche's liking, the more formal structure of the State Department was a different matter. According to Robert Harris, at the State Department Bunche "confronted a rigid bureaucracy and racial prejudice" where "his recommendations were often ignored and even scorned. He was considered a 'do-gooder,' whose pleas for the self-determination of colonial subjects were regarded as impractical."[105] Bunche was present at conferences such as Dumbarton Oaks, where the institutional frameworks for the postwar order were being laid out; however, as Lawrence S. Finkelstein, his colleague at these meetings, has written, Bunche "was not positioned to exert a dominant influence on the issues that remained open for decision."[106] In addition, like his former roommate at Harvard, Robert C. Weaver, and his Howard colleague William Hastie, Bunche was viewed by his Washington superiors as an important source of advice on domestic race relations.[107] Bunche's stay at the State Department was a last stop on the way to his final destination, one that all his experience since his undergraduate days at UCLA had prepared him: in 1946, Bunche left the U.S. government for the Trusteeship Division of the United Nations, thus opening a new chapter in his professional life.

In the fall of 1927, Ralph Bunche had come to Harvard University with the intention, at least initially, of studying law. By the end of his first semester, he had instead chosen to pursue a doctorate in government. Graduate work would serve as a vehicle through which Bunche could examine the intricacies of race relations from the most encompassing perspective possible, the international. In addition, his teaching career at Howard University had brought him into close contact with the foremost thinkers on American race relations in his own country. But the coming of the Second World War interrupted and significantly altered the train of Bunche's thought and career. As the nation moved from the crisis of the Great Depression to preparation for war, Bunche turned his intellectual energies from highly speculative formulations about the restructuring of the American political economy and social order in favor of disciplined attention to the preservation of a particular, if manifestly imperfect, democracy.

These shifts in Bunche's thinking were accompanied by a change of vocation. During the war, Bunche did, at times, look ahead to future academic progress. He remained interested in returning to his original dissertation topic, a study of race relations in Brazil, with an eye toward publishing an ambitious comparative study ranging over several cultures and continents.[108] Bunche was also encouraged by the Rosenwald Foundation to "make a study and report of colonial administration" in the Far East, for which he received a grant.[109] Bunche's immersion in the reorganization of the OSS and his transfer to the State Department placed him at a professional crossroads.[110] Edwin R. Embree, director of the Rosenwald Foundation, argued for the importance of a published study to Bunche's professional future even while sensing the shift in direction that Bunche was contemplating: "In the absence of definite facts, I have no judgment as to the various calls coming to you. It may well be that your duty is to stay in Washington . . . I do feel that you have a contribution to make in a definitive report on colonization in the Far East and for the sake of your own career, I would like to see such a scholarly publication behind you. However, you must decide between the various calls that are pressing upon you."[111]

If the threat to democracy posed by fascism and the prospect of a more effective League of Nations pulled Bunche toward government service, he may also have been pushed away from the university by certain aspects of academic life. More than ten years as a scholar seem to have left Bunche, by the summer of 1940, questioning the value of such a career. In an essay for Howard's *Journal of Negro Education,* Bunche bluntly questioned whether the university was fulfilling its mission in a democracy under threat, writing, "I wish to see us continue to cultivate scholars, but I would also like to see some . . . crusaders for democracy . . . stride forth from our portals." More to the point, Bunche worried that the academy's commitment to the "search for 'Truth' " was really something less: "an escape device—whereby we can divorce ourselves from the rough and dangerous controversies of the world."[112] Although Bunche would officially remain on the faculty of Howard for some years after the war, and although he would tentatively accept an appointment at Harvard in 1949, Bunche would in fact never return to university life. He did, however, remain a teacher. In fact, during the 1950s, he would reach more "students" as a symbol of the United Nations than he ever did as a professor of political science. Such wide visibility as a symbol, however, came at the cost of a loss of autonomy over the use of his own image and his own words.

Ralph Bunche and the Cultural Politics of Race

3

He is a model for all young men to follow. All parents can hold him up to their children as an example to which to aspire. All peoples the world around can see in him the great heights that the human spirit may reach— even in the face of great difficulty . . . I am hoping that there are many young men and also young women who are today thinking very seriously about training for the foreign service of their country . . . It is a field wherein the Negro, as opposed to other ethnic groups in this country, is uniquely fitted, with proper training, to bring peace to our country and to the world.

—Mary McLeod Bethune (1953)

The Negro wanted to feel pride in his race? With tokenism the solution was simple. If all twenty million Negroes would keep looking at Ralph Bunche, the one man in so exalted a post would generate such a volume of pride that it could be cut into portions and served to everyone.

—Martin Luther King, Jr. (1964)

As an African-American troubleshooter with the newborn United Nations, Ralph Bunche became an icon of possibilities: that the Wilsonian vision of international order might be redeemed, shorn of racial condescension, and that the "double V" sought by A. Philip Randolph and W. E. B. Du Bois after World War I might actually be achieved. "Today in this year of war, 1945," Franklin Roosevelt counseled Americans in his final inaugural address, "we have learned that we cannot live alone, at peace; that our own well-being is dependent on the well-being of other Nations, far away. We have learned that we must live as men and not as ostriches, nor as dogs in the manger. We have learned to be citizens of the world, members of the human community."[1]

This expectation was repeatedly expressed throughout the Cold War era and formed the intellectual foundation for American entry into the United Nations, military interventions in Korea and Vietnam, collective security agreements across the globe, and extensive programs of foreign aid and military assistance, along with their cultural counterparts, programs encouraging "cultural exchange." During the early Cold War, public portrayals of Ralph Bunche condensed his life and work into a symbolic testimonial that in the field of race relations Americans were indeed internationalists. A Canadian journalist captured best the fervor with which some opinion leaders used this image of Bunche to promote the hope that the dream of a humane community of free and independent nations might come to pass: "It is remarkable enough that a poor Negro orphan has become one of the most eminent Americans of his time. But Bunche is less important as a man than as a symbol. As a man he has become the most famous figure in the United Nations, but as a symbol he represents the whole meaning of the United Nations. In him, the divided worlds of color are at last joined."[2]

The publicly constructed Bunche, the symbol created by American journalists, Hollywood screenwriters, advertisers, and United Nations publicists, was an important ingredient in the making and remaking of common meanings about race and democracy in the political culture of the early Cold War. Bunche's public accomplishments and personal biography—and, to a lesser extent, his own words—became important narrative set-pieces in the deracialization of the Horatio Alger myth, defining the boundaries of Negro Americanism and modeling a resolute approach to prejudice with which all supposedly could identify. Furthermore, the iconic Bunche came to personify a mode of internationalism that placed great faith in the power—symbolic, potential, and real—of the United Nations to bring about a more stable, just, and humane world order. Of these symbolic roles, the last proved to be the most resonant: only Eleanor Roosevelt, the "first lady of the world," was more recognized as the embodiment of the humanitarian dimensions of this responsibility. In a 1950 cover photograph, the editors of *Ebony* visually captured just this sentiment, showing the pair looking up from a document, presumably the UN charter, that they held jointly in their hands. This image vividly represented how the UN, through Bunche and Roosevelt, was helping to join the historically divided "worlds of color." The editorialists of *Ebony* spoke for millions beyond their readership when they declared that, as an African-American serving as a peacemaker on behalf of the entire world community, "there is no one [in the

United Nations] more symbolic of its worldly ideals" than Ralph Bunche.[3] It was not just that Bunche was a model of basic American values; Americans, in order to be genuine Americans, must act according to his example.[4]

The quotations that open this chapter introduce its subject: Bunche's evolution, in American postwar popular culture, as a collective representation of American aspiration. In its first incarnation, the Bunche image symbolized a world cleansing itself of racial hatred and an imperial past as it created a more just world order through the United Nations. Much of Bunche's initial popularity arose from the belief that, by establishing the competence of the United Nations to mediate a fragile peace between Israel and Egypt, Bunche had prevented the institution from "following the League of Nations into oblivion."[5]

As the most honored African-American in America, Bunche's name came to be invoked by the white press to symbolize the absurdity and the mindless cruelty of racism as well as the universality of the reach of racial injustice—a burden borne by all, from Malcolm X to Ralph Bunche. Such was the case in Charles E. Silberman's *Crisis in Black and White,* one of the first books written to explain the "Negro revolt" to the general public: "The occasional acts of police brutality, however, hurt less than the constant flow of petty indignities—indignities that seem to demonstrate . . . that no matter what a Negro does, no matter what he believes, no matter what he is, the white world will never accept him. He can be Ralph Bunche and still be refused a room in an Atlanta hotel while his secretary's reservation is immediately accepted."[6] In the opinion, however, of his former Howard University colleague E. Franklin Frazier, Bunche's frequent appearances in the black press contained a narrower and not altogether healthy significance for the black bourgeoisie:

> While rejecting any genuine identification with the black race, the black bourgeoisie seeks nevertheless whatever recognition it may enjoy because of the high status of individuals of Negro ancestry in the world. Consequently, the Negro press is compelled to focus attention upon the relatively few Negroes who have gained any form of recognition in the white world. The few Negroes who have gained recognition consist chiefly of entertainers and leaders of organizations

who have contact with whites. Dr. Ralph J. Bunche has a unique position in this respect, since not a week passes that the Negro press fails to carry news about him and his achievements. Every recognition that Dr. Bunche has received has been interpreted as a form of recognition for the black bourgeoisie—who have been all the more inclined to identify with him because he is not black.[7]

As for Bunche's visibility in the white press, some feared that the repeated use of Bunche as a success story created a convenient illusion of progress that could be used by the leaders of white America to postpone, and even thwart, the achievement of fundamental social reform. When Martin Luther King used Bunche's name, it was to bring to light the unintended consequences of Bunche's symbolic ubiquity. Michael Harrington, in *The Other America,* went further, summarizing a report that argued that the hero-worship of Jackie Robinson and Bunche did more harm than good: "The image of Jackie Robinson or Ralph Bunche is a threat to the young Negro. These heroes are exceptional and talented men. Yet, in a time of ferment among Negroes, they tend to become norms and models for the young people. Once again, there is a tragic gap between the ideal and the possible. A sense of disillusion, of failure, is added to the indignity of poverty."[8] By the middle 1970s, Ralph Bunche, to the extent that he was remembered at all, was recalled as part of a discredited era in which African-Americans were required to "fit in" to white America. In 1977, shortly after being appointed the United States ambassador to the United Nations, Andrew Young recalled that Ralph Bunche had been a hero of his youth, that his example had first inspired Young to think about serving in that body. For the middle-aged Andrew Young, now an admired veteran of the civil rights movement and a respected political figure in his own right, the memory of Bunche also recalled the high price of success for blacks in the forties and fifties. For Bunche, as for others of that era, "A lot of . . . energy went into not being black and trying to assimilate."[9]

The late 1940s and early 1950s were a period of dramatic change in the rules governing American political and cultural life. The presumed imperative of fighting a globally expansive communism predicated the blacklist that blighted American life for more than a decade to come. This imperative also provided the rationale for the celebration of figures like Ralph Bunche and Jackie Robinson, who became the two most recognizable emblems of African-American achievement in American culture.[10]

The relationship of these two symbols to each other in the public arena is best captured by a photo essay titled "Two Great Americans" in the February 1951 issue of *The Instructor*. The photo essay was composed of two photographs: the first of Robinson, the champion athlete, suited up in a Brooklyn Dodger uniform, and the second of Bunche, the world-traveling, Harvard-trained intellectual, dressed in a tailored suit, leaning against a bookcase and looking up thoughtfully from the giant book he held in his hands.[11] Robinson and Bunche symbolized for many the two halves of African-American achievement: Robinson, its physical genius, and Bunche, its intellectual brilliance. As icons of possibilities both men served as popular evocations of the hope that the color line had been erased and that America's newfound leadership in redrawing the map of the world—through the Marshall plan, NATO, and a rebuilt and politically reconstructed Japan—would be matched by a parallel willingness to invent a new democracy at home.

American Race Relations on the World Stage

The composite creation from newspaper profiles, magazine cover stories, and television dramas that I call "Ralph Bunche stories" was part of a larger discourse on race and democracy that began during the New Deal, gathered force and legitimacy during the Second World War, and survived, in a weakened form, into the postwar period. During the war, Sumner Welles, Wendell Willkie, Eleanor Roosevelt, Gunnar Myrdal, and a host of others made clear that the elimination of prejudice was both a moral and a strategic necessity. By the Cold War, as the reformist politics of the New Deal era fell out of public favor, the international strategic imperative came to dominate the debate on civil rights. As the President's Committee on Civil Rights (which eventually became the U.S. Civil Rights Commission) admitted in 1947, "Our civil rights record has growing international implications . . . A lynching in a rural community is not a challenge to that community's conscience alone. The repercussions of such a crime are heard not only in the locality, or indeed only in our own nation. They echo from one end of the world to another, and the world looks to the American national government for both an explanation of how such a shocking event can occur in a civilized world and remedial action to prevent its recurrence."[12]

For New Deal liberals, especially those like Henry Wallace, who found themselves on the ideological defensive as the Cold War gained momentum, the United Nations possessed a special significance.[13] In addition to the widely expressed hope that the UN might be able to contribute to the creation of a democratic world community, many seem to have shared the expectation expressed by the sociologists Arnold and Caroline Rose that the UN "will become strong enough to force the United States to give up its most unpopular domestic policy."[14] If the UN charter offered little encouragement for this belief, the location of UN headquarters in New York City insured that each incident of public racism in the United States, especially those involving diplomats from the developing nations, would become a proverbial shot heard round the world.[15] In testimony advocating the desegregation of the armed forces before the Senate Armed Services Committee, A. Philip Randolph made typically masterful use of the new international and strongly anticolonial context in which American leadership was now forced to act: "Negroes want full and unqualified first class citizenship . . . Passage now of a Jim Crow draft may only result in a mass civil disobedience movement along the lines of the magnificent struggles of the people of India against British imperialism . . . In resorting to the principles and direct-action techniques of Gandhi . . . Negroes will be serving a higher law than any passed by a national legislature in an era when racism spells our doom."[16]

This emphasis on what racial equality might gain the United States in goodwill abroad became one point of entry for public reflection on the symbolic meaning of Ralph Bunche. In early 1950, *The Chicago Defender* nominated Bunche for the post of Secretary of State on the theory that Bunche's presence in that high national office "would give the lie to the enemy propaganda that American democracy is limited to those who can pass a color test." In a clear reference to the fall of China only a few months earlier, *The Defender* continued: "We need the kind of leadership that Mr. Bunche could give us to turn the Asiatic our way. It will take more than dollars to win the Cold War. And Dr. Bunche has what it takes." *Colliers,* under the headline "Mr. President, May We Suggest . . .," advised Harry Truman to counter Soviet propaganda by making Bunche the ambassador to that country. Disclaiming that such an appointment would be a propaganda stunt, the editors argued for it as "a logical step in America's progress toward better race relations."[17]

Bunche himself was quite aware of his central place in the discussion of race in the early Cold War era, and had few qualms about using it in the service of a greater cause. In the spring of 1949, Bunche turned down an appointment as Assistant Secretary of State for Near Eastern and African Affairs because, as he told Philip B. Gellman of *Colliers:* "There's too much Jim Crow in Washington for me . . . It is extremely difficult for a Negro to maintain even a semblance of dignity in Washington. At every turn, he's confronted with places he can't go because of his color . . . Washington isn't unique in this regard . . . but it is the national capital and its racial policies have a great symbolic significance."[18]

In an effort to underline the symbolic importance of segregation in the nation's capital, Bunche addressed the nation via a live radio hookup on July 4th, 1949. "I have lived and worked in Washington for almost a score of years," Bunche began, with a rhetorical allusion to the first words of Lincoln's Gettysburg Address. "Living in the nation's capital is like serving out a [prison] sentence for any Negro who detests segregation and discrimination." By refusing to enter government work under these circumstances, Bunche was, in fact, serving his country. In his protest for equality, Bunche argues, the African-American—in this case Bunche—became the quintessential patriot:

> The Negro is a better American than most when he insists on the realization of the ideals set forth in the Constitution. Because the Negro American believes in [the] principles and ideals which make up the American creed, he would certainly fight to protect the country and its ideals. He has always done so, and I believe he always will. But it is the responsibility of the Negro American . . . and of every American citizen, regardless of color or creed . . . to insist relentlessly on the privilege of enjoying his birthright, which is equality of treatment and opportunity.[19]

Bunche's highly public refusal of the State Department appointment moved some to contrast the traditions sanctioned by the American government with the spirit that was being born at the United Nations. As the venerable and respected African-American newspaper *The Pittsburgh Courier* speculated: "We wonder if deep down inside [himself], Dr. Bunche prefers the atmosphere of the United Nations [where] ability, not color, is a measuring rod of achievement."[20]

Bunche not only symbolized the idea that African-Americans were the equal of any American in ability and potential; his accomplishments were also appropriated by the mainstream media to represent the alleged ideological conformity of leading African-Americans with the emerging anticommunist consensus. This objective was accomplished by contrasting Bunche with another distinguished and well-known black figure, Paul Robeson.[21]

In the 1920s and 1930s Robeson had won wide admiration, both as an athletic hero and as a gifted actor and singer. In the late 1940s, however, Robeson came to be portrayed in increasingly negative terms by the media because his stance on the Soviet Union was at odds with the aims of Cold War policy. During the Second World War, Robeson's public warmth toward the Soviet Union had been in accord with the broad ideological outlines of the American war effort, an effort determined to portray the Soviets as freedom-loving allies; within a few years of the war's end, however, these same views would turn Robeson into a pariah. In the war of public opinion waged against Robeson in the press, the extent of Robeson's "heresy" was highlighted by contrasting Robeson to the vocally anticommunist Bunche.

The invidious comparison of Robeson to Bunche was but one manifestation of a larger fact: African-American performers were not necessarily required to "name names" to avoid the blacklist, but the most effective way to avoid entanglement, according to Victor Navasky, was to attack Paul Robeson, whose past accomplishments had, up to the time of the Cold War, transformed him in the eyes of many black Americans into "the sun around which all else revolved."[22] Navasky argues that this "double standard" was caused by the lack of power of African-Americans within Hollywood. Because Robeson possessed considerable power in the black community, however, prominent African-Americans were expected to disassociate themselves from his views. As Navasky has written, "because blacks already lacked stature in the Hollywood scheme of things, nothing was to be gained by subjecting them to the humiliation routinely visited on whites. They were called upon to degrade not themselves, but their star. And he, in turn, granted indulgences to those blacks who chose collaboration over unemployment on the theory that they had enough problems without shouldering the additional burden of opposing the white man's list. It wasn't their fight."[23]

In April 1950, Robeson provoked a major furor—though one, it is interesting to note, restricted primarily to the white press. He expressed the view that "it is unthinkable . . . that American Negroes would go to war against . . . [the Soviet Union] . . . which in one generation has raised our people to full human dignity of mankind [sic]."[24] Like Jackie Robinson, who appeared before the House Un-American Activities Committee to refute Robeson's statement, Bunche had to make clear— both in public and private—his position on Robeson. As Bunche wrote to the State Department's Division of Security Affairs, he and Robeson were friends of long standing, "but during the past few years we have not seen eye to eye on political matters at all."[25] Bunche made much the same point to the readers of *Collier's* when he pointedly suggested, "Paul should stick to singing." "I've known Paul since 1927," Bunche wrote. "He's had some very unpleasant experiences here, as all of us [have]. He's resentful of the injustices, as all of us are. I know that when he went to Russia he was very well received, and that may have influenced him to follow the party line. He's entitled to his opinions, of course, but I think he's radically wrong. His statements represent the attitudes of very few Negroes indeed."[26] Bunche's rather mild statement of disagreement with Robeson reflected the more temperate attitude within the African-American community toward Robeson's political views. As Walter White told the readers of *Ebony,* "No honest American, white or Negro, can sit in judgment on a man like Paul Robeson unless and until he has sacrificed time, talent, money and popularity in doing the utmost to root out the racial and economic evils which infuriate men like Robeson."[27]

The "thunderbolts of displeasure and rage" came from the white media.[28] Editorialists in the white press frequently juxtaposed the genuinely "American" Bunche against the clearly "un-American" Robeson. "Dr. Bunche pleads the cause of the Negro in the name of real American democracy," ventured the *New York Herald Tribune,* while "Mr. Robeson . . . pleads for the Negro cause in the name of . . . the Soviet Union and its satellites." The paper counseled its readers that "Mr.

Bunche and Mr. Robeson are both right in insisting that there cannot be second class citizens in a democracy." The decisive difference—what allegedly gave unchallenged credence to Bunche—was that "Dr. Bunche is devoted to the equality that arises from freedom [while] Mr. Robeson has attached himself to the cause of a country in which all men are equal because they are all enslaved."[29] Rupert Ruark, writing under the stark headline "Bunche Versus Robeson," was even more blunt in his caricature: "Dr. Bunche demonstrates strikingly that an American, no matter what his color, still has an unlimited ceiling for his achievement. His existence makes a liar of Mr. Robeson and the other race screamers."[30]

Such media-generated endorsements of Bunche as a patriotic American, however, did not entirely immunize Bunche from ideological investigation. It was with a keen sense of irony that Bunche recorded in his diary his being notified that a loyalty investigation was underway: "I had just returned from Haiti . . . where I was selling U.S. democracy."[31] In 1953 and 1954, Bunche's activities as a founding member of the National Negro Congress and, for an equally short time, of the International Committee for African Affairs brought him to the attention of a "loyalty review board" set up by the Federal Bureau of Investigation to investigate Americans employed by the United Nations and its affiliated agencies.[32] To add insult to injury, Bunche was told by friends that the FBI was inquiring about whether Bunche was "more pro-UN than pro-U.S." and "whether, because of my success and high position, I had become isolated from my race!"[33] Supported by a lengthy affidavit describing his departure from both the NNC and the ICAA because of Communist infiltration, as well as by testimonials of ideological correctness from Walter White and others, Bunche was publicly cleared the week after the Supreme Court's ruling in *Brown v. Board of Education.* The connection between Bunche's clearance and the *Brown* decision was not lost on the editors of *The Nation:*

> There is deep humiliation in the circumstance that Dr. Ralph J. Bunche should have been called upon to defend his loyalty in the week that followed the Supreme Court's decision outlawing segregation in American public education. Dr. Bunche is a symbol throughout the world of the American Negro's increasingly effective struggle for equality and complete emancipation from every badge of

discrimination based on race or color . . . Pity the "Voice of America" broadcasters who had to announce this humiliating news in the wake of the Supreme Court's decision![34]

"One World" in the Classroom

Given the neat intersection that was perceived to exist between the conduct and objectives of American diplomacy and the visible improvement of American race relations, it might seem unnecessary to look further to explain the centrality of this discourse on race to postwar public life, or of Bunche's key position within it. Even without the goad of the Communist threat, however, the war had created a fundamentally new ideological terrain, one that required changes in racial attitudes and practices that only a few years earlier would have been assumed to be impossible.

Introducing a revised edition of his wartime classic *Brothers under the Skin,* the journalist Carey McWilliams alluded to this vast change in atmosphere when he recalled that, in the early years of the war, he had been "almost entirely concerned with [conveying the] gathering tensions, the ever-widening perspective . . . which the racial problem had suddenly assumed in American life with the onset of World War II." McWilliams judged that a "revolution . . . in the field of what we still call 'race relations' " had made this bit of education largely unnecessary.[35] Charles S. Johnson, with Wendell Willkie's wartime best-seller very much on his mind, wrote that "wise men and women in every country . . . have called upon their fellow men that this has become 'one world'; that what happens to any of us is important to all of us, that the 'white peoples' and the 'colored peoples' are fellow citizens in the world community . . . More and more we are realizing that, in world community, in national community, in local community, we shall build soundly only when all citizens participate." This grand generality seemed to be concretized, Johnson elaborated, by tangible events taking place on the American scene: "Fresh interest is being shown in all our minority groups, Negro, Indian, Mexican, and Oriental, for the better protection of their rights and for their fuller participation in the responsibilities of citizenship. The Department of Justice is increasingly energetic in prosecuting violations of Federal law directed against members of minority groups, and the

Supreme Court in its recent decisions has continued its tradition of upholding the constitutional rights of citizens irrespective of race."[36]

A comprehensive change in the national outlook on race indeed seemed under way. A host of other breakthroughs from 1947 to 1954—the creation of racially integrated public housing, the desegregation of the armed forces, and the abolition of the doctrine of "separate but equal" in American public education—appeared to indicate that American society was moving in a progressive direction. Lee Nichols, whose popular history of the desegregation of the armed forces served as a widely recommended primer in the public mobilization against prejudice, reflected the matter-of-fact sense of inevitability that characterized so much writing on the subject, stating that "families of Negro and white servicemen were coming more and more to live next to one another on military reservations. Their wives gossiped across the clothesline and learned to be friendly neighbors. Their children attended schools together on military bases in the South . . . This tide of integration was inexorably sweeping into the civilian world, where similar currents were at work."[37] This "tide of integration," commentators assumed, would eventually wash over every part of the republic, propelled forward not by spiritually elevating and rigorously logical sermons on civic unity and intergroup relations, but by natural human contacts that would self-evidently affirm that all were indeed equal.

The public school would prove to be the most important vehicle for spreading the internationalist ethos expressed in Willkie's *One World*. As such, the public schools would serve as another point whereby "The Ralph Bunche Story" would enter into postwar political culture. Rachel Davis Du Bois, "the best-known and most persistent experimenter in the field," believed the public school to be the central institution in providing Americans with their necessary "equipment as modern globe-trotters"; the public school served as "a modern means of getting to know people" where citizens could "recapture their tradition of neighborliness" so that they would be enabled to live in the "culturally mixed social worlds" of the modern era. In so doing, the integrated school, Du Bois argued, would "help rebuild our disintegrated community life."[38]

There was wide agreement on the necessity of "seeking to substitute for symbols based on ignorance and narrow interests other symbols that convey the truth."[39] The truth, in this instance, was that "racial differences (pigmentation, hair, eyes) have no significance as far as culture goes . . . but that cultural differences are fascinating and can be appreciated and even shared."[40] Symbols alone, however, no matter how thickly they adorned the public arena, were useless. "We doubt the worth," wrote Lloyd and Elaine Cook in their text *Intergroup Relations,* "of much good-will material, the barrage day and night of news stories, commercial films, radio and telecasts, streetcar and hallway placards, form letters, leaflets, and the like. People respond who already agree with what is said, and other people are hard to . . . impress. Often, too, a propaganda idea gets twisted in perception, or even reversed, so that it comes to sanction whatever prejudice exists."[41]

Such commentators assumed that, in order for changes in racial attitudes to be genuine, it was necessary that the rearrangement and invention of symbols take place within the intimate context of positive one-to-one relationships between individuals. Such interactions would be facilitated by the local school and church and then radiate out from such places into the homes of a community. Symbols taught in the course of such positive human encounters—whether with playmates, neighbors, or fellow parishioners from another race, religion, or culture—were effective, these educators believed, because universal truths were made real by concrete experiences. The public school, staffed with teachers sensitive to the practical applications of democratic and pluralistic values in the classroom situation, would thus be able to play a central role in redefining the meaning of difference in American social life.

According to this line of thought, if the classroom were to play its part in social reconstruction it must, in a sense, *become* the world—a United Nations in miniature—mirroring its diversity and accurately reflecting its problems and crises. Superficially, this involved rearranging the classroom: decorating it, for example, with picture essays and murals reflecting different aspects of community life from the vantage point of various ethnic communities and depicting the origins of significant local folkways; it also meant portraying the extent to which poverty, discrimination, and other social ills existed.

Such a classroom would also be stocked with a "wide collection of the best available biographies of the most successful people of all races," along with pertinent copies of such journals as *National Geographic* and *Survey Graphic.*[42] The democratic message conveyed on the classroom's walls and in its bookshelves was to be reinforced by a teaching style emphasizing the "cooperative effort of teacher and pupils" and by assignments focusing on such questions as "How can the United States solve its minority problems in the most democratic manner?"[43] In such classrooms, "The Ralph Bunche Story" was given a prominent place in lesson plans introducing American's youngest citizens to their responsibilities as pioneers in "intergroup relations."

Ralph Bunche Stories

It is difficult in retrospect to recapture fully the enthusiasm with which progressive educators, UN propagandists, and liberal screenwriters latched on to Bunche as a composite symbol of internationalism. In schools across America children might read in the national elementary school newspaper *Current Events* that Bunche's diplomatic triumph "has given a new sense of self-confidence to American Negroes."[44] Tenth-grade students could read about "the revolution that has never ended" in Bunche's description of "What America Means to Me," included in the textbook *Adventures in Appreciation.*[45] In the wake of the *Brown* decision, the newspaper of the California Teachers Association proclaimed, "Taking the Supreme Court's anti-segregation decision in one hand and the story of Ralph Bunche in the other, most responsible educators stand solidly against prejudice and discrimination."[46] Students could also read Bunche's words themselves as reprinted in publications such as *Reader's Digest* and in didactic volumes such as Leonard S. Kenworthy's *Twelve Citizens of the World,* which introduced the young reader to "a group of world heroes as symbols for the world community which we are now trying to create."[47]

Set beside other internationalist icons such as Albert Schweitzer, Mahatma Gandhi, and Eleanor Roosevelt, Kenworthy introduced Bunche as a poor boy, one who, like Huck Finn, seldom wore shoes. An orphan, Bunche was depicted as having been steeled against prejudice by his grandmother, Lucy Johnson, who was described as "a sage and practical idealist." "Nana's" influence was far-reaching indeed, in Kenworthy's view, for he credited her spirit of determined optimism with having achieved an armistice in the Middle East. In the aftermath of this achievement, Bunche was, Kenworthy plainly stated, symbolic of a world that seemed on the very verge of creation: "By this dramatic event Bunche had been catapulted into public prominence. He had become a symbol. He represented the success of the United Nations. He represented the hope of the world for peace. He represented the yearnings of the colonial peoples for a better life. He represented the Negro race at its best and the possibility that it would increasingly be released to make its contribution to a better United States and a better world."[48]

A teleplay by United Nations Radio also held Bunche up as a new man for a new era—"a new human being of the century—the citizen of the world."[49] A short film commissioned by the Los Angeles Unified School District, in its exploration of "what makes a hero tick," found in Bunche's background the gifts that "showed the world that differences between people need not result in wars."[50] The readers of *Senior Scholastic* were advised that Bunche was "one of America's greatest living diplomats"[51] and read, in his own words, the role that they must assume in the postwar world:

> The youth of our land, as of every other land, have a special responsibility to discharge in the universal effort to achieve a secure and peaceful world. The issue of peace or war is no longer the exclusive concern of governments and rulers. Peace is everyone's business today, and no age group has more at stake than youth, for their future is totally involved. In this international age, youth can play an effective role in determining the future course of events only if it is alert, well-informed and dedicated firmly to high moral values.[52]

Another important ingredient in the didactic campaign to make Bunche known to the next generation was a teleplay broadcast over the ABC network on the evening of October 11, 1955.[53] Written and produced with Bunche's cooperation, "Toward Tomorrow: The Ralph Bunche-Lucy Johnson Story," like "The Jackie Robinson Story" of five years earlier, is less a biography than a series of set-pieces about the daily encounters of individual blacks with prejudice and, equally important, their undimmed faith in the American Dream in the face of such palpably undemocratic behavior.

"Toward Tomorrow" opens upon a "vacant lot ... arid soil littered with rocks and dried weeds," and comes to rest on a small peach tree. This stark visual image is accompanied by a narrator's explanation of the scene: "No matter how rough the soil, a tree—if it is tended, properly nourished, can grow whole and strong. Human beings need care and nourishment." With this cue, the camera moves away from the tree to reveal a larger scene of boys playing baseball amid the rubble. It is a tableau of naturally occurring pluralism and integration made possible by the innocence of childhood. The players are "white, Negro, Mexican," and they are deeply involved in the archetypal national sport. "They are," the stage notes instruct, "alike only in the poverty of their dress." Ralph, "a wiry sensitive boy of twelve, hits a highball," providing a climax to the opening scene, and foreshadowing his future trajectory.

The action shifts to a nearby street outside the Bunche home, where Lucy Johnson ("Nana"), a woman "of small stature, but with a dignity and pride which shows even through the strain of work and grief," is coming home from the hospital, where Olive Johnson Bunche has just died. Once Nana arrives home, the discussion turns to the need to take Ralph into the Johnson family, which will require her to return to work despite her advanced age. When told by the family that she is too old to work, Nana responds, "That's what they told me when your father died, but I did it and I raised you five children . . . I can do it with Ralph." Then Nana announces a crucial decision, one that would, she hopes, heal the family spiritually and improve its material prospects: "I've been thinking all the way home, there's nothing but unhappiness here. We're going to a new place, a city where—" Her announcement is interrupted by Ralph's arrival home from his game. Lucy Johnson wastes little time giving young Ralph the news: "I've got some bad news for you Ralph, and some good to help a little through the bad. We're leaving here. We're going to take you to Los Angeles where you can grow up . . . right and get a college education like your grandfather . . . That's the good, Ralph. Now what I am going to tell you is going to make you cry. But when the crying's done, there's a better day to look forward to." So, like the Joad family later, and like generations of pioneers before them, the Johnsons trek west.

The next sequence finds Bunche in Los Angeles, struggling with his fears and apprehensions about joining the school basketball team. Under close questioning from Nana, Bunche admits that the fear of racial ridicule from fellow teammates and the coach lies behind his reluctance. In response, Ralph receives what amounts to a homespun lesson in "intergroup relations." Echoing the sentiments expressed in Richard Rodgers and Oscar Hammerstein's song from *South Pacific,* "You've Got to Be Taught (to Hate)," as well as the mainstream social science of the day, Nana says, "People are just as bad—or as good—as they are *taught* to be [emphasis in the original] . . . Remember that. But don't make excuses for yourself. People can't give you a chance unless you ask them." Thus spiritually fortified, Ralph goes to the tryout, where he is treated with stern egalitarianism by a coach whose main concern rests not in racial matters, but in putting together a winning team. Soon we see Nana buying a scrapbook to record Ralph's athletic and academic exploits. We also see Bunche working hard at a print shop after school, studying earnestly late in the evening after work. In fact, we learn that Bunche is so diligent that one night when there is no work at the print shop he stops at the local library to study some law books.

The emphasis of the story is on Nana's strenuous efforts to insure that Bunche continues to "grow toward tomorrow." Burdened by poor health and insufficient money to continue at UCLA, Bunche briefly leaves school, returning only in tribute to Nana's importunings about the future. Explaining why she had established a secret college account to help him continue his education, Nana tells the youth, "You're going to be a big man, Ralph, an important man. This [the money] isn't just for you, it's for . . . You know what I mean a whole lot better than I could find words to say it. You got [sic] to grow toward tomorrow."

In this version of Bunche's biography, it is the efforts of Lucy Johnson, not those of the "Send Ralph Bunche to Harvard" community campaign, that are credited with paying for Bunche's first two years of graduate school. In the same way that, as Ossie Davis has argued, the admiring critics of *A Raisin in the Sun* "kidnapped" Lena ("Mama") Younger and made *Raisin* the story of her personal and individual triumph rather than a drama about her son Walter Lee's exclusion from the American Dream (see Chapter 7), the screenwriters of "Toward Tomorrow" centered their narrative around a similar matriarchal figure. This license with Bunche's biography (apparently sanctioned by him) insured that the plot conformed to a larger cultural script, one emphasizing individualistic virtues. This choice foreclosed the portrayal of a more interesting and complex reality, one at odds with prevailing stereotypes: the role of an organized and supportive African-American community in the launching of one of its younger members into the often hostile world of the larger white society.

If this rendition of "The Ralph Bunche Story" was not entirely faithful to Bunche's biography, it was true to the symbolic and narrative conventions governing the representation of racial politics in popular culture. Contained within the Horatio Alger motif that was stretched over the entire script were others of equal importance: the opening sequence depicting a makeshift ball game, composed so as to emphasize the integrating power of competitive sport, or the centering of further plot-turning action upon the school, where athletics continues to exert its equalizing and integrating influence. There is even a discreet bow to the study of the law as the key to future progress.

"Toward Tomorrow" closes with a scene of a giant scrapbook—presumably Nana's—"elegantly bound, beautifully mounted, containing large photographs as [a] hand flips through the pages." As these scenes pass by, the narrator summarizes Bunche's journey to greatness: "So Ralph 'went on' as a teacher. He returned to Harvard for his doctorate, then went into the service of his country and ultimately into the service of the world." Bunche's bureaucratic posts are listed there as well, and the film ends with a voice-over narrator observing that Bunche's "work has taken him to every corner of the world. His honorary degrees number thirty-four in the United States alone. Today, Ralph J. Bunche is the highest ranking American in the United Nations. Nana Johnson's grandson ranks in all the world second only to the Secretary-General himself." As the narrative comes to a close, the camera settles on a picture of Lucy Johnson. Gradually the camera pulls back, revealing Ralph Bunche himself, seated behind a desk, from which he reads a statement summarizing the lessons of his grandmother's life: "This story is a tribute to a truly wonderful woman . . . Wherever I have gone in the world I have found something of my grandmother's simple goodness and nobility of spirit among people of all nations, races and creeds. Nana taught me that people are bad only as they learn bad lessons from the environment around them; they are capable of unlimited good. To her early teaching I owe my firm faith in people and my never-failing optimism about the future."

"Toward Tomorrow" served as yet another vehicle for arguing the pertinence of the Horatio Alger myth to the African-American experience. In this, it delivered to its audience the same themes that the children of this audience would find thirty years later in the miniseries *Roots.* Herbert Gutman's analysis of *Roots* succinctly captures the aims of "Toward Tomorrow": "*Roots* was an adventure story, a success story that pitted the individual . . . against society . . . *Roots* succeeded in redefining the central tensions in slave society in ways that made it possible to integrate the Afro-American slave experience into middle class American culture. What was more 'American' than a small slave family with meager resources . . . making it? *Roots* succeeded in integrating the slave experience into mainstream American ideology."[54]

Television was not the only medium to apply the Alger myth to the popularization of Bunche's biography. Irwin Ross' profile of Bunche, reprinted in the *Reader's Digest,* is just one example of the myth in print. Ross, too, played on the established story line about Bunche's deprived childhood as an orphan, and highlighted the figure of Nana, whom he described as "a tiny woman of vibrant spirit and strong conviction" who "taught the boy to feel pride about his race, and never to accept a slight from anyone, but never to feel bitterness." Following the Alger formula, Bunche is shown as having been employed from a young age: "In Detroit Bunche hawked newspapers and served as a delivery boy. Later, while attending high school in Los Angeles, he worked as a messenger for the *Los Angeles Times* and spent a summer as a house servant in Hollywood."[55]

But Bunche's story is more than that of a disadvantaged lad "bound to rise," for his race proved to be an additional obstacle he was forced to surmount. Bunche's "brilliant record" at Jefferson High School, for example, failed to shelter him from prejudice. Ross, retelling an incident that became a fixed frame in the Bunche story, recalls that Jefferson's principal congratulated its valedictorian with the comment "We never thought of you as a Negro." Bunche's reaction was faithfully recorded: " 'That line stopped me dead,' Bunche recalls. 'I just didn't know what to say. But I have never forgotten it.' " Such condescension, Ross explains, "only spurred Bunche to greater effort . . . He worked his way though the University of California at Los Angeles, where he won his varsity letter in basketball, was elected to the student board of control, and served as president of the debating society. Majoring in political science, he won scholarships for three years, was elected to Phi Beta Kappa, and graduated summa cum laude."[56]

Homer Metz, writing in the *New Republic,* worked this narrative line in a similar manner, although with some significant variations in fact:

> Ralph Bunche is the grandson of a slave, the son of a Detroit barber . . . When he was a small child, his mother . . . got tuberculosis and the family moved to New Mexico. Ralph was twelve years old when his father and mother both died within weeks of each other, and he moved to Los Angeles to live with his maternal grandmother. There, he attended high school, and on graduation day, an incident occurred which he never forgot. The high school principal, meeting him in the hall, slapped him on the back.
>
> 'You're alright Ralph,' said the principal. 'You know, I never thought of you as a Negro at all.'

Contrary to Metz's account, Bunche's parents did not die "within weeks of each other": Fred Bunch disappeared after Olive Bunch's death. Their son was taken to Los Angeles by his grandmother to join his Uncle Charlie's family, who had already established themselves there. In Metz's version of Bunche's encounter with his high school principal, the impact of that event on Bunche was juxtaposed, through Bunche's own words, against a life lived in the shadow of Jim Crow: "This hit me harder than all the many times that I had been told that I wasn't wanted in all sorts of public places. I always knew that something could be done about Jim Crow laws. But what could you do about a man like that principal?"[57] Metz characterized Bunche as following a road to success already well-trod by previous generations of the "excluded." Buffetted by prejudice, Bunche fought back with accomplishments that could neither be denied nor taken from him: "One thing he could do was go ahead in the best education available; luckily, he was in California, which does not practise [sic] segregation in college. He got a scholarship and, to earn extra money, he worked as a janitor, a mess boy on a coastal steamer, as a carpet layer."[58]

For Bunche's iconographers, there also existed an important connection between Bunche's personal struggles against poverty and prejudice and his public success in the Middle East. The secret ingredients of

Bunche's diplomacy were presumed to be contained in the harsh circumstances of his life, particularly in his familiarity with material and ideological adversity; it was these, his chroniclers suggested, that had made him into a natural diplomat and had endowed him with a spirit of tolerance and patience. "In a sense," wrote one observer, "both Jews and Arabs were members of minority groups in Palestine and Dr. Bunche's personal background gave him a better understanding of their problems."[59] The radio show "American Jewish Hour," in a "tribute to greatness," marveled at how the "grandson of a slave, without wealth, without influence" could overcome the "deep-rooted prejudice of centuries" to accomplish "the most successful moment of peacemaking statesmanship since the United Nations was formed."[60]

A small selection of Ralph Bunche's own words—general observations, for example, about the need to keep faith with the United Nations, reflections on the life lessons taught by adversity, and eloquent expressions in support of the "one hundred percent Americanism" of the Negro—also received wide distribution through *Reader's Digest* and other periodicals. Typical of Bunche's own contribution to the American success genre was an essay he wrote for the April 1955 issue of the *Reader's Digest.* In this piece, Bunche celebrated the advice—credited this time to his mother—that had most effectively insulated him from the psychological damage inflicted by prejudice. Carefully reconstructing the poignant details of a faraway moment in the spring of 1916, he sat with his mother on the steps of their adobe home in Albuquerque, New Mexico, with the sun setting in the distance, Bunche quoted what he said was "the best advice I ever had": " 'Ralph,' she said, taking my hand in hers, 'God sends trials and tribulations to test us. But he arms us against them with hope, faith and dreams. Nothing is lost until *they* [emphasis in the original] are lost.' "[61]

Perhaps Bunche's most often reprinted words, which were used in many magazine profiles, were from a commencement address he gave in 1949 to the graduates of Fisk University, subsequently published in *Vital Speeches,* a staple of public and school libraries throughout the country. Titled "The Barriers of Race Can Be Surmounted," the speech summarized Bunche's case for civil rights as "Americanism" and reflected well the assumptions that underlay mainstream discourse about race between the end of the Second World War and the early 1960s.

Bunche's purpose on the occasion of this speech was to "explore just what it means, at this very moment, in this great nation, to be an American, a citizen, and a Negro." Bunche's conclusion is that every American, according to the Constitution, is "at once a benefactor and protector" of the "American Creed." The students of Fisk, like other African-Americans, were "better Americans than they are Negroes." This, Bunche implies, is not a matter of choice but of necessity because blacks, at this moment, were permitted this identity "primarily in the negative sense" of being "deprived of their birthright as Americans." This was the primary encounter of African-Americans with their racial identity: "Remove that treatment and their identification as Negroes becomes meaningless—at least as meaningless as it is to those of English or French, or German or Italian ancestry."[62]

Blacks deserved the designation of "one hundred percent Americans" because they, better than any other Americans, were fulfilling the active obligation that the creed placed upon all citizens. "Who, indeed," Bunche asked rhetorically, "is a better American . . . than he who demands the fullest measure of respect for those cardinal principles which are the pillars of our society?"[63] Drawing heavily from the study to which he had contributed so much less than a decade earlier, Bunche struck a clearly Myrdalian note:

> The democratic framework of our society is [the Negro's] great hope. The Negro American suffers cruel disabilities because of race which are a flagrant violation of the constitutional tenets and ideals of the American democracy. But the saving grace for the Negro is the democratic warp and woof of the society which permits him to carry on his incessant and heroic struggle to come into his own, to claim those rights, that dignity and respect for the Negro, individually and collectively, which are his birthright as an American. And fortunately, the American, white and black alike, has a conscience.

Alluding to the fortified symbolic position of African-Americans in the postwar American and international public spheres, Bunche continued, "The Negro American daily wins increasing support for his struggle from all those other Americans who aspire toward a democratic . . . America

. . . Moreover, the sympathy of the world is with him. The charter of the United Nations endorses his aspirations."[64]

Nearly one quarter of Bunche's speech was reserved for his own account of the story of his grandmother's influence upon his life, what he characterized as his "priceless heritage from a truly noble woman." Bunche testified that her simple advice had been vindicated throughout "the entire history of the Negro in this country": "Your color, she counseled, has nothing to do with your worth. You are potentially as good as anyone. How good you may prove to be will have no relation to your color, but with what is in your heart and your head." Such values, Bunche affirmed, were at the core of "the kind of world the United Nations is working incessantly to bring about: a world at peace; a world in which people practice tolerance and live together in peace as good neighbors; a world in which there is full respect for human rights and fundamental freedom for all without distinction as to race, sex, language or religion; a world in which all men shall walk together as equals and with dignity."[65] This was Bunche speaking as a self-described "missionary for the U.N. and for civil rights."[66] The two endeavors were linked in Bunche's rhetoric as well as his life: the ideal of true and effective democracy was the goal for both the American nation and for the United Nations, and Bunche wove the two together as a way of emphasizing the stakes that existed at home and abroad.

Unlike the Fisk University speech, most of Bunche's spoken words never reached a national audience. To the extent that his speeches and remarks to various groups were covered at all, that coverage was limited almost exclusively to local newspapers. As a result, most Americans did not have access to the full representation of Bunche's ideas, but instead received a narrower set of images promoted by the national press, which contained an overemphasis on Bunche as a model of rags-to-riches success. What was missing in this picture was Bunche's strong and vocal opposition to McCarthyism. By making himself a public figure, it had been Bunche's intention to challenge the reigning common meanings of American life and to replace them with a set of values that was more inclusive. The mode of his challenge was not to summarily dismiss or repudiate ideas such as the Alger myth, but rather to attempt to speak *through* them so as to illuminate the necessity for a more democratic creed.

Bunche's spoken words can be seen as an extension of his commitment, first undertaken in the 1930s, to use whatever public platforms were provided him by virtue of his intellectual training to argue for his ideas not as a specialist, but as a citizen to other citizens. During the thirties, Bunche had believed that the reconstruction of American society and politics was of the highest priority for social activists. A few years later, however, Bunche would temper this stance because of the dramatic rise of fascism in Europe and his judgment that preventing its ascent in America was a greater necessity.[67]

These developments in the late thirties would convince Bunche to refocus his efforts in his search for social change, and he began to move away from calling for a new class-based politics toward a new intellectual project, in which he demanded the redefinition of Americanism. Postwar prosperity had convinced Bunche that "the problem of race is now far less than it used to be a problem of economics and politics and much more a problem of our minds, of our thinking, our concepts and perspectives." "The prejudice of the white American against the Negro" had become, Bunche now believed, "more veneer than deep grain" and could be "peeled off with little enough damage and pain."[68]

Bunche's commentary in the 1950s turned more and more toward perfecting the institution publicly entrusted with the transmission of knowledge and values: the public school. For some, especially those who had been accused by Bunche in the thirties of being overly concerned with the racial rather than the economic plight of the Negro, the idea of Bunche as a spokesperson, let alone a symbol, of the "Negro American" was a strange turn of events. The distinguished historian Rayford Logan, a colleague of Bunche's at Howard, found ironic humor in the fact that "Ralph Bunche, who some years ago went around calling me a 'black chauvinist,' is now making speeches about the treatment of colored races in the world at large and of Negroes in the United States."[69]

In the spring of 1951, Bunche was invited by the University of Chicago to deliver five lectures on "Man, Democracy and Peace." Bunche addressed such topics as the negotiations in the Middle East that had won him (and, in a symbolic sense, the UN) a Nobel Prize and the rights of minorities within national societies. Bunche reserved the last of the five lectures for a discussion of human relations, a subject of enough generality that he could address the position of blacks in American society.

Like the social scientists and practitioners of the human relations and intergroup relations movements, Bunche focused upon the role of the school. Students, Bunche remarked, must be taught "a deep respect for their fellow human beings, to realize the essential dignity and brotherhood of man . . . These are the ABC's of living." Like educators such as Rachel Du Bois, Bunche held that "a heavy social responsibility [is] resting upon the educational system and institutions." And like his professional colleagues in the social sciences, Bunche envisioned schools as model communities that could do for the coming generation of Americans what they had not done for his: "fortify the young so that they can withstand those out-of-school experiences which would induce distorted and perverted attitudes." To fulfill this ambitious mandate, teachers must "enter the classroom with clean hands and strong biases . . . in favor of peace, of justice, of tolerance, of democracy."[70]

Bunche's commentary even highlighted a matter of central concern to those in the human relations movement: the problem of instructional materials. Existing teaching materials, Bunche contended (with a rhetorical assist from Myrdal), distorted "the true conceptions of our democratic creed." Bunche made clear his belief that Americanism was to be considered no longer to be a matter of "ancestry, of national origin, or religion, or even a matter of blind conformity." Americanism, in Bunche's construction, was "a matter of heart and mind, and Americanism is and must always be dynamic."[71] The nation now faced a time when Americanism must be reconstructed to meet the obligations set forth in its profession of democracy, and Bunche, in this speech, signaled his willingness to join the movement to base this reconstructive effort in the public schools.

Speaking to an audience of African-American teachers working in the nation's capital, Bunche contended that the "essential starting point" of "inter-cultural education" for black Americans "is what the individual Negro is learning about himself, his group, his group's history and background, and the explanation of his present distressing status." Education, properly conceived and carried out, would allow its recipients to discard the "decided provincialism of the Negro"—what Bunche characterized as the tendency for African-Americans to perceive all issues only in their racial dimension. Bunche held that, however understandable this viewpoint might be, adopting such a framework only reinforced the feelings of inferiority transmitted to African-Americans from a hostile majority culture. Bunche saw this frame of mind as supporting a corresponding rhetoric of "racial braggadocio," a style of thought overemphasizing the accomplishments of black entertainers and thus obscuring the ways in which such representations allowed white America to relegate blacks to the "artificial world of the Negro behind the curtain." The continuing prevalence of segregation and of racism, Bunche claimed, had forced "too many of us to lead a double life—militant Negroes by night and uncle Toms by day."[72]

Bunche suggested that, since the Civil War, blacks had been consigned to an intellectual ghetto that "has inspired in us a timidity about venturing out to undertake pioneering." Pioneering—eliminating the duality between white and black, and ending the duality within the experience of every African-American—was the new American frontier. African-Americans, as surely as white Americans, must leave the ghettos of "our misconceptions, intolerances, warped views and confusions" about each other. Intercultural education would provide the balance between accurate self-knowledge and knowledge of others, thus giving to every individual and to every group the ability "to hold its head high, [and] walk down the great boulevards of the world in equality and fraternity with other men." In this context, integration was not the surrender of group difference in the name of conformity to some white standard of conduct, but something far more complex and difficult to achieve. Integration meant for Bunche not the simple passive permission or allowance of difference, but instead its affirmation and encouragement. Affirmatively armed with confidence founded in accurate self-knowledge and in the understanding of others, whites and blacks would together achieve the real meaning of integration: a society in which black citizens would find themselves "moving along with everyone else in the mainstream of American life."[73]

In the early 1950s American institutions seemed to be answering the dual call of conscience and necessity. As Bunche told the NAACP in the summer of 1954, the power of the *Brown* decision to effect change lay in the fact that it could become "a new test of Americanism and loyalty."[74] Speaking at a fund-raiser for the Northside Center for Child Development, founded by his Howard students Kenneth and Mamie Clark, Bunche even called for a holiday to mark "the liberation of Negro children from the degradation of Jim Crow schools."[75]

In a very few years, the rhetoric on race and democracy that Bunche promoted would look very different. Bunche's words would appear staid to a younger generation of African-Americans who, while still admiring of Bunche's personal accomplishments, had grown impatient with waiting for the full awakening of the white majority's conscience. What would come to seem particularly egregious was Bunche's lack of emphasis on developing a positive identification with a black or African-American heritage. Indeed, Bunche had explicitly rejected the label "Afro-American" in his widely cited Fisk address. To a degree, this position was merely a reiteration of one Bunche had reached in the 1930s. More important, however, it was part of a self-conscious effort on Bunche's part in the 1950s to legitimize protest for equal rights at a time when any kind of protest against American institutions was held to be suspect. Contemporary with Bunche's emphasis on the "one hundred percent Americanism" of blacks were the actions of the House Un-American Activities Committee, which, along with other official and unofficial forces, was striving with great noise and success to stifle dissent. Acknowledgement of this context was missing from later revisionist appraisals of Bunche.

Bunche's effort to turn the rhetorical tables and reappropriate the meaning of Americanism from the peddlers of McCarthyism is the least known aspect of his public life. After an initial flurry of publicity due to his being awarded the Nobel Peace Prize, Bunche received far less attention from the national press. As a consequence, his injunction that Americans "be deeply concerned . . . that there are those within our midst—and they are not all Communists—who would take advantage of the world crisis to limit our freedom and curtail our democracy" was not widely broadcast.[76] It certainly did not enter into the telling of "The Ralph Bunche Story."

Even at the high point of Bunche's celebrity, in 1949, such clearly heretical sentiments regarding Americanism seldom found an audience beyond the ears of those who heard them in person. Bunche brought this message to bear, for example, before a large hometown crowd gathered

at the Rose Bowl to watch the local hero accept the highest honor bestowed by the NAACP, the Spingarn medal. Bunche seized the occasion
to embrace civil rights as "good Americanism" and to attack its opponents, stating, "There is much hysteria in our midst about strange ideologies. The greatest defense for democracy is its practice. It is a virile
way of life and its defenders need have no fear if democracy is made to
work . . . If those who today sound the alarums about the dangers from
without would only concentrate a little more on perfecting the practice
of democracy from within, and would have a stronger faith in the fun-
damentals of our creed, American democracy would quickly become
permanently invulnerable."[77]

The Symbolic End of Ralph Bunche

By the early 1960s, the power of constructive symbolism to validate
ostensible advances had been tested and found to be, if not empty, then
at least severely wanting. In the ten years between the climactic triumph
of the *Brown* decision and the passage of the Civil Rights Act of 1964,
Martin Luther King, Jr., felt compelled to identify "tokenism"—the cynical manipulation of symbols to create the *illusion* of progress—as perhaps the paramount threat to the work of democracy. A decade of "hard
struggles," culminating in "limited gains," had reduced the symbolic
meaning of the *Brown* decision and its antecedent symbolic landmarks
in the postwar struggle for racial equality to nothing more than "the
glitter of metal symbolizing the true coin."[78]

Tokenism granted the recipient "a short-term trip toward democracy,"
while permitting an infinite deferral on the part of the white majority for
the structural changes necessary to pay for the rest of the journey. Invoking a metaphor common to both the *Brown* case and the Montgomery
bus boycott, King argued that "he who sells you the token instead of the
coin always retains the power to revoke its worth, and to command you
to get off the bus before you have reached your destination. Tokenism
is a promise to pay. Democracy, in its finest sense, is payment."[79] As the
value of tokenism came into question, the symbolic Bunche came into
disrepute as well. Bunche's position as "the most accomplished Negro
in the world" (to quote Sam Pope Brewer in the *New York Times*) made

him the preeminent illustration of the insincerity of the commitment of the white majority to social change.[80]

Freedomways, a leading journal of the civil rights movement, also used Bunche's name to pointed effect in a cartoon satirizing a social type that first gained wide currency in the early sixties: the "white liberal." The drawing showed a hapless African-American employee being waylaid at the water cooler by the office white liberal, who threw out a succession of thoughtless and uncouth questions beginning with "Have you ever been to Africa?" and ending with "Do you know Ralph Bunche?" Bunche's status as white America's "favorite Negro" was not an unmixed blessing.

Malcolm X suggested that Bunche's success in American society had come at the high price of historical amnesia. In an address entitled "Black Man's History," Malcolm held Bunche up as a man without racial self-awareness. Asking his listeners to consider what the difference might be between Bunche and "the black man who just came here from Africa," Malcolm suggested that "the difference is Bunche doesn't know his history and they, the Africans, do know their history. They may come here out of the jungles, but they know their history . . . You and I can come out of Harvard but we don't know our history . . . The American so-called Negro is . . . confined, he's limited, he's under the control and the jurisdiction of the white man who knows more about the history of the Negro than the Negro knows about himself."[81] Malcolm's words, like those uttered by King the same year, were not directed against Bunche, but against the society that had appropriated Bunche's image. According to Malcolm, public prominence, like integration, required the black American, whether rich or poor, whether formally educated or not, to surrender self-knowledge and, most important, the autonomy and pride that such knowledge brings.

By the late sixties, Bunche had become an iconographic footnote, a symbol whose true meaning was understood only to those few with the memory of Bunche's Nobel award and the knowledge of why he had won it. To many, his name had become a convenient shorthand to signify an era in which African-Americans had had white masks placed over them as one of the prices of public renown. A scene indicative of Bunche's reduced stature can be found in the 1967 pilot for the long-running police drama *Ironsides,* in which Raymond Burr portrayed

Robert Ironsides, Chief of Detectives of the San Francisco Police Department, a man who persevered in his chosen vocation despite being confined to a wheelchair by a sniper's bullet. *Ironsides* had the distinction of being among the first network programs to include an African-American character in a leading role, in this case Ironsides' personal assistant. In the pilot, this character is introduced as a young man with a criminal past who needs only a decent break to become a worthy citizen. Ironsides offers him the job, to which this representation of young black anger bitterly responds, "Now you're going to give me a cigarette and tell me about Jackie Robinson, Ralph Bunche, and Booker T. Washington." After a tense exchange about the inherent value of all work, the black man accepts Ironsides' offer of employment.

Writing in 1968, Nathan Hare expressed this same sentiment of rejection when he dismissed Bunche as one of a handful of "acceptable Negroes" promoted as a "white-groomed Negro leader" to black school-children.[82] This latter day Bunche story was the stereotype to which Andrew Young unwittingly gave voice, when he recalled Bunche as "not being black." Summarizing this revisionist attitude toward Bunche, one scholar concluded, "Bunche may well have been the most outstanding black man in the eyes of white society . . . but he was not a leader of black people . . . He served in white society rather than fighting for black needs."[83]

This censorious evaluation of Bunche's legitimacy and effectiveness as a spokesperson and as a symbol was the outcome of a larger sea change in common meanings. Judged by the publicity generated about Bunche by many in the white press, Bunche may well have seemed in retrospect to be a man without ethnic self-awareness and pride. This interpretation, however, confused the man himself with the icon and with the motives of those who created it. Such an estimate pushed aside the fact of Bunche's expertise on Africa as well as that of his commitment to self-determination and nationhood for the entire nonwestern and formerly colonized world (a subject on which Bunche gave hundreds of addresses during the 1940s and 1950s).

In 1960, for instance, while appearing as a guest on Eleanor Roosevelt's television interview program *Prospects of Mankind,* Bunche took Americans to task for their condescending attitude toward African independence, most frequently expressed in the presumptuous question "Is

Africa ready for independence?" In response, Bunche reminded doubters of their own past experience: "We didn't ask that question [of] ourselves, and I think probably a good case could be made for saying that we weren't ready for it when we got it. The people of Africa are moving toward independence. When people are seeking freedom they're always impatient and I think that [it is] good that they're impatient."[84] In a similar vein, Bunche also warned his audience against expecting political and economic development to occur along American or western lines.[85]

For many opinion leaders in the white and the black press, Bunche's significance began and did not extend much beyond being a living refutation of Soviet propaganda on American race relations. As a consequence, Bunche's biography was lightly and often sloppily sketched to fit this requirement, or to conform to the comfortable confines of the Alger myth; his words were quoted only to the extent that they matched either of these cultural formats. Bunche's public image became frozen in 1950, never to be updated or rethought.

In part, the static nature of Bunche's reputation may reflect the failure of the United Nations to live up to the great expectations that were held out for it. Bunche was symbolic not only of American progress on race, but of a new political order as well, one that would be centered upon the mediating powers of the United Nations; these powers would, as one admirer put it, unite the "divided worlds of color." The diplomatic victory on the Isle of Rhodes, however, would prove to be an unique event, and not the first step toward a new era of international order—one in which the United Nations, and presumably Bunche, would have played central roles. With the diminution of one of the essential rationales for thinking about Bunche, the mainstream media had no great reason to revisit "The Ralph Bunche Story."

Perhaps more important—and deeply ironic—is the possibility that the rise of African nationalism, and especially its ideological counterpart in the United States, rendered Bunche, one of the first modern students of Africa and one of the earliest advocates for its decolonization, symbolically irrelevant. Leaders such as Malcolm X were in the forefront of popularizing a new way of thinking about "Negroes," one explicitly tied to the rise of Africa on the world stage. Remarking on the change, Malcolm recalled that "at one time . . . the word *African* [emphasis in the original] was used in this country in a derogatory way. But now, since

Africa . . . [is] getting its independence . . . the image of the African has changed from negative to positive," thus creating a new empowering symbolic resource for American blacks.[86] Malcolm described the historical moment in the following way:

> As the African nations become independent and mold a . . . positive image, a militant image, an upright image, the image of a man, not a boy—how has this affected the Black man in the Western Hemisphere? It has taken the Black man in the Caribbean and given him some pride. It has given pride to the Black man in Latin America and has given pride to the Black man right here in the United States. So that when the Black revolution begins to roll on the African continent it affects the relationship between the Black man and the white man in the United States.[87]

Malcolm viewed the "white liberal" as but the latest generation of insincere spokespeople for an irredeemably white republic, a republic bereft of the humanitarian conscience attributed to it by Myrdal and Bunche. The black counterpart to the white liberal was the Uncle Tom, an individual who "doesn't want to be Black, he wants to be white," and who was willing to "beg you for integration."[88] According to Malcolm, the historical legacy of the African-American in the white republic made integration as Bunche had portrayed it—as a complex transaction of mutual learning and gain—impossible. The evidence of history suggested, instead, that integration in the American context could only be a one-way process governed by whites.

Viewed from within this framework, Bunche's rhetorical confession "I am tired of being identified as an American 'minority' " seemed a rejection of self.[89] In his effort to recast the language of Cold War discourse, Bunche had declared:

> When people speak to me . . . about being a member of a minority group, I strongly deny it. Negro? Yes, that's merely an incident of birth. American? Emphatically yes. This is my birthright and my greatest asset. Minority? No. For *Americans* [emphasis in the original] are a majority in this country, and I am an American. The *real* [emphasis in the original] minority group in this country consists of those who cannot swallow more democracy; who find that democracy cur-

dles their stomach; who wish Negro-Americans, Spanish-Americans and Oriental-Americans—all the hyphenates—to be treated as second rate Americans.[90]

Malcolm's program was a break with the past as embedded in Bunche's rhetoric. It was a break that profoundly offended the integrationist who was schooled in the assumptions and the images of an era that, although barely gone, now seemed distant indeed. James H. Cone describes this intellectual impasse in the following way:

As Martin Luther King and other integrationists accented their American identity, Malcolm refused to identify with the country of his birth. "We're not Americans, we're Africans who happen to be in America . . . We were kidnapped and brought here against our will . . . We didn't land on Plymouth rock—that rock landed on us." Without fail, Malcolm aroused the resentful feelings of integrationists when he spoke like that. No person tried to be *Americans* [emphasis in the original] more than integrationists. They have been called "super Americans" and "exaggerated Americans." When they heard Malcolm denying his American identity, they were greatly embarrassed because he contradicted what they had been telling whites that blacks wanted.[91]

Some of the symbols of racial equality, if not the change of heart demanded by the civil rights movement and the progressive social scientists prominent in the intergroup-relations and intercultural-education movements, had by the late sixties become a firm part of American public life. But even the symbolic triumph fell short of the goal. During World War II, social democrats such as Eleanor Roosevelt, Ralph Bunche, and Wendell Willkie confidently grasped the opening offered by the war to define Americanism more inclusively. But after the war, it was McCarthyism that would define Americanism, and it proved stronger than Ralph Bunche's best efforts to keep his more expansive and challenging vision of Americanism alive. To the extent that the pluralistic and egalitarian interpretation of Americanism retained its visibility, it was as a necessary concession to the requirements of Cold War foreign policy. The Americanism that Malcolm confronted in 1964 was the same explicitly racist and latently fascist creed that Bunche had denounced in memos to

Myrdal a generation earlier: "Being here in America doesn't make you an American," said Malcolm. "No, I'm not an American. I'm one of 22 million Black people who are the victims of democracy, nothing but disguised hypocrisy."[92]

It was not just the emergence of black nationalism, however, that marginalized Bunche as a symbol. By the early 1960s, the mainstream movement for equality had generated a multitude of nationally known representatives. More than ten years had passed since Bunche had won the Nobel Peace Prize and been acclaimed as one of America's most accomplished Negroes. A new generation, one for whom the UN was little more than a symbol of frustrated idealism, had only a vague awareness of Ralph Bunche. Although no polls were taken in 1950 to measure Bunche's name identification, it is perhaps significant that, in 1963, 28 percent of all adult African-Americans could not identify Bunche in a *Newsweek* poll. Bunche and Thurgood Marshall (unknown to 30 percent) were classified, in the words of William Brink and Louis Harris, as "inspirational figures to the leadership group but more as elder statesman to the rank-and-file."[93]

The America that underwent a "second Reconstruction" had been changed in important ways, but the work of reconstruction continued to be glaringly incomplete, with Americans still stymied as how to resolve its most fundamental dilemma. That there remained then—and still remain today—daunting challenges in "intergroup relations" must not obscure the considerable contributions that Ralph Bunche, Jackie Robinson, and others made through their own words and actions as they traversed the terrain of American iconography. We are indebted to this generation of "first Negroes" for personifying the undisputable equality of African-Americans with the larger white society, and in so doing, making white Americans finally confront the indecency of Jim Crow and the need to transform the nation's laws.

These individuals called upon citizens to do more at the same time that they served as role models for a new cultural code of conduct that extended common humanity, respect, and dignity to the "Negro American." Acknowledging the necessity for this treatment—which is only the first step in recognizing the equality and humanity of the Other—has taken the majority of Americans nearly two hundred years. Nonetheless, America did not go the distance scouted out for it by this generation.

This failure weighed heavily on Jackie Robinson. Recalling the holiest and most fulfilling frame in his legend, Robinson, in the final year of his life, made the ultimate commentary on America past and present when, invoking the scene that had inspired a generation, he wrote himself out of it: "There I was, the black grandson of a slave, the son of a black sharecropper, part of a historic occasion, a symbolic hero to my people. The air was sparkling. The sunlight was warm. The band struck up the national anthem. The flag billowed in the wind. It should have been a glorious moment for me as the stirring words of the national anthem poured from the stands . . . As I write this twenty years later, I cannot stand and sing the anthem. I cannot salute the flag; I know that I am a black man in a white world."[94]

Kenneth B. Clark in the early 1960s
(Kenneth B. Clark & Associates)

Kenneth B. Clark and the Cultural Politics of the *Brown* Decision

4

To separate [children] from others of similar age and qualifications solely because of their race generates a feeling of inferiority as to their status in the community that may affect their hearts and minds in a way unlikely ever to be undone . . . We conclude that in the field of public education the doctrine of "separate but equal" has no place. Separate educational facilities are inherently unequal.

> **—The United States Supreme Court (May 17, 1954)**

American children can be saved from the corrosive effects of racial prejudice. These prejudices are not inevitable; they reflect the types of experiences that children are forced to have. Such prejudices can be prevented—and those already existing can be changed—by altering the social conditions under which children learn about and live with others. When human intelligence and creativity tackle the problem and bring about the changes in the society, then these prejudices and their detrimental effects will be eliminated.

> **—Kenneth B. Clark (1955)**

The U.S. Supreme Court's explicit reliance on social science theory to justify its rejection of the legal doctrine of "separate but equal" in American public education was unprecedented. Although the strength of *Brown* was diluted somewhat by the Court's own implementation decision a year later, the 1954 decision advanced American racial discourse in a crucial way. Fourteen years before *Brown* was rendered, E. Franklin Frazier recognized the fundamental truth that was to give the decision its symbolic power: "In our American culture the public school embodies in its very conception and at the same time symbolizes as does no other institution the democratic ideal."[1] The terms of *Brown* transformed the public school into the symbol of a continuing American dilemma for most of the postwar era, recasting it as the principal institutional battle-ground in the achievement of racial equality. Of the indispensability of the public school to our democratic society, Chief Justice Earl Warren wrote: "Today it is a principal instrument in awakening the child to cultural values, in preparing him for later professional training, and in helping him to adjust normally to his environment. In these days, it is doubtful that any child may be expected to succeed in life if he is denied the opportunity of an education. Such an opportunity, where the state has undertaken to provide it, is a right which must be made available to all on equal terms."[2]

Brown was the finest hour for a cohort of activist social scientists who had been working for over a generation to discredit the tenets of scientific racism. From the beginning, they had not restricted their activities to the academy, but had also sought to plant their ideas directly in the public sphere, through books and articles directed to the general reader. The text of *Brown* offered ample proof of the success of their efforts. As the social psychologist Otto Klineberg, one member of this distinguished group, wrote many years later, the *Brown* decision was "the greatest compliment ever paid to psychology by the powers-that-be in our own or any other country."[3]

The fact that the Supreme Court would ground a major part of its de-cision on the existence of an "inferiority complex" or on the importance of the cultural and civic mission of the public school in a democracy is remarkable, given that *Brown* was issued during a decade remembered for its political paranoia and anti-intellectualism. How academic psy-chology came to represent the consensus of enlightened social science and more particularly how it contributed to making Kenneth Clark one of the best-known participants in the discourse that the Court helped bring into being are the subjects of this chapter.

Clark trained during the 1930s at two centers of politically activist social science: Howard University, where he led demonstrations against Jim Crow and developed close personal friendships with the most polit-ically outspoken members of its faculty; and Columbia University, where Clark worked under Otto Klineberg.[4] In the three years prior to *Brown*, Clark took a leading role in recruiting social scientists as expert witnesses in the appellate courts to buttress the NAACP's case against segregation. He was also responsible for summarizing the relevant psychological research for presentation to the Supreme Court. One of his papers the "Effect of Prejudice on Personality Development," was the first source cited by Warren in footnote 11 of his decision; the last in that footnote was Gunnar Myrdal's *An American Dilemma.* Myrdal was another of Clark's friends and mentors.

Clark's involvement with *Brown* grew directly from his years at Howard and Columbia. The words that Warren paraphrased in the most quoted section of *Brown* had originally been written by Clark four years earlier at the suggestion of Alain Locke, for presentation to the Mid-Century White House Conference on Children and Youth. One year later, Klineberg, Clark's chair at Columbia, told Robert Carter of the Legal Defense and Education Fund about Clark's work on the psychological effects of prejudice upon African-American children. From this contact, Clark became the principal advisor on social science to the Legal Defense and Education Fund; as a member of the NAACP's legal defense team, Clark brought the concept of the inferiority complex into the litigation.[5]

During the first half of his public life, Kenneth Clark was a figure little known outside his field; his first attempt to present social science to the general public, a book called *Prejudice and Your Child,* reached few people in its first edition. Ten years after *Brown,* however, a convergence of circumstances were to make Clark's second book, *Dark Ghetto,* a key text in the representation of a racial reality new to large segments of the American public: the conditions of black Americans' life in the long-neglected ghettos of the urban North. A crucial aspect of this convergence would be the rediscovery by the press of Clark's role in the successful outcome of the *Brown* case—an association that would legitimate him as a "new Myrdal."

Just before the end of the Second World War, Gunnar Myrdal had undertaken, in *An American Dilemma,* to explain the nation's troubled conscience to itself. The use of the African-American as a metaphor for interpreting the health of American democracy and the legitimacy of its institutions was made a central fact of postwar culture by the anticolonialist and antifascist terms in which the Second World War had been fought. The war created an opening in the public sphere for expert-interpreters of American race relations: individuals whose words and public identities could symbolically summarize the public's new understanding of the place of race in American democracy. During the war, maverick Republican politician Wendell Willkie filled that role as author of *One World*, his best-selling testament to international brotherhood. After the war, Myrdal was accorded the status of the expert-interpreter, the man above the partisan political fray. For the next twenty years, Myrdal and *An American Dilemma* symbolized all that "average, good, warm-hearted upper and middle class Americans" knew and believed about racial equality.[6]

The wide reception and praise accorded to Myrdal as a public interpreter of American race relations legitimated a new role that others might play in the future. The *Brown* decision created cultural space for the emergence of two "new Myrdals" who might explain the necessity of desegregation to a wary public. The person who filled this role immediately after *Brown* was the historian C. Vann Woodward. Nearly ten years later, Clark would join him.

Woodward, like Clark, had contributed research to the Legal Defense and Education Fund's brief to the Supreme Court in the case challenging the legality of *Plessy v. Ferguson*. The impetus for Woodward's rise in the late 1950s was a compact, elegant, simple book, *The Strange Career of Jim Crow*. Begun as a series of lectures composed in the summer following the *Brown* decision for delivery that fall at the University of Virginia, *Strange Career*'s first audience "consisted," according to Woodward, "of a hundred or so people, academic though unspecialized, and overwhelmingly Southern."[7] Within a few years of their publication by Oxford University Press in 1955, Woodward's lectures, pushed by "an urgent demand for knowledge and explanation of what was obviously a national problem," won widespread success as a mass-market paperback. *Strange Career* would, in the words of Martin Luther King, Jr., become "the historical bible of the civil rights movement," and it was a text from which King himself sometimes read aloud at public meetings.[8]

Woodward sought to serve his audience in two important ways: first, by exploding Northern stereotypes about the white South—reminding Northern whites that, in truth, the South was being asked, for the second time in a century, to "bear the brunt of a guilty national conscience"; and second, by conferring scholarly legitimacy on the claims of the civil rights movement, presenting compelling evidence that "many of those who are presently defending the Jim Crow laws as ancient and imme-morial folkways are older than the laws they are defending."[9]

In the early 1960s Kenneth Clark became the preeminent expert-interpreter of the American dilemma in the New Frontier-Great Society era, an ascension that Myrdal himself confirmed by providing introduc-tory remarks to Clark's *Dark Ghetto.* In 1954, Clark's specific contri-bution to *Brown,* as coordinator of social science testimony for the NAACP Legal Defense and Education Fund and as the principal drafter of the social science statement signed by one hundred psychologists that was submitted to the Court as an appendix to the NAACP's brief, had brought him to the attention of the social science community. To the general press, however, Clark was simply a junior member of a large and distinguished group of social scientists lending their names and rep-utations to the desegregation of American public education.

Ten years later, as a new chapter of protest and the Johnson ad-ministration's War on Poverty through community action moved the center of discourse on race north, *Dark Ghetto* brought Clark national attention. Although some commentators recalled Clark's contribution to *Brown,* Clark was equally noted for his post-*Brown* role as an activist and community organizer, whose experiment, Harlem Youth Unlimited (HARYOU), had played an important part in the formulation of the War on Poverty. In this new discourse, Clark—immigrant New Yorker and African-American social scientist—became a new Myrdal, an interpreter of the northern urban ghetto to the nation's conscience. When Clark published *Dark Ghetto* in 1965 he would become the figure whose words and writings symbolically summarized what enlightened America now understood about the character and extent of racial injustice within their democracy.[10]

Myrdal had staked the credibility of his findings on his status as a thoughtful outsider, as an individual whose detailed mastery of the American system of class and caste was uncolored by what Myrdal per-ceived as American social scientists' all-too-ready sympathy for the ra-tionalizations and unspoken understandings that sustained it. Reviewers warmed to that theme and received Myrdal as a latter-day Tocqueville whose very unfamiliarity with American folkways and culture rendered him uniquely qualified to interpret them.

In contrast, Woodward and Clark's credibility originated from their very location within the American experience—Woodward as a white Southerner, and Clark as a black former resident of the Harlem ghetto. Woodward, for example, was seen by the northern intellectual community as a Southerner who possessed a genuine empathy and intimate understanding of his region. Clark represented, as Myrdal wrote in his foreword to *Dark Ghetto,* the next and most revolutionary chapter of change, and was consequently pressing for "huge reforms . . . far beyond the enactment of civil rights."[11] A worsening national crisis called for an activist social science directly engaged with the "real problems of men and society . . . in quest of truth and social justice."[12] Clark himself described *Dark Ghetto* as "the cry of a social psychologist, controlled in part by the concepts and language of social science." Clark used this space to argue against traditional social scientific notions of relevance and objectivity, which he saw as little more than forms of indifference and denial.[13]

Over the next generation, as Clark emerged as the social scientist most closely associated with the liberal and reformist spirit of *Brown,* he would come to be characterized as an "icon of integration."[14] Clark's development into a collective representative of integration and, more broadly still, of black America would be gradual, not gathering force until the "Negro revolt" of 1963 made racial injustice the singular and overriding domestic issue in national life.[15]

Patterns of Culture

Clark's activist and public vision for social science had been formed during an earlier era of national crisis, between 1930 and 1945. He began college at Howard University in 1931, where he eventually met his wife and closest professional collaborator, Mamie Phipps Clark. Soon, with the support of Ralph Bunche and other progressive faculty, Clark emerged as a major figure on campus—for example, as the author of incisive editorials in the *Howard Hilltop* against militarism, fascism, and unbridled capitalism (see Chapter 1).

The active involvement of many of Clark's mentors in the defining issues of that era—such as the establishment of a broadly based industrial labor movement, the defense of the Scottsboro boys, repelling the threat of fascism at home and abroad—was proof to Clark that the study of social problems and the achievement of social change were not merely desirable and compatible aims; they were inseparable. It was also at Howard that Clark first heard the words of psychologist Otto Klineberg, whose research was overturning racist assumptions about the inferior intellect of Native Americans and African-Americans. After listening to Klineberg's public summary of his work, Clark decided, "I wanted to go into the field that Otto Klineberg was in."[16]

By the late 1930s politically progressive psychologists who were determined to apply the tools of their discipline to a direct assault on a growing fascist menace at home and abroad had organized themselves into the Society for the Psychological Study of Social Issues (SPSSI). Originally founded to assist unemployed and underemployed psychology Ph.D.'s in finding jobs during the Depression, SPSSI had, by the late thirties, become a vehicle for bringing the latest relevant social science, especially relating to prejudice and other social maladies threatening democracy, to the attention of the public. Gardner Murphy, for example, speaking as chair of the Society in the idiom of New Deal reform, argued that its members "must be good enough psychologists to put our material in the hands of society in such a way as to help it defend itself against reaction and to assist it in seeing the full import of scientific findings translated into action."[17] Little more than a decade later, SPSSI constituted the greatest source of social science support to the Legal Defense and Education Fund in the *Brown* case.

It is no accident that when Clark left Howard in 1938 with a Master's degree he proceeded directly to Columbia, which, as the institutional home of Klineberg (also a leader in SPSSI), Murphy, and activist-anthropologists Franz Boas, Ruth Benedict, and Margaret Mead, served as the intellectual capital of what might be called public social science. It was against the backdrop of these disciplinary politics that Kenneth Clark, in a strong partnership with Mamie Phipps Clark, first entered the discourse within academic psychology on prejudice.

If Klineberg and Murphy were Clark's models of how to combine the study of psychology with the study of society, Ruth Benedict exemplified how a member of the academy could establish a relationship with the lay public and successfully communicate the relevance of the new social science to their lives. In both the rhetoric and the philosophical concerns of Benedict's best-selling work *Patterns of Culture,* the Clarks found inspiration for their subsequent undertakings, and, in particular, their doll studies. At the heart of *Patterns of Culture* was Benedict's assertion that "the life-history of the individual is first and foremost an accommodation to the patterns and standards traditionally handed down in his community." Benedict contends that, for each individual, "from the moment of his birth the customs into which he is born shape his experience and behaviour. By the time he can talk, he is the little creature of his culture, and by the time he is grown and able to take part in its activities, its habits are his habits, its beliefs his beliefs, its impossibilities his impossibilities."[18] Many of the leaders of SPSSI shared Benedict's appreciation of culture as the key factor in the making of the individual. Pioneers in the still emerging field of social psychology, such as Ruth and Eugene Horowitz, Kurt Lewin, Gardner and Lois Barclay Murphy, and Lawrence K. Frank (who, as a foundation official, steered financial support to the study of early childhood), shared a keen interest in how patterns of culture became engraved on the individual personality. Through much of the 1930s, these scholars would be at the forefront of attempts to find a technique by which they could, in the words of E. Franklin Frazier, "disentangle the biological from the social determinants in the formation of personality."[19]

The Clarks found the work of Gestalt psychologist Kurt Lewin (who had taken up residence in the United States when Hitler came to power) particularly compelling. Lewin and his colleagues approached the socialization of children by examining the development and gradual extension of the "force field" of social influences that affected their behavior and to which they in turn contributed by their actions. The quality and extent of such fields, or "life-spaces," argued Lewin, "vary greatly, depending especially upon the economic situation, the character of the parents, the number, sex, and kind of children in the family and among his friends." It was essential, if children were to develop soundly, that each individual be provided with the psychological room in which to develop a life-space "dependent only on his *own* sphere of power" (emphasis in the original). Failure to do so, Lewin contended, "may lead to a real oppression of the child or to a particularly violent revolt." A child who had been confined to a restrictive and circumscribed world, Lewin argued, was denied the power to construct a "psychological environment . . . determined by his *own* needs" (emphasis in the original).[20]

Lewinian concepts of the social field were decisive in the thinking of the Clarks as they set out to design studies on the genesis of racial attitudes. What constituted a child-made environment? Could this environment be altered in ways that would encourage children to be more tolerant, more democratic? These questions formed the foundation of the work of the activist-psychologists coming of age in the thirties. Through children raised free of stereotype and prejudice, Elizabeth Lomax suggests, this cohort of psychologists believed that "a new society was to be born dedicated to peaceful and constructive ends."[21] The Clarks' psychological research was aimed at insuring that this new society would also be free of negative and pejorative racial representations and values.

As Kurt Lewin's field theory gained increasing influence in the 1940s and 1950s among those studying the genesis of racial attitudes, so did a methodological innovation that psychologists had developed in the 1930s in order to study the interaction of cultural agents and the individual child: projective techniques.[22] Projective tests for children were not limited to the standard procedure—the Rorschach—but in fact often incorporated some form of line drawings, pictures, dolls, or other miniature representations of the public world. The Clarks would use projective techniques, which had been initially deployed to evaluate subjective processes and thought structures, to trace the incorporation of racial custom by individual children.

It was no accident that those who used projective techniques in the service of tracing social ideology appropriated Benedict's language—especially her imagery of the patterning of culture—to explain what they sought to reveal. In the words of Lawrence Frank, the most influential early advocate for this new mode of research, such techniques were designed to "induce the individual to reveal his way of organizing experience by giving him a field (objects, materials and experiences) with relatively little structure and cultural patterning so that the personality can project upon that plastic field his way of seeing life, his meanings, significances, patterns, and especially his feelings."[23]

The first psychologist to apply these methods to the study of racial consciousness was Ruth Horowitz. Horowitz used line drawings and portraits of black and white children, as well as representations of assorted animals, to study the residue of the encounter with American cultural values among twenty-four children of ages three through five.

Horowitz found that black boys and white girls experienced the earliest and most well-developed consciousness of their own racial identities, and that, by the fifth year, all of the children had assimilated the social valuations assigned to each of their racial identities.[24]

Mamie Phipps Clark was particularly interested in expanding upon the Horowitz test, which had been the subject of her master's thesis at Howard.[25] Working closely with her husband, she repeated the Horowitz test on a sample of 150, and conducted experiments to establish how the development of racial self-identity correlated with the skin color of the recipient and with the degree of segregation in the school setting. The Clarks found that, while children in both segregated and nonsegregated environments attained a well-developed sense of racial self-identity by the age of four, this process occurred at a marginally more abrupt rate among children in segregated learning environments. The shade of the respondent's skin color had only a slight impact on racial identification among Negro children, and the importance of this variable was virtually eliminated by age five.[26]

It is evidence of the caution that existed within the academy on the subject of race that the Clarks' most significant work during the late thirties and forties bore little relationship to the actual doctoral dissertations that each completed at Columbia. Kenneth Clark graduated in 1940, upon the completion of his doctoral thesis, "Some Factors Influencing the Remembering of Prose Material"[27]—research without any reference to race. Similarly, rather than using her dissertation to extend her Howard master's thesis, Mamie Phipps Clark four years later completed "Changes in Primary Mental Abilites with Age," which contained little reference to a racial dimension.[28] It should be remembered that while the Clarks worked in an academic context that was in some ways politically progressive, this setting was still overwhelmingly white. As the first African-American doctorates in psychology from Columbia, the Clarks carried the burden of proving the intellectual competence of their race; such a hurdle meant completing dissertations noteworthy for their mastery of orthodox methodology. For the present, disciplinary presentations of the research most truly reflective of their shared intellectual interests would remain under the auspices of SPSSI, psychology's activist arm.[29]

Despite the institutional constraints within which they worked as doctoral students, the Clarks received significant financial support from the Julius Rosenwald Foundation to continue their work on racial identification. The results of this research, published in 1947 as part of a SPSSI-sponsored textbook, *Readings in Social Psychology,* were the famous doll studies, the most conceptually ambitious use of projective methods to study the genesis of racial attitudes up to that time. The Clarks tested 253 black children: 134 from public schools in Phipps Clark's native Arkansas, and 119 from racially mixed public schools in Springfield, Massachusetts. The children were given one of four dolls, each identical except for gender and skin color. The children were asked eight questions in the following order:

1. Give me the doll that you like to play with.
2. Give me the doll that is the nice doll.
3. Give me the doll that looks bad.
4. Give me the doll that has a nice color.
5. Give me the doll that looks like a white child.
6. Give me the doll that looks like a colored child.
7. Give me the doll that looks like a Negro child.
8. Give me the doll that looks like you.[30]

The study confirmed both Horowitz's and the Clarks' previous findings, that "a basic knowledge of 'racial differences' [is] part of the pattern of ideas of Negro children from the age of three through the age of seven years . . . and that this knowledge develops more definitely from year to year to the point of absolute stability at the age of seven."[31] The "preference test" (questions 1 through 4) suggested that, as early as the third year, African-American children in both the northern and the southern samples expressed a clear and consistent preference for the white doll over the brown doll, and that they held an equally pronounced belief that brown was "bad" and white was good. Perhaps most compelling of all was the Clarks' qualitative finding that question 8, "Give me the doll that looks like you," caused many children to "become somewhat negativistic," with a few even "becoming unconsolable, convulsed in tears."[32]

"There is no social problem," Benedict challenged in 1934, that "it is more incumbent upon us to understand than . . . the role of custom. Until we are intelligent to its laws and varieties, the main complicating facts of human life must remain unintelligible."[33] The doll studies that Kenneth and Mamie Clark conducted endeavored to respond to that imperative by trying to make intelligible the cultural pattern that so consistently induced African-American children to absorb and act out the American cultural hierarchy, at the ultimate cost, the Clarks believed, of their very selves. The Clark research also came as close as possible to fulfilling Horowitz's hope that projective methods might permit social scientists to see personality when it "is in the first stage of becoming, when the texture of the pattern and the color of the strands that go into the final product are still in an individually discernible state."[34]

As Kenneth Clark's graduate career drew to a close, and as Mamie Phipps Clark's began, their work had already found an attentive and admiring audience within SPSSI. The Second World War would interrupt the Clarks' doll studies and their work with children. These years, however, did provide Kenneth Clark with a further opportunity to explore the application of the concept of the inferiority complex to the problem of prejudice.

"Marginal Men Have Marginal Morale"

World War II added urgency to the work of Clark and of the other activist-psychologists within SPSSI. Particularly active was Lewin, who began applying his field theory to the specific study of "democratic" versus "authoritarian" personalities.[35] Lewin posited, in a much-cited experiment utilizing two groups of boys, that the behavior of individuals is most powerfully influenced by the nature of the social climate that surrounds them and with which they interact through their behavior. According to Lewin's findings, for example, the authoritarian atmosphere encouraged "a pattern of aggressive domination toward one another" among the boys and contributed to a relationship of submission toward the authoritarian leader and "persistent demands for [his] attention." The pattern of interaction in the group led by the democratic leader, by contrast, encouraged peer group relations that were "more spontaneous . . . and friendly. Relations to the leader were free and on an 'equality' basis."[36]

An example of this genre of analysis is *The Authoritarian Personality,* an influential textual study of prejudice published in the early postwar era. The émigré social theorists of the Frankfurt School posited that prejudiced individuals had themselves been damaged at an early age by being socialized in settings where "a basically hierarchical, authoritarian, exploitive parent-child relationship" existed. Such socialization, they argued, was antithetical to both self-respect and respect for others, and was likely to carry over into an adult personality that was "power-oriented, exploitive . . . that has no room for anything but a desperate clinging to what appears to be strong and a disdainful rejection for whatever appears relegated to the bottom."[37]

The themes embedded in *The Authoritarian Personality* formed the intellectual core of the Clarks' doll research. They owed an even more explicit debt, however, to another émigré scholar, the Viennese psychoanalyst Alfred Adler. Adler's concept of the inferiority complex served as the foundation of Kenneth Clark's representation of American race relations; Clark would bring Adler explicitly to bear on the problem of American race relations in Clark's writings of the 1950s.[38] Clark's debt to Adler was aptly summarized by the phrase he used to open his analysis of African-American opinion in wartime America: "Marginal men have marginal morale."[39]

The concept of an "inferiority complex" was popularized in America by Adler, whose articles and lecture tours found a receptive audience among progressive educators and social workers. Originally, Adler's theory was directed toward explaining the feelings of those possessing a visible physical malady—an "organ inferiority"—and "problem children," whose poor academic performance and behavior problems at school originated from a need to react to the presumption of inferiority imposed upon them from an early age by prejudice against their low economic status, immigrant background, or (most often) both together.

Adler's belief that the inferiority complex grew from judgments of inferiority transmitted by society was less a sophisticated theory than a phrase that summarized the approach of social scientists such as Kurt Lewin and the Clarks, who were trying to conceptualize the impact of prejudice on the individual personality, especially the African-American personality. This concentration on the idea of inferiority being instilled by the society in individual members of a minority informs the social science scholarship produced from the New Deal through the Great Society.

An example from the New Deal era is *Children of Bondage,* a pathbreaking study of caste and class by Allison Davis and John Dollard. The African-American child, whatever the place of his family in the class structure of Negro America, they observe, "lives in a caste system which from his birth severely limits his opportunities for economic advancement and for social training." Davis and Dollard highlighted the socialization process that binds bound each young black child to the American pattern, stating that, "at an early age, he learns that the economic and social restrictions upon him . . . are maintained by powerful threats of the white society, and any effort to rise out of his caste position will be severely punished . . . The superior power of the white caste is not left to his imagination but is dramatized periodically for the whole society in the form of beatings and lynchings."[40] Whatever their class, these are "children of bondage," whose personal development is burdened by the necessity of pretending that they "are 'accommodated' to their caste status and that they are simply good-natured human beings with childish needs." This elaborate system of intimidation was essential to maintaining racial hierarchy: "It is necessary for the society to inculcate strong defensive teaching of this kind to prevent general human recognition of the basic deprivations and frustrations which life in a lower caste involves."[41]

One of the best-known advocates of the inferiority complex in the 1950s was E. Franklin Frazier, who devoted a chapter to the concept ("Inferiority Complex and Quest for Status") in his controversial volume, *The Black Bourgeoisie.* Drawing heavily upon his earlier study of the black family, Frazier wrote:

> During the more than two centuries of enslavement by the white man, every means was employed to stamp a feeling of natural inferiority upon the Negro in the Negro's soul. Christianity and the Bible were utilized both to prove and to give divine sanction to his alleged racial inferiority . . . When the system of slavery was uprooted . . . a legalized system of segregation was established which stigmatized the Negro as unfit for human association . . . Living constantly under the

domination and contempt of the white man, the Negro came to believe in his own inferiority . . . The black bourgeoisie—the element which has striven more than any other element among Negroes to make itself over in the image of the white man—exhibits most strikingly the inferiority complex of those who would escape their racial identification.[42]

Frazier's most influential work, *The Negro Family,* had argued that Negroes, unlike other immigrants, had lost their previous cultural heritage and identity during the harrowing middle passage, arriving in America without cultural defenses against slavery. This lack of cultural insulation, according to Frazier, had made the stamp of inferiority branded upon the black race by slave masters all the more enduring.

Daniel Patrick Moynihan is the most famous post-1960 popularizer of this thesis; it was a cornerstone of his report *The Negro Family: The Case for National Action,* published at the height of the Great Society in 1965.[43] Fifteen years earlier Abram Kardiner and Lionel Ovesey had relied heavily upon Frazier to portray the Negro personality as bereft of the positive cultural identity that had sustained and fortified the Jewish people over centuries. The culture of the ghetto Jew, argued Kardiner and Ovesey, was transplanted during adversity rather than destroyed. The place of the Jewish minority, difficult though it was, did not inhibit them from creating their own intrinsic culture, one allowing them to reject poisonous interpretations imposed from the "master culture." Blacks, Kardiner and Ovesey claimed, were culturally naked during the period of their greatest oppression, and had endured a sadly different fate: their prior "aboriginal culture was smashed" by slavery and "old types of organization were rendered useless," eliminating the "minimal conditions for maintaining a culture or for developing a new one."[44] In 1959, historian Stanley Elkins advanced this argument in the starkest possible terms, by drawing an all too direct, and curiously ahistorical, parallel between slavery and the Nazi concentration camps, casting them both as "total systems" that rendered their prisoners childlike and pliant.[45]

Kenneth Clark joined these debates on culture and personality by experimenting with using the inferiority complex as a way of looking at the inscription of culture upon the individual personality. During the war, Clark brought Adlerian theory to bear on the race riots that were a jarring part of life on the home front. One such opportunity was provided by the Harlem riot of 1943. In 1945, Clark, now at City College, and James Barker, one of his colleagues there, published a keenly observed personality study of a riot participant. Clark and Barker were particularly struck by the subject's animation, intelligence, and imagination, which, they contended, were being misdirected into "a tendency to engage in exhibitionistic exaggeration, bordering on fantasy" regarding the riot "events in which he was allegedly involved."[46] His behavior was symptomatic of the "zoot effect" in a personality condemned to social isolation by racial prejudice.[47]

The "zoot effect," according to the authors, "appears to manifest itself when the human personality has been socially isolated, rejected, discriminated against and chronically humiliated. It is the consequence of the attempts of the individual to maintain some ego security in the face of these facts."[48] Clark and Barker claimed that social norms, including the maintenance of "domestic tranquility," have a "definite meaning and stabilizing function . . . only . . . for those individuals who are part of, and permitted free interaction with the larger social field." Conversely, these values "seem to have little meaning or function for the individual who has been deliberately and involuntarily isolated and rejected from the functions and the benefits of society as a whole. Socially desirable values . . . [have] no meaning or function for . . . an individual who is forced to develop within a humiliating, contracted social field." The entire social body has a vital stake in widening the field of interaction and participation for African-Americans, they argued, for "the stability of the individual personality and the stability of the larger society are inextricably inter-related and therefore the socially accepted dehumanization of an individual or group must inevitably manifest itself in societal disturbances"[49]—or, as Clark had written two years before, "marginal men have marginal morale."

After the war, Clark began to write for ever larger and less specialized audiences. *Commentary,* then in only its first year of publication, provided Clark with his first forum outside of social science to demonstrate the relevance of the inferiority complex to intergroup relations. In its February 1946 issue, Clark offered "candor about Negro-Jewish relations," arguing that the historical tensions between the two were a man-

ifestation of a shared "insecure status in the dominant American culture."
Clark argued that each:

> suffers from the psychological threats of humiliation; each has been
> the victim of organized bigotry. But it is naive to assume that, because
> Negroes and Jews are each in their own way oppressed and insecure,
> that this will lead to a feeling of kinship and understanding . . . The
> common ground of insecurity itself may lead to antagonism toward
> individuals sharing that insecurity. It may also lead to an intensifi-
> cation of fear, suspicion and active hostility as each group competes
> in efforts to escape relegation to the lowest status. For in each group
> there may be a feeling—usually unexpressed—that the presence of
> another racial group will deflect the full brunt of the antagonism of
> the majority from itself. The other group may be looked upon as a
> buffer . . . with protective value only so long as its marginal, insecure
> status persists.[50]

Such an analysis was entirely within—indeed characteristic of—the consensus on prejudice that had been forming within social science since
the 1930s. Sounding very much like his mentor Ralph Bunche at a similar point in his career, Clark told this leading journal of Jewish intellectual life that the persistence of tension between blacks and Jews "serves
to indicate the extent to which the pathologies of the dominant group
infect all groups within that society." Such tensions reflected, Clark contended, "the general social fact that prejudice has a certain political,
economic and psychological function in the over-all pattern of American
society."[51]

"The following facts," Clark wrote in words cited by the Supreme
Court in *Brown,* "seem clearly established: (1) Children are aware of
observable racial differences as early as the age of three or four . . . (2)
Children make racial self-identifications as early as four or five years of
age in terms of the concrete perceived facts between their own skin color
and the skin color of other individuals in their environment . . . (3) They
also learn quite early the social status assigned to differences in skin
color by the larger society."[52] The essential point—the one that Warren
incorporated into the Court's unanimous decision—was that "children
of minority groups early learn the prevailing stereotypes about the group

to which they belong. They learn the inferior status to which their group is assigned in the larger society. They react with feelings of inferiority, aggressive and hostile impulses toward themselves and toward others; there is a lowering of personal ambition and a general pattern of personality difficulties which seem to be associated with a humiliating and inferior role assigned to minorities."[53]

Clark's formulation of the relationship between socialization and prejudice, the point the Court would emphasize in its decision, was one he had been laboring to popularize for a number of years. One such audience was the readers of *Child Study,* a journal of parent education published by the Child Study Association. There Clark made clear that "the evidence strongly suggests that among minority group children ... are found not only subjective feelings of inferiority, loss of self-esteem, ambivalent attitudes toward their own group, but also patterns of overt behavior which seem to result from an inferior and rejected status." The victims of prejudice, Clark stated, mirrored the behavior of its perpetrators, a process described in *The Authoritarian Personality.* In Clark's words, "This behavior takes the form of direct and indirect hostility; aggressiveness toward individuals of the dominant group, other minority groups, one's own group; compensatory and exhibitionistic patterns; withdrawal and submissive, defensive and repressive and other general patterns of behavior indicating racial hypersensitivity."[54]

Clark counseled parents of children in the dominant racial group that they owed their youngsters honest answers to their questions about the significance of racial differences and of the visible socioeconomic injuries that often result from prejudice. Parents of minority-group children, for their part, had a more difficult task: preventing the child from using "his minority status as an excuse for undesirable personal characteristics," and providing opportunities for their children to express the inevitable feelings of anxiety, hostility, and rebellion that they would possess. Such parents also bore the "additional responsibility of helping their children to develop a fundamental tolerance and compassion for their fellow man."[55] Echoing the findings of Davis and Dollard in *Children of Bondage,* Clark told readers of *The Child,* a "monthly journal of child welfare," that reactions to prejudice among minority children varied by class position:

Some children, usually of the lower socio-economic classes, may react by overt aggression and hostility toward their own group or toward members of the dominant group . . . Middle- and upper-class minority-group children are more likely to react to their racial frustrations and conflicts by withdrawn and submissive behavior. On the other hand, they may compensate by rigidly conforming to the prevailing middle-class values and aggressively determining to succeed in meeting these values in spite of the handicap of their minority status.[56]

Up to May 17, 1954, Clark's objective had been to provide several small and specialized publics—especially the nine members of the Supreme Court, but also social psychologists, clinicians, progressive religious leaders, and others actively interested in various aspects of social reform and child welfare—with persuasive evidence that segregation damaged the personality of every child coming of age in American culture. The *Brown* decision required Clark and his colleagues to start over. There was now an entire nation to convince about the necessity of uprooting racism at the dawn of citizenship, and the need to end the segregationist practices that sanctioned these early lessons.

The *Brown* Decision in American Political Culture, 1954–1960

From the moment of its announcement, the *Brown* decision became a sacred and redemptive chapter in the history of American democracy. But the full implications of what this meant for Americans themselves would not be closely examined until after Little Rock.

The first celebrations of the decision in the predominantly Northern media overlooked the intellectual contribution of Clark and other social scientists in favor of an emphasis on how the decision would change the balance of power between the United States and the Soviet Union. *Time* recreated this moment of ideological epiphany with the rhetorical equivalent of wide-screen cinemascope:

It was 12:52 P.M. At the long mahogany bench sat the nine judges of the U.S. Supreme Court. From the red velour hangings behind the bench to the great doors at the back of the room, every seat was filled.

Earl Warren, the Chief Justice of the U.S. [sic], picked up a printed document from his desk and began to read in a firm, clear voice.

There was an awesome quiet in the high ceilinged, marble-columned court-room. The eight Associate Justices gave Warren rapt attention . . . When Warren finished reading at 1:20 the ruling was crystal clear: the U.S. Supreme Court held that racial segregation violates the Constitution. The decision was unanimous . . . The lives of some 12 million school children in 21 states will be altered, and with them eventually the whole pattern of the South . . . The international effect may be scarcely less important. In many countries where U.S. prestige and leadership have been damaged by the fact of U.S. segregation, it will come as a timely reassertion of the basic American principle that "all men are created equal."[57]

As this last sentence makes clear, *Brown* was seen at first blush as a message to friend and foe abroad that America was as good as its creed. *Newsweek* seconded this view, noting that "world Communism" had used the fact of Jim Crow as a powerful psychological weapon against the United States, and concluded that "now that symbol lies shattered." The editors of *Life* believed that the Supreme Court had "at one stroke immeasurably raised the respect of other nations for the U.S."[58]

Even *The Nation*—which, under the editorship of Carey McWilliams, had devoted more space than most to the substantive, rather than the merely symbolic, injustices perpetuated by segregation—was seized by the international implications. Prefacing a thoughtful analysis of the historical and socioeconomic forces that had helped bring *Brown* about was the news that a spokesman for Kenya's Luo tribe had affirmed the global significance of *Brown*: "America is right . . . If we are not educated together, we will live in fear of one another. If we are to stay together forever, why should we have separate schools?"[59] Norman Cousins, another thoughtful progressive voice, reminded Americans that, whether by choice or by necessity, they now lived in a "continental display case" and that such acts, especially when they betokened a sincere change of heart, "have at least as much to do with the security of this nation as nuclear weapons or intercontinental ballistic missiles."[60]

Public commentators were also struck with Chief Justice Warren's rhetoric: his pronouncement that separate was inherently unequal was widely repeated, and the phrase entered the political vernacular of the postwar era almost immediately, as though the connection between unequal treatment and the internalization of inferiority were self-evidently true.[61] The equation was little remarked upon. Over the next few years, however, as the school became the focal point of racial redress—and especially after Little Rock—the social scientific underpinnings implicit in this phrase would gain prominence.[62]

That there was an initial lack of journalistic attention to the role of social scientists in helping the Supreme Court reach its decision may not be as surprising as it appears at first glance. Far from suggesting the irrelevance of social scientists to this discourse, it may suggest that the inferiority complex had become such an accepted cultural concept that the Court's reliance on that type of analysis was unremarkable to contemporary observers. Journalists reporting the case in 1954 may have agreed with the conclusion of their *New York Times* colleague Anthony Lewis that the Court's unprecedented citation of social scientists to legitimate a legal decision was "at worst pretentious superfluity." As Lewis caustically remarked, "It took no reference to social scientists to know that state-enforced segregation was a calculated device to exalt one group and debase another . . . After Adolf Hitler the world knew, and the Supreme Court would have been blind not to see, that it was invidious to separate out one group in society, whether Negroes, Jews or some other."[63] Making much the same point, the editors of the *Saturday Evening Post* argued that "the current doctrine could certainly be sustained on the basis of plain, ordinary constitutional law, without benefit of sociology or psychology." In their opinion, the Court's reliance on the academy for support was, moreover, fraught with dangerous implications: "Reliance on sociology alone, particularly in view of the socialistic thinking of many sociologists, may well establish the doctrine that 'equal protection of the laws' necessitates equal housing facilities, equal incomes and parity in motor vehicle horsepower . . . Decisions which imply the duty of the federal government to prevent inferiority complexes certainly suggest a tendency to move in on the legislative function."[64]

College textbooks written and revised after *Brown* attest to the degree to which the achievement of racial equality was seen as central to the nation's image among the "uncommitted" nations (those allied with neither the United States nor the Soviet Union) and to the diffusion, especially among the college-educated public who came of age in the decade after the Holocaust, of the concept of the inferiority complex as interpretive shorthand for the complex psychological consequences of prejudice. In *Empire for Liberty,* Dumas Malone and Basil Rauch were unequivocal about the pragmatic motivations behind *Brown:* "No influence was more important in making the status of Negroes the leading issue in American domestic affairs than the success of Communists in creating enemies for the United States among the emergent people of Asia and Africa, by propaganda on the subject of America's treatment of the Negro."[65]

To a greater extent than the national press, textbooks addressed the centrality of the inferiority complex to *Brown.* Samuel Eliot Morison and Henry Steele Commager's *The Growth of the American Republic,* the preeminent college textbook of its era, succinctly blended symbolic and psychological issues in its analysis: "At a time when the colonial peoples of Asia and Africa were bursting their bonds and emerging into the sunshine of liberty, and when the United States was trying to win them to the side of the democracies, it was embarrassing, and even stultifying to maintain at home a policy that made a dark skin a huge badge of inferiority."[66] Henry Banford Parkes, in the second revised edition of *The United States of America: A History,* argued that "it was obvious that Negro children were handicapped by the material deficiencies of the Negro schools and the damaging effect of segregation necessarily implied by the mere fact of segregation."[67] In the narrowest sense, this emphasis reflects the close identity that the textbook writers felt between history, traditionally classified as a humanity, and the more institutionally prestigious social sciences. Far more decisive, however, were circumstances to which *Brown* lent powerful momentum. The emergence of the civil rights movement as the nation's preeminent domestic issue—as opposed to simply a strategic necessity of the Cold War—caused these interpreters of *Brown* to highlight the place of psychological theory in the Court's decision.

For some textbook writers, the approaching centennial of the civil war legitimated the interpretation of *Brown* as a landmark in domestic discourse on equality and reform. Richard Hofstadter, William Miller, and Daniel Aaron, for example, called *Brown* a "monumental decision," one in keeping with the strong tradition of domestic reform begun in earnest during the New Deal; a photograph of Thurgood Marshall walking up the steps of the Supreme Court accompanies their text. The authors devote considerable space to Little Rock and to "massive resistance" movements throughout the South, while the North, in contrast, is portrayed as moving rapidly toward compliance.[68] The best treatment of race in the textbooks of the late fifties is Carl Degler's essay "Dawn without Noon," which begins by establishing the connections between *Brown* and the Civil War:

> In May of 1954, many Americans suddenly recognized, despite the fact that only ninety years had passed since the War for the Union, that the sounds and clashes of that struggle were still echoing. The Supreme Court's decision that Negroes are entitled to equal status with whites in the public schools of the nation was but the latest of the efforts, beginning as far back as the time of Appomattox, to find for the Negro in America a place consistent with the national heritage of freedom and equality . . . For a full two hundred years, the status . . . of the great majority of black men in America [was] defined and molded by slavery . . . Today, almost a century after the Emancipation Proclamation, it has not been finally determined; it is still capable of arousing deep-seated emotions among Americans.[69]

For the historian John Garraty, the Court's action confirmed that American democracy had completed a long journey that had made it worthy of admiration throughout the world: "In 1954, the United States was the most powerful nation on earth, the Court a tribunal of American might, the government's right to act with immense force in order to advance the general welfare unquestioned. The Constitution had proved itself the most stable and respected frame of government in the world."[70]

The Limits of Victory

Behind all the celebratory words concerning *Brown* lay the ultimate question of how the decree would be implemented. While the Supreme Court had fulfilled the highest expectations of those within SPSSI by incorporating the findings of social science into what was potentially the most revolutionary legal decision in American history, the distance between potential and actual was sobering. Before *Brown,* Kenneth Clark had devoted most of his energy to persuading those in the child development movement of the pertinence of his analysis. After the decision, Clark tried to answer the question of how to achieve desegregation. To this end he sought to reach both his own colleagues and the lay public.

"The legal power of the government is now clearly on the side of protecting our children," Clark wrote. He observed that "there remains, however, the problem of translating this legal decision into practical and beneficial social changes. This problem is primarily the responsibility of the individual citizens in their local communities. Parents, social workers, educators, clergymen, and others must now mobilize their energies for the effective implementation of this decision."[71] Writing in a special issue on integration in the Unitarian journal *The Christian Register* the year after the Supreme Court's more equivocal implementation decision of May 1955, Clark set forth five requirements for a successful desegregation experience, based on what had happened in other communities:

(1) Gradual desegregation does not necessarily insure effectiveness or increase the chances of acceptance by those who are opposed to desegregation; (2) Prolonged preparation for desegregation and extended "gradualism" increase the chances of resistance and resentment and provide an opportunity for those opposed to desegregation to mobilize and to strengthen their opposing forces, thereby increasing the chances of . . . violence; (3) "Immediate" desegregation is no more likely to lead to nonviolent resistance or violence than are the various forms of "gradual" desegregation. This is true even when there is quite intense and vocal initial opposition to desegregation; (4) Active, sustained resistance or violence is associated with desegregation under the conditions of ambiguous, inconsistent or apologetic policy, ineffective or conspirational police, and conflict between competing governmental agencies or officials; (5) Effective desegregation with a minimum of social disturbances can occur where there is a clear and unequivocal statement by leaders with prestige and authority; where there is a firm enforcement of the policy in the face of initial resistance; when there is a refusal of the authorities to engage in or tolerate subterfuges or evasions of the principles and the fact of desegregation;

and when the individuals involved can be appealed to in terms of their religious principles of brotherhood or their acceptance of the American traditions of fair play and justice.[72]

Unfortunately, Clark's expectation that social scientists, blessed with the endorsement of the Supreme Court, would be invited to play a significant advisory role in localities in both the North and the South proved entirely unwarranted. Clark was compelled to admit "that the available empirical knowledge of the social scientists will not be accepted and used ... unless it is to the advantage of one or more of the competing power groups. Knowledge, unfortunately, will not be used until passions have been found ineffective."[73] Faced with the unwillingness of President Eisenhower and the Department of Justice to work vigorously to enforce *Brown,* Clark counseled building a common front in support of *Brown* by recasting the issue of racial injustice as "an aspect of the larger issue of civil liberties," arguing further that "if the rights of Negroes can be abridged with impunity, the rights of all Americans are weakened ... This fact is unrelated to positive or negative attitudes toward Negroes."[74]

Clark's suggestion, and the program that flowed from it, was more visionary than politically realistic, given the general indifference to civil liberties in the mid-1950s. His "meeting ground for action" between African-Americans and liberal whites would later inform federal policy under President Lyndon B. Johnson. As Clark put it, "There must be a program to insure the right of the Negro to vote and petition his government without fear for his personal safety ... Finally, I believe that the next step in the legal approach to civil rights should be the bringing of taxpayers' suits to enjoin the southern states and public officials from using public funds, which include taxes paid by Negroes, for the purpose of withholding from the Negro his adjudicated civil rights."[75]

The *Brown* decision gave unquestioned legal sanction, as well as a measure of cultural legitimacy, to desegregation. With his role in the litigation complete, Clark sought to enter the larger cultural stage with intellectual reinforcements for those citizens leading the way to desegregation and eventual integration. His vehicle was a brief text of 139 pages entitled *Prejudice and Your Child.* Written in a warm, plain-spoken style, the text calls to mind the classic child-care manual of the postwar era, Benjamin Spock's *Common Sense Book of Baby and Child*

Care—a book that, in all five of its editions published from 1946 through 1968, was silent on the challenge posed to parents by the pervasiveness of prejudice and stereotyping in American society.[76] Clark intended his audience to be postwar parents, in the belief that "American citizens should have the same type of objective information that was available to the justices of the United States Supreme Court."[77] Whether or not the decision would be implemented would in the end be up to America's parents.

The basic assumption of Clark's text was that prejudice was not the disability of one individual (although its treatment must often be individually administered) but rather that of a whole culture, collectively created, publicly shared, and generationally transmitted: "Racial symbols are so prevalent in the American scene that all American children eventually perceive them. They observe segregated residential areas, segregated and inferior schools for Negro children, segregated recreational facilities, and in some areas of the country, segregated transportation. They see Negroes often only in domestic service or in other menial occupations. Such observations contribute to the young child's attitude toward those individuals whom the society consistently labels as 'inferior.' "[78] These ubiquitous symbols transmitted to its victims (whom Clark identified as not only African-Americans, but Jews and the children of first-generation ethnics as well) feelings of inferiority, even self-hatred. Unlike the white ethnics, whose social mobility as members of the white majority made such psychic injuries less enduring over the course of generations of assimilation and economic success, African-Americans bore a special burden because they would always be racial outsiders.[79]

In *An American Dilemma,* Gunnar Myrdal had argued that the contradiction between the "American creed" and racial discrimination was a historical irritant to the national conscience that would become irrepressibly acute in the postwar era and therefore would necessarily lead to reform. Although Clark shared Myrdal's optimism about the future, he relied on Adler to argue that the dilemma did not exist in the minds of white Americans:

> All white Americans were either immigrants or the descendants of immigrants. Each wave of newcomers had in common with all others

the fact that each group was fleeing either from economic hardships, religious or political persecution, or from social humiliation. The people who made up the new nation, therefore, were driven by some basic form of personal or group insecurity. This insecurity had to be strong enough to compensate for the disadvantages and discomforts involved in leaving the homeland and migrating to a new world . . . The entrenchment in the culture of the expressed ideas of the "American Creed" was determined by the past inferior status that had made the old world intolerable. To . . . white colonizers and immigrants, the "American Creed" . . . was accepted and sustained in order to obtain a security and integrity that had been previously denied. If this is true, it may offer an explanation of the relationship between the American ideology of equality and the American pattern of social and racial discrimination. An individual in quest of security and status may seek to obtain them not only through positive objective methods . . . but through the denial of security and status to another person or group.[80]

Clark's Americans, whether they were the colonists of the seventeenth and eighteenth centuries, the settlers of the nineteenth-century frontier, or the members of the expanding postwar middle class, closely resembled the social types constructed by the reigning public intellectuals of the 1950s, a group seemingly determined, in the words of John Kenneth Galbraith, to "strike an uncouth note in the world of positive thinking."[81]

Clark's Americans were "other-directed," bearing a strong resemblance to the archetype made famous in David Riesman's *The Lonely Crowd.* In Riesman's view, other-directed individuals were conditioned by their social reference group to "seek adjustment" with convention. An other-directed individual strove, for example, to "have the character he is supposed to have, and the inner experiences as well as the outer appearances that are supposed to go with it." Such individuals, while the beneficiaries of an unprecedented prosperity, were made anxious by the fear that the escalating cost of "making it" in the suburbs would force them to "go back."[82] "Psychologically at least," William H. Whyte said of recent business school graduates, "the newcomers to suburbia are living on the brink of a precipice." Whyte observed:

It is true that they are better buttressed than were their parents against a depression, but that much more have their expectations been raised. Broad as the middle class may be, there is a line, a rather firm one, beneath which middle class life is impossible ... It is not, furthermore, a static figure. It is constantly moving up as the couple ages, for while it may be alright to enter suburbia strapped for money, as time goes on, it is abnormal for one's income not to rise, and this will be painfully evident to the family which cannot follow other contemporaries as they expand the little luxuries of their life.[83]

For those slightly older members of the middle class reaching their late thirties, the anxiety over security and status was not simply a fear of decline in relation to faster rising neighbors. For this large cohort, "the memory of the depression is still so vivid that they cannot be sure the cornucopia will remain open; and their outlook was shaped in that distant period when social security, hospital insurance plans, and other such cushions were not a part of life."[84] Daniel Bell encapsulated the peculiar distress so seemingly ubiquitous in American life during this era when, in one of his essays on "the exhaustion of political ideas in the fifties," he observed that "America in mid-century is in many respects a turbulent country ... Contrary to the somewhat simplistic notion that prosperity dissolves all social problems, the American experience demonstrates that prosperity brings in its wake new anxieties, new strains, new urgencies."[85] "Many people," Vance Packard warned, "are badly distressed by the anxieties, inferiority feelings, and straining generated by this unending process of rating and status striving."[86]

These Americans and their cultural context were also Clark's subjects. The phenomenon of prejudice, and its contemporary expression, must be understood as part and parcel of "the larger social climate within which children and within which their families seek status and security." Clark was deeply distrustful of a psychoanalytic approach to prejudice because, in his view, it focused too much on discrete individuals' experiences of prejudice and ignored the larger forces at work. Clark maintained that prejudice in America originated in "the total pattern of striving for status and success which characterizes American middle-class life."[87] He believed that racism was embedded within the pattern of status striving prevalent in American culture:

While American children of respected parents are being taught to pursue the symbols of status and success, they are at the same time being taught to compete with others—and to exclude those who are "obviously inferior." These attitudes are subtly and effectively taught to children from before the time they are required to compete with their classmates for the highest marks, through the inevitable status competition of the adolescent period, up to the time when they are taught the essentials for successful social and economic mobility which should end in a "good marriage" to the "right person."[88]

Despite the fact that its thesis fit well within the conventions of the genre of popular social science in the fifties, *Prejudice and Your Child* failed to reach the mass audience for which it had been written.[89] Despite Clark's role as the link between the activist psychologists of SPSSI and the Warren Court, it was a work by Harvard professor Gordon Allport, one of the deans of academic psychology, entitled *The Nature of Prejudice* that instead served as the textbook summation of SPSSI research on prejudice from the mid-1930s through the mid-1950s.[90]

One of the reasons for the small initial readership of *Prejudice and Your Child* was that it was not widely reviewed outside of the academy. One exception was an unequivocally negative evaluation in the March 1956 issue of *Commentary*. Clark's rejection of psychoanalytic method as too narrow to fully address the problem of prejudice provoked a near-scathing response there from Bruno Bettelheim, the psychoanalyst most closely associated with the study of prejudice at that time. Such a forceful attack from a person who at the time was an icon of European erudition and humanism may have been decisive in limiting the audience for *Prejudice and Your Child* in its first editions.

Clark's principal error, in Bettelheim's judgment, was to have misunderstood the nature of prejudice: "It is a book which removes a problem of social justice from the realm of ethics to that of the social sciences."[91] Bettelheim found Clark's "benevolent, non-scientific intentions" leading him astray at virtually every turn.[92] To Clark's most basic assumption—that prejudice damages its practitioners as well as its victims—Bettelheim responded by stating that, "while our present methods of investigation do indeed permit us to say *why* a person is prejudiced, or *which* personality types tend to harbor racial prejudice, they by no means give us warrant to predict whether such persons would be happier if they were to become tolerant . . . though prejudice is always a social and economic disadvantage to the victim of discrimination, it sometimes serves vital needs for the victimizer by providing an outlet for discharging internal pressures. But the scientific approach to racial discrimination has not yet given us a means of determining whether such an outlet can be justified" (emphasis in the original).[93]

Equally unfounded, according to Bettelheim, was the most cherished assumption of postwar intergroup relations: that exposure to peoples of different races and backgrounds in a nonsegregated context would lead to well-adjusted citizens. Bettelheim called on his own experience to testify personally to the falsity of this conclusion: "Having, as a Jewish boy, attended non-segregated schools in Germany and Austria, I know this to be blatantly untrue. Indeed, it was the non-segregated German public schools where the seeds of racism and ultra-nationalism took firm root, while most children who went to Catholic parochial schools turned out (even under the Nazis) to be much less prejudiced, not only against Jews, but Poles and Czechs as well." Underlying the assumption that exposure to diversity promotes personal stability is the corollary that prejudice is rooted in personal instability. According to Bettelheim, however, "some of the most stable (i.e., conservative) societies in history were based on the exclusion of all foreigners, or on unalterable class or caste distinctions. Why, in any case, should stability be set up as a criterion of social health? Does not [Clark] himself spend most of his book propagandizing for rapid social change?"[94]

The coup de grace was Bettelheim's suggestion that Clark did not even understand the clear implications of his own research. Clark had argued that the greater calmness demonstrated by southern African-American children as opposed to their Northern counterparts in the course of the doll tests suggested an adjustment to a sick environment, while the northern African-Americans' emotional responses, and even unwillingness, to identify themselves with a race widely interpreted as inferior expressed a recognition—and an unwillingness to cooperate in—a social system that was deeply unjust. Bettelheim asserted that Clark's evidence could easily be read as undermining Clark's own argument. Bettelheim's point was not to make the case for the racial status quo, but to suggest that Clark had badly misconstrued the necessary preconditions for uprooting prejudice:

> I have gone to some lengths in pointing out the inner contradictions that inevitably emerge when the demand for racial equality is based on data from the social sciences or individual psychology. Psychologically speaking, it is just not true that what benefits one benefits all, or that what hurts one hurts all. Social and political equality are issues of justice and morality, not of psychological utilitarianism. It is not even true that strides toward greater racial equality will make everybody happier. But it certainly will make a *juster,* more human world to live in [original emphasis].[95]

Bettelheim's invidiously selective analysis of Clark's *Prejudice and Your Child* was an aggressive argument not for the merits of desegregation, but for issues of equal importance: What constituted the most authoritative representation of prejudice and its victims? What were the most effective means for destroying prejudice? And most important, at least for Bettelheim, which discipline—and which of its members—was best fitted to wear the public mantle of "expert"?

Bettelheim's dissent came from his experience of anti-Semitism in prewar Austria and Germany and his imprisonment in a Nazi concentration camp. His strategic use of the argument from his own experience as a student in "non-segregated schools in Germany and Austria" as well as the terms he used to characterize Clark and his position ("moral partisan," "benevolent, non-scientific," "laudable," "false reasoning on the part of a friend" and "reports data in obvious contradiction of his thesis—though he does not always realize it") insinuate that both Clark's professional training and his experience of prejudice as a black American in the twentieth-century urban North were no match for the deep learning and profound suffering of a Jewish émigré who had experienced racism at its most brutally systematic.

To Bettelheim, the language of those like Myrdal and Clark, whom Whyte called the "new utopians," seemed dangerously naive and latently undemocratic. Describing the social engineer's confidence in the ability of trained intelligence to better organize human affairs, Whyte captured pointedly what it was in the wide-eyed enthusiasm of the social scientist that Bettelheim found dangerous: "Social engineers have emboldened themselves to seek the final solution. Now, they say, we will *scientifically determine ethics*" (emphasis in the original).[96]

Bettelheim's dismissal of Clark's "propagandizing for rapid social change" was as close as the renowned psychoanalyst came to addressing Clark's real argument. Clark and his colleagues would probably have agreed with Bettelheim that the prejudiced individual feels in balance with a society whose members are conditioned to think and act in hierarchical and racialist terms—in fact, this was Clark's basic assumption. Clark was propagandizing and arguing from social ethics more than from science because, like Myrdal, Clark was setting out the foundations for a new American culture—far more a moral than a scientific enterprise. Clark's impatience with what he believed to be the overemphasis of psychoanalysis on adjusting individuals to their environment, and Bettelheim's profound skepticism about grand schemes to transform society scientifically were hardly incompatible.[97]

Clark's association with the NAACP and with SPSSI in the end proved more decisive in placing Clark near the forefront of racial discourse than did his attempt to find a voice for himself as a social scientist for society, in writing *Prejudice and Your Child.* The momentum created by *Brown* effectively launched Clark on a path that would culminate in his becoming the "reigning academic" of the civil rights movement.[98] Clark's arrival as a recognized public intellectual occurred not in 1954, and not as a result of *Brown,* but in 1965, when Clark's identification with *Brown* was but one of the legitimating credentials and accomplishments that qualified him, in the eyes of the press, to interpret the civil rights movement, the War on Poverty, and civil disorder in the country's urban ghettos.

The retroactive importance of *Brown* to the political culture of the late sixties can be seen in the June 1968 issue of *Psychology Today,* where Clark was introduced to its readers in the following way: "Among national leaders alive today, Dr. Kenneth B. Clark has no peer in scholarly or applied knowledge of ghetto psychology, or of educational and employment inequalities in every sector of our society. The 1954 U.S. Supreme Court decisions on school desegregation were based in large part on the appendix from the legal briefs ... The poverty approach of the Office of Economic Opportunity was based on a two-year study ...

under his direction . . . He has received as many honors for his work as any man in public affairs."[99] Likewise, Theodore H. White, easily the most widely read political journalist of the 1960s, included Clark in a wide-ranging three-part series on "action-intellectuals" in *Life* magazine; the piece included sketches of Daniel P. Moynihan, Walt Rostow, and several other luminaries of the New Frontier–Great Society era. White recalled Clark as the man who "set down in precise, scholarly terms the true extent of the psychological damage done by [segregation] to both Negro and white students."[100] As the nation grappled in the coming years with the moral challenge set down officially by *Brown,* Clark became the best-known representative of both the decision itself and of the new prominence of social science in American public life.

But this was in the future. From 1954 through 1960 the focus of Clark's activism was more narrowly cast, as a member of SPSSI (of which he became president in 1960), and in implementing *Brown* in New York City.[101] As the chair of the Intergroup Committee on New York's Public Schools, Clark successfully pushed the New York City Board of Education to form a Commission on Integration (on which Clark served).[102] He was also a member of the New York State Youth Commission. "An ardent intellectual and integrationist," wrote one admirer of his place in the New York intellectual and political establishment, "Clark commanded broad respect."[103]

Although it would be a few years before Clark became a nationally known expert-interpreter of the civil rights movement, his involvement with *Brown* did provide him with unusual opportunities to observe and comment on a movement in the making. In February 1956, for example, Clark and Hylan Lewis, a good friend of Clark's from their Howard years, were invited by the Unitarian Service Committee to undertake an inspection of desegregation efforts in Georgia, Alabama, Mississippi, Tennessee, and South Carolina. Clark and Lewis returned with their early optimism about the ability of a Supreme Court decision to end segregation bruised. They were particularly shocked at the facility with which southern political leaders who were opposed to segregation were able to intimidate communities into a seemingly monolithic opposition to desegregation: "They use the methods of incessant newspaper and radio propaganda," Clark and Lewis reported. "They appeal to the passions and latent and overt racial prejudices of the masses of whites; and they are ruthless in preventing any expression of dissenting opinion among moderate or sympathetic whites."[104]

The most important encounter of the trip for Clark and Lewis was a meeting with Martin Luther King, Jr.:

> He is . . . articulate, intelligent . . . with an inherent dignity and calm. He discusses the issues of the Montgomery boycott and the general problem of race relations in Alabama and the South, not only without venom, but without apparent emotion. He . . . recognizes the relationship between the success or failure of . . . the Montgomery Negroes . . . the total problem of racial justice in America and the more complex problems of international relations . . . He is profoundly concerned with the fundamental issues of the nature of justice and democracy. He is neither cynical nor sentimental; he does not expect miracles nor does he accept the cliches of gradualism . . . He contends that human beings are always ready for justice.[105]

Later that year, on December 1, 1956, Clark introduced King to his first New York audience, a gathering of the National Committee for Rural Schools.[106] Clark's consultancy with the Unitarian Service Committee, as well as his work on desegregation in New York, marked a new chapter in Clark's public life—one in which he functioned simultaneously as a resource to the leadership of the civil rights movement and as one of its most visible interpreters to the public.

Clark's involvement with the liberal educational and political establishment of New York in enforcing *Brown* in the North gave him the first clues that the optimism at the center of *Prejudice and Your Child* was misplaced, even in the city reputed to be a capital of cultural cosmopolitanism and political liberalism. The violence in Little Rock powerfully confirmed Clark's growing doubts about the nation's commitment to future progress. Clark viewed the future with a new sense of pessimism:

> The primary tragedy of Little Rock is not to be found in anything that has happened to the Negro children or in any psychological scars which they must bear . . . Apparently centuries of oppression have immunized them and given them the necessary protective defenses for survival. The real tragedy of Little Rock is what is happening to

the white children in Central High School—the fact that potentially decent human beings are being required to bow to the brutality of a tightly organized white minority. And this reflects a larger tragedy: the decency in the whites of the South is not backed by the fervor and conviction or courage which is shown by fanatical racists. Without regard to the integration issues—without regard to what happens to Negroes, for they will survive—this is a serious omen for the region and for the nation as a whole.[107]

Ten years later, after King's assassination, Clark's pessimism had deepened to the point where he was beginning to doubt the efficacy and relevance of the social role he had created for himself a generation earlier. As Clark confessed to an interviewer from *Psychology Today* in June 1968, "to be quite candid about the success of my attempts at being a psychologist for society, I have to state that I have failed. I've produced documents . . . and memorandums [sic]. The involvements in social action and social change that have dominated my life add up to one big failure."[108]

Before *Brown,* the discourse on race and Americanism that had raised up Ralph Bunche had no single focus when it came to the home front. What Lee Nichols had described in the early 1950s as a "tide of integration" seemed to be washing inexorably over the nation and all of its institutions: the armed forces, baseball, the federal government and its capital city, electoral politics, and education from the local school to the state university. The idea that twenty years later Americans would be heatedly debating the merits of court-ordered busing in order to achieve integration would have been simply unbelievable.[109]

In the long run, one of the greatest contributions of *Brown* to the American discourse on race was that it made the public school its primary emphasis: as the focus of Clark's early professional career attests, the public school would come to be seen as the place where fidelity to the American creed would be measured and therefore most vigorously contested. Before *Brown,* the school had been one of several important fronts in the national mobilization against prejudice; after *Brown,* the public school was, institutionally and symbolically, first among equals.

Kenneth B. Clark and Great Society Reform

5

Most social scientists live in a cool world of dispassion, detachment, and demonstrable truths. But as a Negro psychologist studying the corrosive effects of prejudice, Kenneth Bancroft Clark necessarily lives in a world of passion, involvement, and truths that are strongly held but not easily measured. In 1954, the slight, soft-spoken CCNY professor was written into the history books when the Supreme Court, in a now-famous footnote, offered as one of its justifications for outlawing segregation Clark's study of the psychological damage wrought by "separate but equal" schooling.

> —*Newsweek* (**May 31, 1965**)

The new American Dilemma is one of power. The dilemma is a confrontation between those forces which impel a society to change and those which seek to maintain the past.

> —**Kenneth B. Clark (1966)**

Nineteen sixty-three was the year of the "Negro revolt." As William Brink and Louis Harris reminded the public that year, "During the 1950s, there were sporadic incidents . . . There were ugly and ominous trouble spots, such as Little Rock. But as yet the real proportions of the Negro's revolt were not clearly visible." The "Negro revolt" of 1963 ended this era of invisibility: "Then . . . came Birmingham, with its police dogs and fire hoses turned on the Negro marchers; Birmingham, with the bombing that took the lives of four little Negro girls and boys . . . Then also came the march of the Negroes to the capital of their country, the most awesome display of a race in protest that the United States had ever seen."[1]

"The present battle for racial justice in America is in its show-down stage," Kenneth Clark wrote in the September 1963 issue of *Ebony,* which arrived on the newsstands right before the March on Washington. "Negroes and committed whites will either remove the last barriers to racial equality in America within the next year or two, or," Clark warned, "will witness a frightening and revolting form of racial oppression and moral stagnation in a nation which professes to be a leader of the democratic forces of the free world." The *Brown* decision's promise of liberation "from the shackles of psychological slavery" had been successfully thwarted by the South's strategy of "evasion and indefinite postponement," and the North's complicit willingness to "settle for the crumbs of tokenism."[2]

For a time in the late 1950s, Clark's faith in American democracy had been shaken by the prospect that "the American desire for social peace no matter what the ethical cost and some signs of battle weariness among Negro organizations and leadership might have made it possible for moderation to succeed where the more rabid racists were destined to fail; namely, to evade . . . the letter and spirit of the [Brown] decision. Fortunately, however, the passionate impatience of a small group of Negro college students exploded on a complacent America. The sit-in, freedom rides and other methods of direct action . . . seem to have shocked America out of some of its moral stupor."[3]

By 1964, the first of the long, hot summers that would consume America's urban ghettos was abruptly forcing a reorientation and re-representation of the American dilemma. Its symbolic focus now moved to the ghetto of the Northern city. "The Negro problem," Charles Silberman declared in his highly regarded and much reprinted *Crisis in Black and White,*

> is no longer hidden on the plantations of the Mississippi delta nor in the sleepy towns of the "Old South," not even in the bustling cities of the "New South." On the contrary, the most serious social problem confronting America today is to be found in the heart of the nation's ornaments: New York, Philadelphia, Washington, Chicago, Detroit, Milwaukee, San Francisco, Los Angeles—and in a score of smaller cities . . . For there is not a city of any importance that does not now have a large and rapidly growing "Negro problem."[4]

Much had changed since *Brown.* Outright opposition in the South and more subtle and quieter evasions in the North prevented wide implementation of the decision. The ensuing decade had also witnessed the acceleration of other trends equally responsible for keeping blacks both separate and unequal. African-Americans were migrating to Northern cities where, unlike preceding waves of immigrants, they found that they were entering a labor market that was less able to absorb them and was instead becoming increasingly reliant on skilled, rather than unskilled, labor.[5] "On the tenth anniversary of the Supreme Court's integration decision," James Reston of the *New York Times* wrote, "the paradox and tragedy of the Negro are fairly clear. He is gaining legally but falling behind economically. He is slowly getting the rights but not the skills of a modern computerized society. He is getting a better chance at unskilled jobs, but unskilled jobs are being wiped out by the new bossman, the machine."[6]

The reinvigoration of American political discourse forced by the civil rights movement created an opening for Kenneth Clark, African-American social scientist and veteran of the *Brown* litigation, friend and advisor to leaders of the civil rights movement from Whitney Young to Malcolm X, to speak to a broad national audience with the authority of a "new Myrdal." In 1963 Clark was officially recognized as a leading voice of the civil rights movement. As *Ebony* announced in August 1963:

> The voices of essayist James Baldwin and sociologist Kenneth Clark and black supremacist Malcolm X and actor Sammy Davis and author Louis Lomax and gospel singer Mahalia Jackson and comic Dick Gregory and actress Lena Horne—to name a few—are joined in a common plea for equality. Long divorced from the ghetto complex, these, like countless other Negro celebrities and intellectuals, have found a new identity with the unsung and uneducated Negro. They have found new pride in their race as well as a working formula for gaining the equality all Negroes seek.[7]

Before 1963, Clark had been known primarily to two rather special-ized publics. The first was located within social science, especially psy-chology, where his contribution to the NAACP's challenge to *Plessy v. Ferguson* was widely admired. The second was made up of New York opinion leaders interested in the desegregation of their schools, a group that knew Clark as a significant critic, and occasional ally, of the New York City Board of Education's sporadic efforts to reorganize the city's schools to comply with the letter and the spirit of *Brown.* Indicative of Clark's professional reputation after *Brown,* as well as his visibility in these circles, was that Secretary of State Dean Rusk retained Clark to establish a program to recruit blacks into the ranks of the United States foreign service.[8]

Two events in the late spring of 1963 publicly marked Clark as a new Myrdal. The first was his attendance at a highly confrontational meeting with Robert F. Kennedy that had been organized by Harry Belafonte; other participants included writers James Baldwin and Lorraine Hansberry, actor Rip Torn, a representative of the Chicago Urban League, and a young activist from SNCC. Belafonte's intention in arranging the conference had been to open a line of communication between the Kennedy administration and leading figures in the black community; several of those attending, however, brought more pointed agendas with them.[9] Baldwin and Hansberry, for example, used the occasion to express their belief that the administration was totally out of touch with issues of concern to African-Americans. For his part, Clark, who was attending as Martin Luther King's personal representative, lobbied Kennedy for greater federal action on civil rights and strongly criticized the president's appointments to the federal bench in the South.[10]

The second event bringing Clark into wider public view was a televised interview program that he hosted, *The Negro and the Promise of American Life.* This series of conversations with three leading African-American figures was shown over the summer of 1963 by the affiliates of the newly established National Educational Television network. The Kennedy meeting and the TV program were in fact connected, as Clark told his television audience: "Through a strange set of circumstances we managed to record this conversation with James Baldwin immediately after both of us had attended the now famous meeting between a group of Mr. Baldwin's friends and Attorney General Robert Kennedy."[11]

The meeting with the attorney general received wide publicity because it had been such a mutually alienating experience for the two groups of participants. Kennedy left the meeting believing that he had been ambushed by a circle of people who were only superficially informed as to what the administration was actually doing and who had already decided that "the answer was . . . to take to the streets and shoot white people." On the other side, Clark went away distrustful of the Attorney General, "convinced that we had made no impact on Bobby . . . that we had widened the gap [and that] whatever rapport had existed before was disrupted."[12] In the end, however, it seems that the encounter had the

CoRE

opposite effect. Not only did events force the Kennedys to associate themselves quite strongly with the civil rights issue, but the meeting had significance in the longer term as well. According to journalist Nicholas Lemann, the aborted meeting "deepened [Robert Kennedy's] understanding and drew him emotionally closer to the slums; it was something nobody else at his level in Washington had been through."[13]

The Negro and the Promise of American Life grew, like the meeting with Attorney General Kennedy, out of the high regard in which Clark was held by those who, by 1963, were emerging as the most widely known representatives of the "Negro revolt." The program, produced by WGBH, consisted of Clark's one-on-one interviews with Martin Luther King, Malcolm X, and James Baldwin.[14] In the years after *Brown,* Clark had developed friendships of varying degrees of closeness with these three men. Clark's longest friendship was with Baldwin, whom he had met in the late forties as a result of their shared association with *Commentary.*[15] Clark's pilgrimage to the South in 1956 had brought him into contact with King, with whom he developed a warm professional relationship. Clark's high personal regard for Malcolm X stemmed from Clark's experiment with community action, Harlem Youth Unlimited (HARYOU), from 1961 through 1964; Clark later recalled how the youths of HARYOU went to great pains to bring the academic integrationist together with the Muslim leader at HARYOU functions. "They would always find some way of making sure that I would be seated next to Malcolm at things," Clark remembered. "They [the youths] looked upon me as . . . at best . . . a sort of establishment representative, and at worst, a sort of . . . cynical spokesman of the establishment to control their rebellion." Clark's relationship with Malcolm was further deepened because Clark's son, Hilton, was spending a lot of time with Malcolm. Malcolm's sensitivity in allaying the elder Clark's presumed anxieties on this score formed a bond between the two men; they became "quiet, understanding friends."[16]

Baldwin, King, and Malcolm were presented by Clark as various expressions of a collective mood and condition among African-Americans to a nation only just reawakened to the persistent depth of racial injustice. "We have invited three men at the forefront of the Negro struggle to sit down and talk with us," Clark informed his national viewing audience.[17] "Each of these men reflects in his being the quest of all Negroes for a positive identity, a recognition and respect for their individuality and an insistence upon their total humanity."[18] At the same time, Clark explained, "each of these men, through his actions and words . . . is a spokesman for some segment of the Negro people today."[19]

Clark summarized the representational nature of each of his guests in the following manner: "The Reverend Martin Luther King is the symbol of the heroic nonviolent struggle for integration and full rights now, through peaceful direct action. Malcolm X, the Black Muslims' most eloquent spokesman, is an apostle of black racism and separation. His movement appeals most strongly to the most alienated Negroes. We talk with James Baldwin, a writer who through the magic of his words and the purity of his artistry and truth, has communicated the full passion of the Negro existence."[20]

In remarks introducing each conversation, Clark discussed in a more expansive fashion the symbolic role that each figure was playing in the elaboration of a new chapter in the American discourse on race. King, Clark offered, in the aftermath of the assaults and other violence upon him and his followers in Birmingham, embodied "the dignity, discipline and insistence upon the full rights of American citizenship which the present thrust of the Negro people demands." Clark addressed the larger significance of Malcolm X by presenting a socioeconomic interpretation of his movement. Clark claimed that the Muslims' strength among urban blacks derived from the fact that "their basic premise is true": "White America has permitted a system of cruelty and barbarity to be perpetrated and perpetuated on citizens of dark skin color and the Muslims are very effective at saying this over and over again . . . They are dangerous because they use hatred and racism to manipulate their followers. The Muslim movement seems terribly attractive . . . to a disturbing number of young people and the forgotten masses alienated from white America." Baldwin was present, Clark said, as the voice whose words had finally communicated to white Americans "what every Negro has long known and long felt."[21]

Clark's conversations with these three figures (published later that year by Beacon Press as *The Negro Protest*) elicited basic biographical information and explored the relationship between the individual's biography—particularly the formative encounter with racism—and the development of a larger social philosophy. Clark closed the program with some general philosophical comments that drew a universal truth from the singular life stories of his guests: "If one dares to look for the common denominator of such seemingly different forms of Negro protest," Clark summarized, "one sees in each a common reaction to America's attempts to deny its Negro citizens the fulfillment . . . of the American promise." Clark contended that, "by all meaningful indices, the Negro is still and unquestionably the down-trodden, disparaged group and for a long time he was systematically deprived of his dignity as a human being."[22]

When *Brown* burst upon the public discourse, Clark assumed that once the definitive institutions of American democracy—the army, the Supreme Court, the Congress—had spoken, a process of reasonably rapid change would ensue. Ten years later, Clark told his television audience, "the major indictment of our democracy is that [the continued subjection of blacks] is being done with the knowledge, and at times with the connivance, of responsible, moderate people who are not overtly bigots or segregationists." Clark ended the broadcast on a hopeful note, stating: "We have come to the point where there are only two ways that America can avoid continued racial explosions: one would be total oppression; the other total equality. There is no compromise. I believe—I hope— that we are on the threshold of a truly democratic America. It is not going to be easy to cross that threshold. But the achievement of the goals of justice, equality and democracy for all American citizens involves the very destiny of our nation."[23]

The Re-Representation of the American Dilemma

The ascent of Lyndon Johnson to the presidency and his subsequent decision to launch a "war on poverty" further confirmed Clark's place in the center of the American discourse on race. In 1964, in the midst of the country's first summer of racial unrest, Clark received national attention as a participant-expert actively engaged in saving Harlem, the nation's best-known ghetto and the scene of then unprecedented rioting.

Clark's ambitious plan was to do nothing less than rebuild Harlem's psychological and physical environment, political economy, and cultural life through community action on the part of the residents themselves.

Time, in its cover story on the Harlem riot, spoke highly of Clark's work as a prototype for the War on Poverty:

> The most ambitious program of all is the three-year, $110 million HARYOU-ACT program ... It is the brainchild of Kenneth Clark ... a City College Professor whose brief on the effects of discrimination helped shape the Supreme Court's 1954 desegregation decision. It envisions a network of community councils and organizations dedicated to fighting poverty and helping ghetto youngsters by setting up half a dozen businesses that will be run by some 3,000 teenagers, after-school study centers for those with nowhere to go, job information and training centers handling 2,300 youths a year, pre-school academies to get toddlers out of fetid tenements, and a crash remedial reading program for Harlem's schools. "We've got to show them that hard work does pay off," says Clark, "even for Negroes."[24]

In the opinion of *Time,* Clark's efforts were coming none too soon. "There is justifiable fury in Harlem," the magazine reported, and "that fury will be aimed against whatever barriers still exist, and it will take some costly resistance to keep them from falling." To underline the urgency and the legitimacy of these demands, *Time* quoted a black police patrolman on 125th Street: "You have to keep knocking on the door. If you don't knock, they won't hear you." So that its readers would not misunderstand this Harlem-grown allegory—what "knocking" entailed and who "they" were—*Time* underscored the message: "In the long hot summer of 1964, the question for New York and for every major U.S. city with a Harlem of its own was: how hard will Harlem knock next time?"[25]

Newsweek also featured Clark in its own cover story on Harlem; they praised Clark's mobilization, characterizing it as an attempt to revitalize a "powerless colony." The phrase was one that came straight out of Clark's blueprint for reconstructing Harlem, *Youth in the Ghetto,* the predecessor to *Dark Ghetto. Newsweek* relied on Clark himself to explain to its readership how the white police and, by implication, white America, had contributed to the riot:

> They have been playing Russian roulette with us for years ... What disgusts me is the pretense of shock, surprise, horror. The horrible

conditions, the sanitation, the pushing people around—apparently nobody gives a damn about it. They send hundreds and hundreds and thousands of cops. They would do better to send one-third as many building inspectors or a thousand sanitation workers, or just an attempt at proper schooling . . . But you know what I think we're going to get? "Quiet the natives, then go on with business as usual."[26]

Look endorsed *Youth in the Ghetto* as "recommended reading for any white person—public official, commuter, or panicked subway rider—who can still ask 'Why?' in the summer of 1964."[27]

Also in 1964, Clark, at the age of fifty, became known as a "New York intellectual." The occasion was a wide-ranging panel discussion, organized by *Commentary* and carried in its March issue, that explored the relationship between "liberalism and the Negro." The roster of participants included some of the most distinguished members of the New York intelligentsia, including Sidney Hook, Nathan Glazer, and Norman Podhoretz. Also in attendance were Charles Silberman, the author of *Crisis in Black and White,* and two icons of postwar racial discourse, James Baldwin and Gunnar Myrdal. Like the meeting with Attorney General Kennedy the previous May, the exchanges were often adversarial and highly personal, signaling the advent of a new, polarized era in American racial discourse. In his comments, Clark expressed his alienation with the "white liberal" and defended the pessimism of James Baldwin as mere realism: "How do I—a Negro in America who throughout his undergraduate years and the early part of his professional life identified himself with liberalism— . . . now see American liberalism? I must confess that I now see white American liberalism primarily in terms of the adjective, 'white.' And I think [that] one of the important things Negro Americans will have to learn is how they can deal with a curious and insidious adversary—much more insidious than the out-and-out bigot." Noting the presence of Myrdal, Clark continued by challenging the fundamental premise of *An American Dilemma* and the sincerity of those who had appropriated it as an expression of their own far-sightedness:

With all due respect to my friend and former colleague and boss, Professor Myrdal, I have come to the conclusion that so far as the Negro is concerned, the ethical aspect of American liberalism or the

American Creed is primarily verbal. There is a peculiar kind of ambivalence in American liberalism, a persistent verbal liberalism that
is never capable of overcoming an equally persistent illiberalism of
action. And so I am forced to agree with James Baldwin that so far
as the Negro is concerned, liberalism, as it is practiced . . . is an affliction. It is an insidious type of affliction because it attempts to
impose guilt upon the Negro when he has to face the hypocrisy of
the liberal. Mr. Baldwin has been put on the defensive all throughout
this discussion by people who don't want to be made uncomfortable
by him . . . All you've been saying to Mr. Baldwin is: Don't force
me to look behind my own facade. Don't force me to find out that
my Negro friends aren't really giving it to me straight. I'm glad that
James Baldwin is around, because he's helping some of the rest of us
cope with this difficult problem of facing the American liberal with
the fact that in relation to the Negro he has never been as liberal as
he likes to profess.[28]

In 1965, only a few months before the Watts riot, Clark would cement
his position as the preeminent public expert in this new chapter in American race relations with the publication of *Dark Ghetto,* a book that,
unlike the first edition of *Prejudice and Your Child,* found its public
almost immediately.[29] Frank Cardasco, writing in the *Saturday Review,*
paid Clark the highest possible compliment: "*Dark Ghetto* is a classic
which will be held as important for our day as Jacob Riis' *How the Other
Half Lives* and Jane Addams' *The Spirit of Youth and the City Streets*
were for another." And Robert Coles wrote, "As much as any American
of either race, Kenneth Clark has done his share to expose this nation's
terrible wounds."[30]

The "rediscovery" of poverty by Michael Harrington, the brutality of
the pictures transmitted from Birmingham to the nation and to the world,
and the willingness of President Johnson to explicitly cast civil rights
legislation as the most fitting living memorial to President Kennedy
placed the issue of racial justice above partisan politics and dramatically
enlarged the space devoted to racial redress and social reform within
American political culture. As Clark himself wrote to the readers of the
Saturday Review: "Civil rights has become so fashionable and books
about the Negro are now so plentiful that they repeat themselves, and
even the attempts at novelty seem banal."[31]

This rising tide of public interest not only lifted *Dark Ghetto* into prominence, but also over the course of the decade brought an audience to an expanded edition of *Prejudice and Your Child.*[32] Myrdal's contribution of a foreword to *Dark Ghetto* vouched for its status as a work of import; if there remained any doubt about Clark's renown as a social scientist speaking to the public on race, it was dispelled with the publication of *The Negro American,* a collection of essays on race relations coedited by Clark and sociologist Talcott Parsons. Clark and Parsons envisioned the work as "the most comprehensive survey of the problem and status of the American Negro in American society since *An American Dilemma.*"[33]

As the author of *Dark Ghetto,* as an intellectual with strong connections to the civil rights establishment, and as the architect of an ambitious model for community action, Clark was well positioned to alter Myrdal's formulation and to speak to current circumstances: "The new American Dilemma," Clark wrote, "is one of power. The dilemma is a confrontation between those forces which impel a society to change and those which seek to maintain the past."[34] The new "American Dilemma," Clark contended, was caused by the "benign intransigence" of the certifiably liberal establishment of the urban North. Recounting his experiences in trying to implement *Brown* in New York City, Clark asked:

> What do you do in a situation in which you have the laws on your side, where whites smile to you and say to you that they are your friends, but where your white "friends" move to the suburbs leaving you confronted with segregation and inferior education in the schools, ghetto housing, and quiet and tacit discrimination in jobs? What is the appropriate form of protest? One can "sit-in" in the Board of Education Building and not a single white child will come back from the suburbs ... One can link arms with the Mayor of Boston and march on the Commons and it will not affect the housing conditions of Negroes in Roxbury. One can be justifiably hailed as a Nobel Prize hero by the Mayor of New York City, but this will not in itself change a single aspect of the total pattern of pathology which dominates the lives of the prisoners of the ghettos of New York.[35]

There is no better proof of Clark's observation that civil rights had reached a zenith in public visibility and acceptance than the fact that

Clark and Parsons were able to launch their book with a symbol of legitimacy that had been beyond the reach of even Myrdal in 1944: a foreword by the president of the United States. Clark's last appearance in the official narrative on race relations came in 1968, when the President's Advisory Commission on Civil Disorders devoted most of its one-page conclusion to a quotation from Clark's testimony before the commission on the cycles of racial violence followed by short-lived periods of ritualized official introspection that had recurred throughout the twentieth century.

From Child Guidance to Community Action

Clark's point of entry into Great Society political culture came as the most noted "poverty warrior" in Harlem, an area periodically discovered by the media, this time as the most common representation of the Northern ghetto. "Harlem," as Daniel P. Moynihan wrote in his controversial report on the black family, "is the center and symbol of the urban life of the Negro American."[36] Clark's embrace of community action was a departure from the benevolent optimism he had offered in *Prejudice and Your Child*—as expressed by his conviction that white parents would "demand, in the name of their children, non-segregated public education" once the psychological consequences of segregation were made clear to them.[37] The exasperation he experienced in trying to ensure that the New York City Board of Education implemented measures to conform to the letter and the spirit of *Brown* was one reason for Clark's subsequent alienation.

Clark believed that the myriad plans that had been devised over the years by the board to selectively alter attendance areas in order to achieve a semblance of "physical integration" were "misleading the public" because the plans did not address the exodus of middle-class whites to private schools and the suburbs, which would render integration impossible. In Clark's judgment, the board had engaged in halfhearted efforts and dilatory strategies, all the while protesting that the achievement of integration was being made more impossible year by year. All of the board's proposals ignored what, to Clark, was the most compelling fact of all:

Over eighty percent of Negro children [in New York City] are being educated in predominantly, if not exclusively, Negro schools. Almost invariably these schools have and perpetuate woefully and intolerably low educational standards. These children cannot be abandoned. They cannot be ignored. They have only one lifetime in which they can be educated. It does not seem to be a responsible position to maintain that their predicament of educational inferiority must be endured until the society finds the will and the method of providing them with an integrated school experience.[38]

Clark advocated a crash program to transform the inner-city segregated schools into "citadels of excellence."[39] The challenge of desegregation, Clark told the Urban League, would require unprecedented efforts on the part of the African-American community to accomplish what the white majority could not and would not: "Something must be done to salvage the bulk of these young people and provide them with the strength of personality and stability of character needed to obtain and function effectively in a nonsegregated American society . . . It seems mandatory that [such a] program . . . must be initiated and directed and eventually financed by Negroes themselves."[40]

Clark envisioned a community-based approach that would "mobilize all of the relevant and available resources and skills within the Negro community . . . and the organization of machinery and the development of methods whereby various agencies, institutions, individuals and governmental agencies can work together toward agreed upon common goals."[41] Harlem Youth Unlimited was Clark's effort to achieve this goal. HARYOU had its genesis in Kenneth and Mamie Clark's earlier experience in community service, their Northside Child Development Center, which served Harlem residents. Founded on February 28, 1946, Northside was located in one room of the Dunbar Apartments at 226 West 150th Street, an address that had long been at the center of Harlem political and cultural life. It had originally been conceived by the Clarks as a supplement to services provided by such organizations as the Urban League. These organizations, however, had rejected the Clarks' proposals, believing that their existing programs adequately met community needs. Thus, the Clarks created their own institution.[42]

Funded in its first year by Mamie Phipps Clark's parents, Northside became a well-known institution in New York, attracting an eclectic group to its board of directors. Among the notables who served on the board were Mrs. Jackie Robinson; J. Raymond Jones, an influential Harlem political figure; Mrs. E. Frederick Murrow, the wife of President Eisenhower's advisor on Negro affairs; Robert L. Carter, who had recruited Clark to the NAACP Legal Defense and Education Fund; and Trude Lash, a close friend of Eleanor Roosevelt and the wife of Joseph P. Lash, Mrs. Roosevelt's biographer. Members of the first families of East Coast philanthropy were also prominently represented; among them were Miriam Ascoli, the daughter of Julius Rosenwald and the wife of Max Ascoli, the publisher of the respected liberal periodical, *The Reporter;* and Mrs. Alfred P. Stern, of the Stern Family Fund.[43] As the center's financial base stabilized, and its constituency grew within Harlem and beyond, Northside's mission grew beyond traditional psychological therapy and diagnostic testing to include a remedial reading program, a nutrition program, and workshops to improve both children's study skills and the parenting skills of their elders.[44]

Northside strove to have a multiracial staff and clientele in the belief that the resulting intercultural exchange would facilitate healthy personality development. Demographic trends, however, made this an increasingly difficult goal to achieve.[45] Kenneth Clark's growing sense of what integration would require from African-Americans led him to view Northside's emphasis on treating the wounds of social injustice by focusing upon the individual child or family unit as necessary, but too slow a process when weighed against the social and political forces arrayed against it. Rather than satisfying Clark, Northside's success in treating children provoked him to look beyond it and to formulate a more ambitious program. As Clark remarked, "our successes at Northside were more and more disturbing to me . . . Every time I saw a child who was helped to be more constructive in his role in the community because of the skillful staff at Northside . . . I grew more and more sad that children could be saved, and that there was no possibility of our having enough . . . clinical facilities to save them."[46]

Northside's clinical approach was also powerless to reverse the exodus of whites from Northside's service area, thus jeopardizing the intercultural emphasis of the clinic.[47] The press of these issues caused Northside to broaden its charge beyond its original emphasis on "behavior problems," such as those listed in an early report ("the disruption of classroom work, loss of interest in school, truancy, excessive lying, stealing, enuresis, aggressive behavior bordering on delinquency, withdrawn behavior bordering on psychosis") to a wider mission as "a vigorous advocate, ready with the commitment and skills to help ghetto families transform the context as well as the content of their lives."[48]

By the early 1960s, the focus of Northside (whose staff had contributed heavily to the HARYOU planning document) began to sound more and more like a community action program: a publicity pamphlet explains that the center was "evolving in the direction of a multi-service community center, its program determined not only by the needs of the individual but by the situation of the whole community."[49] The movement of Northside in this direction did not come solely from the Clarks. At a board meeting late in 1965, Mamie Phipps Clark observed that, "if the agency doesn't move with the times, the parents . . . will be far ahead of the agency." She noted that parents were becoming angry and impatient. "The parents want action," Phipps Clark reported, "and [they] question 'how far Northside' . . . is going to go with them."[50]

The creation of HARYOU in 1962 was an admission of the limitations that constricted the scope of a small social service agency dependent on philanthropic funding. In addition to problems of scale were the strings that were sometimes tied to gifts. In the most serious crisis of this kind, Northside lost the support of Miriam Ascoli, chair of its board of directors and its first significant donor, over the shift in Northside's mission away from psychiatric treatment and toward educational remediation and community advocacy.[51] "The families we were working with," Phipps Clark later told Nat Hentoff, "were not going to respond to umpteen years of lying on the couch . . . They needed help with housing, welfare, health, money, all of those things."[52]

The specific event that brought HARYOU into being, however, was the announcement in early 1961 that the Jewish Board of Guardians had been awarded a municipal grant to set up a social service program in Harlem. Angered that a group outside of Harlem had been given such funding while Northside was struggling, Clark attacked the grant as an example of "social work colonialism," a stance that caused great controversy among the Lady Bountifuls populating Northside's Board. "This was a revolt . . . the natives were clearly restless," Clark said of community reaction within Harlem: "And I was the most restless of the natives."[53]

The vehicle for pressing this revolt was HANA, the Harlem Neighborhood Association. HANA insisted that any psychiatric program in Harlem must result from close consultation with the community. By the fall of 1961, New York Mayor Robert F. Wagner had endorsed HANA's demand.[54] To fund his "experiment in community psychiatry," Clark approached the President's Committee on Juvenile Delinquency, which had just funded Mobilization for Youth, a pilot program developed as part of the Ford Foundation's "grey areas" project. Clark's bid for exploratory funds was successful, and he received a planning grant of $230,000, which was to run from June 1, 1962 to December 31, 1963.[55] HARYOU's stated goal was to develop "such programs which will seek to discourage delinquency through an increasing sense of pride, confidence and initiative in the youth themselves." "HARYOU therapy" was designed to teach young people "how to work for social change themselves" and was therefore aimed at treating the individual by employing "techniques for the treatment of the society." The assumption behind this method was that, "as the individual sees the possibility of being a part of meaningful social action, he not only develops a more positive self-image, supported by the reality of his social action, but he also contributes to the movement of the society toward greater stability and justice."[56]

The result of the HARYOU experiment was a voluminous blueprint, published under the imprint of HARYOU, entitled *Youth in the Ghetto*. Its contents were the most detailed survey yet of Harlem's social conditions, completed with the help of two hundred Harlem youths, who served as "HARYOU associates." These associates were at the heart of Clark's program. Their role was not merely to collect data for others to analyze or to create a documentary record of what it was like to be a youth in the ghetto, but to gain the community organizing experience and self-confidence that were prerequisites for successful community leadership. In addition to providing employment, HARYOU, like Mobilization for Youth, also sponsored social events—mixers, dances, and other opportunities for constructive recreation. Like MFY, HARYOU viewed itself as a an alternative to gangs, a role that it assumed down to offering an alternative uniform with the HARYOU insignia and publishing a comic book explaining the HARYOU program.

What HARYOU envisioned as its goal was not far outside the mainstream of American reform (except perhaps in its estimated cost of $110 million to be spent in Harlem alone): a job-training program, an arts and culture program reminiscent of the various Works Progress Administration (WPA) projects, and a network of tutoring and remedial education programs (expanding upon those begun at Northside) to raise the level of academic achievement. Another proposal was the establishment of "pre-school academies," to be team-taught primarily by the parents themselves.[57] These "academies" were an early example of the thinking that would create Headstart, a program that, second only to Medicare, would become the most revered legacy of the Great Society.

HARYOU's departure from the tradition of American reform can be found in the language that framed its planning document, *Youth in the Ghetto.* The text begins unremarkably enough—given the rhetorical conventions of the era—with the observation that "a century after Emancipation and a decade after the *Brown* Decision, Negro Americans still wait on the fulfillment of great hopes." The denial of these hopes was made all the more unacceptable by "the flags of newly sovereign peoples flying before the United Nations" and by the fact that "freedom and equality have come to twice as many peoples as were in the family of nations only two decades ago. The glacial slowness with which freedom and equality come to minorities within our own nation heightens the contrast, converts hopes into expectations, and expectations into demands. The American Revolution waits to be completed." Very quickly, however, the rhetoric changes: "Ghettoes in contemporary America may be defined primarily in terms of racial and color-determined restrictions on freedom of choice and freedom of movement. Ghettoes are the consequence of the *imposition of external power and the institutionalization of powerlessness. In this respect they are in fact social, political, educational, and—above all—economic colonies. Those confined within ghetto walls are subject peoples. They are victims of the greed, cruelty, insensitivity, guilt, and fear of their masters*" (emphasis added). It is difficult to imagine a document that, at least in its description of the racial crisis, was further from *Prejudice and Your Child.* Clark now finds that "concrete indications" of powerlessness are not merely those of an internalized "inferiority complex," but are the result of "deteriorated housing, overcrowdedness, infant mortality and high disease rates."[58]

Clark's blueprint, hailed as a breakthrough by no less than Sargent Shriver, the commander of President Johnson's War on Poverty, ran head-on into political reality. First, Clark's was not the only Harlem community plan competing for funds. The most important of these other applicants was Associated Community Teams (ACT), the brainchild of Representative Adam Clayton Powell, then at the height of his power as the chair of the House Committee on Education and Labor. The President's Committee on Juvenile Delinquency, under the guidance of David Hackett, a close associate of Robert Kennedy (its nominal chair), hoped to "work with the city and base our decisions on the merits of the programs," a noble goal complicated by ACT and by Powell's direct power over the commission's appropriations.[59] By the summer of 1962, a fragile resolution had been achieved. ACT's initial application was withdrawn "after consultation with staff since it overlapped with another project in Harlem [HARYOU]" and was "redrawn requesting a grant" to create a "domestic peace corps" in central Harlem. By July 1962, HARYOU and ACT had merged to "develop a comprehensive program to serve the youth of Central Harlem for submission to City, State, Federal and private funding sources."[60]

The merger existed, however, only on paper. During the intensive research and planning that resulted in *Youth in the Ghetto,* Clark and the HARYOU staff worked on the document alone. With the research and planning process at an end and application to the Office of Economic Opportunity complete, Powell, according to Clark, made clear that Clark was to serve as the professional figurehead, with Powell providing the political muscle—thus insuring a generous congressional appropriation, a substantial portion of which could be split between them. Clark refused, expecting his friendship with Hackett to strengthen his hand: "[Powell] made it very clear [that] if I made a public fight of this I'd be out on a limb without any support from the President, from Bobby Kennedy or from any of the people on the President's Committee on Juvenile Delinquency." Powell's blunt evaluation of the situation proved more accurate than Clark's. Clark later summarized his experience: "He really gave me a brilliant lesson in practical, corrupt politics."[61] Clark's presumed victory with Powell was also doomed because it came at a politically improvident time, coinciding as it did with Robert F. Kennedy's entry into the race for the U.S. Senate in New York, for which he would need Powell's support.[62]

Clark's showdown with Powell was but the first of hundreds of contentious battles between poverty warriors and local political establishments in cities around the nation; not surprisingly, the outcomes of these other confrontations proved to be much the same. By 1967, after two years of politically embarrassing and costly battles between poverty warriors and big-city mayors, community action programs, if they existed at all, did so as distinctly marginal bodies, operating far from the centers of municipal power.[63] "When conflict between the poor and vested interests has occurred," Clark testified before the Senate Subcommittee on Employment, Manpower and Poverty in 1967, "the resolution seems invariably to have been in the direction of the dilution of social action and . . . a substitution of social service benevolence for community action."[64]

Representing the Ghetto

Clark resigned from HARYOU-ACT on June 8, 1964. He turned immediately to the revision of *Youth in the Ghetto,* crafting it into a broader analysis of the plight of black Americans "imprisoned" in the "dark ghettos" of America's cities. As Clark embarked on *Dark Ghetto,* his second effort to write as a "psychologist for society," Bettelheim's review of *Prejudice and Your Child* was very much in mind. Bettelheim had fortified his critique of Clark's analysis by recalling his own experience in the desegregated schools of Austria and Germany, which, according to Bettelheim, had been incubators of racial hatred, rather than instillers of practical tolerance and pluralism.

Nine years after Bettelheim's review in *Commentary,* Clark established the legitimacy of his own representation of prejudice by embedding it, as Bettelheim had, in the authority of his own life experience. *Dark Ghetto* opened with a brief summary of the HARYOU experiment (minus a discussion of its demise), and then quickly shifted to a more personal history. Clark framed his personal experiences to evoke a parallel between the European Jew in the concentration camp and the African-American's isolation in the Northern urban ghetto:

> But I could never be fully detached as a scholar or participant. More than forty years of my life had been lived in Harlem. I started school in the Harlem public schools. I first learned about people, about love, about cruelty, about sacrifice, about cowardice, about courage, about bombast in Harlem. For many years before I returned as an "involved observer," Harlem had been my home. My family moved from house to house, and from neighborhood to neighborhood within the walls of the ghetto in a desperate attempt to escape its creeping blight. In a very real sense, therefore, *Dark Ghetto* is a summation of my personal and lifelong experiences and observations as a prisoner within the ghetto long before I was aware that I was really a prisoner.[65]

Clark analogized his return to Harlem as an "involved observer" to the experiences of Victor E. Frankl and Bettelheim, "who used their skill and training to provide us with some understanding of the nature of the horror and barbarity of the German concentration camps." "The circumstances of their initial observation were involuntary," Clark admitted, while his own return to Harlem "appears to be a matter of personal choice." Clark argued for the relative unimportance of this difference by recalling the "gnawing self-doubt," the "equivocation and broken agreements" of allies, and the "defensiveness" that accompanied his return, asking: "Who can say how free the choice really is . . . Can the prisoner ever fully escape the prison?"[66] *Newsweek,* in a profile of Clark written to coincide with the publication of *Dark Ghetto,* borrowed Clark's choice of metaphor to describe him as "the prison psychologist of the ghetto."[67]

Clark's "dark ghetto" was a direct institutional descendant of the original European ghetto created to isolate and confine Jews. The American variation merely extended "the restriction of persons to a special area and limit[ed] their freedom of choice on the basis of skin color." The European ghetto had been constructed to contain, if not to extinguish, the cultural and economic power of a people. At this point, on page eleven of his text, Clark replaced his analogy between African-Americans and European Jews with an analogy emphasizing the connection between the American racial ghetto and another European institution, the economic and political colony: "the dark ghetto's invisible walls have been erected by the white society, by those who have power, both to confine those who have *no* power [emphasis in original] and to perpetuate their powerlessness. The dark ghettos are social, political, educational, and—above all—economic colonies. Their inhabitants are subject peoples, victims of the greed, cruelty, insensitivity, guilt, and fear of their masters."[68]

The colonial metaphor did not displace the principal theme of Clark's professional writing, the inferiority complex. Feelings of inferiority were powerfully implanted and reinforced by the "paradox of the ghetto." Clark maintained that, while the white community could "blind itself to the conditions of the ghetto," its residents were "bombarded by the myths of the American middle class, often believing as literal truth their pictures of luxury and happiness, and yet at the same time confronted by a harsh world of reality . . . The discrepancy between the reality and the dream burns into their consciousness. The oppressed can never be sure whether their failures reflect personal inferiority or the fact of color. This persistent and agonizing conflict dominates their lives."[69]

Clark argued that this self-doubt disabled initiative and confidence. The inhabitants of the ghetto, Clark surmised, embarked upon life as "ghetto youth"—individuals caught in a precarious liminal state—who "have neither succumbed totally to the pathology nor have they been able to emerge from it." As adults, Clark contends, these individuals form a kind of "silent majority," trying, against great odds, to survive in a condition of ever more "unstable equilibrium":

> They are the ones who listen to Malcolm X but do not join; who vote Democratic if they bother to register but recognize at the same time that City Hall will do little for them. They are momentarily stimulated by the verbal militance of certain Negro newspaper editors and soapbox orators; they gain vicarious satisfaction through temporary identification with the flamboyance and anti-white verbal extremisms of charismatic Negro politicians. They send their children to bad public schools reluctantly because they do not have the money for private schools. They are the great potential who could engage in constructive social action or who could become the pawns of the demagogues. They have no inner-determined direction. Whoever develops any movement toward power in the ghetto finally does so

through winning the allegiance of this group—the largest in the ghetto—not of the semicriminal and certainly not of the elite and comfortable.[70]

This pervasive resignation to the social forces that created and maintained the ghetto was essential, Clark thought, to understanding the riots of 1964. Far from representing the "mobilization of effective power" or the actions of "the lower class of Harlem residents," Clark argued that these events were instead the spontaneous expression of a "weird social defiance" on the part of "marginal Negroes who were upwardly mobile" and "bent on irrational destruction."[71] Rather than a riot in pursuit of a specific political goal or a category of redress, the Harlem riot of 1964, as Clark read it, was an "eerie, surrealistic" piece of political theater, performed to transmit a message through the transparent wall:

> His was an oddly controlled rage that seemed to say, during those days of social despair, "We have had enough. The only weapon you have is bullets. The only thing you can do is to kill us." Paradoxically, his apparent lawlessness was a protest against lawlessness directed against *him*. His acts were a desperate assertion of his desire to be treated as a man. He was affirmative up to the point of inviting death; he insisted upon being visible and understood. If this was the only way to relate to society at large, he would die rather than be ignored [emphasis in original].[72]

Clark saw colonialism as the definitive fact of the dark ghetto. The ghetto's colonialist political structure was heavily personal, with the leaders it sent to the representative bodies of American government acting as conveyors of black votes to the Democratic Party in exchange for crumbs of patronage. As a colonial entity, the ghetto's economy was "geared toward the satisfaction of personal needs . . . it does not produce goods or contribute to the prosperity of the city as a whole."[73]

Clark stated that slavery and postbellum economic and social exclusion had similarly marginalized the Negro male. Denied a place in the productive economy, the black colonial "was compelled to base his self-esteem . . . on a kind of behavior that tended to support a stereotyped picture of the Negro male—sexual impulsiveness, irresponsibility, verbal bombast, posturing, and compensatory achievement in entertainment and athletics." "The pressure to find relief from his intolerable psychological position," Clark elaborated, "seems directly related to the continued high incidence of desertion and broken homes in Negro ghettos." To live in the ghetto was to live in a diseased environment: "The dark ghetto is institutionalized pathology; it is chronic, self-perpetuating pathology; and it is the futile attempt by those with power to confine that pathology so as to prevent the spread of its contagion to the 'larger community.' "[74]

The schools were also colonial outposts, serving as sites for administrators to reinforce the ghetto's disintegrative structure by offering "acceptable alibis for . . . educational default." If social science had done away with biological explanations, educators had replaced them with superficially compassionate and "enlightened" theories, which saw ghetto children as irremediably damaged by an equally immutable condition: that of "cultural deprivation." The facility with which social science could invent such explanations, Clark indicates, exposed little more than the class interest of supposedly neutral investigators: "Speculation appears to reflect primarily the status of those who speculate. Just as those who proposed the earlier racial inferiority theories were invariably members of the dominant racial groups . . . those who . . . propose the cultural deprivation theory are, in fact, members of the privileged group who inevitably associate their privileged status with their own innate intellect . . . Such association neither proves nor disproves the theory in itself, but the implicit caste and class factors in this controversy cannot and should not be ignored."[75]

The rhetoric and ambiance of *Dark Ghetto* make it easy to overstate its distance from Clark's *Prejudice and Your Child*. *Dark Ghetto* was striking in its range of metaphors; still, the idea of an "inferiority complex" is central to the scaffolding of *Dark Ghetto,* just as it had been essential to *Prejudice and Your Child*. In fact, Clark's new public stature allowed him to repackage the essential argument of *Prejudice and Your Child* for *Ebony* magazine in August 1965, in an essay entitled "What Motivates American Whites." In *Dark Ghetto,* Clark used Adler's concept of the inferiority complex from the 1920s and 1930s, but it shares textual space with franker, indeed harsher, metaphors of repression, many of which were invented by others to describe the morally incomprehensible excesses of World War II and the horrific scenarios generated in the nuclear age: the concentration camp; the specter of an ill-

contained social contamination that threatened to explode in the equivalent of a mushroom cloud; and the barely suppressed tension that existed
between the colony and the center of empire.

Dark Ghetto contained no detailed blueprints; like Harry Caul's *Night
Comes to the Cumberlands,* Harrington's *The Other America,* and Moynihan's *The Negro Family: The Case for National Action,* Clark's text
was intended as a spur to conscience and as a call to action to end an
injustice, not as an argument for a defined program. To some, this was
a discrediting flaw, rendering *Dark Ghetto* "vague and rhetorical"; such
characterizations, however, misunderstood Clark's purpose.[76] *Dark
Ghetto* was written to supply a representational base capable of making
the "anguish of the ghetto . . . is in some way shared not only by its
victims but by the committed empathy of those who now consider themselves privileged and immune to the ghetto's flagrant pathologies."[77] In
its motive, mode of presentation, and broad social influence, *Dark Ghetto*
was to the Great Society what *The Jungle* and *Shame of the Cities* had
been to the Progressive era, or *Grapes of Wrath* and *Let Us Now Praise
Famous Men* had been to the New Deal: *Dark Ghetto* was part of a
sequence of impassioned tracts that sought to utilize and direct the
idealism of the middle-class public toward specific ends. In the New
Frontier–Great Society era, books such as *Dark Ghetto, The Other
America,* and *Night Comes to the Cumberlands* also stood beside the
published indictments of other citizen-activists; well-received works by
such authors as Ralph Nader and Rachel Carson did as much as any
policy documents or presidential addresses to determine the content of
domestic policy in the Kennedy-Johnson years.

Attuned as he was—indeed, as self-consciously a representative as he
sought to be of the "Northern Negro . . . rejected, segregated, discriminated against . . . in spite of a plethora of laws that imply the contrary"—
Clark articulated with a succinct clarity the "common meaning" that by
1965 had become the jewel in the crown of the Second Reconstruction:[78]

> The great tragedy—but possibly the great salvation, too—of the
> Negro and white in America is that neither one can be free of the
> other. Each Negro is a little bit white and every white is a little bit
> Negro, in the sense that neither is totally alien from the other. Both
> are caught in a common human predicament. Each needs the other,

the white to be free of his guilt, the Negro to be free of his fear; guilt and fear are both self-destructive . . . The Negro alone cannot win this fight that transcends the "civil rights struggle." White and Negro must fight together for the rights of human beings to make mistakes and to aspire to human goals. Negroes will not break out of the barriers of the ghetto, unless whites transcend the barriers of their own minds, for the ghetto is to the Negro a reflection of the ghetto in which the white lives imprisoned. The poetic irony of American race relations is that the rejected Negro must somehow find the strength to free the privileged white.[79]

Dark Ghetto sought to convey the dimensions of the racial crisis that remained, even though laws guaranteeing equality of opportunity and legal treatment had been enacted. The earlier struggle for civil rights laws had succeeded in part because it had been represented in the mind of Northern whites by "neatly dressed Negroes carrying books," a picture that "fitted neatly into the middle-class white image more adequately than the vulgar whites who harassed them." For a relatively brief period between Little Rock and Watts, "the middle-class white . . . identified with the oppressed, not the oppressor." The "dark ghettos" symbolized by Harlem and Watts, however, required a more rigorous degree of commitment from whites in eradicating the social injustices they contained. The outrage expressed by whites over civil disorder left little doubt in Clark's mind that the sympathy engendered among Northern whites by Little Rock had been a mere commodity, "a reward for respectable behavior." "Understanding," Clark cautioned, "can only be tested when one's own interests are threatened." The interests of northern whites were now directly at issue, and a "deeply repressed prejudice" was now being expressed, belying the "warmth of public support for civil rights." "These feelings must be exposed," according to Clark, "as the prelude to realistic programs for change."[80]

In response to white outrage, Clark repeated a theme that he had developed in describing the personality of a participant in the Harlem riot of 1943—that reproaches against violence constitute "racist condescension." Clark once again assumed the role of defender and interpreter of the rioter as a legitimate political actor who had been pushed to violence by white racism:

One cannot expect individuals who have been systematically excluded from the privileges of a middle-class life to view themselves
in middle-class terms or to behave in terms of middle-class values . . .
Negroes see only the continuing decay of their homes, many of them
owned by liberal whites. He sees he does not own any of the means
of production, distribution and sale of goods he must purchase to live.
He sees his children subjected to criminally inefficient . . . public
schools . . . often administered and staffed by liberal whites. He sees
liberal labor unions which either exclude him, accept him in token
numbers, or even when they accept him en masse, exclude him from
leadership or policy-making roles.[81]

The next phase in the struggle for racial equality required more than
expressions of support from northern whites, a group now frightened by
their proximity to social unrest:

Fortunately, love is not a prerequisite for the social reorganization
now demanded. Love has not been necessary to create livable working
arrangements among other ethnic groups in our society. It is no more
relevant to ask Negroes and whites to love each other than to ask
Italians and Irish to do the same as a prerequisite for social peace and
justice . . . The Negro must be included within the economy at all
levels . . . thereby providing the basis for a sound family life and an
opportunity to have an actual stake in American business and property
. . . The social organization of our educational system must be transformed so Negroes can be taught in schools which do not reinforce
their feeling of inferiority. The reorganization, improvement and integration of our schools is also necessary in order to re-educate white
children and prepare them to live in the present and future world of
racial diversity . . . The conditions in which Negroes live—bad
housing, infant mortality and disease, delinquency, drug addiction—
must be drastically reduced . . . Until these minimum goals are
achieved, Americans must accept the fact that we cannot expect to
maintain racial ghettos without paying a high price. If it is possible
for Americans to carry out realistic programs to change the lives of
human beings now confined within their ghettos, the ghetto will be
destroyed by rational acts. Only then will American society not re-

main at the mercy of primitive, frightening, irrational attempts by prisoners in the ghetto to destroy their own prison.[82]

The Shifting Politics of the Moynihan Report

Nat Hentoff's criticism of *Dark Ghetto* as "vague and rhetorical" in its prescription for change was also applied to another effort to represent the plight of the black ghetto—a report issued by the Department of Labor under the title *The Negro Family: The Case for National Action.* Issued in March 1965 as a confidential document for use within the Johnson administration, the report had been leaked to the press the following summer (a leak initiated, it was widely assumed, by its principal author, Daniel Patrick Moynihan).[83] By the fall, the document, now widely known as the Moynihan report, had provoked a bitter public debate over how best to think about the plight of African-Americans in the "post–civil rights era," a debate made all the more urgent and vigorous by the Watts riots in August 1965. How should Americans understand the worsening socioeconomic gap between the "two Americas" once the most visible legal barriers to political and economic participation had been removed? Did white Americans have a responsibility beyond extending the prospect of opportunity—to creating, for example, mechanisms to encourage greater equality in socioeconomic outcomes?

Moynihan's report, like Clark's *Dark Ghetto,* was deliberately stark and frankly polemical. Moynihan's primary objective, again like Clark, was to reach the white liberal conscience and to combat a complacency that might come to the white majority with the early legislative successes of the Great Society. As Moynihan told *Newsweek,* his goal was to "grab the attention of the men of power": "There was a lot of euphoria . . . when I started this thing in January and I was trying to say, 'Wait, it's not over, don't start celebrating yet.' I was trying to tell them the problem in a different terminology, in a way where they would say, 'Wow, we can't let that happen to *people!*' " (emphasis in original).[84] According to Moynihan, the struggle to achieve racial equality had entered a new period of rising expectations. As Moynihan put the matter: "The expectations of Negro Americans will go beyond civil rights . . . They will now expect that in the near future equal opportunities for them as a group will produce roughly equal results, as compared with other groups. This is not going to happen. Nor will it happen for generations to come unless a new and special effort is made."[85]

A discussion of what such a "new and special effort" might entail was absent from Moynihan's text. What it contained instead was a succession of statistics and graphs supposedly supporting his thesis that "the Negro family in the urban ghettos is crumbling." Moynihan contended that a small and fragile African-American middle class was being over-whelmed by a "vast number of unskilled, poorly educated city working class," for whom "the fabric of conventional social relationships has all but disintegrated." To legitimate this unrelenting picture of "massive deterioration," Moynihan drew upon *Youth in the Ghetto,* the report of his colleague and friend since the late 1950s, Kenneth Clark.[86]

Moynihan succeeded admirably in capturing the attention of the na-tion. His findings were the basis of a major address by President Johnson at Howard University in June 1965. Announcing that the nation had reached "the end of the beginning" in the struggle toward racial equality, Johnson told his audience that the time had come to focus on the deep social scars left by two centuries of slavery and legally enforced segre-gation. Foremost among these wounds, the president declared, was the "breakdown of the Negro family structure," a condition for which "white America must accept responsibility."[87]

The Howard speech stands second only to Johnson's "We Shall Over-come" address of March 1965 as perhaps the most warmly received of his presidency. Ralph Ellison, a vocal critic of the Moynihan Report, regarded Johnson's speech, which Moynihan himself had helped to draft, as marking a truly majestic moment: "President Johnson spelled out the meaning of full integration for Negroes in a way that . . . no president, not Lincoln nor Roosevelt, no matter how much we love and respect them, has done before. There was no hedging . . . no escape clauses."[88] Whitney Young also lauded the President's candor and courage: "He has acknowledged the prime responsibility for the problem. He has put it at the white man's door, and he's right."[89]

When the document upon which the speech had been based was re-leased, the outcome was very different. Especially in the months after Watts, Moynihan's insistent focus on what he saw as the internal weak-nesses of the black family seemed to many within the civil rights com-munity to be a cynical, subtle effort to shift the focus of blame from white society to its black victims. Moynihan's omission of positive reform strategies, as well as his resignation from the administration to seek elective office, were taken as powerful confirmation of Moynihan's opportunism and mixed motives. Moynihan's broadbrush rhetoric, Young complained, "stigmatized an entire group of people when the majority of that group of people do not fall into the category of the Negro family that Moynihan describes." Martin Luther King, Jr., responded to Moynihan's report by warning that "the danger [of focusing on the shortcomings of the Negro family] will be that problems will be attributed to innate Negro weaknesses and used to justify neglect and rationalize oppression."[90]

Ellison, in the same interview in which he had endorsed Johnson's words, took strong exception not only to the Moynihan report, but to the whole intellectual structure that had supported social science thinking on race, beginning with Myrdal's *An American Dilemma.* Ellison's alienation from this tradition extended back to the publication of *Dilemma* in 1944. In an unpublished essay intended for the *Antioch Review,* Ellison scored Myrdal for treating African-Americans as a people shaped only by "reactions . . . to . . . more primary pressures from the side of the dominant white majority." Ellison countered by asking: "Are American Negroes simply the creation of white men, or have they at least helped to create themselves out of what they found around them? Men have made a way of life in caves and upon cliffs, why cannot Negroes have made a life upon the horns of the white man's dilemma?"[91]

In their eagerness to amass and present the evidence of what white society had done to Negroes—undermining their economic strength, distorting their family lives, inflicting feelings of great inferiority upon them—American social scientists from Frazier and Myrdal to Stanley Elkins and Kenneth Clark, Ellison asserted, had contributed to a representation of African-Americans as powerless and pathological:

> I don't deny that these sociological formulas are drawn from life, but I do deny that they define the complexity of Harlem. They only abstract it and reduce it to proportions which the sociologists can manage. I simply don't recognize Harlem in them . . . Which is by no means to deny the ruggedness of life there, nor the hardship, the poverty, the sordidness, the filth. But there is something else in

Harlem, something subjective, willful, and complexly and compellingly human. It is that "something else" that challenges the sociologists who ignore it, and the society which would deny its existence. It is that "something else" which makes for our strength, which makes for our endurance and our promise.[92]

Ellison concludes that in their determination to prove the massive cruelty of slavery, these scholars argued, perhaps inadvertently, for the inhumanity of its victims. These analysts had, in Ellison's words, simply assumed that "slaves had very little humanity because slavery destroyed it." But despite the historical past upon which Moynihan had built a representation of African-American "pathology," "there is," Ellison claimed, "something further to say. I have to *affirm* my forefathers and I *must* affirm my parents or be reduced in my own mind to a white man's inadequate—even if unprejudiced—conception of human complexity" (emphasis in original).[93]

In Ellison's view, the emergence of social science as the primary mediator and legitimator of the African-American experience to the nation meant that one set of negative stereotypes had been replaced with another. Out of sight was another side of the African-American experience that neither the social scientist nor the caricaturist of traditionally popular stereotypes knew or understood:

Over and over again when we find bunches of Negroes enjoying themselves . . . and in a mood of communion, they sit around and marvel at what a damnably marvelous human being, what a confounding human type the Negro American really is . . . We exchange accounts of what happened to someone [we] once knew . . . His crimes, his loves, his outrages, his adventures, his transformations, his moments of courage, his heroism, buffooneries, defeats, and triumphs are recited, with each participant joining in. And this catalogue soon becomes a brag, a very exciting chant celebrating the metamorphosis which this individual . . . underwent within the limited circumstances available to us . . . In the process the individual is enlarged. It's as though a transparent overlay of archetypal myth is being placed over the life of an individual, and through him we see ourselves. This, of course, is what literature does with life; these verbal jam sessions are indeed a form of folk literature and they help us to define our own experience.[94]

When African-American writers take up their pens to write about the "black experience" for the public, however, "this wonderful capacity for abstracting and enlarging life" is lost; Ellison finds these black writers asking instead, " 'How do we fit into the sociological terminology?' Gunnar Myrdal said this experience means thus and so. And Dr. Kenneth Clark, or Dr. E. Franklin Frazier, says the same thing . . . And we try to fit our experience into their concepts." Ellison charged such expert-interpreters with elitism, stating that "whenever I hear a Negro intellectual describing Negro life and personality with a catalogue of negative definitions, my first question is: How did you escape, is it that you were born exceptional and superior? If I cannot look at the most brutalized Negro on the street, even when he irritates me and makes me want to bash his head in because he's goofing off, I must still say within myself, 'Well, that's you too, Ellison.' And I'm not talking about guilt, but of an identification which goes beyond race."[95]

Ellison's criticism of the primacy of social science in the representation of the African-American experience spoke especially to Moynihan's broadbrush generalities and one-dimensional presentation of the life of complex human communities. Ellison's mention of Clark in this connection is a more complicated matter, especially because much of Clark's work; certainly the most innovative SPSSI research on prejudice from the 1930s on was engaged in finding ways to strengthen the individual personality against the effort, often sanctioned by whole societies, to erase or distort the self through stereotyping and prejudice.

Implicit in Ellison's criticism is a vital larger question: how should the "other" be represented by those seeking to bring their existence, and the processes that so define them, to the center of the collective conscience? In writing *Dark Ghetto,* Clark had to reach some accommodation with what T. V. Reed identifies as the principal dilemma posed by attempts at representing those excluded individuals whose existence is, by and large, unimagined by the larger community. How, especially if the intended venue is the wide screen of popular culture, can this be done without erasing individuals, leaving them as nothing more than symbols of their tragic circumstances? How does one avoid "appropriation and reduction through representation," especially when the prevailing cultural politics may sanction, or even depend upon, "leaving these 'others' unrepresented or represented less scrupulously and less justly"?[96] Clark's response to this difficulty can be seen in the brief biographical discussion with which he opens *Dark Ghetto;* the words of his personal testimony are meant to make the point that compassion, love, and heroism coexist with pathology in the ghetto, and that survival there requires rare personal strength.

The tenor of the remainder of the text bears witness to a rhetorical style befitting a political culture, which, as William Leuchtenburg observes, had used the "analogue of war" to mobilize against the Great Depression.[97] *Dark Ghetto* reached back for a rhetoric that dominated the public world of Clark's youth, and it was shaped to fit the next great mobilization for reform. Indeed, this new mobilization was one whose animating symbols, such as Lyndon Johnson's War on Poverty, and Whitney Young's still-popular formulation of a domestic Marshall Plan, were conceived by figures whose political education and sensibilities were formed, as Leuchtenburg phrases it, "in the shadow of FDR."[98] In the end, Ellison's rhetorical inclusion of Clark in the same category as Frazier and Myrdal may be less an implicit criticism of *Dark Ghetto* than evidence of the hazards that accompanied Clark's emergence as the Myrdal of the Great Society.

The debate over the Moynihan report was not over whether a crisis existed in the "dark ghetto" or of the consequences that the harshness of slavery had visited upon African-Americans. As historian Herbert Gutman, one of the most outspoken critics of Moynihan, Frazier, and Elkins, pointed out: "Moynihan, it should be emphasized, had not created a fictive history: he had reported what was then conventional academic wisdom. His most severe critics shared that historical perspective with him."[99] The Moynihan report became the focal point for a debate that was already under way. It played this role, in large measure, because it had been designed to do so by an individual well placed, as an action-intellectual whose ideas were respected within the Johnson administration, to enter that discourse at its center.

In the narrowest and most personal of terms, as Lemann argues, Moynihan had hoped that the report's bold and polemical rhetoric would create a sensation and "establish his place in the first rank of American intellectuals," thus winning him recognition in the media as a "famous racial seer." The idea, propagated in the press, that the confidential report had been suppressed by the administration because of its impolitic content added a conspiratorial edge to the drama.[100] The argument provoked in these circumstances really concerned how racism would be explained and characterized, now that a villainous southern political leadership had been fatally undermined by passage of the Voting Rights Act. "With these events behind us," Moynihan wrote in the first chapter of his report, "the nation now faces a different set of challenges, which may prove more difficult to meet, if only because they cannot be cast as concrete propositions of right and wrong . . . The fundamental problem . . . is that the Negro revolution, like the industrial upheaval of the 1930s, is a movement for equality as well as for liberty."[101]

Moynihan's most vigorous opponents believed that his hyperbolic language, coupled with a seeming fixation on rates of illegitimacy among young African-Americans, was an effort to reverse the villains as the civil rights movement moved closer to home—the home, that is, of northern liberal academics like Moynihan. In the aftermath of Watts, clinical psychologist William Ryan was the most eloquent articulator of the fear that the Moynihan report inspired among many in the civil rights community: "Evidence of improvements in American race relations is to be found all the way from Birmingham lunch counters to national television commercials. As yet, however, the change has had little impact on the life of the average American Negro. He remains badly housed, badly educated, underemployed and underpaid. The terms of the discourse change, but the inequality persists; and we spend more time in explaining this inequality than in doing something about it." The Moynihan report expressed a "new ideology" tailored to sustaining these subhuman conditions in the urban North, because it located the cause of "unemployment, poor education and slum conditions" in the "cultural deprivation" of its victims, Ryan charged, rather than in the "racist structure of American society." In its design, the Moynihan report served as an essential mechanism in maintaining this ideology of avoidance and denial. In Ryan's words, the report exploited a willingness to "engage in the popular new sport of Savage Discovery and, to fit the theory, savages are being discovered in great profusion in the Northern urban ghetto. The all-time favorite 'savage' is the promiscuous mother who produces a litter of illegitimate children in order to profit from AFDC [Aid to Families with Dependent Children]."[102]

In the late nineteenth century, northern political leaders and philanthropists could fairly easily abandon the African-American by refusing to look south. The Great Migration of the twentieth century had closed this geographic distance. Now, as a white backlash continued to gather force, Ryan and others feared that the Moynihan report was the Johnson administration's strategy for abandoning the African-American after an incomplete "Second Reconstruction."[103]

Moynihan found it ironic that intellectuals and civil rights leaders embraced President Johnson's speech on the crisis of the black family in June 1965 even as they assaulted Moynihan for presenting the same argument only a few months later. Moynihan interpreted this as an indication that the permissible subjects and boundaries of cultural politics had radically changed; writing in 1967, he stated that "it is essential to keep in mind how much attitudes have changed since the Spring of 1965 . . . what a person might have said two or three years ago he possibly could not say today."[104] In fact, these opposing reactions to two very similar representations of the African-American family reflected the fact that Johnson had done two things that Moynihan had not: he had laid the responsibility for the condition of the poor black family on the racist structure of American society, and he had underscored this reality by promising measures to aid those who were being harmed by these structural injustices.

Clark himself defended Moynihan, with whom he had been friends since the late fifties, both publicly and privately. In February 1966, Clark wrote to Moynihan, "I don't believe that this report needs any defense either from you or from me." At the time Clark was at work on an essay intended for *Commentary* (but one that he never completed) on the "implications of the controversy surrounding this report . . . What does the controversy tell us about some aspects of the civil rights movement? What does it reveal about levels of anxiety, conflicts, ambivalence, and a type of quiet hysteria . . . among many of us who have been identified with a social science approach to the attainment of social justice in America? To what extent have some of us become contaminated with the very irrationalities and tendency toward seeking scapegoats which consciously we are fighting?"[105] The previous December, as the controversy spilled over from the journals of liberal opinion into the general press, Clark had strongly defended his colleague in *Newsweek*. "The attacks on Moynihan as a racist are merely foolish," *Newsweek* told its readers; in support of this conclusion, the magazine quoted "tough-minded Negro psychologist Kenneth Clark." Clark characterized Moynihan's critics as a "wolf-pack operating in a very undignified way" and endorsed Moynihan unequivocally: "If Pat is a racist, I am. He highlights the total pattern of segregation and discrimination. Is a doctor responsible for the disease simply because he diagnoses it?"[106]

Within a few years, however, Clark reversed his view of Moynihan. The decisive event was Moynihan's later service as a domestic policy advisor in the first Nixon administration, in particular his recommendation, again stated in the most provocative possible language—and again leaked to the public in a period of great political polarization—that it was time to practice a strategy of "benign neglect" in racial matters. This counsel of benign neglect, as Lemann translates the phrase, served as shorthand for the belief that "racial progress was to continue, but very quietly" and that it was to be discreetly focused on school desegregation in the South, while desegregation in the North was to be vocally opposed by the Nixon administration.[107] Responding to Moynihan's memo, again in *Newsweek,* Clark this time was condemnatory: "He has left out the cruelty and barbarity of the ghetto . . . He left out the truth of American racism, of which he now unfortunately is a symptom."[108]

Moynihan's catchphrase became public in the spring of 1970, at a time of mutual suspicion between the Nixon administration and the civil rights community. The year of "benign neglect" was also the year in which Patrick Buchanan, then a Nixon speechwriter, announced, "The Second Era of reconstruction is over; the ship of integration is going down; it is not our ship . . . and we cannot salvage it; and we ought not be aboard."[109] The anger aroused in Clark and others by the phrase "benign neglect" was not due to a misunderstanding on their part of what Moynihan had meant; rather it was an expression of frustration at the political cynicism exhibited by the administration, a cynicism exemplified by Moynihan's own choice of words. On the one hand, Nixon, unlike Eisenhower, praised *Brown* from the White House—albeit sixteen years after the fact—as "right in both constitutional and legal terms."[110] On the other hand, as Tom Wicker recounts, in 1968 candidate Nixon opposed federal action to desegregate southern schools as "going too far." Furthermore, very soon upon entering office, President Nixon "became the first president to send federal attorneys into court to argue for *postponement* of school desegregation already ordered" (emphasis in original).[111]

To Clark, Moynihan came to represent a crude caricature of the public social scientist. Moynihan, Clark would come to imply, had successfully sought to parlay the trappings of academic distinction into high political office. The public social scientist, as Clark understood the role, must represent those noble truths and ideals whose exacting nature insures that they will never be fashionable. In the mid-1970s, as Moynihan served as the U.S. ambassador to the United Nations, Clark pointedly suggested that those social scientists striving to be public social scientists by "being obsequious and begging acceptance by the people in power" were unworthy of the title. In a choice of words constructed to remind his audience of Moynihan's ambassadorial tours under Nixon and Ford, as well as Moynihan's achievement of intellectual celebrity as a result of leaks to the national press, Clark was particularly adamant that such figures "can't go around begging the press and the media to say what they are [doing] and [that they] deserve to be given ambassadorships or special assistantships to this or that politician."[112]

Ten years after Clark had publicly supported Moynihan in the imbroglio over Moynihan's representation of the African-American family, and six years after attacking Moynihan's memo advocating benign neglect, Clark again felt compelled to weigh in on Moynihan's activities, this time in the midst of Moynihan's first campaign for the United States Senate: Clark actively opposed Moynihan as "a successful opportunist" who "is a danger to my people and would not serve the basic human and democratic needs of the people of New York state." Clark felt so strongly on this point that he endorsed the Republican incumbent, James Buckley, the brother of William F. Buckley, the conservative columnist and television personality.[113]

Dark Ghetto was not tainted in the controversy over the Moynihan report, in part because, like Johnson's speech, it was unambiguous on the question of the central role of white culture in creating and sustaining the ghetto. Charles A. Valentine, a leading critic of Moynihan and of the body of work upon which he had unreflectively relied, welcomed *Dark Ghetto* for this reason. Although Valentine criticized Clark for drawing some of the same kind of overly broad conclusions from census data that had weakened *The Black Family*—and for solely defining Harlem by its "pathologies" rather than "in terms of its *own* social order, cultural idiom or life style"—he also found that *Dark Ghetto* was clearly distinguishable from the Moynihan report in its frank admission that the ghetto was created from the injustices and "pathologies" of the larger white society. "[T]his man," Valentine concluded of Clark, "is one of the few students of lower class Negro life who has begun to break the spell of the Frazier tradition."[114]

What was Clark's relationship to Frazier, the man who, until *Dark Ghetto,* had been the social scientist most cited—if not the most carefully read—by white intellectuals? On the purely personal level, Frazier had been part of that powerful nucleus of intellectuals at Howard during the 1930s who had introduced Clark to the world of ideas and to the relationship between ideas and social activism. This academic association did not, however, include the close personal friendship of the kind that Clark enjoyed with Ralph Bunche.

As social theory, the writings of Frazier and Clark were separated chiefly by a contrast in tone and rhetoric that perhaps bespoke a deeper difference in their backgrounds and temperaments. Although it is correct that Frazier's work was seriously misrepresented by both Moynihan and his critics, it is nonetheless true that the often acid and condescending language that Frazier invoked—whether describing the "pathologies" of the black "lower class" or the pretensions of the "black bourgeoisie"— unwittingly abetted this intellectual misuse. Clark, by contrast, strove to convey an empathy and a respect for exactly those people at the bottom of society for whom many social scientists of the preceding generation— Frazier included—reserved their most unreflective, judgmental, and condescending language. Virtually every piece of public writing by Clark was composed in direct relationship to where he had come from and who he believed himself to be as a consequence: a son of the northern ghetto, and, in adulthood, its representative to the academy and to the nation. These qualities in Clark's text were what separated *Dark Ghetto* from the Frazier tradition.

Dark Ghetto also won another audience because its central metaphor had been that of "internal colonialism" rather than that of the "tangle of pathology" (although this latter was also a Clark phrase). Stokely Carmichael and Charles V. Hamilton found eloquent support in *Dark Ghetto* for their belief that African-Americans must begin to understand how an internal colonialism every bit as insidious and profitable as its international counterpart had shaped their lives, and therefore must shape their strategy of liberation.[115]

In Clark, the Black Power movement had, if not an advocate, then at least a sympathetic interpreter. According to Clark, Black Power was a natural response to the "racial cynicism" of the post-*Brown* era. Especially cynical, according to Clark, was the sentiment, widely expressed in the media, that Carmichael was bringing the prospect of violence to the "nonviolent" civil rights struggle. "Stokely Carmichael and his followers," Clark reminded an audience of newspaper publishers in 1966, "cannot with justice be accused of introducing violence into the civil rights controversy." Clark pointed out that

> they are not responsible for the unpunished bombings of scores of Negro churches in communities throughout the South. They are not responsible for the fact that the masses of Negro children are still condemned to attend segregated and intolerably inferior schools in the North and in the South . . . They are not responsible for the persistent unemployment and underemployment of Negroes—particularly Negro males and Negro youth . . . What is now called the white backlash is merely the continuation of the persistent and long-standing resistance of the majority of American whites to any positive change in the social, economic and political status of the American Negro . . . The racism of . . . black power is the offspring of the pervasive racial cynicism and the present moral emptiness of our nation . . . Negroes are now being asked to behave themselves and to control their verbal excesses or else their rights as Americans will be denied or taken away from them.[116]

Upholding the Spirit of *Brown*

By the mid-1960s Clark felt compelled by white flight from urban centers and the political realities of white backlash at the ballot box to concede that "it is now time for us to reexamine the strategy and tactics required to bring about effective desegregation of the public schools."[117] Given the resistance that was developing to busing students across town in order to achieve racial balance, some argued for a new emphasis on making racially separate schools equal in their educational resources.

Despite the expression of such sentiments, Clark found that "school boards and public officials [in the North] seem as resistant to developing and implementing programs . . . for Negro children in segregated schools as they are deaf to all requests for effective desegregation plans and programs."[118] In comments prepared for the White House conference called by President Johnson in his Howard University commencement address of June 1965 (remembered in the press primarily for the snubbing of Moynihan by the invited participants), Clark endorsed the reorganization of urban schools into "educational parks" to be funded by federal grants and centrally located in "neutral" areas between the predominantly black neighborhoods of the inner city and the white suburbs. "The neighborhood school," Clark suggested, "may have no more advantage in contemporary education in the metropolis than did the one-room school in the country."[119]

Such ideas seemed doomed in the aftermath of the presidential election of 1968. George Wallace, then an avowed segregationist, and Richard Nixon, who pursued a blander and more subtle strategy of reassuring a "silent majority" that he would look kindly upon dismantling the Great Society while also downgrading as a priority the rigorous enforcement of judicial decisions and legislation in the areas of civil rights and desegregation, had together won nearly 60 percent of the vote. Three weeks later, Clark offered the "considered judgment that the attempt on the part of Negroes in the North and in the South to free their children from the burdens of dehumanizing inferior public education through desegregation of the schools has been thoroughly defeated."[120]

By 1968, the discourse on desegregation and integration that had been moved to the forefront of American public life by *Brown* seemed to be nearing an impasse, the hopes for desegregation resting primarily in the hands of sympathetic federal judges. Whites, Clark charged, had used their power over local schools to "reduce any attempt at desegregation of their schools to tokenism, sham [and] evasiveness." In a reference to the famous footnote in *Brown*, Clark continued: "The masses of whites, North and South . . . in spite of the Supreme Court's declaration of the damage . . . inherent in racially segregated schools . . . had absolutely no intention of remedying this damage by a serious desegregation of the schools."[121]

Clark's career would continue into the 1970s and 1980s. Indeed, during this later period, Clark would receive the highest honor that his discipline could bestow: the presidency of the American Psychological Association. The APA also honored Clark with the Award for Distinguished Contributions to Psychology, as well as a Gold Medal Award for contributions "by a Psychologist in the Public Interest." In the arena of direct social action, Clark was appointed to the New York Board of Regents, the body responsible for setting that state's policy for primary and secondary education.

Nonetheless, any prospect that the ideas articulated by Clark as a "psychologist for society" might actually become realized as social policies that would improve the classrooms and empower the communities of the "dark ghetto" left the national scene with Lyndon Johnson. In spite of the honors and the advisory positions that would come his way, Clark's career as a public social scientist with influence at the federal level came to an end, "because," as Clark himself said in 1975, "the kinds of policies that I would formulate are not the kinds of policies that people who have the right to make policies want me to formulate."[122]

Kenneth Clark, unlike Ralph Bunche and Lorraine Hansberry, has been largely spared explicit diminution of his historical contribution to the legitimation of racial equality. Clark's early advocacy of community action and his telling use of the colonial metaphor to illuminate the "dark ghetto" drew the respect of potential adversaries such as Stokely Carmichael, Charles A. Valentine, and other critics of the civil rights establishment of which Clark was a member. By 1968, in fact, Clark had become his own revisionist critic. In an interview conducted after the assassination of Martin Luther King, Jr., published in *Psychology Today,* Clark expressed the fear that American society might be inherently incapable of transcending its racism:

> Our disease could be terminal. Race conflict in America is the most flagrant, visible form of dry rot in our country . . . Look at our educational systems. They are organized and operated on the irrelevant factor of race . . . the superstition and mystique of race are the cardinal factors around which all our educational systems still function . . .

Our churches make words; they pass resolutions. But there has been no evidence that the churches have found the strength, the courage or the practical know-how to use religious institutions as instruments for bringing about the kind of maturity that our schools have not provided ... Our labor unions, with a history of fighting for justice for the working man, are now among the most conservative if not reactionary elements in our society ... And our political figures merely reflect the permeating moral schizophrenia of the larger society. They are practical, pragmatic exploiters of it.[123]

In *Prejudice and Your Child,* Clark had expressed the belief that if white Americans could be made to understand the depth of the damage inflicted by their prejudice, they could be moved to change. The events of the subsequent decade appeared to Clark to refute this thesis.

In the 1940s, 1950s, and 1960s Clark had been a frequent guest speaker and consultant to church groups and labor unions in an effort to build a constituency to support the comprehensive change that ending the American dilemma required. The enlarging dimensions of the American racial crisis in the late sixties, however, raised the fundamental question of whether it was indeed possible to be an effective psychologist for society; and Clark wondered if perhaps he had played an unwitting part in official America's elaborate dance of alarm and avoidance on race. As he said in 1968: "To be quite candid about ... my attempts at being a psychologist for society, I have to state that I have failed. I've produced documents ... The involvements in social action and social change that have dominated my life add up to one big failure. I fear the disease has metastasized."[124] Refusing to leave the field of battle, Clark fought on with a clearer understanding of the full range of the defensive resources available to the "enlightened" establishment—including, on occasion, the tactic of ceding time and recognition to its most eloquent critics.

With Thurgood Marshall, Kenneth Clark remains one of the best-known participant-symbols of the *Brown* decision and of the civil rights movement. His recollections of those days have become part of public retrospectives on the Second Reconstruction, such as the PBS television series *Eyes on the Prize*. In 1991, Clark's doll studies were reenacted in *Separate but Equal,* an Emmy-winning television film dramatizing Marshall's legal crusade against school segregation. Such attention demonstrates that Clark is, to this day, an elder statesman, and an icon of integration.

Such recognition bestows opportunity and imposes limitations. Elder statesmanship confers a broad respect within the intellectual community and offers a dignified public platform for personal reflection when past milestones are remembered and new ones passed. The "icon emeritus" of an era that is fondly remembered, but gone nonetheless, may find that the public demand for his voice extends more to an ability to evoke, if only by his presence, the past in the present, and less to receiving any wisdom that he might currently possess about contemporary problems.

Sometimes the icon can simultaneously evoke a mood and teach some lessons. Such was the case in early May 1992, in the aftermath of the upheaval in Los Angeles surrounding the Rodney King verdict, when television journalist Ted Koppel recalled the last occasion of national introspection on racial injustice by reading from the Kerner report. With a sketch of the "distinguished black scholar Kenneth B. Clark" providing a visual backdrop, Koppel quoted from Clark's testimony: "I read that report of the 1919 riot in Chicago, and it is as if I were reading the report of the investigating committee on the Harlem riot of '35, the report of the investigating committee on the Detroit riot of '43, the report of the McCone Commission on the Watts riot. I must again, in candor, say to you members of this commission it is a kind of Alice in Wonderland, with the same moving picture reshown, over and over again, the same analysis, the same recommendations, and the same inaction."[125]

On this and other occasions, Clark was continuing in the tradition of public education and agitation that he had first observed in the lives and teachings of his Howard University mentors. A generation after Ralph Bunche became the most widely broadcast symbol of American progress toward racial equality, Kenneth Clark found himself before a microphone at the Voice of America, teaching a new generation. In 1950, Bunche could urge Americans forward with a double sense of confidence: first, that the cause he symbolized was profoundly just, and second, that the momentum of history ran in its favor. Thirty years later, the cause remained just and its fulfillment urgent; the prospect of its achievement, however, seemingly remained out of reach. In 1980, nearly thirty years after *Brown,* as the consensus that had supported modest progress was nearing dissolution, Clark restated the symbolic centrality of the public school and the ghetto to the enduring American dilemma: "The main form that racism takes in America is the criminal[ly] inferior segregated schools of the Northern communities. You do not have 'benign neglect,' you have . . . malignant neglect in the basic education of the masses of blacks."[126]

Lorraine Hansberry
(Library of Congress)

The Political Education of Lorraine Hansberry

6

The play contains no comments of any nature about Communism as such but deals essentially with negro aspirations, the problems inherent in their efforts to advance themselves, and varied attempts at arriving at solutions . . . From [my] observations of the plot and the dialogue, nothing specific was found that is peculiar to the CP program . . . Comments overheard from whites appeared to indicate that they appreciated the drama and the quality of the acting . . . Relatively few people appeared to dwell on the propaganda messages.

—An FBI Memo (February 5, 1959)

Miss Hansberry's play is a social protest, but it is such a consummate work of art that the objects of the protest applaud it vigorously each night on Broadway.

—John A. Davis (January 1960)

"A Raisin in the Sun," Doris Abramson writes in her history of African-Americans in the American theater, "was the first play by a Negro about which one is tempted to say, 'Everyone knows it.' Thousands of Americans have seen it on stage . . . Many more thousands have seen it on the screen. And finally, millions of Americans who might not seek it out have seen the movie on their television screens . . . Americans who read could have read *A Raisin in the Sun* in hardcover, in a very inexpensive paperback . . . or in anthologies."[1]

The debut of *Raisin* and the public's embrace of Lorraine Hansberry, was a final celebratory frame in postwar America's coming of age on race, taking its place beside Jackie Robinson's integration of baseball, Ralph Bunche's winning of the Nobel Prize for bringing peace to the Middle East, and the Supreme Court's seemingly unequivocal renunciation of segregation in *Brown v. Board.* One of the few reviewers who took on the challenge of talking about the symbolic issues that seemed to overtake the consideration of *Raisin* and its young, unknown author was Gerald Weales, writing in the June 1959 issue of *Commentary:*

> On the day that the New York Drama Critics' Award was announced, a student stopped me . . . and asked a sensible question. Had *Raisin* won because it was the best play of the year, or because its author, Lorraine Hansberry, is a Negro? Even if the play is a good one (and, with reservations, I think it is), even if it were indisputably the best of the year, the climate of award-giving would make impossible its consideration on merit alone . . . Even if the balloting had been purely aesthetic, the award to Lorraine Hansberry would have been greeted as the achievement of a Negro—hailed in some places as an honor to American Negroes, dismissed in others as a well-meaning gesture from the Critics' Circle. Such reactions are inevitable at this time. Any prominent Negro—Marian Anderson, Jackie Robinson or Ralph Bunche—becomes a special hero to the Negro community . . . an example of what the Negro can do in the United States; such figures are heroes also to white Americans who feel a sense of guilt about what the average American Negro cannot be and do . . . So long as the Negro remains an incompletely integrated part of American society (equal but separate, in the non-legal meaning of the phrase), the achievements of a singer, baseball player, or diplomat may be admired as such, but his race will not be ignored—by Negro or white.[2]

Hansberry, like her contemporary Martin Luther King, Jr. (they were one year apart in age), recognized both the didactic importance of these cultural conventions and the fact that the failure of the nation to move beyond such tokens of progress to progress itself was, by the late 1950s, an even more salient fact. Her father's inability to implement his own Supreme Court victory, *Hansberry v. Lee* (see Chapter 1), had left her dubious about the efficacy of the established civil rights movement's "obsessive over-reliance on the courts"; nonetheless, she understood the crucial significance of what *Brown* had, by 1959, already accomplished: placing the children and the public schools of the South at the very center of public attention.[3] In an essay deconstructing the rhetoric of southern resistance published two months after *Raisin* had become a hit, Hansberry told the readers of *Liberation,* an influential journal of the New York left:

I have dwelt so much on the racial problem of the South that one might suppose that I did not know that we have all the kindred rigors right here in New York. I assure you that I do know this. And not for one moment should our feelings about the desperate situation in the South make us blind to our ugly failings in our own city . . . But the nature of the struggle is such that one must begin. And for my part I can think of no better place to begin than with the Little Ones. The Little Ones in the Southland. The Little Ones and the Young Ones who must create the New South. The Little Ones and the Young Ones who must first of all have education and plenty of it, free and equal and integrated.[4]

These words recall the revolutionary meaning that integration held for many in the civil rights movement: Hansberry understood integration to be the removal of all barriers to the construction of solidarity among the children of the American working class—both white and black.[5] Hansberry, in the spirit of the Howard intellectuals of the preceding generation, understood the push for integration not as a sign that African-Americans wished to be "absorbed into 'this house,' " but rather that, as Hansberry put it, "the Negro people would like to see this house rebuilt."[6] For Hansberry, as for Michael Harrington, Martin Luther King, Jr., and others on the left, racial injustice was only the most obviously repugnant and easily understood symptom of a deeper crisis within American society. The conquering of racism would signal the existence of a significant constituency for tackling problems such as poverty, militarism, materialism, and the vast inequality of power between labor and capital.

Hansberry spent her political and professional apprenticeship under FBI surveillance as an associate of Paul Robeson, the most well-known leader of the African-American left in the late 1940s and early 1950s. From the pages of Robeson's monthly newspaper, *Freedom,* Hansberry celebrated the victories of the new nations against their former European colonizers; defended colleagues under ideological assault from the FBI; explored the origins of the American political economy, delineating the expression of this system in the maintenance of racial ghettos; and learned how to write political literature, be it journalism, fiction, or drama.

In this chapter I focus on Hansberry's moment of arrival and on *A*

Raisin in the Sun as a social document of unappreciated political radicalism and thematic complexity. In Chapter 7, I examine Hansberry's efforts to reclaim her text from those who had celebrated it as an affirmation of the American dream.[7] In that chapter I also take up another text completed by Hansberry immediately after *Raisin: The Drinking Gourd,* a script on the Civil War commissioned by the National Broadcasting Company. *The Drinking Gourd,* though privately applauded by network executives as brilliant, was never produced, because these same network executives also believed that the work was too controversial.

Hansberry, who died in 1965 at the age of thirty-four, left two bodies of work: what she had completed by the time of her death; and a number of other manuscripts that, according to Margaret B. Wilkerson, Hansberry's biographer, the playwright left behind unfinished.[8] Although I draw upon some of this draft material to indicate the direction of Hansberry's thinking, I concentrate on the two works directly related to racial issues that Hansberry considered completed and ready for immediate entry into public discourse: *A Raisin in the Sun* and *The Drinking Gourd.*

Negotiating the Terms of a Classic

John A. Davis's tribute to *Raisin* in 1960 as such "a consummate work of art that the objects of the protest applaud it vigorously each night" confirms the truth of Helene Keyssar's observation twenty years later that Hansberry had written the "archetypal script" of her era.[9] *Raisin,* Richard G. Sharine argues, "is still the best protest play ever written because of its ability to turn an audience's perception of them into a mutual 'we.' "[10] Hansberry's extraordinary fluency in the elements of American drama, especially the "drama of arrival" pioneered by Clifford Odets, among others, was as much a burden as it was a strength. Gerald Weales found Hansberry's reliance on such tried-and-true devices to be especially unfortunate:

> From the moment that Walter Lee mentions his plans for a profitable liquor store, his connections, the need for spreading money around in Springfield, the audience knows that the money will be stolen; supposedly, in good naturalistic tradition, the audience should sit, collective fingers crossed, hoping that the inevitable will not come,

hoping that he might be spared, that the dream might not be deferred and shrivel, like a raisin in the sun, as the Langston Hughes poem has it. I found myself, fingers crossed, hoping that the inevitable would not come, not for the sake of Walter Lee Younger, but for the sake of the play, of which the solid center was already too hedged with contrivances. No one's crossed fingers did any good.[11]

For many who saw the play in 1959, these qualities operated as a kind of ideological safety net that allowed them to observe a situation far outside their own experience without entirely losing their balance. As Hansberry herself discovered almost immediately, some of those who shouted "Bravo" most lustily could do so in part because they were able to bring their "prior attitudes into the theater from the world outside" as interpretive screens. In seeing through these screens, uncomfortable audiences could ignore representations too far afield from well-worn stereotypes, and instead fasten onto a superficially familiar theme or plot device, elevating it to the play's center—an act tantamount, in Ossie Davis's words, to "kidnapping" the play's discomfiting "message" so that they could avoid feeling the moral injunction to unclutch tightly held stereotypes in the name of a "mutual 'we.' "[12]

Davis persuasively argues that critics, by focusing their attention on Lena Younger, the widowed head of the Younger clan, were able to sidestep a theme central to the play and of prime importance to its author: the illusory and, consequently, destructive quality of American platitudes about equality and opportunity—clichés that, in their falsity, deny the economic, political, and social power of American racism, whether in the North, South, East, or West. In *Raisin,* these themes are articulated through the experiences of Lena Younger's son, Walter Lee, Jr. As Davis concluded in 1965, however, "the people who sit in judgment made their choice. Walter's dream and the threat it contained for our society ended for them when the curtain went down . . . Success and the great American audience decreed that Walter and his dream was Mama's problem."[13]

The praise for *A Raisin in the Sun* began long before it reached Broadway. In a review of its first out-of-town performance, Daniel Gottlieb of the *Hartford Times* was moved to write: "Where has Miss Hansberry been? If she writes nothing else her place is secure. She has not only taken hold of what is bothering our society today, but she has tried to offer a credo for living, come what may."[14] Philadelphia welcomed *Raisin* with a full house and warm reviews. The *Philadelphia Daily News* lauded the play as "explosive in content . . . and extraordinarily well performed." Hansberry had crafted a play, the review noted, that "looks bleakly upon the facts of integration. The action takes place in the North, an area which piously prefers to segregate this problem in the South." Hansberry, just shy of her twenty-ninth birthday, was hailed as the rare "political" playwright who "never lets preachment impede the progress of the play."[15] The *Philadelphia Daily Bulletin* christened Hansberry's work "the best play in a decade about Negro life."[16]

Raisin is an intriguing play, one that appropriates a traditional narrative form to press a point entirely alien to the mainstream of 1959: that the liberation of the American Negro required confronting economic forces and arrangements that according to Hansberry, racism exists to perpetuate. This, however, was not the reason for the enthusiasm with which the play was greeted by the white critical establishment.

The basic plot—an exploration of the many implications of a family matriarch's decision to use the $10,000 payment on her late husband's life insurance policy to purchase a home in a white neighborhood— conformed, at first glance, to the story lines of previous ethnic dramas of arrival. One example of the genre is Philip Yourdan's *Anna Lucasta,* a play about a Polish family's struggles in Pennsylvania, which had been reconditioned into an African-American drama by the American Negro Theater ten years before *Raisin;* another is Clifford Odets's *Awake and Sing.*[17] Recalling the historic ambiance of *Raisin*'s opening night, critic Kenneth Tynan was among the first to draw a comparison between *Raisin* and Odets's earlier effort: "I was not present at the opening twenty-four years ago of Mr. Odets' *Awake and Sing,* but it must have been a similar kind of occasion, generating the same kind of sympathy and communicating the same kind of warmth."[18] Conversely, plot details that were outside this familiar mold and specifically rooted in the world of 1959 (such as the inclusion of an African student who speaks of anticolonial revolution) were either ignored or devalued. One critic, for instance, dismissed the African subtheme as "impotent chatter."[19]

When *Raisin* reached Broadway in March 1959, Frank Ashton of the *New York World-Telegram* honored it as an "honest drama" that "has no axe to grind" and "will make you proud of human beings."[20] Walter Kerr of the *New York Herald Tribune* praised the "vital, restless, decently ambitious members of a chauffeur's family . . . caught in a no-man's-land between helplessness and hopelessness."[21] In her widely syndicated column *My Day*, Eleanor Roosevelt, speaking in the rhetorical style of Wendell Willkie's *One World* and Gunnar Myrdal's *An American Dilemma*, thanked both Hansberry and the play's star, Sidney Poitier, "for an evening that had real meaning, and I hope meaning that will sink into the conscience of America."[22]

Among the national media, *Life* made the oft-repeated suggestion that Hansberry had created a "Negro" play that had transcended the particulars of that experience to become "universal." Hansberry's "Negroes," *Life* held, were "human beings rather than social problem cases."[23] A few years later, Harold Isaacs would capture well the price that Hansberry was forced to pay when *Raisin* was appropriated by the critical establishment as a "universal" classic: "She was being praised so highly for creating 'real' people . . . that hardly anybody has given her credit for trying to deal symbolically with some important ideas."[24]

The cultural politics of race placed a special significance on the facts of Hansberry's biography and, indeed, a special burden on Hansberry herself. Tynan, in his judgment that the "supreme virtue" of *A Raisin in the Sun* lay in its "proximity to life as the dramatist has lived it," spoke for a wide section of the critical establishment, who took the play to be an autobiographical account of Hansberry's experience as an "American Negro."[25] This assumption explains the great public attention given during a brief period in the summer of 1959 to a report (leaked to the press by the administration of Chicago's mayor, Richard Daley) that the Hansberrys, unlike the Youngers, had not only been property owners but, it was alleged, slum landlords who were in violation of a number of building codes.[26]

The compliment that would come to haunt *Raisin* most tenaciously was the idea that the script's greatest strength was that it was not a "race" drama or a "social" drama, but one that spoke to "universals" of the human condition. As the actor and playwright Loften Mitchell remembered, the label of "universal" caused problems from the very beginning. According to Mitchell, the praise that *Raisin* received for being "universal" (that is, beyond race) was a common mechanism by which white critics looked past the uncomfortable fact that *Raisin* was, among other things, part of a national discourse on race:

> Negroes got tired of hearing whites say: "Even though I'm of such-and-such a background, I could identify with the Negro family." And some Negroes answered bluntly, "Yes, I could identify with the Nazi victims and the victims of the potato famine." Then—someone accused the play of being too much like O'Casey's *Juno and the Paycock*. Right behind that accusation came another—that it was really a Jewish play with a Negro cast and that is why it did so well. And there were Negroes who became angry because critics said the play really said nothing about the Negro plight, that it was not an angry play, and they lauded the playwright for balance in her writing . . . *A Raisin in the Sun* crystallized the era Negro playwrights began to call the "nots." The critics said *In Splendid Error* was *not* a message play. *Trouble in Mind* was *not* vindictive. *Take a Giant Step* was *not* just about Negroes, *Simply Heaven* was *not* an angry play, *A Land beyond the River* was *not* a propaganda play, and *A Raisin in the Sun* was *not* a Negro play. In other words, black playwrights were being praised for *not* making white people uncomfortable in the theater [all original emphases].[27]

During the 1960s and 1970s, as a mass-market paperback and as an assigned text in high school English courses, *Raisin* would become a symbol—as the image of Ralph Bunche had been—of the mainstream's appropriation and domestication of the struggle for racial equality. Following the verdict of the critics, academics would situate *Raisin* within the literary canon of postwar America as a "crucial document" of the early civil rights movement, its "sociologically ideal family" sharing that movement's alleged political naiveté and comfortably middle-class aspirations and orientation.[28] Werner Sollors, in his 1978 monograph on Amiri Baraka, cast Hansberry as Baraka's aesthetic opposite:

> When Amiri Baraka . . . turned toward writing, he defied the restrictive "philistine" aesthetic of the Black Bourgeoisie which defined art as an artifact, an "object," and a credit to the race. When Amiri Baraka broke into print in the "placid" decade of the 1950s, Afro-American

literature had reached the peak of its integrationist universalism, middle-class orientation, sexual inhibition, and naturalistic conventionality. Lorraine Hansberry's Broadway and Hollywood success, *A Raisin in the Sun,* epitomized this literature, and it was an anathema to later black writers that Hansberry insisted on interpreting the characters of her play as "honest-to-God, believable, many-sided people who happened to be Negroes," and herself not as a "Negro playwright," but as a writer who "happens to be a Negro." Despite Baraka's own contradictory relationship to his bourgeois background, he never published a work of similar aesthetic and social orientation, and very early in his career began polemicizing against Christianized middle-class, middle-brow, integrationist and naturalist "Negro literature."[29]

Sollors' staging of Baraka's entry onto the public stage as a dramatic rejection of a brand of cultural assimilationism that allegedly reached its apotheosis with *Raisin* summarized the view of Hansberry held by many academics by the late 1970s. Some of these critics went so far as to dismiss Hansberry's work as "an Odets play with Negro replacements," in which the particularities of the African-American experience were overlooked or muted in order that the "Negro" could be portrayed "as a human being faced with the same problems of survival as the white man, but with these problems intensified by the pressures of discrimination."[30]

Harold Cruse codified this revisionist trend in his widely read *The Crisis of the Negro Intellectual,* with the assertion that *Raisin,* shorn of its symbolic significance—that is, marking the arrival of integration on Broadway—represented little more than a shopworn ethnic soap opera of the kind that predominated on radio during the 1930s and 1940s.[31] Critics such as Cruse found *Raisin*'s allegedly derivative quality originating from a deeper flaw in the African-American left: the fact that their class background and experience differentiated them from the great mass of African-Americans—especially the northern urban proletariat whose plight Hansberry had portrayed in *Raisin.* This line of class analysis contended that Hansberry—the daughter of a major figure in Southside Chicago real estate, rather than, for example, of a stockyard laborer—had no genuine roots in black America, and that this fact rendered *Raisin* sociologically false. Applying a minutely honed sense of class gradation,

Cruse judged the Youngers to be, at worst, members of the "lower middle-class" rather than the "working class"—the "lower middle-class" still being too far below Hansberry's "privileged" status for her to be able to write "authentically" about them.[32]

The very fact that the white critical establishment of 1959 had found so much to praise in *Raisin* suggested to the politically committed students of 1969 not that its author had been misunderstood, but that she had told a basically racist public the comforting story it so wanted to hear. Looking no further than the superficial form of Hansberry's play as a domestic drama, one academic, writing in 1971, held that Hansberry's success with *Raisin* merely confirmed the truism that "it is easier for American audiences . . . to confront the Negro problem . . . through the familial pleasantness of *A Raisin in the Sun,* rather than through the sweeping and brutal *Blues for Mr. Charley* or the sustained insult of LeRoi Jones' *The Dutchman.*"[33]

John Rodden's delineation of how the "terms of repute" that frame the interpretation, recollection, and reputation of a work in the public sphere are established offers a useful way to understand the unstable place of *Raisin* within the canon that evolved between 1965 and 1980. Rodden describes three "spheres of literary repute":

> "Academic" reputation institutionalizes the author in school curricula. His or her work becomes a "classic" or pedagogical staple, lectured about, set for examinations, anthologized in school or college readers. "Intellectual" or "avant garde" reputation often precedes reputation in the academy; it may or may not lead to it—usually depending on whether the avant garde becomes the establishment (whether by transforming it or being coopted by it). Here the author is respected by other writers and receives attention chiefly in the non-specialist "intellectual" quarterlies or "advanced" magazines, rather than in the specialist academic journals . . . "Popular" or "public" reputation involves sales and public recognition. The author's books sell beyond academic and intellectual circles; often his name or personal history gets publicized by the mass-media.[34]

By the early sixties, *Raisin* was well-established as a "classic" text in the high school curriculum; it, along with Richard Wright's *Black Boy* (or either of these alone) was assigned to represent the work of the

African-American writer.[35] *Raisin* was, however, less favorably situated in the academy, serving there primarily as telling documentary evidence of an era whose limitations were, it was believed, fast becoming evident. In the general public sphere there was ready access to *Raisin,* both as a play published in paperback and as a film starring Sidney Poitier. Through its mass-market audience the text had by 1966 (the year in which the New American Library edition was published with textual additions approved by Hansberry before her death) entered not only what the playwright George C. Wolfe describes as the "colored museum . . . where the myths and madness of black / Negro / colored Americans are stored," but also what we might call the "museum of American enlightenment," constructed by educators and the media over the course of the postwar era.[36]

Hansberry's essays and other published comments on culture and politics—which are the strongest evidence against the way in which the academy chose to interpret her and her best-known work—were words that were not heard much beyond the New York audiences to whom they had been delivered. While some of these vital texts are becoming more broadly available in anthologies, during the crucial years when the terms of repute were being set, these essays remained secluded in the pages of the advanced journals and intellectual magazines where they first appeared.[37]

Freedom

It may well have been that the FBI's venture into theatrical criticism, from which one of this chapter's epigraphs was taken, reflected a general practice of the bureau toward any new play dealing with African-Americans. It is equally probable, given the size and extent of Hansberry's FBI file, that the review of *Raisin*—before it reached New York, no less—was part of the FBI's effort to monitor the activities of this particular radical journalist, who only four years earlier had been listed on the masthead of Paul Robeson's monthly Harlem newspaper, *Freedom.*

Whatever the particular circumstances that brought a special agent to the Walnut Theater in Philadelphia on the night of February 4, 1959, the memo that resulted from it is an enduring reminder of the first fact of American politics and culture during the 1950s: the systematic purging of Hollywood, schools, politics, and government of people whose politics were, in many cases, only fractionally left of center. In this connection, it should not be forgotten that Lorraine Hansberry was the second generation of her family to draw the interest of the FBI; her father, Carl A. Hansberry, had come under surveillance in 1943 (see Chapter 1).

For African-Americans, there existed a double blacklist. Frederick O'Neil, one of the founders of the American Negro Theater, which had briefly realized the cherished dream of establishing a broadly based, community-supported theater company in Harlem, described how McCarthyism destroyed the guarded progress against Jim Crow in the New York theater community: "The McCarthy era . . . made being black controversial [again]. White people who had black friends were suspected of being Communist-influenced. And the easiest way around the 'black problem' was to avoid it."[38]

Lorraine Hansberry arrived in New York in the late summer of 1950, as the dramatic constriction of American political life from its more open and freely contentious condition during the 1930s and 1940s was well under way; she joined the staff of Robeson's *Freedom* soon after her arrival in the City. Robeson, like Langston Hughes, Walter White, and W. E. B. Du Bois, had been a friend of the Hansberry family in Chicago. Influenced, perhaps, by her father's inability to obtain enforcement of his legal victory against racial covenants in housing and by his decision to live his final years in self-imposed exile in Mexico, Hansberry joined the *"Freedom* family," becoming a committed opponent of American adventures abroad and political repression at home.[39] Hansberry got started as "subscription clerk, receptionist, typist and editorial assistant." "And in between," the editors noted, "she finds time to write fine poetry and an occasional article."[40] Hansberry was quickly promoted to the post of associate editor.

Freedom was a distant point indeed from the centrist celebration of Jackie Robinson and Ralph Bunche. An unsigned editorial titled "What Are You Doing Out There," published in August 1951, spoke out strongly against the indictment of Du Bois as a "foreign agent," the revocation of Robeson's passport, and the harassment of Harlem city council representative Benjamin J. Davis. The piece charged that these leaders were being pursued by the full apparatus of the national security state because "they have soberly decided that the path to Negro liberation lies with the Communists rather than the Democrats, Republicans or Dixiecrats." This pattern, the editors warned, was a symbolic act whose major purpose was to telegraph a warning to established African-American leaders that they had better hew closely to the emerging anti-communist and pro-militarist consensus or face the same fate: "The axe that today hangs over the heads of Negro radicals is sharpened for the necks of our 'safe and sound' leaders as well; that is, unless the Walter Whites, Lester Grangers, Ralph Bunches and Edith Sampsons are prepared to yield in unquestioning conformity with every iota of Truman's foreign policy and domestic policy as the price for the honorary degrees, continental junkets, and 15 minute meetings with the President with which they have been rewarded."[41]

Hansberry's four years at *Freedom*—beginning in 1951 and ending with the paper's demise in 1955—were her equivalent of a college education. At *Freedom,* she had regular contact not only with Robeson, but also with Du Bois and John O. Killens and Julian Mayfield, authors who would loom large in the discourse of the 1960s and 1970s. Under the mentorship of *Freedom*'s editor, Louis Burnham, Hansberry became an all-purpose essayist—book reviewer, theater critic, and social analyst.[42] Among her comprehensive commentaries on the American scene was an examination of the cultural structures that preserve racism through the generations. One year after *Brown* had given currency to a very similar line of argument, Hansberry wrote: "From the time he is born the Negro child is surrounded by a society organized to convince him that he belongs to a people whose past is so worthless and shameful that it amounts to no past at all . . . Awaiting our youth in every area of American life is a barrage of propaganda which distorts and disparages their identity . . . In a land where the Grace Kelly–Marilyn Monroe monotyped 'ideal' is imposed on the national culture, racist logic insists that anything directly opposite—no matter how lovely—is naturally ugly."[43]

The intellectual example of Robeson, Du Bois, and Burnham can be readily seen in Hansberry's numerous articles chronicling the decolonization of the African continent, such as an essay endorsing President Nkrumah's $211 million plan to rebuild the infrastructure of the former Gold Coast, now Ghana, as proof that Nkrumah "wants no part of Marshall Plan hypocrisy and political enslavement." "The people of Ghana," Hansberry counseled readers, "clearly see their struggles and victories in connection with black folk on the rest of their continent as well as in the United States."[44] Hansberry was also profoundly impressed by the rise of nationalism in Egypt, proof that "the Egyptian people, like other African peoples, are tired of the exploitation and humiliation" of Great Britain, a "white supremacist imperialist nation."[45]

Hansberry as Dramatist

Throughout her first years in New York, while taking on steadily increasing responsibilities at *Freedom* and holding down various odd jobs, Hansberry studied drama assiduously and made several starts at writing her own plays, only to discard each attempt, unfinished. Among these efforts was *The Final Glory,* the story of a trade union leader framed for the murder of an African-American strikebreaker, as well as an adaptation of Charles Chesnutt's *Marrow of Tradition.*[46] According to one scholarly study, Hansberry ceased full-time work at *Freedom*—which folded at the end of 1955—because she had come to the conclusion that she could best serve social change as a dramatist.[47]

Hansberry took up *Raisin* shortly thereafter. "I started work on the play in 1956," says Hansberry, and, according to her former husband and literary executor, Robert Nemiroff, she kept at it for six months.[48] "If it weren't for him," Hansberry confessed, "this play would never have hit the boards." At one point in the writing, Hansberry became convinced that the manuscript was "the worst effort I'd ever made at anything," and threw the accumulated pages up into the air. Hansberry later recalled that "Bob didn't rebuke me at all except with a look. He just got down on the floor and picked up every sheet of it. He put it back in order and kept the whole thing out of my sight for several days. And then one night, when I was moping around, he got it out and put it in front of me. I went to work and finished."[49]

Hansberry's apprenticeship at *Freedom* gave her ample opportunity to think about the key ingredients of frankly political and polemical art. As early as 1952, Hansberry, then aged twenty-two, set down the properties of a politically relevant and effective literature of revolution in the course of a review of Howard Fast's historical novel, *Spartacus.* Fast, Hansberry thought, had wisely chosen as his subject "the story of the Thracian gladiator . . . who at one moment in history threw his weapon into the bloody sand of a Roman arena . . . Forty thousand slaves followed this man and destroyed the powerful Roman armies in an early move for human freedom which shook the foundations of the mighty Roman empire." Hansberry judged, however, that Fast had erred by choosing to tell this drama so much from the angle of the "degenerate slave-holding class and so little through the eyes and hearts of the slaves who were the heroes of both the book—and of history." Fast's error had not been in his interpretation but in its expression. Hansberry contended that the novelist's emphasis on the slaveholding class undermined his didactic purpose—to celebrate the slaves' will to freedom—and thus might reinforce in readers a fatalism about the possibility of revolution. The prospect of just this kind of misreading was fortified, Hansberry feared, by Fast's closing scene, in which the "heroic Jewish gladiator" asks, "Spartacus—who did we fail?" In her own conclusion, Hansberry responds that "the whole book is an implication of the answer: that this was the morning time of human history, that concepts of freedom and slavery were fresh and raw, that many centuries had to pass before all men would see that chains are not the only symbols of slavery. Somewhere this might have been put more concisely and clearly, lest the reader conclude that human struggle is romantic and idealistic—but futile and foolish."[50]

If Hansberry could not prevent the selective appropriation of *Raisin* seven years later, it is nonetheless clear that she followed her own advice to Fast by creating a drama centered not on the comfortable middle class but instead on the working class, whose struggles and decisions are "more pertinent, more relevant, more significant . . . more *decisive* [emphasis in original]—in our political history and our political future."[51] This emphasis did not prevent Hansberry from suggesting in *Raisin* how the African-American working class interacted with other classes. For instance, she chose to give Beneatha Younger two suitors: one, George Murchison, is the epitome of careerism and crude assimilationism into the middle class; the other, Joseph Asagai, is a wise Nigerian student whose educational attainments are directed toward achieving progress for his homeland. Another character, Karl Lindner of the Clybourne Park Improvement Association, represents, first, the self-described white moderate whose racism hides behind pleas for understanding and accommodation, and, second, the modestly propertied lower middle class whose economic vulnerability makes its members especially susceptible to diversionary appeals to race.

The action of *Raisin* takes place in the living room of one of the Southside's many "kitchenette" apartments. Hansberry elaborately describes its depleted ambiance—as well as the exhausted condition of its inhabitants:

> The Younger living room would be a comfortable and well-ordered room, if it were not for a number of indestructible contradictions to this state of being. Its furnishings are undistinguished and their primary feature now is that they have clearly had to accommodate the living of too many people for too many years—and they are tired. Still, we can see, at some time, a time probably no longer remembered by the family (except for Mama), the furnishings of this room were actually selected with care and love and even hope—and brought to this apartment and arranged with taste and pride . . . Weariness has, in fact, won in this room. Everything has been polished, washed, sat on, used, scrubbed too often. All pretenses but living itself have long since vanished from the very atmosphere of this room.[52]

As a child of relative privilege who nonetheless attended the segregated and vastly underfunded public schools of the Southside, Hansberry had, no doubt, seen the interior of more than one of the walk-up flats she describes here.[53]

As the play begins, Ruth Younger wakes up her husband Walter Lee, a chauffeur. The couple and their ten-year-old son Travis share this small space with Walter's younger sister Beneatha, a premed student at an unnamed local university, and their mother, Lena Younger. "Mama" is a woman who, according to Hansberry's screenplay (written in 1960), "was born someplace in the border South about 1890" and who had come to Chicago during the Great Migration of the First World War with her husband, Big Walter, a man who had "worked hisself to death . . . fighting with this here world."[54] Within the first few lines of dialogue between Ruth and Walter, Jr., Hansberry introduces a third force, a check for $10,000 from Walter Younger's life insurance policy, the anticipation of which has intensified the already strained relations between the Youngers.

C. W. E. Bigsby, echoing Gerald Weales' critique in *Commentary,* has faulted Hansberry's treatment of the check as far too narrowly instrumental: the check, Bigsby argues, acts as a mere "enabling device whose moral and social implications remain largely unexamined."[55] It is certainly quite accurate to see the insurance check as an enabling device, but its operation is considerably more subtle than Bigsby suggests. The money—the prospect of its arrival, its eventual appearance, and the loss of much of it to a street hustler—broadly illuminates the American dream in a few of its forms and implications; the discourse thus generated creates the opportunity for Hansberry to expose the ways in which class and race shape and inhibit aspirations.

In *Raisin*'s first moments we are introduced to the family that Walter, Jr., is being forced, by economic necessity alone, to raise in the cramped quarters of his parents' flat, which, thirty years before, even his parents had viewed as only a temporary accommodation. Hansberry uses a quarrel between Walter and Ruth—the themes and outcome of which had become well established over time—to disclose the dimensions of his dream as well as the limited mechanisms available to him for its achievement. The doors to the traditional networks of acquaintance and finance that run business and politics—white and black—in Chicago and everywhere else are quite surely locked to the likes of Walter Lee. He tells Mama in scene 2 of act 1, that, as he holds doors open for his employer, standing outside "them cool, quiet looking restaurants," he sees the system at work, sees white men younger than he "turning deals worth millions of dollars." As an outsider to this world, Walter Lee must do business with his own network—two street hustlers—in his living room late at night, while his son is kept awake in a daybed nearby (pp 47–48).

On this particular morning, Ruth, who has seen her own hopes for the future ground down by the exigencies of daily life and who, unbeknownst to her husband, is both pregnant and planning an abortion, is tired—too tired to engage in what has now become a weary ritual between her and her husband: an argument about Walter's "business partners" and his grand plans for gaining a foothold on upward mobility for his family. Ruth attempts to break off the conversation, but Walter Lee presses on—covering old territory between them, but this time perhaps more explicitly than in the past:

You see that? Man says to his woman: I got me a dream. His woman say: Eat your eggs. Man say: I got to take hold of this here world,

Baby! And woman will say: Eat your eggs and go to work. Man say—
I got to change my life, I'm choking to death, Baby. And his woman
say . . . your eggs is getting cold! . . . This morning I was lookin' in
the mirror and thinking about it—I'm thirty-five years old; I been
married eleven years and I got a boy who sleeps in the living room—
and all I got nothing to give him, nothing but stories about how rich
white people live. (p. 16)

Soon after, Hansberry introduces Beneatha Younger, who, Hansberry
told interviewer Studs Terkel, "is myself eight years ago."[56] Walter and
Beneatha tangle over the money, to which Beneatha lays no claim, but
who, Walter surmises, will receive a substantial portion to attend medical
school (to which Beneatha replies, "What do you want from me,
brother—that I quit school, or just drop dead, which?"—p. 19). Beneatha's ambition to step beyond her place—one to which she has been
relegated by society's devaluation of her race and her gender—is another
threat to Walter, one made all the more personally humiliating by the
fact that Beneatha's education has been supported by Ruth's willingness
to "get up and go to work in somebody's kitchen for the last three years,"
a reality that the much younger Beneatha, Hansberry seems to suggest,
doesn't always fully appreciate (p. 19).[57]

The relationship of Walter Lee to Beneatha, all but absent from previous commentary on *Raisin,* deserves closer attention. Their dreams—
and their often opposed understandings of the world—are intimately
connected. First, of course, there is the fact that, at *Raisin*'s beginning,
Beneatha's dream has the family's financial support, while Walter Lee's
is universally disparaged: by Mama because the sale of liquor goes
against her religious faith; by Beneatha because the proprietorship of a
liquor store represents a collaboration in one of the worst institutions of
the ghetto economy; and by Ruth because she realizes the many risks to
which Walter, in his entrepreneurial enthusiasm, is blind.

In a larger sense, the pitched disagreement between Walter Lee and
Beneatha also permits Hansberry to explore two strategies of advancement. The first is traced by Walter Lee, who, at his lowest point, seeks
to recover his bearings by making a solitary pilgrimage to the steel mills
and smokestacks on the outskirts of Chicago, to the great dairy farms of
Wisconsin, and to the Green Hat (an unpretentious watering hole on the

Southside that represents the most attainable version of Walter Lee's grand dream of being one of the "big men" of capitalism). Walter Lee, like his father before him, envisions a future built directly upon his own formally untutored acumen.[58]

Beneatha, in contrast, has invested her hopes in an equally venerated strategy in the American tradition: the pursuit of education and a place in one of the great professions, from which one might also exert power and leadership. On a more pointedly ideological plane, Walter Lee's admiration for the master builders of capitalism, and Beneatha's distrust of them—and her corresponding affinity for the anticolonial movement that was sweeping across Africa—represent the poles of debate between Hansberry, Robeson, and the "*Freedom* family" on the one hand and the leaders of the African-American establishment on the other. The most profound chasm between Beneatha and Walter Lee, however, is created when Walter Lee is informed that the nest egg remaining after Lena's down payment on the house in Clybourne Park—money that Mama had given to him in a redemptive and courageous gesture of confidence in her son's judgment—has been stolen by one of Walter Lee's "partners." Walter Lee's error in judgment kills—at least for the moment—not only his dream but Beneatha's as well.

The deep contention between Walter Lee and Beneatha, however, is also the product of a shared restlessness among their generation—many of whom would soon become the foot soldiers of SNCC. Like Walter and Beneatha, many of these young people did not share the devotion to the black church or to the "American way" of their parents. In the final moments of act 2, Mama asks Walter: "Son, how come you talk so much 'bout money?" to which, "with immense passion," Walter replies, "Because it is life, Mama." To Mama's observation that the world had changed, Walter responds by saying: "No—it was always money, Mama. We just didn't know it" (p. 49). This point of view is one that both he and Beneatha, as children of the Great Migration who have grown up in the ghettos of the urban North, share intuitively. Through Mama, Hansberry, whose parents had themselves come to Chicago from the unreconstructed South, brings this theme to a clear and eloquent conclusion: "No . . . Something has changed . . . You something new, boy. In my time we was concerned about not being lynched and getting to the North if we could and how to stay alive and still have a pinch of dignity too

... Now here come you and Beneatha—talking 'bout things we ain't never even thought about hardly, me and your daddy." Giving expression to some of the tensions that would, in a few years, become evident in the movement for equal rights, Hansberry closes with the following words for Lena Younger: "You ain't proud or satisfied or proud of nothing we done. I mean that you had a home; that we kept you out of trouble till you was grown; that you don't have to ride to work on the back of nobody's streetcar—You my children—but how different we done become" (p. 49).

Mama enters the play a figure nearly overwhelmed with the enormity of her burdens—especially her inability to end the polarization between her two children. The heaviest weight Mama carries is the prospect that she and Walter Lee will fail to realize their own modest dreams. Like her son, Lena Younger once had a dream—a dream so strong that she and her young husband trekked north to Chicago. In answer to Ruth's dismissal of their overcrowded kitchenette as a "rat trap," Mama remembers back to her and Big Walter's arrival:

> "Rat trap"—yes, that's all it is. [*Smiling*] I remember just as well the day me and Big Walter moved in here. Hadn't been married but two weeks and wasn't planning on living here no more than a year. [*She shakes her head at the dissolved dream*]. We was going to set away, little by little ... and buy a little place out in Morgan Park. We had even picked out the house. [*Chuckling a little*] Looks right dumpy today. But Lord, child, you should know all the dreams I had 'bout buying that house and fixing up and making me a little garden in the back. [*She waits and stops smiling.*] And didn't none of it happen. [*Dropping her hands in a futile gesture.*] (pp. 25–26)

At the beginning of *Raisin,* family disunity has a greater power to keep the Younger family imprisoned than a check for $10,000 has to liberate them. As no one else in the family possibly can, Mama sees in her son—and in her daughter-in-law's plan to obtain an abortion—the repetition of traumas that had killed her husband and defeated their dreams:

Honey, Big Walter would come in here some nights back then and slump down on the couch and just look at the rug, and look at me and look at the rug and then back at me—and I'd know he was down then . . . really down. [*After a second very long and thoughtful pause; she is seeing back to times that only she can see.*] And then, Lord, when I lost that little baby—little Claude—I almost thought I was going to lose Big Walter too . . . God knows there was plenty wrong with Big Walter—hard-headed, mean, kind of wild with women— plenty wrong with him. But he sure loved his children. Always wanted them to have something—be something. That's where brother gets all these notions, I reckon. Big Walter used to say . . . "seem like God didn't see fit to give the black man nothing but dreams—but He did give us children to make those dreams seem worth while." (p. 26)

Only near the end of the play does Lena Younger come to perceive the vital connection between her own exhausted—and often over-bearing—efforts to keep the family from falling in upon itself and her own son's feelings of powerlessness. Brought to her senses by Walter Lee's brief and angry departure from the family, Lena comes to terms with her past and thus empowers the present. After Walter returns from his solitary drive to the stockyards and the farms, Mama finally admits her unwitting complicity in his rage:

I say I been wrong, son. That I been doing to you what the rest of the world been doing to you . . . Walter—what you ain't never understood is that I ain't got nothing, don't own nothing, never really wanted nothing that wasn't for you. There ain't nothing as precious to me . . . There ain't nothing worth holding on to, money, dreams, nothing else—if it means it's going to destroy my boy . . . I paid the man thirty-five hundred dollars down on the house. That leaves sixty-five hundred dollars. Monday morning I want you to take this money and take three thousand dollars and put it in a savings account for Be-neatha's medical schooling. The rest you put in a checking account— with your name on it. And from now on any penny that come out of it or go into it is for you to look after. For you to decide. It ain't much, but it's all I have in the world and I'm putting it in your hands. I'm telling you to be the head of this family from now on like you supposed to be. (pp. 70–71)

If this were *Raisin*'s climactic scene, the play would certainly conform to the derogatory stereotype of it that developed through the 1960s and

1970s. But it is not; and Hansberry takes the drama in an unexpected direction, one that argues that injustice casts a long shadow and inflicts deep wounds, neither of which can be lifted or salved by one great gesture of goodwill, no matter how financially generous or emotionally genuine.

Walter Lee does not deposit the money for his sister's medical education in a bank account; instead, he hands over the $6,500 to one of his partners—only to find out that the partner has disappeared with it. After years of having to live at the level of bare spiritual subsistence, feeling his rage grow and his dreams metastasize into grotesquely swollen and self-obsessed delusions as steadily as his ability to realize them fell, Walter Lee could not instantly be free of them and assume the leadership of his family.

The disclosure of Walter's loss of the family nest egg comes on the heels of another manifestation of injustice—the appearance on the Younger family doorstep of Karl Lindner of the Clybourne Park Improvement Association (representing "hardworking, honest people who don't really have much but those little homes and a dream of the kind of community they want to raise their children in"—p. 78). Lindner has arrived to attempt to buy back—at a handsome profit to the Younger family—the property on which Lena Younger had made a down payment. The Youngers, not yet aware that the remainder of their insurance money has been lost, stand fast; Walter Lee orders Lindner out of their house.

The disappearance of the family's remaining financial stake threatens to destroy this solidarity. Walter's act of betrayal is so profound a wound that even Mama, the keeper of the dreams and the bedrock of the family, temporizes, conceding that "me and Big Walter just didn't never learn right . . . Just aimed too high all the time— . . . I see things differently now. Been thinking 'bout some of the things we could do to fix this place up . . . Sometimes you just got to know when to give up some things . . . and hold on to what you got" (p. 96).

The news that he has been sold out by Willy Harris leads Walter Lee, again without consulting anyone, to invite Lindner back to accept the association's offer, which Walter Lee rationalizes as a canny recognition of "what counts in this world" (p. 97). To Mama, Walter's act is a betrayal of the generations and represents the spiritual death of her son:

"Son—I come from five generations of people who was slaves and share-croppers—but ain't nobody in my family never let nobody pay 'em no money that was a way of telling us we weren't fit to walk the earth. We ain't never been that poor. We ain't never been that dead inside." To which Beneatha adds: "Well—We are dead now. All the talk about dreams and sunlight that goes on in this house. All dead" (p. 99). Walter is defensive—and unmoved; unmoved until Mama forces Walter Lee's ten-year old son Travis to witness his father's sellout of the family: "You make him understand what you are doing, Walter Lee. You teach him good. Like Willy Harris taught you. You show him where our five generations done come to, Go ahead, son" (p. 102).

Face to face with the next generation, Walter Lee, uneasily and un-certainly taking hold of that sense of self that he had only briefly expe-rienced when Mama had invested him with the substance of the family's dreams, rejoins the family—and his race's—historical struggle forward by turning back Lindner once again, with words that are meant not only for Lindner but for himself and for his son:

> WALTER: Well, Mr. Lindner . . . We called you—[. . . *there is a pro-found, simple groping quality in his speech*] because, well, me and my family [*He looks around and shifts from one foot to the other*] Well—we are very plain people—
> LINDNER: Yes—
> WALTER: I mean—I have worked as a chauffeur most of my life— and my wife here, she does domestic work in people's kitchens. So does my mother. I mean we are plain people. . .
> LINDNER: Yes, Mr. Younger—
> WALTER: [*Really like a small boy, looking down at his shoes and then up at the Man*] And—uh—well, my father, he was a laborer most of his life.
> LINDNER: [*Absolutely confused*] Uh, yes—
> WALTER: [*Looking down at his shoes once again*] My father almost beat a man to death once because this man called him a bad name or something, you know what I mean?
> LINDNER: No, I'm afraid I don't.
> WALTER: [*Finally straightening up*] Well what I mean is that we come from people who had a lot of pride. I mean—we are a very

proud people. And that's my sister over there and she is going to be a doctor—and we are very proud—

LINDNER: Well—I am sure that is very nice, but—

WALTER: [*Starting to cry and facing the man eye to eye*] What I am telling you is that we called you over here to tell you that we are very proud, and that this is—this is my son, who makes the sixth generation of our family in this country, and that we have all thought about your offer and we have decided to move into our home because my father—he earned it . . . We don't want to make no trouble for nobody or fight no causes—but we will try to be good neighbors. [*He looks the man absolutely in the eyes*] We don't want your money. (pp. 102–103)

The Younger family's solidarity is restored by Walter Lee's act of courage. Lindner appeals to Mama, who stands with her son and, Hansberry writes, "shaking her head with double meaning," says to Lindner, "You know how these young folks is nowadays, mister. Can't do a thing with 'em. Good-bye" (pp. 103–104). Lindner exits with words possessing an equally strong double meaning: "I sure hope you people know what you're doing" (p. 104).

Raisin did not promise its audience that the Younger family's resolution to take possession of their dream would mean its attainment; the Youngers, while they have decided to move to Clybourne Park, have been warned by Lindner that they will encounter a new round of escalated resistance. By the same token, the action of the play makes clear that Walter Lee's journey to manhood and to a fuller consciousness of the consequence of his actions has only just begun; Hansberry's script gives little basis for the belief that Walter Lee's struggle is complete—only that it has emerged. That so many interpreters of the play—New York critics, playwrights, and university intellectuals—read into this scene an entirely unproblematic happy ending confirms Robert H. Grant's conclusion that "the political sensibilities of an audience have a way of impinging on the interpretation of almost any arbitrarily chosen black drama." *Raisin* was only one play among many to share this fate in the history of the American theater.[59]

One of Hansberry's boldest moves is the introduction of Joseph Asagai, a Nigerian student at Beneatha's university and an aspirant for her hand in marriage. Asagai represents Africa and the disciplined intellectual commitment that had been made scarce by the Cold War and rendered unfashionable by the vogue of fatalism among European intellectuals, epitomized most completely for Hansberry by Albert Camus.[60] Asagai's role in *Raisin* is to educate Beneatha about Africa and the hard work of revolution: seeking to guide humankind in its halting, erratic, and easily reversed pursuit of the best and most hopeful prospect of its destiny. When the family's dream seems all but lost, and Beneatha's normally abundant idealism seems to be slipping into fatalistic self-pity, Asagai gently reproaches her and offers her a compelling synthesis of idealism and realism—which, in a later edition of the play, Hansberry would christen the "religion of doing what is necessary in the world." Asagai explains:

> In my village at home it is the exceptional man who can even read a newspaper . . . or who ever *sees* [original emphasis] a book at all . . . I will go home and much of what I will have to say will seem strange to the people of my village—But I will teach and work and things will happen, slowly and swiftly. At times it will seem that nothing changes at all—and then again—the sudden dramatic events which make history leap into the future. And then the quiet again. Retrogression even. Guns, murder, revolution. And even I will have moments when I wonder if the quiet was not better than all that death and hatred. But I will look about my village at the illiteracy and disease and ignorance and I will not wonder long. And perhaps . . . perhaps I will be a great man . . . I mean perhaps I will hold on to the substance of truth and find my way always with the right course . . . and perhaps for it I will be butchered in my bed some night by the servants of empire . . . or perhaps I will live to be a very old man, respected and esteemed in my new nation . . . And perhaps I will hold office and . . . perhaps the things I believe now for my country will be wrong or outmoded, and I will not understand and do terrible things to have things my way or merely to keep my power . . . [And] there will be young men and women, not British soldiers then, but my own black countrymen . . . to step out of the shadows and slit my then useless throat.[61]

A Raisin in the Sun testifies to the ambition and depth of Hansberry's self-education during the 1950s, aimed as it was toward the creation of literature that addressed the central social, philosophical, and political questions of late fifties American life. Hansberry sought to reestablish the salience and legitimacy of the leftist and Marxian critique that had been publicly purged from American discourse during the early fifties by constructing a drama that spoke authoritatively, knowingly, and fluently of the American dream that is the cultural cornerstone of American capitalism.

Hansberry's mission in *Raisin* had been very different from that of Myrdal in *An American Dilemma* fifteen years earlier. Myrdal had presented the fact of racial injustice in America as a stark and simple contrast between the tenets of an egalitarian and democratic American creed and the failings of American democracy in practice. The unsuccessful struggle of Carl Hansberry, a man of some wealth and influence, to implement *Hansberry v. Lee,* a landmark Supreme Court decision striking down racial discrimination in housing, was tangible evidence to his youngest daughter that the American dilemma was not that simple, and that it never had been. The crux of the problem as Lorraine Hansberry saw it was American capitalism itself: the social and cultural engine that had simultaneously produced both the idealized expression of the creed and the social context in which it was used.

The script that Hansberry believed that she had written was not the one that the public would receive. *Raisin,* as with any other public text, was not simply *delivered* to an audience: it was *presented,* wrapped in the interpretations of those critics, academics, and others who constructed the terms of repute in which *Raisin* would be framed and remembered, not only by the relatively small number of people who saw the Broadway stage production, but also by the significantly larger public that encountered it as a motion picture or as a part of a high school or college curriculum. The critical establishment of 1959 read Hansberry's text as fundamentally a confirmation of, rather than a challenge to, the American ethos. During the next few years, Hansberry would strive to reclaim her classic and to produce a successor text that would not share *Raisin's* fate.

7

The Dialectical Imagination
of Lorraine Hansberry

Popular idiom deals best with race prejudice: "who needs it?" It too is a killer. Negroes, for instance, simply do not live as long as white people in America. I think we must begin to remember facts like that and chatter less about the sensibilities of our bigots. We have been pathetically overgenerous with their malignant whimsy for three centuries. I hope that in the next ten years we will begin to recognize the void that racism has left in the character of white Americans. The sorry absence of courage on the race question presents terrifying implications for our culture. I also hope that a new spirit will charge the ranks of Negro leadership. The current plantation-paced dance of gratitude for crumbs shames the heart.

   —Lorraine Hansberry (1960)

Lorraine Hansberry, whose political and professional initiation had been gained on the front lines of the Cold War battles being waged against the African-American left during the late 1940s and early 1950s, was welcomed onto the center stage of American culture at an important moment in the relationship between America and the world and in the expression of Americanism and the striving for racial equality. The gradually quickening tempo of grass-roots civil rights activism, as represented to the public by the Little Rock Nine and by the emergence of Martin Luther King, Jr., was beginning to force Americans to widen the parameters of their political consciousness after ten years of obedience to a repressive brand of Americanism. This activism, which would hit full stride by 1963, was in its early stages in 1959; among its earliest consequences would be the clearing of an opening just large enough for *A Raisin in the Sun* and its author to pass into the mainstream of American cultural and intellectual life. Hansberry sought to deploy the unaccustomed visibility and cultural legitimacy conferred upon her by *Raisin*'s success to extend the boundaries of American political discussion and action to include Marxian and socialist themes that had not been given a hearing since the thirties.

Hansberry used the platform created by *Raisin*'s commercial and critical success to continue the work of public commentary that she had begun at *Freedom*. The passages that frame this chapter are taken from Hansberry's public contributions as a "New York intellectual." In this role, she sought to return to the public arena the themes advocated a generation earlier by the young Ralph Bunche and his close friend Abram Harris—themes that had been driven from the public realm by the Red Scare of the late forties and early fifties. In 1964, Hansberry set forth a challenge that the young Bunche would have seen as closely resembling his own. The movement for racial equality, Hansberry wrote, now as then, was in desperate need of:

> a new and presently-developing young Negro leadership—a leadership which must absolutely, if the present Negro revolt is to turn into a revolution, become sophisticated in the most advanced ideas abroad in the world, a leadership which will have had exposure to the great ideas and movements of our time, a Negro leadership which can throw off the blindness of parochialism and bathe the aspirations of the Negro people in the realism of the 20th century, a leadership which has no illusions about the nature of our oppression and will no longer hesitate to condemn, not only the results of that oppression, but also the true and inescapable cause of it—which of course is the present organization of American society.[1]

Among the most eloquent testimonies to Hansberry's effort to reawaken Americans—particularly the young—to the systemic injustices in American society was *The Movement,* a documentary text developed in cooperation with SNCC and, perhaps not coincidentally, reminiscent of Richard Wright's Depression-era *10 Million Black Voices. The Movement,* like so much of Hansberry's public work, was an effort to reclaim for the Marxian left a significant, legitimate place in the analysis of the nation's problems. In *The Movement,* Hansberry sought to remind those Americans who were only now discovering poverty that underneath the stark superstructure of the conflict between white and black and North and South lay a substructure of economic oppression. Beneath one portrait in the text, Hansberry, in an allusion to the firefighters who had assaulted protesters in Birmingham, reminded readers that "the men in helmets are from a class of Southerners who are themselves victims of

a system that has used them and their fathers before them for generations." Below Hansberry's words, written in 1964, was a passage that
had been penned thirty years earlier by W. E. B. Du Bois, once a leading
target of the Cold War Red Scare:

> In the South, the great planters form proportionately a quite small
> class, but they have, singularly enough, at their command, some five
> million poor whites; that is, there were actually more white people to
> police the slaves than there were slaves. Considering the economic
> rivalry of the black and white worker, it would have seemed natural
> that the poor white would have refused to police the slave. But two
> considerations led him in the opposite direction. First of all, it gave
> him work and some authority as overseer, slave driver and member
> of the patrol system. But above and beyond this, it fed his vanity
> because it associated him with the masters. To these Negroes he trans-
> ferred all the dislike and hatred he had for the whole slave system.
> The result was the system was held stable and intact by the poor
> white.[2]

Hansberry received *Raisin*'s success as a sign that, after "a decade . . .
[of] imposed intellectual impoverishment," Americans were again ready
to listen, and that the ideological rigidification that had all but destroyed
Robeson's career was breaking down.[3] "I think," she told Studs Terkel
in the spring of 1959, that "it reflects . . . a new mood. We went through
eight to ten years of misery under [Joseph] McCarthy and all that non-
sense, and to the great credit of the American people, they got rid of it
. . . There's a new affirmative political and social mood in our country
having to do with the fact that people are finally aware that Negroes are
tired, and it's time to do something about it."[4]

Hansberry debuted in her newly enlarged public role in a speech before the American Society of African Culture only a few weeks before
Raisin opened on Broadway. In uncompromising language, she took on
the many "illusions rampant in contemporary American culture," among
them the sentiments that "women are idiots . . . people are white . . .
Negroes do not exist," and, most of all, "that the present social order is
here forever and this is the worst of all possible worlds but there-is-
nothing-we-can-do-about-it-anyway—'human nature' being what it is."[5]
The Negro writer, Hansberry argued, has a special obligation to lead the

battle against this encrustation of social illusions and political fictions, because "those who say they do not wish to have 'social' material on the stage, motion picture or t.v. screen are the same persons who in the past have not hesitated to relegate *all* [original emphasis] black material, save hip-swinging musicals, to the 'social' category." Hansberry contended that this illusion was of a piece with an even broader fiction: "the idea that our country is made up of one huge, sprawling middle-class whose problems . . . are considered to represent the problems of the entire nation and whose values are thought to be not only the values of the nation but . . . of the entire world."[6]

As the 1950s drew to a close, and as large portions of the world were fighting their way out from under European colonialism, Hansberry uttered perhaps the ultimate heresy of the fifties:

> The simple fact is that sections of the world's peoples remain unimpressed . . . and even aloof from our efforts at demonstrating leadership and seem, at this point, perfectly capable of omitting from their historical destinies much of what we have thought was the very essence of the American past and the great American Dream. That is to say—our particular organization of industrial society. It is idle to argue the patriotism of those who call this question to our attention. It is more relevant to recognize the truth and to alert the people of this nation to that truth.[7]

Finally, there was "the last great illusion that . . . still clings to the cultural fabric of the country like dampness to wool on a rainy day": "the all-important illusion that there exists an inexhaustible period of time during which the nation may leisurely resurrect the promise of our Constitution and begin to institute the equality of man within the frontiers of this land . . . When the questions are asked in Bombay and Peking, and Budapest and Laos and Cairo and Jakarta—so I will tell it. And as of today, if I am asked abroad if I am a free citizen of the United States of America, I will say only what is true: NO."[8]

Those who had heard Hansberry's speech before the American Society of African Culture two weeks before she would become known to the nation through *Raisin*'s success came away convinced that, in the words of Loften Mitchell, "the decade which began as the fearful fifties had developed into one of optimism and output."[9] *Raisin* symbolized this change in atmosphere not only in its text but also in the manner of its arrival: *Raisin* was produced on Broadway by Philip Rose, a songwriter, and Daniel J. Cogan, an accountant, neither of whom had any prior experience in theatrical production; was directed by Lloyd Richards, who with *Raisin* would become the first African-American to direct on Broadway; and was financed by 147 individual investors who had contributed an average of just $250 each.[10]

Reclaiming Her Classic

If the signature images of the politics of the early 1950s had been the HUAC hearings and Joseph McCarthy waving his lists of "subversives," the end of the decade had a different feel. Although the politics of ideological suspicion outlived Martin Dies and McCarthy in the post-Sputnik rhetoric of the "missile gap" and national decline and in television footage of civil defense drills, it is also true that the years between 1957 and 1963 provided new images that distilled an emerging anxiousness regarding pressing challenges to democracy at home: the rapid rise of Martin Luther King, Jr., as the most powerful countersymbol to the Americanism of Joseph McCarthy; Little Rock; the sit-ins across the South; Birmingham; and the March on Washington. And if the Soviet-American relationship remained tense, there was a change even there: the visit of Premier Khrushchev and his wife to the American heartland—and to Disneyland—had given communism a human face and legitimated the phrase "peaceful coexistence" as a much-repeated term in the political lexicon.

It was into this changing public realm that Hansberry brought her play. If, however, there was sporadic evidence that the intellectual repression and the crude, easily caricatured anticommunism of the early fifties was beginning to recede, it is equally true that the opening created by these developments was quite limited. The nearly instant misreading of *Raisin* as a traditional ethnic drama with a happy ending was one sign of this.

Hansberry spent the first months of her celebrity seeking to reclaim the meaning of her classic. "When Lorraine Hansberry read the reviews," her former husband, Robert Nemiroff, remembered, she was "delighted by the accolades, grateful for the recognition," but disturbed by the critical consensus that was developing about *Raisin*'s meaning.[11] What disappointed Hansberry most was that Walter Lee "remains, despite the play, despite performance, what American racial traditions wish him to be: an exotic." Hansberry expounded at length about the response her play had evoked, focusing particularly on the characterizations that had been put forward of Walter Lee:

> Some writers have been astonishingly incapable of discussing his purely *class* aspirations and have persistently confounded them with what they consider to be an exotic longing to "wheel and deal" in what they further consider to be (and what Walter never can) "the white man's world." Very few people today must consider the ownership of a liquor store as an expression of extraordinary affluence, and yet, as joined to a dream of Walter Younger, it takes on for some, aspects of the fantastic. We have grown accustomed to the dynamics of the "Negro" personality as expressed by white authors. Thus, de Emperor, de Lawd, and of course Porgy, still haunt our frame of reference when a new character emerges. We have become romantically jealous of the great image of a prototype whom we believe is summarized by the wishfulness of a self-assumed opposite. Presumably there is a quality in human beings that makes us *wish* we *were* capable of primitive contentments; the *universality* of ambition and its anguish can escape us only if we construct elaborate legends about the rudimentary of *other* men . . . America, for this reason, long ago fell in love with the image of the simple, lovable, and glandular "Negro" [original emphasis].[12]

Hansberry contended that this thick interpretive screen prevented most reviewers from seeing the dreams and the pain that linked Walter Lee with his nearest relative in American drama: Willy Loman, Arthur Miller's symbol of the closing of America's psychic frontier. Walter Lee, like Willy Loman, Hansberry argues, are fated "to see their problems only in the terms which the culture presents to them." Hansberry suggests, "Walter accepts . . . the 'world' as it has been presented to him . . . Within himself, he is encouraged to believe, are the only seeds of defeat or victory in the universe. And when opportunity, haphazard and rooted in death, prevails, he acts."[13] As a product of his culture, and as a symbol of its reigning values and illusions, Walter Lee's decision to lead the Younger family to Clybourne Park represents the full measure of a self-consciously revolutionary and liberating act. "Elsewhere in the world," Hansberry contends, Walter Lee might have dealt with the tragedy of his family's circumstances by donning "saffron robes of acceptance and [sitting] on a mountain top all day contemplating the divine justice of his misery. Or, history being what it is turning out to be, he might wander down to his first Communist Party meeting." History and culture, however, had not created these possibilities for Walter Lee, for:

> here in the dynamic and confusing postwar years on the Southside of Chicago, his choices of action are equal to those gestures only in symbolic terms. The American ghetto hero may give up and contemplate his misery in rose colored bars to the melodies of hypnotic saxophones, but revolution seems alien to him in his circumstances (America), and it is easier to dream of personal wealth than a communal state wherein universal dignity is supposed to be a corollary. Yet his position in time and space does allow for one other alternative: he may take his place on any one of a number of frontiers of challenge. Challenges (such as helping to break down restricted neighborhoods) which are admittedly limited because they do not threaten the basic social order.[14]

If Willy Loman and Walter Lee Younger were too deeply of their culture to see its strong hand in their tragedies, they did not share an equal fate. Arthur Miller did not create for his quintessential American the scene of personal redemption that Hansberry gives to Walter Lee. Walter Lee is redeemable because Mama has reactivated the moral and historical compass deep within him, a history of struggle and resistance that, "despite his lack of consciousness of it," has "inextricably wedded" Walter Lee to his people.[15] By contrast, Hansberry believes, Willy Loman's "section of American life" (by which Hansberry means the white ethnic working- and lower-middle classes to whom the New Deal still spoke) could find no such spiritual sanctuary—not because they had been oppressed or struggled any less severely, but because they had bought into the myth that, in America, all white men at least have an equal start toward the American dream. Thus brainwashed, the Willy Lomans of the world cannot "draw on the strength of an incredible people who, historically, have simply refused to give up." As a "representative hero" of the African-American working class, Walter Lee, whatever other illusions he chooses to sustain, is "forced . . . by the very nature of the situation . . . to recognize that he must ultimately be at cross-purposes with at least certain of his culture's values."[16]

If the pages of the *Village Voice* gave Hansberry the space in which to clarify and forcefully restate the significance of Walter Lee, her remarks before the annual meeting of the American Academy of Psychotherapists four years later gave her the chance to "rescue" Mama, whom, Ossie Davis charged, had been "kidnapped" by the white critical establishment and held up as the sole center of the play. Hansberry and the critics agreed that "Lena Younger is the black matriarch incarnate; the bulwark of the Negro family since slavery," but, Hansberry asserted, she also symbolized "the Negro will to transcendence," whose sacrifices make possible the publicly celebrated achievements of role models and icons like Ralph Bunche: "It is she who . . . scrubs the floors of the nation in order to create black diplomats and university professors. Seemingly clinging to traditional restraints, it is she who drives the young into firehoses. And one day she simply refuses to move to the back of the bus in Montgomery."[17]

Hansberry also sought to counter misreadings of *Raisin* by adding previously deleted material to the 1959 and 1966 published editions of the play, and by creating some new material for the 1960 movie screenplay. Hansberry's additions to the 1959 Random House text were modest. The most important of these was a sequence of dialogue in act 1, scene 1, where Hansberry, speaking through Beneatha, draws a clearer picture of the class difference that exists between the Younger family and that of Beneatha's beau, George Murchison, Hansberry's representative of the black bourgeoisie. As Beneatha now tells her mother: "The Murchisons are honest-to-God-real live-rich colored people, and the only people who are more snobbish than rich white people are rich colored people. I thought everybody knew that. I've met Mrs. Murchison. She's a scene!"[18]

When Hansberry prepared *Raisin* for the screen in 1960, she added scenes that, as Margaret Wilkerson argues, would require white Americans to confront the "conditions and circumstances that drive a man like Walter to strike out at his family, that motivated Walter's father to quite literally work himself to death, that led Ruth to risk abortion rather than add another child to the family, and that impel a Lena Younger to move into a hostile neighborhood. The camera's eye would be irrefutable as it swept the panorama of Chicago and, by implication, America's major cities where the majority of African-Americans reside."[19] These scenes—such as Lena Younger working as a domestic and paying exorbitant prices for inferior goods at a Southside supermarket, and Walter Lee appealing unsuccessfully for business advice from a white liquor store owner, only to be rebuffed with condescension and barely concealed dislike—never made it into the final film.[20] A clear sense of what Hansberry hoped to achieve in the film version survives in her many detailed and eloquent instructions to the director, the first of which reads in part:

> This is the ghetto of Chicago . . . Not indolence, not indifference, and certainly not the lack of ambition imprisons [the Younger family], but various enormous questions of the social organization around them which they understand in part, but only in part.[21]

Despite the limitations imposed by the extremely confining rules of the reigning cultural politics, Hansberry was able to preserve some lines from her original screenplay that clearly establish the Younger family's class and historical place. For instance, words originally written for Lena Younger to say to her white employer, Mrs. Holiday, are amended slightly and spoken to Ruth Younger instead: "Big Walter always hated the idea of being a servant. He was always talking about how a man's hands wasn't meant to carry nobody's slop jars and make their beds and all. Always said they were meant to turn the earth with or make things . . . And that husband of yours is just like him."[22]

In another adept blending of old and new material to clarify the social and historical context, Hansberry takes lines originally in act 2, scene 2, of the play, where Lena gives Walter the balance of the insurance money to handle for the family, and makes them the heart of a new scene set in Walter Lee's favorite bar, the Green Hat. Hansberry builds to these lines by having Lena describe to her son why she and Walter Sr. had left the South forty years earlier. In response to Walter's query about why his parents had left the South, Lena Younger says:

> I 'spect for the same reason everybody did. I thought I might be able to do more with myself up here. And I don't say I exactly took over the world in the years since then—but—

Walter interrupts and finishes the thought—

But you didn't give nobody the right to keep you there when you decided you had to go, did you, Mama? Even if you wasn't really goin' no place at all—you felt like you was, didn't you, Mama, didn't you?[23]

With these lines, Hansberry emphasizes again the historic context and historic significance of Walter Lee's decision at the conclusion of the drama to follow the precedent set by his parents and thus to lead his generation of the family to a better life. This dialogue also reinforces the point that the Youngers' decision to take possession of their home in Clybourne Park is not a manifestation of a crude impulse toward social climbing or a need for validation by the white mainstream, but rather an assertion of the fullness of their autonomy, come what may.

At the time of her death, Hansberry had, according to Nemiroff, decided to restore two more segments of dialogue to *Raisin*.[24] A few lines are added to Asagai's final exchange with Beneatha, which serve to sharpen the expression of Beneatha's despair and of Asagai's own position as a believer in "the religion of doing what is necessary in the world—and of worshipping man—because he is so marvelous, you see."[25] Most important of all, Hansberry restored a key scene between Walter Lee and his son, Travis. Immediately following Mama's admission to Walter Lee that she had unwittingly contributed to his sense of powerlessness, this scene foreshadows Walter Lee's gamble with the family's money and shows Walter Lee looking toward the day when he can pass on a better world to his child. The scene begins with Walter Lee asking his son what kind of future he envisions for himself. Travis's wish to be a bus driver shocks Walter Lee, and moves him to share with his son the wider vistas that he is hoping to create for him:

WALTER: [*Gathering him up in his arms*] You know what, Travis? In seven years you going to be seventeen years old. And things is going to be very different with us in seven years, Travis . . . One day when you are seventeen I'll come home from my office downtown somewhere—

TRAVIS: You don't work in no office, Daddy.

WALTER: No—but after tonight. After what your daddy gonna do tonight, there's gonna be offices—a whole lot of offices. . .

TRAVIS: What you gonna do tonight, Daddy?

WALTER: You wouldn't understand yet, son, but your daddy's gonna make a transaction . . . a business transaction that's going to change our lives. That's how come one day when you 'bout seventeen years old I'll come home and I'll be pretty tired . . . after a day of conferences . . . And I'll pull the car up on the driveway . . . And I'll come up the steps to the house and the gardener will be clipping away at the hedges and he'll say, "Good evening, Mr. Younger." And I'll say, "Hello Jefferson, how are you this evening?" And I'll go inside and Ruth will come downstairs and meet me at the door and we'll kiss each other and she'll take my arm and we'll go up to your room to see you sitting on the floor with the catalogues of all the great schools in America around you. And—and I'll say, all right son, it's your seventeenth birthday, what is it you've decided? . . . Just tell me where you want to go to school and you'll *go*. Just tell me, what it is you want to be—and you'll *be* it . . . Whatever you want to be—Yessir! . . . You just name it, son . . . and I hand you the world! [original emphasis][26]

Hansberry envisioned *Raisin* as the first work of many that would test the seemingly fixed boundaries of American political discourse in the postwar era. In that first play, she had tried to represent the dreams and the life experience of the African-American working class, with whom, she believed, the future of black America rested. What Hansberry had perhaps not fully anticipated was exactly the fate that, seven years earlier, she had feared would befall Howard Fast's *Spartacus:* that her work would be read in such a way that it would seem to be consistent with, rather than in opposition to, the conformist political atmosphere of its day. Her first acts as a widely known public figure were all directed to one objective: amplifying her original intent so as to regain some measure of control over the interpretation of her text, which had instantly become an icon of racial progress. Hansberry did not, however, allow these efforts to distract her from work on new projects, scripts whose structure would make the ideological challenge she meant to pose harder to ignore or to discount. As a young political journalist at *Freedom,* Hansberry had been fascinated by the anticolonial revolutions sweeping the world. In the work that followed *Raisin,* she enlarged her focus in order to explore this global development and to ponder the relationships that she believed tied it to the American past and present.

Beyond the Borders

Hansberry's emergence as an intellectual force came at an important moment in the American discourse on race. By 1959 five years had passed since *Brown,* and it was clear to all that school desegregation was still many years away from achievement, in the North and in the South. And while the 1950s had been a period of general prosperity, it had not lifted all classes, much less all races, with equal vigor. With the seeming stagnation of progress on race—a major Supreme Court case ignored and a weak civil rights act on the books to little effect—optimism among some black intellectuals came to be tempered with a growing sense that progress had been largely a matter of symbolic acts designed to obscure the absence of real change.

Speaking at the same conference at which Hansberry had issued her artistic and political creed, Julian Mayfield gave eloquent voice to this concern. "The dream has proved elusive, and," Mayfield held, "there is reason to believe that it never had a chance of realization." A decade and a half after the Second World War, African-Americans had received and could expect little more than the "trappings that other citizens already take for granted."[27] It was time, Mayfield argued, for African-American political and cultural leaders to reevaluate the dominant postwar meaning of "integration," that is, of "completely identifying the Negro with the American image—that great-power face that the world knows and the Negro knows better." In their "fervid pursuit" of such legitimacy, Mayfield claimed that Negro leaders had thought nothing of saying, "Take our youth and they will prove their worth as Americans . . . If the dream he has chased for three centuries is now dying even for white Americans," said Mayfield, the African-American would be well advised to "consider alternative objectives" and lead a charge away from the "stultifying respectability [that] hangs over the land [and] inhibits the flowering of new ideas . . . and cultural regeneration." Black artists were ideally suited to this new task, because their detachment from the mainstream placed them "in a better position to illuminate contemporary American life," thus rendering them "more sensitive to philosophical and artistic influences that originate beyond our national cultural boundaries."[28]

In the early 1960s, Hansberry would work energetically to produce a new work that would expand on the great themes expressed in *Raisin* but ignored by critics. Among these efforts was an opera on Toussaint L'Ouverture and the liberation of Haiti; *Les Blancs,* a representation of the conflict between colonialism and nationalism in Africa; and *The Drinking Gourd,* a teleplay that sought both to return slavery to the front of centennial reflections on the Civil War and to reassert the notion that it was American capitalism that made that conflict inevitable. Of these projects, only *The Drinking Gourd* (1960) was finished at the time of her death, and ready, in Hansberry's judgment, for entry into the public arena. To the network executives who, with great fanfare, had commissioned *The Drinking Gourd* right after *Raisin,* the work was considered beautifully realized, but too controversial, too far beyond the borders of conventional American discourse. In *The Drinking Gourd,* as in all of her work from this period, Hansberry strove to create art that was accessible to a general American audience and also an authentic reflection of the American past and the conflicts sweeping the globe:

> Chinese peasants and Congolese soldiers make drastic revolutions in the world while the obtuse and myth-accepting go on reflecting on the "inscrutability and eternal placidity" of those people. I believe that when the blinders are dropped, it will be discovered that while an excessively poignant Porgy was being instilled in generations of Americans, his truer-life counterpart was ravaged by longings that were, and are, in no way alien to those of the rest of mankind . . . He is waiting yet for those of us who will but look more carefully into his eyes, and listen more intently to his soliloquies. We must not be intimidated by the residue of the past; the world is paying too large a price for the deception of those centuries; each hour that flies teaches that Porgy is as much inclined to hymns of sedition as to lullabies and love songs; he is profoundly complicated and interesting; everywhere he is making his own sounds in the night.[29]

Raisin was the first—and, in her lifetime, the only—public chapter in Lorraine Hansberry's effort to liberate from stereotype those denied the power to represent themselves, either in politics or in culture. Even before *Raisin*'s debut Hansberry was in the preliminary stages of "my epic," the theatrical dramatization of the life of Toussaint L'Ouverture, who liberated Haiti from Napoleon.[30] Of this project Hansberry wrote in December 1958, "I was obsessed with the idea of writing a play (or at that time even a novel) about the Haitian liberator Toussaint L'Ouverture when I was still an adolescent and had first come across his adventure with freedom. I thought then, with that magical sense of perception that sometimes lights up our younger years, that this was surely one of the most extraordinary personalities to pass through history. I think so now." Hansberry envisioned a script shorn of the "exotic voodoo mysticism, the overrich sensuality which springs to mind traditionally with regard to Caribbean peoples" and which had been used by European dramatists of this event to "distort the entire significance and genuine romance of the incredibly magnificent essence of the Haitian Revolution and its heroes." Like the Youngers' tenacious struggle to hold fast to five generations of hopes and ideals, the story of Toussaint would serve as "testimony to purpose and struggle in life."[31] Hansberry completed an opening scene (which was nationally broadcast by public television in June 1961), but the rest of the play remained only generally sketched out in some fragmentary notes.[32]

In the late spring or summer of 1960, according to Nemiroff's estimate, Hansberry again took up these themes in another script, this time in a drama on colonial revolution in Africa, a continent that was beginning to overtake Asia and India as the preferred American metaphor for understanding what were then called the "developing nations." Perhaps it was coincidence, but Hansberry's first tentative steps toward the play she envisioned as the successor to *Raisin* were taken as world attention came to be increasingly focused on the standoff between the Belgian armed forces and the nationalist government of Patrice Lumumba in the Congo. By April 1961, Hansberry's script had a title: *Les Blancs,* an ironic reference to Jean Genet's *The Blacks,* then running to strong reviews on Broadway.[33] Hansberry found Genet's play not a thoughtful meditation on the postcolonial era, but rather a vehicle that, in the guise of radical and intellectually engaging drama, recycled stereotypes of "the black" as libidinous, romantic, the quintessential hipster.[34]

The setting of *Les Blancs* is a missionary hospital in an outermost African locale, a symbolic meeting place between white and black, Africa and the West. The hospital is run by a saintly European doctor and humanitarian whose care of the African ends where the African's desire for autonomy begins. In prior years, the mission had been an essential and honored part of the community, one whose staff (all white European disciples of the great doctor) had become valued friends to the village and whose chapel on Sundays was a center of Christian services. In more recent times, however, friendships had dissipated into cold formality, and the chapel was no longer a place of congregation. Now the mission and its staff were caught between their former friends, who were now fighting a war of liberation, and the brutal colonial forces arrayed against them.

Into this scene Hansberry places Tshembe Matoseh, an African Europeanized by his many years of study in Britain. Married to a European woman of unspecified nationality and father to a son, Matoseh's thoughts are far from his native Africa and from the possibility of revolution. Matoseh has come home to bid farewell to his dying father, but he arrives too late. Like *Raisin,* the action of the play becomes telescoped upon the situation of one man who faces a choice. Matoseh's dilemma lies in choosing between his illusion that Europe has given him the best of both worlds—a strengthened foundation for his anticolonial nationalism and a universal and color blind perspective that he believes has allowed him to look beyond history and its fleeting causes—and his intellectual awareness that, in *his* historical time and place, revolution is both inevitable and necessary. By the play's end, Matoseh, like Joseph Asagai, has synthesized those parts of him that matured in the West with that part of him born in Africa, and has chosen action over detachment; and, like Walter Lee, Matoseh stands with his father's struggles, ready to lead the fight toward their future.

Hansberry worked on the play intermittently between 1960 and her death in January 1965, a process severely hampered by her rapidly declining health and the work of mounting her second Broadway production, *The Sign in Sidney Brustein's Window,* which opened to mixed reviews at the Longacre Theater on October 15, 1964, and closed 101 performances later on January 12, 1965, the day of Hansberry's death from cancer.[35] According to Nemiroff, Hansberry left behind a work that was still very much in the throes of conception: some scenes had reached a late stage of development (indeed, one had been performed at the

Actor's Studio in 1963); others had been sketched in writing; still others, although discussed, had not yet been committed to paper.[36]

After *Raisin in the Sun,* Hansberry used her symbolic status as the first black woman playwright to conquer Broadway in the service of supplanting the discourse of American exceptionalism in which she and *Raisin* were being wrapped with a more provocative image of her moment's cultural politics. Hansberry aimed to replace this discourse by forging literary works that were more faithful to America's real past and present than the conceptual boundaries of American exceptionalism had sanctioned. Nowhere was this goal more fully manifest than in her teleplay, *The Drinking Gourd.*

Unmaking *Gone with the Wind*

In *The Drinking Gourd,* Hansberry took special aim not only at the Sambo and Porgy stereotypes through which African-Americans had been represented, but also at the cultural system that projected them to the nation a century after the end of the Civil War. "I am profoundly concerned," Hansberry told a radio audience in early 1961, "that in these hundred years since the Civil War very few of our countrymen have really believed that their Federal union and their defeat of the slavocracy . . . is an admirable fact of American life." One sign of this national ambivalence was the way in which the centennial celebration of the Civil War avoided the central issue of that conflict—slavery—in favor of an antiquarian fascination with old battlefields and military strategy. "It is possible today," Hansberry commented, "to get enormous books that are coming out on the Civil War . . . and not find the word slavery, let alone Negro."[37] Mainstays of popular culture such as *Gone with the Wind* remained intact as elaborate false fronts of "beautiful ladies in big fat dresses" concealing the real engine of the still-defended "southern way of life . . . a culture drawn from unpaid labor, near-starvation, brutalization and the enactment of atrocity upon four million people in bondage."[38]

"The time has come," Hansberry argued, "for us to stop speaking of the Southern problem only as it relates to the Negro question and to demand an accounting of the reasons why the Southern people, all of them, black and white, do not enjoy the same standard of living as the rest of us." Hansberry pointedly asked: "Why are there fewer and poorer schools, fewer hospitals, lower wages, and fewer services for the people of the South; why is there less utilization of the natural resources of the region, more illiteracy, more disease and more poverty[?]"[39] Having established herself as a leading figure in American letters, Hansberry was presented with a seemingly ideal opportunity to compose a drama around these themes when she was commissioned by Dore Schary to create a ninety-minute "spectacular" for NBC to commemorate the centennial of the civil war. She was promised a free hand.[40]

Hansberry produced a drama set in the few days before the attack on Fort Sumter that, though half the length of *Raisin,* made full use of the wider scope and greater technical resources of film to present a comprehensive portrayal of slavery as a social system and as a way of life: the slave master, pressed by the necessities of a maturing capitalist economy; the slave family, held together by the constant contemplation of escape and by sweet hymns of sedition; and the poor white hardscrabble farmer, whose dreams of land in a distant frontier are virtually all that separate him from the chattel slave.[41] In an effort, perhaps, to protect her script from selective appropriation by audiences wishing to see anything *but* its politics, Hansberry fused a generous narrative sequence to the beginning and to the end of the drama, to be delivered by a mysteriously distinguished and universally representative figure—"not Lincoln but perhaps Lincolnesque . . . suggesting a certain idealized generality," clad in informal military attire "in no way recognizable as to rank or particular army . . . his voice . . . markedly free of identifiable regionalism." "His imposed generality," Hansberry's script advises, "is to be a symbolic American specificity."[42] Standing somewhere along the southeastern coastline, Hansberry's generic American sets down the rudiments of historical materialism:

This is the Atlantic Ocean . . . Over there, somewhere, is Europe. And over there, down that way, I guess, is Africa. [*Turning and facing inland*] And all of this, for thousands and thousands of miles in all directions, is the New World. [*He bends down and empties a pile of dirt from his handkerchief into the sand*] And this—this is soil. Southern soil. [*Opening his fist*] And this is cotton seed. Europe, Africa, the New World and cotton. They have all gotten mixed up together to make the trouble. [*He begins to walk inland . . .*] You see, this seed and this earth [*gesturing to the land around him*] only have meaning—potency—if you add a third force. That third force is labor. (pp. 167–168)

Like *Gone with the Wind,* Hansberry begins her drama at "quittin' time," with a panoramic survey of the plantation and the surrounding countryside; unlike *Gone with the Wind,* Hansberry's lens closes in not on an equivalent of Tara—"a magnificently columned, white manor house"—but instead on the "little white painted cabins" that constitute the slave quarters (p. 168). As exhausted slaves stream into the quarters, the narrator resumes his commentary, and in words quite opposed to the preamble of *Gone with the Wind* ("There was a land of cavaliers and cornfields called the Old South. Here in this pretty world gallantry took its last bow") he describes the real Old South—whose most important members were not its "cavaliers," but its slaves:

Labor is so plentiful that, for a while, it might be cheaper to work a man to death and buy another one than to work the first one less harshly . . . These people are slaves. They did not come here willingly. Their ancestors were captured, for the most part, on the West Coast of Africa, by men who made such enterprise their business . . . Few of them could speak to each other. They came from many different peoples and cultures. The slavers were careful about that. Insurrection is very difficult when you cannot even speak to your fellow prisoner. All of them did not survive the voyage. Some simply died of suffocation; others of disease and still others of suicide. Others were murdered when they mutinied . . . That trade went on for three centuries . . . Some planters will tell you with pride that the cost of maintaining one of these human beings need not exceed seven dollars and fifty cents—a year . . . There are of course no minimum work hours and no guaranteed minimum wages. No trade unions. And, above all, no wages at all. (pp. 169–170)

In Hansberry's script, southern slavery was not treated as a heinous aberration restricted to one region but as part and parcel of an entire national system that countenanced child labor in mines and factories and "did not yet believe that women are equal citizens who should have the right to vote." Alluding to the doctrines of George Fitzhugh, a noted theoretician of the slavocracy who argued that chattel slavery represented a humane alternative to unbridled northern capitalism, and to those contemporary defenders of the "southern way of life," Hansberry acidly concludes: "It is a time when we still punish the insane for their madness. It is a time, therefore, when some men can believe and proclaim to the world that this system is the . . . highest form of civilization" (p. 170).

With these interpretative foundations firmly in place, Hansberry then draws viewers into the slave quarters at dinner, and to a family headed by Rissa, a character who, like Lena Younger, is "a woman of late years with an expression of indifference that has already passed resignation." She is the cook, and a trusted figure of some influence in the Big House. The family is awaiting the arrival of Uncle Hannibal, "a lean, vital young man" whose unquenchable appetite for freedom leads him to run off and otherwise tangle with the "marster" (pp. 170, 172).

Sarah, one of the children, is sent out to find him. We are introduced to Hannibal in a clearing where Sarah finds him lying, "arms folded under his head, staring up at the stars with bright commanding eyes" (p. 172). Hannibal's interest in the stars is not merely aesthetic, but another expression of his unrelenting desire for freedom: he is particularly mesmerized by the Big Dipper—"the old Drinkin' Gourd pointin' straight to the North Star . . . Sure is bright tonight," Hannibal confides to Sarah. "Sure would make good travelin' light tonight" (pp. 173–174). Hannibal is the hero of the piece, firmly convinced that "all marsters come from hell" and who thus works diligently to be "the only kind of slave I could stand to be—a *bad* one! . . . Every day that come and hour that pass that I got sense to make a half step do for a whole—every day that I can pretend sickness 'stead of health, to be stupid 'stead of smart, lazy 'stead of quick—I aims [*sic*] to do it. And the more pain it give *your* marster and the more it cost him—the more Hannibal be a man!" (pp. 201, 202; emphasis in original). The conversation between Sarah and Hannibal soon discloses that Hannibal's brother, Isaiah, had escaped when his wife had been sold after just having given birth to a baby boy (pp. 175–176).

From these scenes testifying to the strength of slave family life and the slaves' passion for seeking freedom, Hansberry cuts to the ornate dining room of the Big House. This scene also bears a resemblance to another establishing shot in *Gone with the Wind,* in which Rhett Butler seeks to sober up confederate hotheads drunk with war fever. Hansberry's rendition of this staple scene of Civil War drama introduces Hiram Sweet, the aging and desperately ill patriarch of the Sweet family, surrounded by the equivalent of his court, holding forth at the head of his "well-laden table," counseling reason to his son, Everett (p. 176).

Everett, the quintessence of the temperament driving the South toward secession, is committed to war against northern industrial hegemony and to the preservation of an institution that he believes to be in need of no more than a greater efficiency of method. Blinded by such illusions, Everett foolishly boasts that the confederacy "can have 600,000 men in the field without even feeling it" (pp. 176–177) and win the war in a matter of months, a claim his father tries to counter in the worldly-wise tone he shares with Rhett Butler. Unlike Margaret Mitchell's Butler, however, who rests his case on the manufacturing might of the industrial North, Hansberry's lines for Hiram Sweet go to the nub of the issue: "And may I ask something of you, my son? When *you* and the rest of the white men of the South go off and fight your half of the war, who is going to stay home and guard your slaves? Or are they simply going to stop running away because then, for the first time in history, running away will be so easy?" (p. 178; emphasis in original). The elder Sweet goes on to note that, even in times of relative peace, there are "reward signs up on every other tree in this county" (p. 178).

Hiram Sweet is the best face of an evil institution, an intelligent man whose moral faculty is stunted by the conviction that "other men's rules are a part of my life," (p. 215). He is among the last representatives of a slave economy that, though cruel, was not administered in a systematic and single-mindedly capitalistic fashion. Hansberry writes Sweet as a holdout against the regional trend of turning over plantations to a "pack of overseers" hired to drive slaves beyond their present exhausting nine-and-a-half hour days in the fields (p. 184).

The class to which Hansberry turns last is the poor white sharecropper. In place of the omniscient narrator, Hansberry invents a figure of equal moral authority, a traveling preacher, to act as the conscience of Zeb Dudley, a hardscrabble farmer who clings to a dream of slaveholding and an open frontier as the instruments of his liberation. The preacher presents the classic rationale for a solidarity between the groups most imprisoned by American capitalism—the black slave and the poor white: "Seems to be three things the South sends out more than anything else. A steady stream of cotton, runaway slaves and poor white folks. I guess the last two is pretty much lookin' for the same thing and they both runnin' from the first" (p. 193).

With Hiram Sweet's illness leaving him on the threshold of death, Everett takes the reins of the plantation and begins immediately to implement his more severe regime, hiring Zeb Dudley to serve as a hard-driving overseer. To Dudley's misplaced belief that his collaboration with the slavocracy will bring him within reach of his yeoman's dream, the preacher reminds him of the truth, to no avail: "Them people hate our kind. Ain't I heard 'em laughin' and talkin' 'mongst themselves when they see some poor cracker walkin' down the road—about how Ne-gras was clearly put here to serve their betters but how God must have run clear out of ideas when He got to the poor white! . . . Cotton and slavery has almost ruined our land, 'n' some of us got to hold out 'ginst it. Not go runnin' off to do their biddin' every time they need one of us" (p. 195). This appeal to conscience and to farsighted pragmatism means little to Dudley, whose family has been pressed against the margins of subsistence for generations. Dudley's narrow conception of his political interests, James V. Hatch argues, reflects not Hansberry's low estimate of Dudley and others of his class, but rather her view that "religious precepts without pragmatic economic power were valueless to the poor Southern white."[43]

Dudley takes up his new responsibilities, ordering the slave force out an hour and one-half early and whipping Hannibal across the face—"That's right, for nothin'!"—in a calculated show of force to the rest of the slaves. This flogging, however, does nothing to dissuade Hannibal from running off. Later that day, Hannibal leaves again, this time to meet Everett's younger brother in a clearing, where Hannibal gives a banjo lesson in exchange for learning to read and write. When Everett and Zeb are informed of Hannibal's latest departure from the crew (by a black overseer, not coincidentally named Coffin—recalling Lena and Beneatha Younger's cautions to Walter Lee about being made "dead inside" by an equally mercenary strain of ambition), they head for Hannibal's clearing. There the two men discover the slave committing the greatest breach of the slavocracy; learning to read. What happens next establishes with a shrill finality that the leadership of the Sweet plantation has passed into more callous hands: Everett forces Dudley to blind Hannibal with the butt of his whip. The scene permits Hansberry to bring the key figures together in one scene—Everett, the cowardly savage; Coffin and Dudley, the uncomprehending instruments of Everett Sweet's despotic rule; and Hannibal, the embodiment of the slave-rebel—for one final commentary on the political economy of American slavery:

EVERETT: [*Truly outraged*] You have used your master's own son to commit a crime against your master . . . There is only one thing I have ever heard of that was proper for an "educated" slave. It is like anything else: when a part is corrupted by disease . . . One cuts out the disease—. . .

HANNIBAL: [*Screaming at him, at the height of defiance in the face of hopelessness*] You can't do nothing to me to get out my head what I done learned . . . I kin read! And I kin write! You can beat me and beat me . . . but I kin read . . . [*To Zeb*] I kin read and *you* [original emphasis] can't—

[*Zeb wheels in fury and raises his whip. Everett raises his arm.*]

EVERETT: He has told the truth. [*To Zeb coldly*] As long as he can see, he can read. . .

[*Zeb arrests his arm slowly, looking at Everett with disbelief*]
   You understand me perfectly. Do it now.

[*Astonished and horrified, Zeb looks from the master to the slave. Everett nods at him to proceed and the man opens his mouth to protest.*]
   Proceed.

[*Zeb looks at the master one more time, takes the butt of his whip and advances toward the slave, who comprehends what is to be done to him. Everett turns on his heel away from the scene, and with a long traveling shot, we follow his face as he strides through the woods and as, presently, the tortured screams of an agonized human being surround him . . . Fade out.*] (p. 210)

The Drinking Gourd draws to a close as the shots at Fort Sumter announce the coming of a second American revolution. Alone among his circle, the dying Hiram Sweet understands that the end of slavery has arrived. Of the meaning that this conflict will have for his slaves, Sweet says:

They do not know who or how or why this army is coming. They do not know if it is *for* them or indifferent to them. But they will be with it. They will pour out of the South by the thousands—dirty, ignorant and uncertain about what this whole matter is about. But they will be against *us*. And when those Yankee maniacs up there get up one fine morning feeling heady with abolitionist zeal and military necessity and decide to arm any and every black who comes ambling across Confederate lines . . . it will be all over . . . My time is over. I don't think I want to see that which is coming. I believed in slavery. But I understood it; it never fooled me . . . It's just as well that we die together. (pp. 213–214; emphasis in original)

Hiram Sweet finally meets his death after going to Rissa's cabin to apologize for the blinding of her son, trying feebly to explain that "I had nothing to do with this . . . some things do seem to be out of my hands after all . . . Other men's rules are a part of my life" (p. 215).

The Drinking Gourd's final scene (like the climax of act 2 quoted at length above) brings together in one long frame the elemental forces—personal, ideological, social, economic—that, even in 1960, continued to test the American republic. As Everett and his mother contemplate the straight path to greater prosperity that they believe has been cleared by his father's death, Hansberry guides us past their veranda and through to the "darkened dining room" where Rissa has removed a gun from Hiram's gun cabinet. The camera follows her as she moves "rapidly across the dining room into the dark kitchen and out the back way." She is met by Joshua, the youngest of what remains of her family. She takes his hand as they "half run" to Hannibal's clearing, where they meet Sarah, "poised for traveling, and trembling mightily" and "just beyond her . . . the blind Hannibal." Rissa entrusts the gun to Sarah. "There is a swift embrace," writes Hansberry, "and the woman [Sarah] and the child and the blind man turn and disappear into the woods" (p. 217). Unlike the centennial celebrations appearing in other cultural arenas, Hansberry asks her viewers to see and judge the larger import of the war. The teleplay ends as "Rissa watches after them and the singing of 'The Drinking Gourd' goes on as we pan away from her to the quarters, where the narrator has left us. Only now, his musket leans against the fireplace. Once again the slaves are gone. He walks into the scene . . . He looks at us as he completes the attire of a private of the Grand Army of the Republic." Speaking through the voice of her representation of the American conscience, Hansberry's closing words make clear that the demise of slavery was caused not by a humanitarian awakening on the part of either the North or the South, but by an underlying dialectic of expansion and empire that is both the engine and the substance of history, and that still drives social relations:

> Slavery is beginning to cost this nation a lot. It has become a drag on the great industrial nation we are determined to become; it lags a full century behind the great American notion of one strong federal union which our eighteenth-century founders knew was the only way we could eventually become one of the most powerful nations of this world . . . And now, in the nineteenth-century we are determined to hold on to the dream . . . And so— . . . We must fight; there is no alternative. It is possible that slavery might destroy itself—but it is more possible that it would destroy these United States first. That would cost us our political and economic future. . . . It has already cost us, as a nation, too much of our soul. (p. 217)

Cast in these terms, the Cold War republic of 1960 was not so distant from the slaveholding, industrializing republic of 1861.

Lorraine Hansberry's arrival to the center stage of American culture only four years after the folding of Paul Robeson's publication *Freedom* is evidence of the way in which the struggle for racial equality was once again fast becoming an irrepressible conflict. This time—in the actions of the Montgomery bus boycotters, of the Little Rock Nine, and, shortly, of those participating in the sit-ins of SNCC and the Freedom Rides of CORE—it was to be the most publicly resonant challenge yet to the reactionary Americanism promoted by the House Un-American Activities Committee and McCarthyism. The massive resistance of the political leadership of the South gave a morally indefensible face to right-wing Americanism as well.

In the late 1940s, Ralph Bunche, Jackie Robinson, and A. Philip Randolph had worked strategically against the paranoid, antidemocratic currents that predominated in the political culture of the early Cold War.

Within this context, their accomplishments, including their strategic invocation of Americanism, had been largely symbolic. Still, their contributions provided part of the necessary framework that would support greater progress when the political atmosphere became more favorable to the work of democracy. *A Raisin in the Sun* was among the first signs that a fresh and more open political dialogue was indeed getting under way; within a very few years, the nationally visible activism of the civil rights movement would help to create a public willing not just to rediscover islands of want in a sea of affluence, but to acknowledge the reality of systemically created poverty compounded by racism, as presented in Michael Harrington's *The Other America* and in Kenneth Clark's *Dark Ghetto.*

While it is true that timing is everything, it is also true that people play a part in making their times. Because *A Raisin in the Sun* first entered public awareness before the discourse that made its entry possible had been fully realized, it was rather unimaginatively categorized as a timely turn on the genre of immigrant arrival. Would the arbiters of reputation in the era of *Dark Ghetto* and *The Fire Next Time* have given *Raisin* a fairer first reading than did their counterparts of 1959? As it was, by the mid-1960s, Hansberry's play had come to symbolize the supposedly naive world existing before Birmingham, before the March on Washington, before Selma, and before Watts. Not until the 1980s would *A Raisin in the Sun* and Lorraine Hansberry get the fresh reading they both deserved.

The American public has never been given the opportunity to see *The Drinking Gourd* in its entirety. Despite Dore Schary's best efforts (according to Robert Nemiroff, Schary had secured Henry Fonda's commitment to play the narrator and Laurence Oliver's interest in the role of Hiram Sweet), *The Drinking Gourd* was but one casualty of a decision by all three networks to steer clear of the civil war. Nearly ten years later, portions of the screenplay eventually received a measure of national exposure as part of Robert Nemiroff's stage play and remembrance of Hansberry's life and works, *To Be Young, Gifted and Black.* The script of *The Drinking Gourd* was eventually published in 1972 as part of Nemiroff's compilation, *Lorraine Hansberry: The Collected Last Plays.*

Perhaps the change that most insures that Hansberry's words and name remain within our reach is the rise of black feminism, which embraces her as a pioneering voice and *To Be Young, Gifted and Black* as a foundational text. Black feminists are also bringing to a wider audience Hansberry's early writing on the then-taboo subject of sexuality. Gloria T. Hull and Barbara Smith note that Hansberry, in a 1957 letter penned to *The Ladder,* "a pioneering lesbian periodical," not only attacked the structural sexism of American society, but also came out forcefully against "homosexual persecution" as a practice rooted "not only in social ignorance, but a philosophically active anti-feminist dogma." Writing twenty-five years later, Hull and Smith honor these words as "an amazingly prescient anticipation of current accomplishments of lesbian-feminist political analysis . . . Hansberry was speaking, without knowing it, directly to us."[44] But if Walter Lee's importance to *Raisin* has come to be more firmly established over the years, Jewelle L. Gomez argues convincingly that Walter Lee's younger sister, Beneatha, has yet to be appreciated as a fully developed character, one who conveyed important themes of Hansberry's own radical politics, especially her feminism. Nearly thirty years after her death, Hansberry's work and life are taking on renewed significance, in relationship to a later generation's articulation of black feminism. The regeneration of Hansberry's status as a participant-symbol in current cultural debates is testified to by Gomez, who writes that Hansberry "has lately become an insurgent again . . . She knew that people/women would study the specifics of her life and find the universal truths we needed and that we would claim her."[45] Gomez is also correct in suggesting that Hansberry hoped her ideas would resonate beyond her own life and times.

Lorraine Hansberry conceived herself—and believed it to be within the capacity of every person—to be a "citizen of life." The role of the "citizen of life" was one that demanded "participation in the intellectual affairs of all men, everywhere," in a commitment to confront "the most pressing issues of our time—war and peace, colonialism, capitalism vs. socialism," in search of answers to the great questions "which plague the intellect and the spirit of man."[46] In being true to her own injunction as she worked at finding and developing her voice, Hansberry gathered up and incorporated into her labors a number of different analytical projects from both the past and the present. In her intellectual inquiries, for example, Hansberry worked to return to the center of American discourse the themes and experimental spirit that had animated Ralph Bunche and the Howard intellectuals of the 1930s. In her best-known work, *A Raisin in the Sun,* Hansberry's quest led her to explore territory familiar to Kenneth Clark, another African-American intellectual who, like Hansberry, had first encountered American racism and its social and economic coefficients in the segregated communities of the urban North. In devising a post-Myrdalian representation of the American dilemma that cast this image in starker and more demanding terms, Hansberry, like Clark, argued that in the twentieth century American racism was most powerfully expressed and institutionalized in the "dark ghettos" that segregated African-Americans into economic, social, cultural—and sometimes invisible—colonies.

In the end, Hansberry mapped out the way toward a new consciousness: one that traveled the distance from "American Negro" to "African-American." The experience of American Negroes and Africans with western racism (which originated in the appropriation of Africans for slavery in America) led Hansberry to what she believed to be "the most robust and important . . . conclusion . . . of our time: that the ultimate destiny and aspirations of African people and twenty million American Negroes are inextricably and magnificently bound up together forever."[47] Hansberry believed that only when all Americans, white and black, come to terms with the ways in which slavery, imperialism, and racism divide and particularize the experiences of Western life can they understand and embrace what is fundamentally shared and universal in their common historical experience and future destiny.

Conclusion

They only let . . . one or two of us through at a time, and when that one
person comes through, then he becomes, whether he wills it or not, a representative of his people.

    —Ossie Davis (1972)

In the generation between 1935 and 1965, most Americans—certainly
the almost exclusively white leadership of culture and politics—came to
understand that racial discrimination was inconsistent with the nation's
cherished egalitarian ethos. In the early years of this process, during the
1930s and 1940s, the contrast between the nation's founding principle
that "all men are created equal" and the routine practice of explicit racial
discrimination was often only tentatively and obliquely acknowledged
by the white establishment; the increasing outspokenness on this issue
by some of its members—such as Eleanor Roosevelt and Wendell
Willkie—was widely dismissed as impractical utopianism. The ideological terms of the Second World War and the subsequent Cold War established both the pragmatic and moral necessity that American society
make more explicit and systematic efforts to fight racism at home and
actively encourage an ethic of pluralism and tolerance.

    The process by which American society strove to come to terms with
what Gunnar Myrdal posed as the "American dilemma" has been prob-
lematic, uneven, and at times superficial and illusory. In these pages, I
have examined the contradictory nature of the ascent of racial equality
in postwar American culture by following the public lives of three people
who each came to symbolize a defining moment in its legitimation. The
award of the Nobel Peace Prize to Ralph Bunche, the Supreme Court's
seemingly unequivocal declaration that separate was inherently unequal,
and the debut of Lorraine Hansberry's *A Raisin in the Sun* each served
as a thematic frame within which the hoped-for resolution of racial injustice was set and presented to the American public. As living representatives of the new common meanings celebrated by these scenes,
Ralph Bunche, Kenneth B. Clark, and Lorraine Hansberry each achieved

unusual legitimacy as contributors to the American discourse. If it is true that they were able, by their association with a moment of national moral affirmation, to speak to a public beyond their immediate peers, it is also true that that legitimacy acted as a kind of rapidly hardening concrete in which their lives and reputations became set in the public mind.

The experiences of Bunche and Hansberry especially confirm the burden placed upon the African-American symbol or role model. To a degree that was not true of their white counterparts, the image of each that became known to the public was the one created by what John Rodden calls the "institutional network of production, distribution and reception," the members of which create and constitute the mainstream of a given culture.[1]

Those who learned the basic lessons of human relations from the symbolic representation of Bunche put forward by the media heard very little of Bunche's chosen message. Instead they received a rags-to-riches success story of a man whose world-class achievements allegedly proved the universality of the Alger myth. The significance of this fact lies not in whether Bunche actually was a rags-to-riches success (he was), nor in whether Bunche was resistant to this reading of his experience (he concurred in and at times overtly encouraged it). What is important is that the Alger myth became something that Bunche neither intended nor anticipated: the single prism through which he would be viewed, to the exclusion of the rest of his ideas and public accomplishments. "The Ralph Bunche Story" overwhelmed and nearly completely overshadowed the other ways in which Bunche sought to use the platform built from the public's admiration, namely his efforts to appropriate the symbols and rhetoric of Americanism from anticommunist crusaders in order to legitimate the goal of racial equality. Instead, by choosing to confine Bunche's significance in such simple terms, the authors of "The Ralph Bunche Story" were performing the classic work of the mythmaker, which, as Philip Fisher notes, is the taming of "the variety of historical experience, giving it familiarity while using it to reaffirm the culture's long-standing interpretation of itself."[2]

An even more dramatic example of the way in which the force of the mythmaking process threatens to overtake the authorial voice of its subject is presented in the politics of arrival that surrounded Lorraine Hansberry's play, *A Raisin in the Sun.* The drama critics who established the terms in which Hansberry was raised to the center stage of American culture, and the university-based literary critics who a few years later cleared a small, grudging place for *Raisin* in the literary canon, shared a perception of her script as a fairly traditional text, one smoothly congruent with convention, that extolled the virtues of hardworking, God-fearing people moving purposefully toward entry into the mainstream. Swimming against the currents that bounded her place and time in American culture, however, Hansberry had actually written a drama of unusual thematic ambition and frankly subversive political and social content. So strong, however, was the desire of mainstream critics to make *Raisin* conform to the surrounding cultural landscape that Hansberry's evocation not only of racism, but of working class life as well, was misunderstood, distorted, or altogether ignored. Very quickly after *Raisin*'s premiere, Hansberry sought to arrest the crystallization and hardening of this consensus, although with little success. As gifted a cultural pugilist as she was, Hansberry, like Bunche, was denied her due as a leading citizen of her times. In her lifetime, Hansberry's political unconventionality necessitated that it was her play, and not its author, that would become iconic. It was only during the 1970s and 1980s that Hansberry herself emerged as a symbol, when she came to be widely understood as a model of black feminist activism.

If Bunche and Hansberry were each robbed of their chosen messages, who committed these crimes? The answer lies not merely in conjuring up the image of a self-conscious elite bent on appropriating all discordant movements and voices, but also in recognizing that such acts of appropriation reflect the power of certain of what Raymond Williams characterized as "common meanings."[3] These common meanings are the bedrock of a culture and provide the formative interpretations of collective experience through which we first come to know and understand the world. That a shared culture necessitates that a people hold certain understandings in common does not preclude intense social and cultural conflict. As Warren Susman argues, "cultures can actually be arguments or debates themselves . . . This way of seeing culture as a debate still assumes some measure of common understanding and even common language, as well as separate and special understandings and languages that belong almost singularly to those [competing] groups, classes, factions, and parties."[4] These points of contention often become the intellectual and cultural structures and fault lines around which a society develops. If the arguments as much as the agreements about common meanings and shared values define a culture, the contest between them is seldom between equally matched opponents. The legitimacy and explanatory power that certain common meanings—such as the Alger myth—accrue over time allows them to become so integrated into cultural modes of understanding that challenging their continuing utility and clearing a way past them becomes enormously difficult.

This is especially the case in a period like the 1950s, when public rituals of ideological purification and homogenization—the HUAC hearings, the McCarthy witch-hunt, and the addition of the phrase "In God We Trust" to the national currency—were the order of the day. Seen from the present, the fifties have been too easily stereotyped as a time of prosperity and tranquility. In some ways, and for some people, no doubt they were. But what also cannot be overlooked is the degree to which there existed a general uneasiness about the rest of the world, especially those new nations whose revolutions and programs for nation building did not, in the end, much resemble the American precedent. To the extent that Bunche and Hansberry articulated ideas and issues that pressed for a more constructive engagement with that alien and threatening world, they shared the fate of Ralph Ellison's "invisible man": "I am invisible . . . simply because people refuse to see me . . . It is as though I have been surrounded by mirrors of hard distorting glass. When they approach me they see only my surroundings, themselves or figments of their imagination—indeed, everything and anything except me."[5]

As a heavily credentialed expert in the Myrdal tradition, Kenneth Clark's thoughts would be subjected to less translation by the media than were those of Bunche and Hansberry. As a certified "expert" with recognition and stature derived from within a scientific discipline, Clark enjoyed a greater latitude in choosing the words in which his case was presented to the public. More often than not, when Clark at the peak of his public prestige had something to say to *Time* or *Newsweek,* his own words were directly quoted rather than being summarized or analyzed for the reader. Set against this greater media deference is the fact that the range of Clark's influence and his access to institutions of the mass media expanded and contracted drastically over time. If Clark's invocation of the colonial analogue to describe the "pathology of the ghetto" substantially inoculated him against the invidious revisionism by others that devalued the work of Bunche and Hansberry from the late 1960s through the 1970s, it is equally true that Clark became, in a sense, his own revisionist, concluding that he had been naive to expect that social change could be nurtured by "speaking the truth to power." By 1968, Clark had become convinced that it was impossible to be a psychologist to society because the afflicted patient refused to summon the resources necessary to seek a lasting cure.

Finally, there is the issue of postwar cultural politics. Those who gave themselves to the legitimation of racial equality in the difficult years between the Second World War and the Vietnam conflict were neither unsophisticated in their thinking nor dupes of the establishment center. The work of Bunche, Clark, and Hansberry reflects the continuing relevance and vitality of the social democratic values of the 1930s into the postwar era. Bunche, Clark, and Hansberry each worked to publicly preserve these values during the height of the politically reactionary circumstances of the Cold War.

The oversimplifications and distortions that are an inevitable part of cultural contestation have made this point difficult to see. Kenneth and Mamie Clark, for example, never argued from their doll studies that black children should be taken away from their neighborhoods and cultures in order to be integrated into white suburban schools. Instead, the Clarks fought for alternate arrangements that would both vitalize the schools of the inner city and create educational parks—located neither in the "dark ghetto" nor in the "lily-white" suburbs—where children of different backgrounds could come together on an equal footing, none of them having to travel to the home ground of the other, thus forging a new political reality. Similarly, arguments over whether or not Lorraine Hansberry had experienced the depth of hardship and suffering that was the alleged prerequisite to her portraying the aspirations of the African-American working class overlooked the fact that her father's position in the black community did not insulate her from the structural racism imposed by the white community, especially in the public schools. In addition, such criticism unfairly discounts her strong connection to the African-American left, as well as her years of service on the front lines of the war against the blacklist. The obsession of some with the fact that the Hansberrys were not the Youngers has until recently totally obscured the dimension of the challenge that she sought to place before the public.

Over the years, Americans have come to see the era between the Great Depression and the Great Society not as a cohesive unit of historical experience, but as three separate, even dramatic, indeed convulsive, periods: the Great Depression, the Second World War, and the Cold War. In academic writing as well as in the popular imagination, the Second World War sweeps away virtually everything before it. By the same token, the Cold War obliterates the notion of the United Front and the progressive atmosphere, if not the programs, of the New Deal period.

In coming to terms with the work of the three participant-symbols that are the subject of this book, I have, instead, come to see the years between 1933 and 1965 as a cohesive period in American culture, politics, and social life. What gives this stretch of time a distinctive historical coherence is a culturewide debate that occurred over defining Americanism: what its appropriate principles should be, and who was to be counted as being "in" America and who was to be counted as "out." Mass media—the resurgent black press and the rise of motion pictures, radio, and television—not only made such a national discussion possible, but recreated it in the life of every American to an extent unprecedented in history. Jim Crow was overturned in part because the magnifying power of these media made its reality impossible to deny, much less sustain. Finally, these media created a global village in which human rights and self-determination emerged as irrepressible issues.

In addition, Americans have yet to fully understand the general significance of the civil rights movement as a rejuvenator of American public life after the fall of Joseph McCarthy. The contrast between the quietly heroic Little Rock Nine and the cynical defiance of Governor Faubus and his mob may in the end have done more to knock down the dominoes supporting reactionary Americanism than any other single factor. The ascendance of Martin Luther King, Jr., in the late 1950s and early 1960s as an icon of democratic aspiration, and the activism of SNCC and CORE, forced open public debate and created a constituency for, and a fuller national engagement with, long-deferred issues such as racism and poverty.

Finally, the period from the 1930s through the 1960s witnessed the demise of the idea of experiential universalism in American racial discourse. In the late forties, Jackie Robinson and Ralph Bunche were portrayed in the mainstream media of both races as representing the irrelevance of race: although their lives had been complicated and hardened by the cruel irrationality of prejudice it was assumed that, underneath their skins and underneath the protective armor that they required to survive racism, they like African-Americans in general, had the same aspirations and expectations of life as white Americans. The belief that black and white Americans share a universal experience of life was at the core of Clark's initial embrace of *Brown v. Board*. Within ten years, however, Clark had become convinced that racism was a structurally comprehensive social problem. American racism, in Clark's view, had created an American system of colonial oppression that forced African-Americans to experience the American reality very differently than did others. Hansberry argued that in the realm of political consciousness, Negro Americans shared an experience of oppression and colonialism with Africans that was beyond the understanding of most whites.

Many of those who reconsidered the nation's uneasy progress on race from the vantage point of the late sixties and early seventies tended to devalue Bunche, Clark, and Hansberry because each had allegedly been or had become representative of the failings of a movement and of an era. In contrast, I believe that Bunche, Clark, and Hansberry's negotiations of the cultural politics of race testify both to the practical necessity of such public work and to the iron strength of the cultural forces arrayed around them—ready to appropriate and re-create, sometimes beyond recognition, the ideas that each of these three individuals held dear. Despite these forces, each advanced the conversation, at profound personal sacrifice, in ways that continue to radiate in American culture. It is left to us to be educated but not dispirited by their defeats and miscalculations, and to be respectful of their measured victories in difficult times as we take our place on the line, performing the work of democracy.

Notes

Acknowledgments

Index

Notes

1. Representatives, Representations, and the Cultural Politics of Race

The epigraph is from Richard Wright, *Twelve Million Black Voices: A Folk History of the Negro in the United States* (New York: The Viking Press, 1941), p. 35.

1. King uses the term in *Why We Can't Wait* (New York: New American Library, 1964), p. 141.
2. Ibid., pp. 138–146.
3. Among the works that model and exemplify the study of cultural politics, I found the following especially instructive: Warren I. Susman, *Culture as History: The Transformation of American Society in the Twentieth Century* (New York: Pantheon Books, 1984); Raymond Williams, *Key Words: A Vocabulary of Culture and Society* (New York: Oxford University Press, 1976) and *Resources of Hope: Culture, Democracy, Socialism* (New York: Verso, 1989); Lawrence W. Levine, *Black Culture and Black Consciousness: Afro-American Folk Thought from Slavery to Freedom* (New York: Oxford University Press, 1977) and *Highbrow/Lowbrow: The Emergence of Cultural Hierarchy in America* (Cambridge: Harvard University Press, 1988); George Lipsitz, *Time Passages: Collective Memory and American Popular Culture* (Minneapolis: University of Minnesota Press, 1990); and Herbert G. Gutman, *Power and Culture: Essays on the American Working Class* (New York: Pantheon, 1987). Two recent anthologies that address issues of cultural politics are Lynn Hunt, ed., *The New Cultural History* (Berkeley: University of California Press, 1989) and Richard Wightman Fox and T. J. Jackson Lears, eds., *The Power of Culture: Critical Essays in American History* (Chicago: University of Chicago Press, 1993).
4. Ralph Ellison, "The Myth of the Flawed White Southerner," in *Going to the Territory* (New York: Random House/Vintage, 1986), p. 78.
5. James Baldwin, "Many Thousands Gone," in *Notes of a Native Son* (Boston: Beacon Press, 1984; originally published 1955), pp. 25–26.

6. James Weldon Johnson, *Negro Americans—What Now?* (New York: The Viking Press, 1934), p. 93.

7. On the ways in which cultural representations still deny the reality of African-American individuality, see Jeffrey Prager, "American Political Culture and the Shifting Meaning of Race," *Ethnic and Racial Studies* 10(1987):62–81, and "American Racial Ideology as Collective Representation," *Ethnic and Racial Studies* 5(1982):99–119. For other sensitive discussions of the place of race in contemporary American discourse, see Robert Bellah et al., *Habits of the Heart* (Berkeley: University of California Press, 1986), and Bob Blauner, *Black Lives, White Lives* (Berkeley: University of California Press, 1989).

8. Nicholas Lemann, *The Promised Land: The Great Black Migration and How It Changed America* (New York: Alfred A. Knopf, 1991), p. 7. For an early survey of the African-American migration, see also Carter G. Woodson, *A Century of Negro Migration* (New York: AMS Press, 1970; originally published 1918); Leonard Dinnerstein et al., eds., *Natives and Strangers: Ethnic Groups and the Building of America* (New York: Oxford University Press, 1979); and E. Marvin Goodwin, *Black Migration in America from 1915 to 1960: An Uneasy Exodus* (Lewiston, NY: The Edward Mellen Press, 1990). The most recent research is presented in Joe William Trotter, Jr., ed., *The Great Migration in Historical Perspective: New Dimensions of Race, Class and Gender* (Bloomington: Indiana University Press, 1991).

9. Alain Locke, *The Negro in America* (Chicago: American Library Association, 1933), pp. 34–35. On the Harlem Renaissance and its vast implications for American life, begin with Locke's compilation, *The New Negro: Voices of the Harlem Renaissance* (New York: Albert and Charles Boni, 1926), and the still essential Nathan I. Huggins, *The Harlem Renaissance* (New York: Oxford University Press, 1971). Other helpful and evocative works are David Levering Lewis, *When Harlem Was in Vogue* (New York: Alfred A. Knopf, 1981), and Jervis Anderson, *This Was Harlem* (New York: Farrar, Straus & Giroux, 1982).

10. E. Franklin Frazier, *Negro Youth at the Crossways: Their Personality Development in the Middle States* (New York: Schocken Books, 1971; originally published 1940), pp. 178–179.

11. Levine, *Black Culture and Black Consciousness,* p. 440.

12. See especially Hamilton Cravens, *The Triumph of Evolution: American Scientists and the Heredity-Environment Controversy, 1900–1941* (Philadelphia: University of Pennsylvania Press, 1982). Another survey of this development is Carl N. Degler, *In Search of Human Nature: The Decline and Revival of*

Darwinism in American Social Thought (New York: Oxford University Press, 1991).

13. Richard Weiss, "Ethnicity and Reform: Minorities and the Ambience of the Depression Years," *Journal of American History* 66 (1979): 566–585.

14. Participant-symbols certainly existed in earlier eras, but the slower speed of communication made the interactions between resonant public figures, their symbolizers, and the public more deliberate and static. The drastic foreshortening of all distances that is a by-product of modern communications networks has made this process more immediate, omnipresent, intimate, and complex.

15. As Chapters 4 and 5 make clear, Clark, unlike Bunche and Hansberry, was not an instant icon. Rather, his "arrival," which culminated in the publication of *Dark Ghetto,* took ten years, during which time successively larger and less specialized audiences were introduced to his work. Nonetheless, *Dark Ghetto,* like Gunnar Myrdal's *An American Dilemma,* was informed and framed by the developments discussed above.

16. Theodore G. Vincent, ed., *Voices of a Black Nation: Political Journalism in the Harlem Renaissance* (San Francisco: Ramparts Press, 1973), p. 20.

17. Johnson, *Negro Americans—What Now?,* pp. 31, 27. The most detailed and authoritative account of the black press in the interwar years remains Arnold Buni, *Robert L. Vann of the Pittsburgh Courier: Politics and Black Journalism* (Pittsburgh: University of Pittsburgh Press, 1974). For an excellent survey of the black press from its earliest beginnings to the present, see Clint C. Wilson II, *Black Journalists in Paradox: Historical Perspectives and Present Dilemmas* (New York: Greenwood Press, 1991).

18. See Winthrop Jordan, *White over Black: American Attitudes Toward the Negro, 1550–1812* (Chapel Hill: University of North Carolina Press, 1968); Edmund S. Morgan, *American Slavery, American Freedom* (New York: W. W. Norton, 1975); Gary B. Nash, *Forging Freedom: The Formation of Philadelphia's Black Community, 1720–1840* (Cambridge: Harvard University Press, 1988); Thomas F. Gossett, *Race: The History of an Idea in America* (Dallas: Southern Methodist University Press, 1963); Gary B. Nash and Richard Weiss, eds., *The Great Fear* (New York: Oxford University Press, 1969); George M. Fredrickson, *The Black Image in the White Mind: The Debate on Afro-American Character and Destiny, 1817–1914* (Middletown: Wesleyan University Press, 1987; originally published 1971); Ronald T. Takaki, *Iron Cages* (New York: Oxford University Press, 1979); Reginald Horsman, *Race and Manifest Destiny* (Cambridge: Harvard University Press, 1981); Alexander Saxton, *The Rise and Fall of the White Republic* (New York: Verso Press, 1990); and Joseph Boskin, *Sambo: The Rise and Demise of an American Jester* (New York: Oxford University Press, 1986). Gary Wills

painstakingly reconstructs the Gettysburg Address as a signal contribution to the legitimation of racial equality as an inherently American value in *Lincoln at Gettysburg: The Words that Remade America* (New York: Simon and Schuster, 1992). The representations that govern contemporary racial discourse are powerfully addressed in Bob Blauner, *Black Lives, White Lives* (Berkeley: University of California Press, 1989); Studs Terkel, *Race: How Blacks and Whites Feel about the American Obsession* (New York: The New Press, 1992); and Andrew Hacker, *Two Nations: Black and White, Separate, Hostile, Unequal* (New York: Charles Scribner's Sons, 1992). Hacker presents the most recent statistical survey of the various dimensions of the "American dilemma." Lawrence Levine explores how African-Americans constructed a brilliant, vital, and subversive culture to counter the exclusionary tendencies of the larger national culture in *Black Culture and Black Consciousness.*

19. Henry Louis Gates, Jr., "The Trope of the New Negro and the Reconstruction of the Image of the Black," *Representations* 24 (1988): p. 129. This essay has been reprinted in Philip Fisher, ed., *The New American Studies: Essays from Representations* (Berkeley: University of California Press, 1991).

20. Gunnar Myrdal, *An American Dilemma: The Negro Problem and Modern Democracy,* 2 vols. (New York: Harper & Brothers, 1944), p. 1015.

21. Students of the American discourse on race are fortunate to have two exceptional studies of Myrdal's impact: Walter A. Jackson's *Gunnar Myrdal and America's Conscience: Social Engineering and Racial Liberalism, 1938–1987* (Chapel Hill: University of North Carolina Press, 1990) and David W. Southern's *Gunnar Myrdal and Black-White Relations: The Use and Abuse of "An American Dilemma," 1944–1969* (Baton Rouge: Louisiana State University Press, 1987).

22. Richard B. Gellman, "Ralph Bunche: American Peacemaker," *Colliers,* June 11, 1949, p. 35.

23. Pamphlet announcing Horatio Alger Award, Box 143, Ralph J. Bunche Papers, University of California at Los Angeles, Special Collections (hereafter Bunche Papers), p. 12.

24. Ralph J. Bunche, speech before the League for Industrial Democracy, March 31, 1951 (Box 47, Bunche Papers), pp. 1–2.

25. I am indebted to family member Jane Johnson Taylor for informing me that Ralph Bunche's birth was never officially registered in Detroit. It was misrecorded as 1904 in the family Bible, although his early school records list the correct birthdate of 1903. This error was repeated in all of Bunche's biographical documents.

26. The most reliable source on Bunche's early years is John D. Weaver, "Ralph Bunche: The Early Years," *Westways,* May 1975, pp. 18–23. I am also in-

debted to the late Jane Johnson Taylor, a historian of the family, who shared her research with me.

27. According to Jane Johnson Taylor, Bunche's Aunt Ethel, the author of a family history included in the Bunche papers, believed that these stories—and Bunche himself—had overdramatized the economic plight of the family, an interpretation that was a small bone of contention between the two in later years.

28. Undated (but apparently from 1927) letter to Raymond Buell from Allena Hollwood Hunter (Box 126, Bunche Papers).

29. Ralph J. Bunche, "The Young Negro" (Box 43, Bunche Papers).

30. Ibid., p. 3.

31. Ibid., pp. 7, 4.

32. *California Eagle,* February 2, 1922, p. 8; *California Eagle,* February 25, 1922, p. 8.

33. The UCLA years are covered well in John D. Weaver, "Ralph Bunche: Seasons of Influence," *Westways,* June 1975, pp. 18–23.

34. Ralph J. Bunche, "That Man May Dwell in Peace," p. 4 (Box 43, Bunche Papers); the year is 1926.

35. Ibid.

36. Ibid., p. 6.

37. Ralph J. Bunche, "The Fourth Dimension of Personality," June 1927 (Box 126, Bunche Papers), pp. 4, 3.

38. For details of the community campaign to send Bunche to Harvard, see issues of the *California Eagle* for the summer of 1927.

39. On the wide use of *Dark Ghetto* in American universities, see Richard Kluger, *Simple Justice* (New York: Vintage Books, 1977), p. 315. An instructive overview of the race relations curricula in postwar higher education is provided in Peter I. Rose, *The Subject Is Race* (New York: Oxford University Press, 1968).

40. Letter to the author from Russia Hughes (on behalf of Kenneth Clark), December 11, 1989.

41. Ibid.; Kenneth Clark Oral History, Columbia University Oral History Research Office (hereafter Kenneth Clark Oral History).

42. Robert A. Hill, General Introduction, in *The Marcus Garvey Papers,* vol. 1 (Berkeley: University of California Press, 1983), p. xxxix.

43. For an overview of Jamaican immigration to New York, see Nancy Foner, "The Jamaicans: Race and Ethnicity among Migrants in New York City," in Nancy Foner, ed., *New Immigrants in New York* (New York: Columbia University Press, 1987), pp. 195–217. Of the Jamaican arrival to New York, Foner writes that "the most jarring change was that being black took on a new and more powerful meaning" (p. 202).

44. One of many examples detailed in *The New Amsterdam News* during the 1920s

involves Chandler Owen, co-editor with A. Philip Randolph of *The Messenger*. Owen reportedly accused West Indian immigrants of agreeing to work for absurdly low wages, thus "crowding out" native-born African-Americans. Owen also allegedly asserted that West Indians' facility at "boot-licking," in addition to their disdain for African-Americans, served West Indian immigrants well in their relations with American whites; see *The New Amsterdam News*, February 28, 1923, p. 2.

45. Hill, General Introduction, p. xli.

46. Nat Hentoff, "The Integrationist," *New Yorker*, August 23, 1982, pp. 40–44.

47. Kenneth Clark Oral History, pp. 60–61, 82.

48. Ibid., pp. 71–72; Ralph Bruner, "About Ralph Bunche and Others," interview of June 1973 (Box 4356, Kenneth B. Clark Papers, Library of Congress, Manuscript Division) (hereafter Clark Papers), pp. 2–4.

49. *Howard Hilltop*, May 26, 1933, p. 4.

50. Clark defeated Ulysses Lee by a vote of 252 to 217 (*Howard Hilltop*, May 26, 1933, p. 1).

51. Kenneth Clark, "Sambo's Idea of the Universal Jig-saw," *Howard Hilltop*, February 23, 1934, p. 2. Lawrence Levine's "Hollywood's Washington: Film Images of National Politics during the Great Depression," *Prospects*, 10 (1985): 169–195, suggests that this kind of rhetoric and the concern with fascism and militarism it expressed were central features of the culture of the 1930s; see especially pp. 170–171 and pp. 175–177.

52. On Johnson's successful campaign for federal funding, see Rayford Logan, *Howard University: The First Hundred Years* (New York: New York University Press, 1969), pp. 239–270.

53. Ibid., pp. 278–279; Kluger, *Simple Justice*, pp. 129–131.

54. Kenneth Clark Oral History, pp. 74–75; Kluger, *Simple Justice*, pp. 129–130; Bruner interview, p. 2.

55. Oral history of Mamie Phipps Clark, Columbia University Oral History Research Office, pp. 1–16 (hereafter Mamie Clark Oral History); Mamie Phipps Clark, "Mamie Phipps Clark," in Agnes O'Connell and Nancy Felipe Russo, eds., *Models of Achievement: Reflections of Eminent Women in Psychology* (New York: Columbia University Press, 1983), pp. 267–269. This essay incorrectly lists Phipps's birthplace as Hot Springs, Arizona.

56. "The Hansberrys of Chicago: They Join Business Acumen with Social Vision," *The Crisis* 48 (1941): 106–107.

57. Lorraine Hansberry, *To Be Young, Gifted, and Black*, adapted by Robert Nemiroff (New York: New American Library, 1969), pp. 45, 63.

58. Ibid., pp. 50, 51. On the Hansberry Foundation, see "The Hansberrys of Chicago: They Join Business Acumen with Social Vision," pp. 106–107.

59. "The Hansberrys of Chicago: They Join Business Acumen with Social Vision," pp. 106–107.

60. War Department report to Herbert Hoover on the Hansberry Foundation, September 30, 1943. Declassified and released to the author on April 8, 1991.

61. "Talk of the Town," *New Yorker,* May 9, 1959, p. 34.

62. Ibid.

63. Hansberry, *To Be Young, Gifted, and Black,* p. 45.

64. Ibid., p. 63.

65. James V. Hatch taped interview of Robert Nemiroff, May 7, 1975 (Hatch-Billops Theater Archives, New York City) (hereafter Nemiroff interview).

66. On the activities of Robeson, Du Bois, and others on the black left, see Mark Solomon, "Black Critics of the Cold War and Colonialism," in Thomas G. Patterson, ed., *Cold War Critics: Alternatives to the Cold War in the Truman Era* (Chicago: Quadrangle Books, 1971), pp. 205–239, and especially Gerald Horne, *Black and Red: W. E. B. Du Bois and the Afro-American Response to the Cold War, 1944–1963* (Albany: State University of New York, 1984).

67. Nemiroff interview.

68. Peter J. Kellog, "Northern Liberals and Black America: A History of White Attitudes, 1936–1952," (Ph.D. diss, Northwestern University, 1971), pp. 384–385; the re-representation of Bunche by influential African-American intellectuals and political leaders is detailed in Chapter 3. Cruse's negative assessment of Clark's public contribution (especially, Cruse argues, when compared to the scholarship of E. Franklin Frazier) can be found in his *Plural but Equal: Blacks and Minorities in America's Plural Society* (New York: William Morrow, 1987), pp. 42, 50, 248, 358–359; I quote from p. 358. In *The Crisis of the Negro Intellectual: A Historical Analysis of the Failures of Black Leadership* (New York: Quill, 1984; originally published 1967), Cruse dismisses Clark and James Baldwin as intellectually muddled men who "talked as if all they read about American race problems and liberalism is what they themselves published"; see p. 195. Baraka's recollections are from his essay "A Critical Reevaluation: *A Raisin in the Sun's* Enduring Passion," in Lorraine Hansberry, *"A Raisin in the Sun": Expanded 25th Anniversary Edition and "The Sign in Sidney Brustein's Window"* (New York: New American Library, 1987), pp. 18–19. In the course of his eloquent defense of Hansberry, Baraka refers unfavorably to Bunche on p. 18 as the "spiritual father" of George Murchison, a character in *Raisin* who represents the unimaginative black bourgeoisie.

69. Diana K. Marre, "Traditions and Departures: Lorraine Hansberry and Black Americans in Theater" (Ph.D. diss., University of California at Berkeley, 1987), pp. 2–3. Marre reports that when she interviewed playwright Ed

Bullins, founder of the National Black Theater, in the fall of 1984, he was unfamiliar with any Hansberry play other than *A Raisin in the Sun.* When asked for his opinion of that work, he responded with the comment "I don't write kitchen melodrama."

70. Hank Aaron (with Lonnie Wheeler), *I Had a Hammer: The Hank Aaron Story* (New York: HarperPaperbacks, 1992), p. 309. Beating Babe Ruth's record had many repercussions for Aaron. Among them is that, as Aaron approached Ruth's record, the volume of hate mail addressing Aaron as "Dear Nigger" increased dramatically. Aaron's own acute awareness of the dynamics that come into play in the making of a participant-symbol resulted in his decision, as he approached the record, to become more publicly outspoken on racial issues.

71. Audre Lorde, "Learning from the 60s," *Sister Outsider: Essays and Speeches* (Trumansburg, NY: The Crossing Press, 1984), pp. 136–137.

72. George Lipsitz, "The Struggle for Hegemony," *Journal of American History* 75 (1988): 149.

73. For a cogent discussion of how the civil rights movement became the model for later social movements, see Aldon Morris, "Centuries of Black Protest: Its Significance for America and the World," in Herbert Hill and James E. Jones, Jr., eds., *Race in America: The Struggle for Equality* (Madison: University of Wisconsin Press, 1993).

2. Ralph Bunche and American Racial Discourse

The epigraphs are from W. E. B. Du Bois, *The Correspondence of W. E. B. Du Bois: Volume 1, Selections, 1877–1934,* ed. Herbert Aptheker (Amherst: University of Massachusetts Press, 1973), pp. 353–354; Bunche's letter can also be found in Benjamin Rivlin, ed., *Ralph Bunche: The Man and His Times* (New York: Holmes and Meier, 1990), pp. 217–219.

1. Du Bois's comments before the American Jewish Congress, though not covered in the *New York Times,* appeared in the African-American newspaper of Bunche's hometown, the Los Angeles–based *California Eagle;* see "Dr. Du Bois Criticizes Bunche, UN Negro Mediator in Palestine," December 9, 1948, pp. 1, 5. For a discussion of Du Bois's passionate support of Israel and his surprisingly vitriolic attitude toward Arabs, see Gerald Horne, *Black and Red: W. E. B. Du Bois and the Afro-American Response to the Cold War, 1944–1963* (Albany: State University of New York Press, 1984), pp. 283–284.

2. Letter from Bunche to E. Franklin Frazier, January 29, 1951 (Box 127, Ralph J. Bunche Papers, University of California at Los Angeles, Special Collections) (hereafter Bunche Papers). The "apology" to which Bunche alludes in

the letter is quoted directly on p. 5 of the *California Eagle* article cited in n. 1. Despite Du Bois's attack, Bunche was much sought after as a speaker by the Jewish Anti-Defamation League and other prominent Jewish organizations. For a clear account of Bunche's role in the partition negotiations, see Shabtai Rosenne, "Bunche at Rhodes: Diplomatic Negotiator," in Benjamin Rivlin, ed., *Ralph Bunche: The Man and His Times* (New York: Holmes and Meier, 1990). Rosenne was a member of the Israeli delegation to the 1949 armistice negotiations.

3. James Weldon Johnson, *Negro Americans, What Now?* (New York: The Viking Press, 1934), p. 100.

4. Clifford L. Muse, Jr., "An Educational Stepchild: Howard University during the New Deal, 1933–1945," (Ph.D diss., Howard University, 1989), p. 12; Rayford W. Logan, *Howard University: The First Hundred Years* (New York: New York University Press, 1969), p. 239.

5. Vincent J. Browne, "Ralph Bunche: Teacher and Political Scientist," unpublished paper delivered at "Ralph Bunche: The Man and His Times," conference held at the City University of New York, May 5–6, 1986, p. 2.

6. Letter of recommendation from Alain Locke on behalf of Bunche, Bunche Fellowship File (Reel 1, Rosenwald Foundation Microfilm).

7. W. E. B. Du Bois, *The Souls of Black Folk* (New York: New American Library, 1969; originally published 1903), p. 54.

8. Letter from Bunche to his doctoral committee chair at Harvard, Arthur N. Holcombe, February 28, 1931 (Box 126, Bunche Papers).

9. Holcombe to Bunche, January 17, 1931. Holcombe quotes a letter from Embree to him dated September 15, 1930. In his letter to Holcombe dated February 28, 1931, Bunche reports that Alain Locke and Mordecai Johnson both advised him to drop the project because of probable difficulties in obtaining foundation support for a project involving Brazil. Embree later vehemently denied making the statements attributed to him by Holcombe and, in support of his position, noted the many Brazilian-based studies funded during the period of Bunche's initial application. For these documents and Bunche's other dissertation correspondence, see Box 126 of the Bunche Papers. Frazier's 1944 contribution to this new and soon flourishing comparative genre, "A Comparison of Negro-White Relations in Brazil and the United States," is reprinted in G. Franklin Edwards, ed., *E. Franklin Frazier on Race Relations* (Chicago: University of Chicago Press, 1968), pp. 82–102.

10. Bunche to Embree, April 5, 1931 (Box 126, Bunche Papers).

11. Embree to Bunche, July 1, 1931 (Box 126, Bunche Papers). Twelve years later, Bunche was forced to turn down a $5,000 Rosenwald grant because the Office of Strategic Services was unable to find a replacement for Bunche as

head of its Africa section; see Bunche to Embree, October 25, 1943 (Box 126, Bunche Papers).

12. Bunche to George Arthur, September 28, 1932 (Reel 1, Rosenwald Foundation Microfilm).

13. Bunche to Arthur, October 3, 1932 (Reel 1, Rosenwald Foundation Microfilm).

14. Bunche was less than impressed with the quality of the existing French literature on colonial administration. As he wrote to George Arthur of the Julius Rosenwald Foundation: "The French books on colonial administration (and they are legion!) are rather frothy—highly emotional, spirited, some of them critical, but few of them really based on intelligent, painstaking, detached and scholarly research. My way becomes more clear to me each day—I must primarily devote myself to running down the cold facts and figures and conduct an entirely original analysis of conditions, quite objectively" (Bunche to Arthur, Aug. 16, 1932; Reel 1, Rosenwald Foundation Microfilm).

15. Bunche's dissertation is fully discussed in Rivlin, *Ralph Bunche;* in that volume see especially Nathan Huggins, "Ralph Bunche the Africanist," and Lawrence S. Finkelstein, "Bunche and the Colonial World: From Trusteeship to Decolonization."

16. Ralph J. Bunche, "French Administration in Togoland and Dahomey" (Ph.D. diss., Harvard University, 1934), p. 82.

17. Ibid., pp. 420–421.

18. Ibid., pp. 73, 74.

19. Bunche's field notes are contained in Box 65 of the Bunche Papers. A useful survey of Bunche's work in Africa, from his graduate and postdoctoral studies through his work at the OSS and the State Department, is provided in Robert Harris, "Ralph Bunche and Afro-American Participation in Decolonization," in Robert A. Hill, ed., *Pan-African Biography* (Los Angeles: UCLA African Studies Center / Crossroads Press, 1987).

20. Ralph Bunche, application to the Social Science Research Council, p. 5 (Box 126, Bunche Papers).

21. Ralph Bunche, application for funding of "An Analysis of the Political, Economic and Social Status of the Non-European People in South Africa," p. 6 (Box 126, Bunche Papers).

22. The phrase "unemployed men and women, students and graduates" is from a speaking invitation located in Box 43 of the Bunche Papers; the reference to "Fort Hare students" is Bunche's, and refers to a talk on "group self-confidence and pride" that Bunche presented to them late in 1937 (Box 65, Bunche Papers).

23. Ralph Bunche, "Report on the Needs of the Negro," memorandum prepared

for the Republican Party Program Committee, June 1939 (Box 60, Bunche Papers).

24. Richard Weiss, "Ethnicity and Reform: Minorities and the Ambiance of the Depression Years," *Journal of American History* 66 (1979): 566–568; for a discussion that follows this cultural development from the 1930s to the present, see Philip Gleason, *Speaking of Diversity: Language and Ethnicity in Twentieth Century America* (Baltimore: Johns Hopkins University Press, 1992), especially pp. 91–122 and 153–187. Evidence of concern during this era with questions of national identity is the emergence of phrases such as the "American way of life" and the "American dream"; see Warren I. Susman, *Culture as History: The Transformation of American Society in the Twentieth Century* (New York: Pantheon Books, 1984), pp. 156–158.

25. The progressive possibilities held out for air transport, for example, are discussed in Joseph Corn, *The Winged Gospel: America's Romance with Aviation, 1900–1950* (New York: Oxford University Press, 1983). On the role of radio in establishing an intimate bond between the public and FDR, and the public and world events, see William Stott, *Documentary Expression and Thirties America* (New York: Oxford University Press, 1973), pp. 80–91. The utopian hopes invested in radio are discussed by Susan J. Douglas in "Amateur Operators and American Broadcasting: Shaping the Future of Radio," in Joseph J. Corn, ed., *Imagining Tomorrow: History, Technology, and the American Future* (Cambridge: MIT Press, 1986). Warren I. Susman presents a provocative analysis of the definitive role of movies, radio, and other forms of mass communications in the culture of the thirties in "Culture and Communications," in his *Culture as History.*

26. Robert E. Park, Introduction, in Everett V. Stonequist, *The Marginal Man: A Study in Personality and Culture Conflict* (New York: Russell & Russell, 1961; originally published 1937), p. xiv.

27. Ibid., p. 213.

28. Charles S. Johnson, *The Negro in American Civilization: A Study of Negro Life and Race Relations in Light of Social Research* (London: Constable and Company, 1931), pp. 478, 479.

29. Johnson, *The Negro in American Civilization,* p. 478.

30. Sterling A. Brown, Arthur P. Davis, and Ulysses Lee, eds., *The Negro Caravan* (New York: Arno Press and the New York Times, 1969; originally published 1941 by the Dryden Press), p. 371.

31. Blacks and ethnic immigrants also shared an involuntary membership in what Sterling Brown calls the "comic gallery" of American culture, as the "humorous butts" of American society. (Brown et al., *The Negro Caravan,* p. 3). For an excellent analysis of Brown's work and career, see Joanne V. Gabbin,

Sterling A. Brown: Building the Black Aesthetic Tradition (Westport, CT: Greenwood Press, 1985).

32. Alain Locke, *The Negro and His Music* (Port Washington, NY: Kennikat Press, 1968; originally published 1936 by Associates in Negro Folk Education), pp. 12, 24.

33. Melville J. Herskovits, "The Ancestry of the American Negro," in Frances S. Herskovits, ed., *The New World Negro: Selected Papers in Afro-American Studies* (Bloomington: Indiana University Press, 1966), pp. 121–122.

34. Brown et al., *The Negro Caravan*, p. 3.

35. Abram Harris, *Race, Radicalism, and Reform: Selected Papers* (New Brunswick: Transaction Publishers, 1989), p. 173. Many intellectuals of the early twentieth century who were working toward the eventual transcendence of racism came to that project from within a racialist framework—but one that understood skin color and other supposedly racially derived physical traits to betoken a shared social and historical experience rather than a shared inheritance of an inferior intellectual capacity. Among these thinkers were Robert Park, W. E. B. Du Bois, and Alain Locke, whose definition of race covered not only Negroes and Caucasians, but also subdivisions including the Irish and the various ethnicities of Southern, Eastern, and Central Europe, all of whose cultural inventions were interpreted as reflecting their shared racial identity. Even Bunche, although he eschewed most forms of racialism, carried the imprint of this mode of thought in his judgments of nonwestern groups as culturally, economically, and politically backward. This more elastic genre of thought about race has yet to be fully explored. For an especially provocative and thoughtful critique of this mode of analysis generally, as well as its influence on Du Bois, see Kwame Anthony Appiah, *In My Father's House: Africa in the Philosophy of Culture* (New York: Oxford University Press, 1992), pp. 28–46.

36. Robert E. Park, *Race and Culture* (Glencoe: The Free Press, 1950), p. 116.

37. Nancy J. Weiss, *Farewell to the Party of Lincoln: Black Politics in the Age of FDR* (Princeton: Princeton University Press, 1983), p. 37.

38. On Brown's role in the Writers' Project, see Gabbin, *Sterling A. Brown*, p. 70. Bunche appears to have served as one of several unofficial advisers on this project to Brown; see Brown to Bunche, April 16, 1936 (Box 1, Bunche Papers).

39. Brown et al., *The Negro Caravan*, p. vi.

40. Alain Locke, "Freshman Humanities: Negro Thought and Leadership," lecture notes, p. 3; "Locke Writings," Alain J. Locke Papers, Moreland-Spingarn Research Center, Howard University (hereafter Locke Papers).

41. Alain Locke, "Resume of Talk and Discussion: Alain Locke Sunday After-

noon Session: National Negro Congress," p. 1, "Locke Writings," Locke Papers. This manuscript is undated, but appears to be circa 1935 or 1936.

42. Locke, "Freshman Humanities," p. 2.

43. Alain Locke, "Minority Group Strategy," seminar dated February 17, 1941, p. 2 ("Locke Writings," Locke Papers).

44. Ibid., p. 4.

45. E. Franklin Frazier, *The Negro Family in the United States* (Chicago: University of Chicago, 1939), p. 475.

46. Ralph J. Bunche, "Memorandum on Conceptions and Ideologies of the Negro People," p. 10 (Box 81, Bunche Papers).

47. Ralph J. Bunche, "General Critique of Negro Organizations," p. 1 (Box 80, Bunche Papers).

48. Ralph J. Bunche, "Futility of Racialism in a Period of Social Change," manuscript dated March 24, 1935, p. 11 (Box 43, Bunche Papers).

49. Ralph J. Bunche, "Some Implications of the Economic Status of the Negro for Negro Education," address dated October 27, 1936, given before an audience of the Princeton School of Public and International Affairs (Box 43, Bunche Papers).

50. Ibid., p. 3.

51. Ralph J. Bunche, *A World View of Race* (Washington, DC: Associates in Negro Folk Education, 1936), pp. 67, 11–12.

52. Abram Harris, *Race, Radicalism and Reform,* pp. 198–199, 173.

53. For a brilliantly suggestive discussion of the rationale and the significant successes of "selective buying" campaigns, see Lizabeth Cohen, *Making a New Deal: Industrial Workers in Chicago, 1919–1939* (Cambridge: Cambridge University Press, 1990), pp. 147–155.

54. Abram L. Harris, *The Negro as Capitalist: A Study of Banking and Business among American Negroes* (College Park, MD: McGrath Publishing Co., 1968; originally published 1936 by the American Academy of Political and Social Science), p. 101.

55. Ralph J. Bunche, speech before the Institute of Education dated June 11, 1937 (Box 43, Bunche Papers).

56. Ralph J. Bunche, "Modern Policies of Imperialistic Domination of Subject Peoples," manuscript dated April 5, 1935, p. 6 (Box 43, Bunche Papers). On the subject of African retentions, Frazier used a very similar rhetoric. Africanisms were mere "scraps of memories" forming "an insignificant part of the growing body of traditions in Negro families . . . Probably never before in history has a people been so nearly completely stripped of its social heritage as the Negroes who were brought to America"; see Frazier, *The Negro Family in the United States,* p. 21.

57. Ralph J. Bunche, "The Political Status of the Negro," vol. 4, unpublished manuscript, p. 8 (Box 80, Bunche Papers). Anthony M. Platt, in his fine study *E. Franklin Frazier Reconsidered* (New Brunswick: Rutgers University Press, 1991), discerns a similar pattern of thought in Frazier's work; see especially pp. 126–128.

58. For a detailed discussion of Du Bois's thought prior to the Depression era, see Eric J. Sundquist, *To Wake the Nations: Race in the Making of American Literature* (Cambridge: Harvard University Press, 1993), pp. 457–625.

59. W. E. B. Du Bois, *The Correspondence of W. E. B. Du Bois,* vol. 2, *Selections, 1934–1944,* Herbert Aptheker, ed. (Amherst: University of Massachusetts, 1976), pp. 90, 91.

60. W. E. B. Du Bois, "Social Planning for the Negro, Past and Present," *Journal of Negro Education* 5 (1936): 125. On Du Bois's economic program see also his essay "A Nation within the Nation" in the June 1935 issue of *Current History and Forum,* and especially his intellectual autobiography *Dusk of Dawn* (Millwood: Kraus-Thompson Organization, 1975; originally published 1940), pp. 197–220. On the debate between Du Bois, Bunche, and Harris, see Raymond Wolter's *Negroes and the Great Depression: The Problem of Economic Recovery* (Westport: Greenwood Publishing Corp. 1970), pp. 219–258; James O. Young, *Black Writers of the Thirties* (Baton Rouge: Louisiana State University Press, 1973), pp. 41–63; and John B. Kirby, *Afro-Americans in the Roosevelt Era: Liberalism and Race* (Knoxville: University of Tennessee Press, 1980), pp. 189–197.

61. Ralph J. Bunche, "A Critique of New Deal Social Planning as It Affects Negroes," *Journal of Negro Education* 5 (1936): 60, 59, 61.

62. Ralph J. Bunche, "An Analysis of Contemporary Negro Leadership," speech given at St. Augustine's College, Raleigh, North Carolina, February 8, 1941, p. 6 (Box 43, Bunche Papers).

63. Ralph J. Bunche, comments before the "New Negro Alliance," April 23, 1939 (Box 43, Bunche Papers).

64. "Call to Attend the National Negro Congress," in Joanne Grant, ed., *Black Protest: History, Documents and Analyses, 1619 to the Present* (New York: Fawcett Publications, 1968), p. 242.

65. See John B. Kirby, "Race, Class, and Politics: Ralph Bunche and Black Protest," in Rivlin, *Ralph Bunche,* as well as Kirby, *Afro-Americans in the Roosevelt Era,* pp. 164–168; Martin Bauml Duberman, *Paul Robeson* (New York: Alfred A. Knopf, 1988), pp. 247–248; Mark Naison, *Communists in Harlem during the Great Depression* (Urbana: University of Illinois Press, 1983), pp. 177–182, 294–297; Young, *Black Writers of the Thirties,* pp. 58–61; and Lawrence Wittner, "The National Negro Congress: A Reassessment,"

American Quarterly 22 (1970): 883–901. Generally useful on the personal relationships and issues that characterized the black community in Washington, DC, is Lewis Newton Walker, Jr., "Struggles and Attempts to Establish Branch Autonomy and Hegemony: A History of the District of Columbia Branch of the NAACP" (Ph.D. diss., University of Delaware, 1979), especially pp. 171–173, 177–179, and 186–187.

66. Ralph J. Bunche, "The Role of the University in the Political Orientation of Negro Youth," *Journal of Negro Education* 9 (1940): 573.

67. Ralph J. Bunche, "Education and Minority Group Citizenship," speech at Miner Teacher's College, November 13, 1935 (Box 43, Bunche Papers).

68. Bunche, "The Political Status of the Negro," vol. 4, p. 1549; Judy A. Kutulas, "Toward the Beautiful Tomorrow: Intellectuals on the Left and Stalin's Russia," (Ph.D. diss., University of California at Los Angeles, 1986), p. 127.

69. Ralph J. Bunche, "Democracy and Servitude," undated essay; references to current events suggest that it was written in the spring of 1940 (Box 60, Bunche Papers).

70. Ibid., p. 3.

71. Ralph J. Bunche, "Constructive Suggestions: Extended Memorandum on Tactics," pp. 1–8 (Box 80, Bunche Papers).

72. Untitled remarks by Ralph J. Bunche, March 26, 1940, p. 2 (Box 60, Bunche Papers).

73. Ralph J. Bunche, address before the Association of Negro Colleges and Secondary Schools, December 6, 1940, p. 2 (Box 43, Bunche Papers).

74. Bunche, "Constructive Suggestions: Extended Memorandum on Tactics," p. 15.

75. Ibid., p. 16. Bunche repeated this passage exactly in his speech before the Association of Negro Colleges and Secondary Schools, December 6, 1940, pp. 10–11.

76. Ibid., pp. 10–11.

77. Ibid., p. 12.

78. Ralph J. Bunche, "World Problems of the Negro," speech at the 75th anniversary of Lincoln University, Jefferson City, MO, February 18, 1941, p. 19 (Box 43, Bunche Papers).

79. Ralph J. Bunche, "The Next Decade in American Foreign Policy," April 1, 1941 (Box 60, Bunche Papers).

80. Bunche, address before the Association of Negro Colleges and Secondary Schools, December 6, 1940, p. 17.

81. Bunche, "The Role of the Negro University in the Political Orientation of Negro Youth," p. 573.

82. Bunche, "World Problems of the Negro," p. 3.
83. Myrdal called Bunche his "coordinator of information" in a letter to him dated May 5, 1942 (Box 81, Bunche Papers).
84. Ralph J. Bunche, "The Political Status of the Negro," pp. 13, 21 (Box 80, Bunche Papers).
85. Ibid., p. 21.
86. Ibid., pp. 21–22.
87. On this point, see also Walter A. Jackson, *Gunnar Myrdal and America's Conscience: Social Engineering and Racial Liberalism, 1938–1987* (Chapel Hill: University of North Carolina Press, 1990), p. 129.
88. Gunnar Myrdal Oral History, Carnegie Foundation Oral History, p. 97 (Columbia University Oral History Research Office). On the Bunche-Myrdal relationship, see also Jackson, *Gunnar Myrdal and America's Conscience,* pp. 121–134.
89. Myrdal, *An American Dilemma,* pp. 4, 831.
90. Bunche, Preface to "Political Status of the Negro," p. 2. On the writing of *Dilemma,* see Jackson, *Gunnar Myrdal and America's Conscience,* pp. 88–134 and 161–173, and especially David Southern, *Gunnar Myrdal and Black-White Relations: The Use and Abuse of "An American Dilemma," 1944–1969* (Baton Rouge: Louisiana State University Press, 1987), pp. 29–48.
91. Donald Young Oral History, Carnegie Foundation Oral History, p. 56 (Columbia University Oral History Research Office).
92. Myrdal to Bunche, January 14, 1942 (Box 81, Bunche Papers).
93. Ralph Ellison was one of the few reviewers who objected to Myrdal's "running battle with Marxism" in the text, and in particular to Myrdal's dismissal of the more class-based analyses promoted by Bunche and others. Ellison's unpublished essay, originally written for the *Antioch Review,* is included in Ellison's *Shadow and Act* (New York: Random House, 1964), pp. 303–317.
94. This memo from Roy Wilkins to Walter White, dated March 12, 1941, was forwarded to Myrdal (Box 81, Bunche Papers).
95. Myrdal to Bunche, May 5, 1942 (Box 81, Bunche Papers).
96. Ernest W. Burgess, "Social Planning and Race Relations," in Jitsuichi Masouka and Preston Valien, eds., *Race Relations: Problems and Theory, Essays in Honor of Robert E. Park* (Chapel Hill: University of North Carolina Press, 1961), p. 21. An excellent discussion of Myrdal's place in the contemporary discourse on race is contained in Alexander Saxton, *The Rise and Fall of the White Republic: Class Politics and Mass Culture in Nineteenth Century America* (New York: Verso, 1990), pp. 1–18.
97. Alain Locke, "The Unfinished Business of Democracy," *Survey Graphic,* November 1942, pp. 455–456. On Locke's importance to the study, see Jackson,

Gunnar Myrdal and America's Conscience, pp. 112, 131; and Southern, *Gunnar Myrdal and Black-White Relations,* p. 21. Locke's correspondence confirms that Myrdal met with Locke on numerous occasions to discuss the project. In recognition of his intellectual debt to Locke, Myrdal wrote Locke to request an autographed photo "for inclusion in a corner [of my office] reserved for colleagues as well as friends who have influenced my work"; Myrdal to Locke, August 21, 1947 (Locke Papers).

98. Wendell L. Willkie, *One World* (New York: Simon and Schuster, 1943), pp. 187–195.

99. Carey McWilliams, *Brothers under the Skin,* rev. ed. (Boston: Little, Brown, 1951), p. 11. On Willkie's evolution into an icon of internationalism, see John Morton Blum, *V was for Victory: Politics and American Culture during World War II* (New York: Harcourt Brace Jovanovich, 1976), pp. 262–279; Robert Dallek, *The American Style of Foreign Policy* (New York: New American Library, 1983), pp. 128–130; and the essays by Harvard Sitkoff, Howard Jones, and A. S. Manykin in James H. Madison, ed., *Wendell Willkie: Hoosier Internationalist* (Bloomington: University of Indiana Press, 1992).

100. Clayton R. Koppes and Gregory D. Black, *Hollywood Goes to War: How Politics, Profits and Propaganda Shaped World War II Movies* (Berkeley: University of California Press, 1990), pp. 319–323.

101. Richard Dailfume, "The Forgotten Years of the Negro Revolution," *Journal of American History* 60(1968):90–106.

102. The Mydral book was also backed by an effective public relations campaign. See Jackson, *Gunnar Myrdal and America's Conscience,* pp. 242–263; and Southern, *Gunnar Myrdal and Black-White Relations,* pp. 71–125.

103. Gunnar Myrdal, *An American Dilemma: The Negro Problem and Modern Democracy,* 2 vols. (New York: Harper Brothers, 1944), p.xliii.

104. Memo to Conyers Read, February 6, 1942 (Box 73, Bunche Papers). This memo also mentions the use of the Phelpes-Stokes Foundation.

105. Robert Harris, "Ralph Bunche and Afro-American Participation in Decolonization," in Robert A. Hill, ed., *Pan-African Biography,* (Los Angeles: UCLA African Studies Center/Crossroads Press, 1987), p. 128.

106. Lawrence S. Finkelstein, "Bunche and the Colonial World: From Trusteeship to Decolonization," in Rivlin, *Ralph Bunche,* p. 117.

107. Bunche, with Robert Weaver and others, had an official advisory role in the establishment of the Fair Employment Practices Commission (FEPC); a memo to Conyers Read, dated December 28, 1941, discusses an early conclave with Weaver, Attorney General Biddle, and others (Box 73, Bunche Papers). Bunche also offered advice on how to handle the delicate racial situation that existed between Britons and African-American servicemen sta-

tioned in Great Britain. Bunche recommended that a series of highly visible lectures on race be undertaken in Britain, utilizing American experts of both races; he also advocated that a free and open discussion between both governments about racial friction be held. Although Bunche did furnish advice on domestic race relations to the Office of War Information, he resisted many other efforts—including an appointment as Assistant Secretary of Labor—to involve him in this topic, one he felt was outside his chosen area of expertise; see Bunche memo to Edward Dale of the OWI, dated September 30, 1942, and a Bunche memo to Conyers Read, dated December 31, 1942 (both Box 73, Bunche Papers).

108. In July 1941, only a few months before Bunche's transfer to the OSS, he wrote to Lewis Hanke that, upon completion of his work for Myrdal, he would apply for a foundation grant "which would make possible a trip of several months to Brazil and several other Latin American countries, where I would devote myself particularly to the political status of the nonwhite elements in their population. I have a wealth of data on this subject for most other important areas of the world as a result of previous trips in Africa and the Orient. I hope some day to be able to continue the collection of data with a view toward publishing a broad comparative analysis"; Bunche to Hanke, July 3, 1941 (Reel 1, Rosenwald Foundation Microfilm).

109. Edwin Embree to Bunche, April 29, 1943 (Reel 1, Rosenwald Papers).

110. On Bunche's burdens at the OSS, see Bunche to Edwin Embree, October 25, 1943 (Reel 1, Rosenwald Foundation Microfilm). Bunche was awarded a Rosenwald Fellowship of $5,000 in 1943 for the Far East project, but Bunche's OSS and State Department duties prevented him from using it, and the fellowship was withdrawn the following year.

111. Embree to Bunche, May 12, 1943 (Reel 1, Rosenwald Papers, and Fisk University Library Special Collections).

112. Bunche, "The Role of the Negro University in the Political Orientation of Negro Youth," p. 573.

3. Ralph Bunche and the Cultural Politics of Race

The epigraphs are from Mary McLeod Bethune, column in the *New York Age,* October 3, 1953, preserved in Box 190 of the Bunche Papers; and Martin Luther King, Jr., *Why We Can't Wait* (New York: New American Library, 1964), p. 31.

1. Samuel I. Rosenman, ed., *The Public Papers and Addresses of Franklin D. Roosevelt, 1944–45* (New York: Harper Brothers, 1950), p. 524.

2. Editorial by Bruce Hutchinson, *Ottawa Evening Citizen,* May 29, 1951 (Box

195, Ralph J. Bunche Papers, University of California at Los Angeles, Special Collections; hereafter Bunche Papers).

3. Eleanor Roosevelt's papers testify to the existence of a warm personal and intellectual friendship with Bunche. These two icons of progressive internationalism traveled in the same professional circles, sharing not only the January 1950 *Ebony* cover, but the dais at many events on behalf of the UN as well. Bunche was also an occasional guest on Mrs. Roosevelt's public affairs programs during the 1950s and 1960s. The citation is from *Ebony,* May 1947, p. 6.

4. That Bunche was a role model of democratic possibility to both black and white Americans is seen first by Andrew Young's recollection that "I really did have the UN in the back of my mind for a long time. That's because of Ralph Bunche. He was the first black man in public life that I identified with as a kid" (interview of Andrew Young by Peter Ross Range, "Playboy Interview: Andrew Young," *Playboy,* March 1977, p. 70), and second by the request of twenty-five-year-old Robert F. Kennedy, then a student at the University of Virginia Law School, for an autographed portrait of the Nobel laureate (see Box 6, Bunche Papers).

5. Henry F. and Katherine Pringle, "The Man Who Stops Fights," *Saturday Evening Post,* August 13, 1949, p. 25. In an ironic coincidence, the treaty that Bunche successfully negotiated between Israel and Egypt was taken, in the aftermath of the Los Angeles riots forty-three years later, as the model of a treaty preserving a truce between Los Angeles gangs; see Jesse Katz and Andrea Ford, "Ex–Gang Members Look to Mideast for a Peace Plan," *Los Angeles Times,* June 17, 1992, p. B-1. It seems, however, that Bunche's involvement in the negotiation of the earlier treaty played no role in its selection by ex–gang members. In a separate interview with the author, Andrea Ford confirmed that Ralph Bunche was never mentioned as an influence by those involved in writing the Los Angeles treaty.

6. Charles E. Silberman, *Crisis in Black and White* (New York: Random House, 1964), p. 52.

7. E. Franklin Frazier, *The Black Bourgeoisie: The Rise of a New Middle Class* (New York: The Free Press, 1957), p. 190.

8. Michael Harrington, *The Other America: Poverty in the United States* (New York: Penguin Books, 1981; originally published 1967 by Macmillan), p. 82.

9. Andrew Young, in Peter Ross Range, "Playboy Interview: Andrew Young," *Playboy,* March 1977, p. 70.

10. For the definitive treatment of Jackie Robinson's experience, see Jules Tygiel, *Baseball's Great Experiment: Jackie Robinson and His Legacy* (New York: Oxford University Press, 1983). An evocative incident of how Robinson (and

his Brooklyn Dodgers) stood for all outsiders in the late forties is provided by Joel Oppenheimer in Jonathan Kaufman, *Broken Alliance: The Turbulent Times between Blacks and Jews in America* (New York: New American Library, 1989): "We had heard about all the great black ball players and how they weren't allowed to play, and for me Jackie was all of those guys rolled into one, and he was going to lead my Dodgers to glory . . . During the game Jackie made a good play in the field, at which point everyone was yelling, 'Jackie, Jackie, Jackie,' and I was yelling with them. And suddenly I realized that behind me someone was yelling, 'Yonkel, Yonkel, Yonkel,' which is Yiddish for Jackie. With great wonderment and pleasure, I realized that here was this little Jewish tailor . . . the only white face in a crowd of blacks, aside from me, and he's yelling, 'Yonkel, Yonkel, Yonkel.' It was a very moving moment" (pp. 82–83).

11. Photo essay, "Two Great Americans," *The Instructor,* February 1951, p. 27. Another instance of this pairing occurs in a column by Mary McLeod Bethune in *The Baltimore African-American,* in which she designated both Bunche and Robinson as "the outstanding Americans of 1947" (Box 190, Bunche Papers). Bethune lauds Bunche for exemplifying "the triumph of peaceful preparation and acknowledged merit over racial barriers" and Robinson for driving "a dramatic wedge in a long-standing racial barrier, which warmed the hearts of people all over the world." Examples of Bunche's image as a man of "Negro cosmopolitanism and intellect" include an *Ebony* poll of prominent black women to discover "Negro America's most exciting men"; the June 1949 issue describes Bunche as an "inspiring personality with oodles of charm and sophistication" (p. 50). Bunche's stature is also confirmed by a poll of some three hundred thousand Pittsburgh-area college students, which established Bunche as that year's recipient of radio station WWRL's Collegiate Forum of the Air Collegiate Peace Award, according to *The Pittsburgh Courier,* March 5, 1949 (Box 190, Bunche Papers).

12. The President's Commission on Civil Rights, *To Secure These Rights: The Report of the President's Commission on Civil Rights* (Washington: U.S. Government Printing Office, 1947), pp. 100–101.

13. Wallace, according to John Morton Blum, was Wendell Willkie's opposite number, a "Democratic heretic" whose own visionary rhetoric would not wear well during the Cold War; see Blum, *V was for Victory: Politics and American Culture during World War II* (San Diego: Harcourt Brace Jovanovich, 1976), pp. 279–292. See also John Morton Blum, ed., *The Price of Vision: The Diary of Henry A. Wallace* (Boston: Houghton Mifflin, 1973). Among other New Deal liberals who placed great faith in the UN as an agent of international order and reform were Eleanor Roosevelt, Adlai Stevenson, Chester Bowles,

Hubert Humphrey, Dean Rusk, and J. William Fulbright. The division between Fulbright and Rusk over Vietnam has obscured the degree to which their careers were both devoted to the common goal of strengthening the UN so that it might live up to the aspirations that its most idealistic advocates held for it.

14. Arnold Rose and Caroline Rose, *America Divided: Minority Group Relations in the United States* (New York: Alfred A. Knopf, 1948), p. 328.

15. Former Secretary of State Dean Rusk discusses this dimension of American public diplomacy at length in his memoir, *As I Saw It* (New York: W. W. Norton & Co., 1990), pp. 579–592.

16. U.S. Senate, *Hearings before the Armed Services Committee,* 80th Cong., 2nd sess., March 31, 1948, p. 687.

17. *Chicago Defender,* February 11, 1950; *Collier's,* June 10, 1950, p. 86.

18. Philip B. Gellman, "Ralph Bunche: American Peacemaker," *Collier's,* June 11, 1949, p. 14.

19. "Radio Broadcast," dated July 4th (no year) (Box 44, Bunche Papers).

20. *The Pittsburgh Courier,* June 4, 1949.

21. The definitive biography of Robeson is Martin Bauml Duberman, *Paul Robeson* (New York: Alfred A. Knopf, 1988).

22. Victor S. Navasky, *Naming Names* (New York: The Viking Press, 1980), p. 194. Navasky discusses the effect of the blacklist on Robeson, Jackie Robinson, Canada Lee, Langston Hughes, Lena Horne, Joshua Daniel White, and Harry Belafonte on pp. 186–194; on Robeson, see also David Caute, *The Great Fear: The Anti-Communist Purge under Truman and Eisenhower* (New York: Simon and Schuster, 1978), pp. 164–166, 247–248.

23. Navasky, *Naming Names,* p. 194.

24. The statement was reported in the April 4, 1949, *New York Times* and can also be found in Philip S. Foner, ed., *Paul Robeson Speaks: Writings, Speeches, Interviews, 1918–1974* (New York: Brunner Mazel Publishers, 1978), p. 537.

25. Bunche to Harding Bancroft (Box 129, Bunche Papers).

26. Gellman, "American Peacemaker," p. 33. Although Navasky does not discuss Bunche in the section of *Naming Names* addressing the relationship of African-Americans to the blacklist, the evidence he presents supports the conclusion that Bunche's comments fit within a format widely used by African-Americans when called upon to respond to Robeson's political statements. According to Martin Duberman, Robeson was "never more than marginally acquainted" with Bunche, although they remained on cordial terms throughout the fifties (Duberman, *Paul Robeson,* pp. 651, 745–746).

27. Quoted in Paul Robeson, *Here I Stand* (New York: Othello Associates, 1958), p. 37.

28. Ibid., p. 36.

29. *New York Herald Tribune,* July 19, 1949.

30. *New York World Telegram,* October 3, 1950.

31. Bunche diary, entry dated January 9, 1954 (Bunche Papers).

32. While Bunche and others among his colleagues in the UN secretariat publicly protested the intervention of the McCarran Committee in UN hiring practices, their words cannot obscure the fact that the UN's first Secretary General, Trygve Lie, cooperated enthusiastically in rooting out "subversives" on behalf of the U.S. government; see Caute, *The Great Fear,* pp. 325–338, and Shirley Hazzard, *Countenance of Truth: The United Nations and the Waldheim Case* (New York: Viking Press, 1990), especially pp. 19–36. On Bunche's own loyalty hearings, see Caute, *The Great Fear,* pp. 43, 128–129. For the case against Bunche's loyalty, see Harold Lord Varney, "Who and What Is Ralph Bunche?" *American Mercury,* May 1956, pp. 29–35. Bunche is portrayed in the Varney article as an opportunist whose "major talent has always been . . . [an] intuitive gift for picking the 'winning side,' and for making himself conspicuously useful to those who are promoting it." For a thorough discussion of how political discourse on racial issues was systematically narrowed and constricted during the Cold War, see Gerald Horne, *Black and Red: W. E. B. Du Bois and the Afro-American Response to the Cold War, 1944–1963* (Albany: State University of New York Press, 1986).

33. Bunche diary, entry dated March 28, 1954 (Bunche Papers).

34. "Now Ralph Bunche," *The Nation,* June 5, 1954, pp. 474–475.

35. Carey McWilliams, *Brothers under the Skin,* rev. ed. (Boston: Little, Brown, 1951), p. 4.

36. Charles S. Johnson, *Into the Main Stream: A Survey of the Best Practices in Race Relations in the South* (Chapel Hill: University of North Carolina Press, 1947), p. 3.

37. Lee Nichols, *Breakthrough on the Color Front* (New York: Random House, 1954), p. 8; the standard academic history is Richard M. Dailfume, *Desegregation of the Armed Forces: Fighting on Two Fronts, 1939–1953* (Columbia: University of Missouri Press, 1969).

38. Rachel Davis Du Bois, *Neighbors in Action: A Manual for Local Leadership in Intergroup Relations* (New York: Harper Brothers, 1950), pp. x, 104, 3. The most influential postwar guide toward "helping children . . . learn to live democratically" (p. xi) was Helen G. Trager and Marian Radke Yarrow's summary of the work of the Philadelphia Early Childhood Project, *They Learn What They Live* (New York: Harper Brothers, 1952).

39. R. M. McIver, *The More Perfect Union: A Program for the Control of Inter-group Discrimination in the United States* (New York: The Macmillan Company, 1948), p. 188.

40. Du Bois, *Neighbors in Action,* p. 104.

41. Lloyd and Elaine Cook, *Intergroup Education* (New York: McGraw-Hill Book Company, 1954), p. 169.

42. Ruth Benedict and Mildred Ellis, *Race and Cultural Relations: America's Answer to the Myth of a Master Race* (Washington, DC: National Association of Secondary School Principals/National Council for the Social Studies [Departments of the National Education Association], 1942), p. 50.

43. Ibid., p. 52.

44. *Current Events,* May 14–18, 1951, p. 259.

45. Walter Loban, Dorothy Holmstrom, and Luella B. Cook, eds., *Adventures in Appreciation* (New York: Harcourt Brace, 1958). This piece stresses the universality of American principles and makes virtually no mention of race. The essay was exported throughout Europe and the Middle East by the Department of State (Box 60, Bunche Papers).

46. "Ralph J. Bunche," *CTA Journal,* October 1955, p. 12.

47. Leonard S. Kenworthy, *Twelve Citizens of the World* (Garden City: Doubleday & Co., 1953), p. 9.

48. Ibid., pp. 23, 25, 33; quote on pp. 33–34.

49. United Nations Radio, "Citizen of the World: Ralph Bunche," p. 14 (Box 127, Bunche Papers).

50. "The Successful Diplomat," script prepared by the UCLA Theater Arts Department for Los Angeles City Schools, p. 16 (Box 127, Bunche Papers).

51. Bill McDade, "Ralph Bunche: Peacemaker," *Senior Scholastic,* May 23, 1951, p. 15.

52. Ralph Chapman, "Meet Ralph Bunche," *Senior Scholastic,* February 20, 1952, p. 4. Bunche was a symbol of how to cultivate an international sensibility for adults as well. His views are among those solicited by *House and Garden,* for example, for the article "Education of an American" in the August 1953 issue. His words appear side by side with those of three other postwar symbols of progressive cosmopolitanism, Eleanor Roosevelt, Bernard Baruch, and Robert Hutchins. See also Lynn Baron's interview with Bunche in the January 1961 issue of *Seventeen.*

53. "Toward Tomorrow: The Ralph Bunche–Lucy Johnson Story" (Box 127, Bunche Papers).

54. Herbert G. Gutman, "Historical Consciousness in Contemporary America," in his *Power and Culture: Essays on the American Working Class* (New York: Pantheon Books, 1987), p. 401.

55. Irwin Ross, "Ralph Bunche, Mediator," *Reader's Digest,* March 1950, pp. 147–148.

56. Ibid.

57. Homer Metz, "He Made Peace in Palestine," *New Republic,* May 30, 1949, p. 9.

58. Ibid. See also Sam Pope Brewer, "Palestine Solvent," *New York Times Magazine,* November 14, 1948, p. 25.

59. Thomas J. Hamilton, "Peacemaker Extraordinary," *Americas,* November 1950, p. 15.

60. "Tribute to Greatness," p. 1 (Box 127, Bunche Papers).

61. Ralph Bunche, "The Best Advice I Ever Had," *Reader's Digest,* April 1955, p. 133.

62. Ralph J. Bunche, "The Barriers of Race Can Be Surmounted," *Vital Speeches,* July 1, 1949, p. 572.

63. Ibid., pp. 572–573.

64. Ibid., p. 573.

65. Ibid., p. 574.

66. Ralph J. Bunche, speech at Tougaloo College, October 23, 1963, p. 4 (Box 56, Bunche Papers).

67. Furthermore, during this period, according to his friend and Harvard roommate Robert C. Weaver, Bunche became convinced that the New Deal—in particular the Wagner Act and the Social Security Act—was indeed more genuinely social democratic than he had originally believed. Interview by the author with Robert Weaver, New York City, March 26, 1990.

68. Comments at the Sinai Temple, Michigan City, Indiana, January 22, 1956, pp. 29, 28(Box 52, Bunche Papers). These lines were repeated in several of Bunche's commencement speeches for 1956.

69. Rayford Logan, diary, January 28, 1951 (Rayford Logan Papers, Library of Congress).

70. Ralph J. Bunche, Walgreen Foundation Lecture no. 5, pp. 21, 22 (Box 46, Bunche Papers).

71. Ibid, p. 22.

72. Ralph J. Bunche, Remarks at Armstrong High School, Washington D. C., pp. 1, 3, 6 (Box 44, Bunche Papers).

73. Ibid, pp. 6, 9, 12, 20.

74. Ralph J. Bunche, Remarks before the 45th Annual Convention of the NAACP, Dallas, Texas, July 14, 1954 (Box 50, Bunche Papers).

75. Ralph J. Bunche, Remarks at the 10th Anniversary of Northside, May 17th, 1956 (Box 52, Bunche Papers).

76. Ralph J. Bunche, Speech at Roosevelt College, p. 5-A (Box 48, Bunche Papers).

77. Ralph J. Bunche, Remarks at Spingarn Ceremony, July 17, 1949, pp. 3–4 (Box 45, Bunche Papers).

78. Martin Luther King, Jr., *Why We Can't Wait* (New York: New American Library, 1964), p. 31.

79. Ibid.

80. Brewer, "Palestine Solvent," p. 24.

81. Iman Benjamin Karim, ed., *The End of White World Supremacy: Four Speeches by Malcolm X* (New York: Arcade Publishing, 1971), pp. 27, 28.

82. Nathan Hare, "Brainwashing of Black Men's Minds," in Amiri Baraka, ed., *Black Fire: An Anthology of Afro-American Writing* (New York: William Morrow and Co., 1968), p. 183.

83. Peter J. Kellog, "Northern Liberals and Black America: A History of White Attitudes," (Ph.D. diss., Northwestern University, 1971), pp. 384–385.

84. *Prospects for Mankind,* Program 6: "Africa: Revolution in Haste," p. 1. Recorded March 6, 1960, at WGBH and broadcast throughout the country beginning March 14, 1960 (Box 1, Henry Morgenthau III Papers, Franklin Delano Roosevelt Library). The other guests on the program were Julius Nyerere (president of Tanzania), Barbara Ward (noted author on issues related to economic and political development in the so-called Third World), and Saville Davis (managing editor of the *Christian Science Monitor*).

85. Ibid., pp. 6, 14.

86. Bruce Perry, ed., *Malcolm X: The Last Speeches* (New York: Pathfinder Press, 1989), p. 95.

87. Ibid., p. 128.

88. Ibid., p. 32.

89. Bunche, Remarks at Spingarn Ceremony, p. 4. By 1963, Bunche was publicly speaking out against the Muslim "fantasy of separation," which he understood to be "simply a new version of the Garveyites of the thirties" (see p. 6 of the Bunche speech "Race in World Perspective," delivered at Texas Christian University, May 6, 1963; Box 56, Bunche Papers). In a speech before the Houston Council on Human Relations on March 25, 1964, Bunche lumped Malcolm X and Adam Clayton Powell together as cynical racial demagogues (Box 56, Bunche Papers); speaking before the Southern Conference on Human Welfare, Bunche reiterated this view, arguing that "we have the White Citizens' Council on the one hand, and the Black Muslims, Malcolm X, and Adam Clayton Powell on the other" (comments reported in the *Daily Texan,* March 25, 1964, p. 1; see Box 56, Bunche Papers).

90. Ralph J. Bunche, Remarks at Roosevelt College, March 29, 1952, p. 6 (Box 48, Bunche Papers).
91. James H. Cone, *Martin and Malcolm and America: A Dream or a Nightmare?* (Maryknoll, NY: Orbis Books, 1991), pp. 197–198.
92. George Breitman, ed., *Malcolm X Speaks* (New York: Pathfinder Press, 1989), p. 26.
93. William Brink and Louis Harris, *The Negro Revolution in America* (New York: Simon and Schuster, 1964), p. 123.
94. Jackie Robinson and Alfred Duckett, *I Never Had It Made* (New York: G. P. Putnam's Sons, 1972), p. 12.

4. Kenneth B. Clark and the Cultural Politics of the *Brown* Decision

The epigraphs are from Leon Friedman, ed., *Argument: The Oral Argument before the Supreme Court in* Brown v. Board of Education of Topeka, *1952–1955* (New York: Chelsea House Publishers, 1969), p. 330 (this passage became the most quoted section of *Brown,* and the final sentence has become a signature phrase in American political discourse); and Kenneth B. Clark, *Prejudice and Your Child* (Middlebury, CT: Wesleyan University Press, 1988; originally published 1955 by Beacon Press), p. 130.

1. E. Franklin Frazier, *Negro Youth at the Crossways: Their Personality Development in the Middle States* (New York: Schocken Books, 1967; originally published 1940), p. 91.
2. Leon Friedman, ed., *Argument: The Oral Argument before the Supreme Court in* Brown v. Board of Education of Topeka, *1952–1955* (New York: Chelsea House Publishers, 1969), p. 329.
3. Otto Klineberg, "SPSSI and Race Relations, in the 1950s and After," *Journal of Social Issues* 42 (1986): 54.
4. On Howard, see Chapters 1 and 2.
5. Richard Kluger, *Simple Justice* (New York: Random House/ Vintage, 1977), pp. 315–345, 353–356; see also Ralph Bruner, "Ralph Bunche and Some Others . . .," interview with Clark, June 1973, p. 7 (Box 4336, Kenneth B. Clark Papers, Library of Congress, Manuscript Division) (hereafter Clark Papers), and Kenneth Clark Oral History, Columbia University Oral History Research Office), pp. 111–113.
6. The description of this public is Myrdal's; see Gunnar Myrdal, *Challenge to Affluence* (New York: Pantheon, 1963), p. 50. After the war, Myrdal and his wife, Alva, like many other progressive social scientists, devoted considerable energy to achieving social change through the United Nations, UNESCO in

particular. American social scientists connected with UNESCO programs against prejudice included sociologist E. Franklin Frazier, philosopher Alain Locke, social psychologists Otto Klineberg, Gordon Allport, and Lois and Gardner Murphy, and historian Rayford Logan.

7. C. Vann Woodward, *Thinking Back: The Perils of Writing History* (Baton Rouge: Louisiana State University Press, 1986), p. 82.

8. Ibid., pp. 90–92.

9. C. Vann Woodward, "Equality: The Deferred Commitment," in *The Burden of Southern History* (Baton Rouge: Louisiana State University Press, 1960; originally published 1958 in *The American Scholar*), p. 86; C. Vann Woodward, "Young Jim Crow," *The Nation*, July 7, 1956, p. 10. For a full discussion of Woodward's scholarship, the debates it fostered, and his ambivalence about the popularity of *Strange Career*—as well as the other professional burdens and problems that intellectual celebrity brought him—see John Herbert Roper, *C. Vann Woodward: Southerner* (Athens: University of Georgia Press, 1987), especially pp. 194–196, 232–235, and 249–250. John Hope Franklin recalls the contribution of historians to answering key questions raised by the court in "The Historian and the Public Policy" in his collection *Race and History: Selected Essays, 1938–1988* (Baton Rouge: Louisiana State University Press, 1989), pp. 309–320. For a more wide-ranging discussion of the contributions of historians as consultants and activists in American politics and public policy, see William E. Leuchtenburg, "The Historian and the Public Realm," *American Historical Review* 97 (1992): 1–18.

10. The dilemmas now posed were, as Myrdal himself acknowledged, northern and urban; they were most urgently symbolized for Myrdal by the creation of an "under-class of unemployed and, gradually, unemployable and under-employed persons and families," including both black and white Americans; see Myrdal, *Challenge to Affluence*, p. 34. On African-Americans, see pp. 26, 44–45, and 163–172.

11. Gunnar Myrdal, Foreword, in Kenneth Clark, *Dark Ghetto: Dilemmas of Social Power* (New York: Harper & Row, 1965), pp. x–xi.

12. Clark, "Introduction to an Epilogue," in *Dark Ghetto*, p. xxiv.

13. Clark, "Introduction," *Dark Ghetto*, pp. x–xii.

14. David Maraniss, "Icon of Integration and the Durability of Racism," *Washington Post*, March 5, 1990.

15. For an elaboration of these issues in regard to Clark's image as a public social scientist, see Chapter 5.

16. Richard I. Evans, *The Making of Social Psychology: Discussions with Creative Contributors* (New York: Gardner Press, 1980), p. 65.

17. Gardner Murphy, "The Research Task of Social Psychology," in "Bulletin of

the Society for the Psychological Study of Social Issues," *Journal of Social Psychology* 10 (1939): 119.

18. Ruth Benedict, *Patterns of Culture* (Boston: Houghton Mifflin, 1934), pp. 2–3.

19. Frazier, *Negro Youth at the Crossways,* p. 275.

20. Kurt Lewin, "Environmental Forces," in Carl Murchison, ed., *A Handbook of Child Psychology,* rev. 2nd ed. (Worcester, MA: Clark University Press, 1933), p. 613.

21. Elizabeth Lomax, "The Laura Spelman Rockefeller Memorial: Some of its Contributions to Early Research in Child Development," *Journal of the History of the Behavioral Sciences* 13 (1977): 284.

22. See Morton Deutsch, "Field Theory in Social Psychology," in Gardner Lindzey, ed., *Handbook of Social Psychology* (Cambridge: Addison-Wesley, 1954), pp. 181–222. For an appreciation of Kurt Lewin's contribution to the study of prejudice by a leading figure in SPSSI, see Gordon W. Allport, "The Genius of Kurt Lewin," in Allport's *The Person in Psychology: Selected Essays by Gordon W. Allport* (Boston: Beacon Press, 1968), pp. 361–370.

23. Lawrence K. Frank, "Projective Methods for the Study of Personality," *Journal of Psychology* 8 (1939): 402–403. My understanding of progressive psychologists during this era owes much to Katherine Ann Pandora, "Dissenting Science: Psychologists' Democratic Critique during the Depression Era" (Ph.D. diss, University of California at San Diego, 1993).

24. Ruth Horowitz, "The Development of Attitudes toward the Negro," *Archives of Psychology* (1936), no. 1944; Ruth Horowitz, "Racial Aspects of Self-Identification in Nursery School Children," *Journal of Psychology* 7 (1939): 91–99.

25. Mamie K. Phipps Clark, "An Investigation of the Development of Consciousness of Distinctive Self in Pre-School Children," unpublished master's thesis, Howard University, May 12, 1939.

26. Kenneth B. Clark and Mamie P. Clark, "The Development of Consciousness of Self and the Emergence of Racial Identification in Negro Pre-School Children," *Journal of Social Psychology* 10 (1939): 591–599; Kenneth B. Clark and Mamie P. Clark, "Segregation as a Factor in Racial Identification of Negro Pre-School Children," *Journal of Experimental Education* 8 (1939): 161–163; Kenneth B. Clark and Mamie P. Clark, "Skin Color as a Factor in Racial Identification of Negro Pre-School Children," *Journal of Social Psychology* 11 (1940): 159–169.

27. Kenneth B. Clark, "Some Factors Influencing the Remembering of Prose Material," *Archives of Psychology,* no. 253 (July 1940), R. S. Woodworth, ed.

28. Mamie P. Clark, "Changes in Primary Mental Abilities with Age," *Archives*

of Psychology, no. 291 (May 1944), R. S. Woodworth, ed. Of the 320 children tested, 6 were black.

29. Nor was the status of social psychology, the still-emerging subfield in which their doll studies fell, firmly established in the larger discipline. Social psychology, although well represented in the literature of psychology, would lack a firm institutional footing within the discipline until the postwar era.

30. Kenneth B. Clark and Mamie P. Clark, "Racial Identification and Preference in Negro Children," in Theodore M. Newcomb and Eugene L. Hartley, eds., *Readings in Social Psychology* (New York: Henry Holt, 1947), p. 602.

31. Ibid., p. 604.

32. Ibid., pp. 603–611; quote on p. 611. Another segment of the Rosenwald studies was a "coloring" test administered to 160 Negro children aged five through seven. The children were given crayons and line drawings and told to first color the figure "the color that you are" and then to color the figure "the color you like little girls or boys to be." The results followed a pattern similar to that of the doll tests. A significant number—ranging from 63 percent among five-year-olds to 35 percent among seven-year-olds—rejected the brown color in the preference tests. See Kenneth B. Clark and Mamie P. Clark, "Emotional Factors in the Racial Identification and Preferences in Negro Children," *Journal of Negro Education* 19 (1950): 341–350.

33. Benedict, *Patterns of Culture,* p. 3.

34. Horowitz, "Racial Aspects of Racial Self-identification," p. 91.

35. For Lewin's career before his exile see Mel Van Elteren and Helmut E. Luck, "Kurt Lewin's Films and Their Role in the Development of Field Theory," in Susan A. Whelan, Emmy A. Pepitone, and Vicky Abt, eds., *Advances in Field Theory* (Newbury Park: Sage Publications, 1990), pp. 39–61.

36. Kurt Lewin, Ronald Lippitt, and Ralph K. White, "Patterns of Aggressive Behavior in Experimentally Created 'Social Climates,' " *Journal of Social Psychology,* 10 (1939): 277; see also Jean Matter Mandler and George Mandler, "The Diaspora of Experimental Psychology: The Gestaltists and Others," in Donald Fleming and Bernard Bailyn, eds., *The Intellectual Migration: Europe and America, 1930–1960* (Cambridge: Harvard University Press, 1969), pp. 399–405.

37. T. W. Adorno, E. Frenkel-Brunswik, D. J. Levenson, and R. N. Sanford, *The Authoritarian Personality* (New York: Harpers, 1950), p. 971. For a detailed discussion of these thinkers see Martin Jay, *The Dialectical Imagination: A History of the Frankfurt School and the Institute of Social Research, 1923–1950* (Cambridge: Harvard University Press, 1984).

38. Kenneth B. Clark, "The Implications of Adlerian Theory for the Understanding of Civil Rights Problems and Action," *Journal of Individual Psy-*

chology 23 (1967): 181–189. My appreciation for Adler as a significant figure in American culture between the wars owes much to Richard Weiss's "Early American Uses of Adlerian Psychology," unpublished paper delivered at the conference of the International Society of Political Psychologists, Tel Aviv, Israel, June 18–22, 1989.

39. Kenneth B. Clark, "Morale among Negroes," in Goodwin Watson, ed., *Civilian Morale* (Boston: Houghton Mifflin, 1943), p. 228.

40. Allison Davis and John Dollard, *Children of Bondage: The Personality Development of Negro Youth in the Urban South* (Washington, DC: American Council on Education, 1940), p. 247.

41. Ibid., p. 245.

42. E. Franklin Frazier, *The Black Bourgeoisie: The Rise of a New Middle-Class* (New York: Free Press, 1965; originally published 1957), pp. 130–131.

43. U.S. Department of Labor, Office of Policy Planning and Research, *The Negro Family: The Case for National Action,* March 1965 (Ann Arbor: University Microfilms, 1982).

44. Abram Kardiner and Lionel Ovesey, *The Mark of Oppression: Explorations in the Personality of the American Negro* (New York: World Publishing Co., 1951), pp. 39–41.

45. Stanley M. Elkins, *Slavery: A Problem in American Institutional and Intellectual Life,* 2nd ed. (Chicago: University of Chicago Press, 1968); originally published 1959). For a thorough review and critique of Elkins's use of psychological and psychoanalytic theory to describe the personality of the African-American in slavery, see Kenneth M. Stampp, "Rebels and Sambos: The Search for the Negro's Personality in Slavery," *Journal of Southern History* 37 (1971): 367–392.

46. Kenneth B. Clark and James Barker, "The Zoot Effect in Personality: A Race Riot Participant," *Journal of Abnormal and Social Psychology* 40 (1945): 147.

47. Ibid., p. 143.

48. Ibid.

49. Ibid., p. 148. See also Clark's earlier informal survey of Harlem public opinion about the riot, "Group Violence: A Preliminary Study of the Attitudinal Pattern of Its Acceptance and Rejection: A Study of the 1943 Harlem Riot," *Journal of Social Psychology,* 19 (1944): 319–337, in which he makes a similar argument.

50. Kenneth B. Clark, "Candor about Negro-Jewish Relations," *Commentary,* February 1946, pp. 11–12.

51. Ibid. The black press insured that Clark's comments would reach well beyond the readership of *Commentary:* in a short sketch of the Clarks in its issue of

March 2, 1946, the *Chicago Defender* endorsed the article as "must reading for any understanding of American brotherhood," and the Clarks as "nice folks." The *Pittsburgh Courier* carried extensive excerpts from the article in its issue of March 23, 1946 (clippings from the fellowship files of Kenneth and Mamie Clark, Reel 1, Rosenwald Foundation Microfilm, Reel 1).

52. Kenneth B. Clark, "Summary: Effect of Prejudice and Discrimination on Personality Development of Children," pp. 1–2 (Box 350B, Clark Papers). This box contains a typescript of Clark's text, with handwritten revisions. Originally completed for presentation to the Mid-Century White House Conference on Children and Youth, the findings are only generally summarized in the conference proceedings. No copies of the report were found among the papers of the Justices relating to *Brown,* which are preserved in the manuscript division of the Library of Congress.

53. Ibid., p. 3.

54. Kenneth B. Clark, "How to Protect Children against Prejudice," *Child Study,* Spring 1951, p. 9.

55. Ibid., p. 11.

56. Kenneth B. Clark, "Race Prejudice in Children," *The Child,* March 1953, p. 113.

57. "To All on Equal Terms," *Time,* May 24, 1954, p. 21.

58. "Historic Decision," *Newsweek,* May 24, 1954, p. 26. "A Historic Decision for Equality," *Life,* May 31, 1954, p. 11.

59. Carey McWilliams, "Climax of an Era," *The Nation,* May 29, 1954, p. 453. *The Nation*'s coverage of the issues relating to *Brown* was extensive, far more so than that of the similarly progressive *New Republic. The Nation* carried one article that mentioned the expert testimony of Jerome Bruner of Harvard in the litigation leading to *Brown* (Horace Bond and Morton Puner, "The Battle for Free Schools: Jim Crow in Education," *The Nation,* November 24, 1951, pp. 446–449); see also the unsigned editorial "Human Rights Are Now," which endorsed Judge J. Waties Waring's dissent at the circuit court level, July 14, 1951, pp. 24–25. Less than a month after *Brown, The Nation* carried an article devoted entirely to the psychological implications of segregation by Frederic Wertham, a noted psychoanalyst and the founder of the La Fargue Clinic, "the first psychiatric clinic established in the Harlem district." Wertham had been asked by the NAACP to examine both black and white children, and to testify about the psychiatric consequences of segregation (Frederick Wertham, "Nine Men Speak to You: Jim Crow in the North," *The Nation,* June 12, 1954, pp. 497–499).

60. Norman Cousins, "The New Ordeal," *Saturday Review,* February 26, 1956, p. 25.

61. Only *Newsweek*, among the national news weeklies, reported the insertion of psychological evidence into the series of cases grouped under *Brown*. In the issue of June 11, 1951, *Newsweek* reported: "Monday and Tuesday of last week, the NAACP presented 'expert' witnesses, to prove that segregation was psychologically damaging to both white and Negro children. Through segregation, 'we build into the Negro the very characteristics which we then use to justify prejudices,' said David Krech, visiting associate professor of psychology at Harvard" (p. 30).

62. As *Brown* passed significant anniversaries, the role of social science was given greater attention. The tenth anniversary of *Brown* was commemorated by two journalistic surveys of *Brown* and the social and political confrontations it had caused: Anthony Lewis, *Portrait of a Decade: The Second American Revolution* (New York: Random House, 1964); and Benjamin Muse, *Ten Years of Prelude* (New York: The Viking Press, 1964). In honor of the fifteenth anniversary of *Brown*, the full oral arguments were published as Friedman, *Argument*, which included an essay by Clark entitled "Social Scientists, the *Brown* Decision, and Contemporary Confusion," pp. xxxi–l. See also Friedman's *Civil Rights Reader* (New York: Walker and Co., 1968), which includes Clark's "The Effects of Segregation and the Consequences of Desegregation: A Social Science Statement," pp. 154–163; the decision itself was also reprinted in Joanne Grant, ed., *Black Protest: History, Documents, and Analyses, 1619 to the Present* (New York: Fawcett Publications, 1968), pp. 261–268. The definitive account of *Brown* remains Richard Kluger, *Simple Justice: The History of* Brown v. Board of Education *and Black America's Struggle for Equality* (New York: Random House, 1975), published with the passing of *Brown*'s twentieth birthday. Marking its thirtieth is Raymond Wolters, *The Burden of Brown: Thirty Years of School Desegregation* (Knoxville: University of Tennessee Press, 1984), which argues that desegregation decisions after 1968 went significantly—and Wolters believes deleteriously—beyond *Brown*'s call for desegregation to efforts to achieve integration through measures (such as busing) to achieve a statistical racial balance. Such measures, Wolters contends, did nothing to raise the level of academic achievement among African-Americans. In fact, Wolters finds that the level of funding devoted to predominantly African-American schools has not risen appreciably since that before *Brown*. The *Brown* case has also been the subject of two dramatic treatments. Loften Mitchell wrote a three-act play on the genesis of the South Carolina litigation entitled *Land beyond the River* (Cody: Pioneer Drama Service, 1963). That text focused upon the role of the Reverend Dr. Joseph A. Delaine in mobilizing Clarendon County African-Americans behind a legal action to obtain bus transportation for children residing in rural

areas. Envisioned originally as a one-act piece to raise funds for the African-American community in Clarendon, Mitchell, with the active encouragement of Ossie Davis, expanded *Beyond the River* into a three-act play. The play opened at the Greenwich Mews Theater in New York City in March 1957 to enthusiastic reviews and ran for a year. For a plot summary and critique of *Beyond the River,* see C. W. E. Bigsby, "Three Black Playwrights: Loften Mitchell, Ossie Davis, Douglas Turner Ward," in C. W. E. Bigsby, ed., *The Black American Writer,* vol. 2 (DeLand, FL: Everett / Edwards, 1969), pp. 138–144. One generation later, in 1991, the ABC television network presented a dramatization of the NAACP's legal fight in Clarendon under the title *Separate but Equal,* which included a dramatization of Kenneth Clark administering the doll test, and then testifying in the *Briggs* case. Clark's participation in *Brown* was also prominently featured in the PBS docudrama *Simple Justice,* which aired in January 1993.

63. Lewis, *Portrait of a Decade,* p. 30.

64. "Segregation Was Doomed before the Court Acted," *Saturday Evening Post,* June 19, 1954, p. 10.

65. Dumas Malone and Basil Rauch, *Empire for Liberty,* vol. 2 (New York: Appleton-Century-Crofts, 1960), p. 840.

66. Samuel Eliot Morison and Henry Steele Commager, *The Growth of the American Republic,* 5th ed. (New York: Oxford University Press, 1962), p. 968. The fourth edition had been published in 1950. The decision itself was reprinted in the sixth, seventh, and eighth editions of Commager's companion volume, *Documents of American History* (New York: Appleton-Century-Crofts, 1958), pp. 799–802.

67. Henry Banford Parkes, *The United States of America: A History,* 2nd rev. ed. (New York: Alfred A. Knopf, 1959), p. 733.

68. Richard Hofstadter, William Miller, and Daniel Aaron, *The American Republic,* vol. 2 (Englewood Cliffs, NJ: Prentice-Hall, 1959), pp. 659–663.

69. The essay is contained in Carl Degler, *Out of Our Past: The Forces that Shaped Modern America* (New York: Harper Brothers, 1959), pp. 208–237.

70. John Garraty, ed., *Quarrels that Have Shaped the Constitution* (New York: Harper and Row, 1964), p. 243. Garraty's words introduce an essay by Alfred H. Kelly, "The School Desegregation Case," pp. 243–268. For a discussion of the role of social scientists in the case, including that of Clark, see pp. 258–259.

71. Kenneth Clark, *Prejudice and Your Child* (Middlebury, CT: Wesleyan University Press, 1988; originally published 1955 by Beacon Press), p. 12.

72. Kenneth B. Clark, "A Struggle for Complete Human Dignity," *The Christian Register,* July 1956, p. 11. For a specific discussion of the experience of the

other communities, see "Desegregation: An Appraisal of the Evidence," *Journal of Social Issues* 9 (1953): 1–77.

73. Clark, "Struggle," p. 11.
74. Ibid., p. 37.
75. Ibid.
76. Benjamin Spock, *The Common Sense Book of Baby and Child Care* (New York: Duel, Sloan and Pierce, 1946). See also the paperback editions published by Pocket Books in 1951, 1957, 1960, and 1968. Spock's first published advice on prejudice was a twenty-four-page pamphlet, "Prejudice in Children: A Conversation with Dr. Spock" (New York: Anti-Defamation League of the B'nai B'rith, 1963). His most extensive discussion of race prejudice is included in *Raising Children in a Difficult Time: A Philosophy of Parental Leadership and High Ideals* (New York: W. W. Norton and Co., 1974), pp. 103–114. Spock introduces that discussion with a brief summary of the findings of the Clark doll studies: "Children are affected by prejudice in various ways. Psychological studies have shown that by four or five years of age, black children in America become convinced that they are inferior people because of the color of their skin . . . Black children become prejudiced against themselves at the start of life, by accepting the white man's prejudice against them" (p. 103).
77. Clark, *Prejudice and Your Child*, p. 13.
78. Ibid., p. 28.
79. Ibid., pp. 28, 50.
80. Ibid., pp. 7–8.
81. John Kenneth Galbraith, *The Affluent Society* (Boston: Houghton Mifflin Co., 1958), p. 5.
82. David Riesman, *The Lonely Crowd: A Study of the Changing American Character* (New Haven: Yale University Press, 1950), p. 286; William H. Whyte, Jr., *The Organization Man* (Garden City: Doubleday and Co., 1956), pp. 339–341.
83. Whyte, *The Organization Man*, p. 338.
84. Ibid., p. 353.
85. Daniel Bell, *The End of Ideology: On the Exhaustion of Political Ideas in the Fifties* (New York: The Free Press, 1960), p. 103.
86. Vance Packard, *The Status Seekers: An Exploration of Class Behavior in America and the Hidden Barriers that Affect You, Your Community, Your Future* (New York: David McKay Co., 1959), p. 7. The best-known historical exposition of status anxiety as a force in American society is Richard Hofstadter's *Age of Reform: From Bryan to FDR* (New York: Random House/ Vintage, 1955); see especially pp. 33–38 and 148–173. David M. Potter, in

People of Plenty: Economic Abundance and the American Character (Chicago: University of Chicago Press, 1954), was more optimistic about the future of status politics in American society and less concerned than Riesman over the alleged problem of "other-directedness." Potter held out the prospect that "the fulfillment of abundance . . . opens the way for a more beneficent form of status which would emphasize the concepts of membership . . . identity . . . of place in the community, and would minimize the hierarchical aspects, as, indeed the new abundance has already minimized them by diminishing the physical differences in standards of dress, of diet, of housing, and of recreation among the various elements in society" (p. 105). For another influential essay on the cultural consequences of "skipping the feudal stage of history," see Louis Hartz, *The Liberal Tradition in America* (San Diego: Harcourt Brace Jovanovich, 1955).

87. Clark, *Prejudice and Your Child,* pp. 73–74.

88. Ibid.

89. From 1955 through early 1963, *Prejudice and Your Child* sold just 1,428 copies (letter to the author from Miriam Levinson of Beacon Press, October 23, 1991).

90. Gordon W. Allport, *The Nature of Prejudice* (Garden City: Doubleday, 1958; originally published 1954 by Addison-Wesley). Allport was a former president of SPSSI and of the American Psychological Association as well as a past chairman of Harvard University's Department of Psychology. Allport was also one of the founders in the United States of the subfield of personality psychology; see his highly regarded *Personality: A Psychological Interpretation* (New York: Holt, 1937).

91. Bruno Bettelheim, "Discrimination and Science," *Commentary,* March 1956, p. 384.

92. Ibid., p. 385.

93. Ibid., p. 384.

94. Ibid., p. 385.

95. Ibid., p. 386.

96. Whyte, *The Organization Man,* pp. 33, 32.

97. Robert Coles's *Children of Crisis: A Study of Courage and Fear* (Boston: Little, Brown, 1967), a pioneering effort to use psychoanalytic techniques to understand the motivations of the opposing forces in the southern struggle over school integration, exemplifies this point. Although Clark did not answer Bettelheim himself at length, his response to critics of his research and of his role in the *Brown* case is contained in "The Desegregation Cases: Criticism of the Social Scientist's Role," an appendix to the 1988 Wesleyan University Press edition of *Prejudice and Your Child,* pp. 185–206.

98. The phrase belongs to Taylor Branch; see his *Parting the Waters: America in the King Years, 1954–1963* (New York: Simon and Schuster, 1989), p. 809.

99. Mary Harrington Hall, "A Conversation with Kenneth B. Clark," *Psychology Today,* June 1968, p. 19.

100. Theodore H. White, "Action-Intellectuals: The Idea Men of American Politics," *Life,* June 9, 1967, p. 52. Parts 2 and 3 appeared in the issues of June 16 and June 23, 1967.

101. Clark, *Prejudice and Your Child,* p. 134.

102. Clark chaired the Sub-Commission on Educational Standards and Curriculum. His public charges that New York City schools were severely segregated preceded the conclusion of the *Brown* case (see the *New York Times,* April 25, 1954, p. 84). On the Board of Education's response to *Brown,* see the *New York Times,* July 14, 1954, p. 1, and July 15, p. 23. On the Commission's work, see the *New York Times,* May 18, 1956, p. 27.

103. Diane Ravitch, *The Great School Wars* (New York: Basic Books, 1974), p. 252; for an excellent explanation of why integration was politically impossible to achieve in New York City, see pp. 251–378.

104. Kenneth Clark and Hylan Lewis, "Report to the Unitarian Service Committee," May 15, 1956, pp. 3–4 (Kenneth Clark, personal papers).

105. Ibid., p. 5.

106. The text of Clark's introduction of King, and King's own remarks that evening, have been reprinted in the January 12, 1981, issue of the MIT student newspaper, *Tech Talk,* p. 2.

107. Kenneth B. Clark, "Observations on Little Rock," *New South,* June 1958, p. 8.

108. Hall, "A Conversation with Kenneth B. Clark," p. 21.

109. For a sampling of the optimism that was felt about the prospect of desegregation in the years immediately following *Brown,* especially among the experts, see the essays by Oscar Handlin, George B. Tindall, C. Vann Woodward, and Roy Wilkins in the May 1957 issue of *Current History.*

5. Kenneth B. Clark and Great Society Reform

The epigraphs are from "Light on the Ghetto," *Newsweek,* May 31, 1965, p. 79; and Kenneth B. Clark, "The Dilemma of Power," in Kenneth B. Clark and Talcott Parsons, eds., *The Negro American* (Boston: Houghton Mifflin, 1966), p. xi.

1. William Brink and Louis Harris, *The Negro Revolution in America* (New York: Simon and Schuster, 1964), p. 20; for a similar account of public

opinion see Samuel Lubell, *White and Black: Test of a Nation* (New York: Harper and Row, 1964). Lubell's discussion of the dangers of the race issue to the Democratic Party in the North—a danger forestalled somewhat by the Kennedy assassination—is incisive and highly prescient; see pp. 7–10, 120–152, 172–174.

2. Kenneth B. Clark, "A Relevant Celebration of the Emancipation Proclamation," *Ebony*, September 1963, pp. 24, 23.

3. Kenneth B. Clark, "A Challenge to Desegregation," speech delivered to a meeting of the National Urban League, Grand Rapids, Michigan, September 5, 1962, pp. 2–3 (Box 89, Kenneth B. Clark Papers, Library of Congress, Manuscript Division) (hereafter Clark Papers).

4. Charles E. Silberman, *Crisis in Black and White* (New York: Random House, 1964), pp. 7–8.

5. Ibid., pp. 19–20, 41–45, 165–166. Silberman relies heavily on Nathan Glazer and Daniel P. Moynihan's *Beyond the Melting Pot* (Cambridge: MIT Press, 1963), pp. 24–85. Silberman sets up Oscar Handlin's *The Newcomers* (Cambridge: Harvard University Press, 1959), one of the last books to argue that African-Americans were following the same pattern of adjustment set by previous immigrants from Europe, as his principal intellectual foil. Silberman, however, significantly overstates the degree of Handlin's optimism about both the present and the future trend of developments. Handlin's optimism that African-Americans would follow other immigrants into the middle class was conditioned on his very cautiously held hope that prejudice would decline significantly in the coming decade (see pp. 42–59, 68–92, 103–104).

6. James Reston, "Education and Integration," in James Reston, *Sketches in the Sand* (New York: Alfred A. Knopf, 1967), p. 164. This piece originally ran in the *New York Times* on May 15, 1964.

7. "Outgrowing the Ghetto Mind," *Ebony*, August 1963, p. 98; reprinted in Alan F. Westin, ed., *Freedom Now!* (New York: Basic Books, 1964), pp. 26–29.

8. See Kenneth B. Clark, "The Social Programs of the Kennedy and Johnson Administrations," paper delivered at the Lyndon Baines Johnson Library, Austin, Texas, September 13, 1976 (Files of Kenneth B. Clark and Associates, Hastings-on-Hudson, New York) (hereafter Clark and Associates); Kenneth B. Clark Oral History, Columbia University Oral History Research Office (hereafter Kenneth Clark Oral History), pp. 259–260. James Booker's political column, "Uptown, Low-down Political Pot," *New Amsterdam News*, August 10, 1963, p. 9, announces the prospect of Clark's involvement in foreign service recruitment and speculates that the State Department's interest is in direct response to the new wave of activism on civil rights. After his retirement from teaching in 1976, Clark founded Kenneth Clark and Associates, a con-

sulting firm advising government agencies and corporations on the recruitment of minorities.

9. For the most detailed account of this meeting see Taylor Branch, *Parting the Waters: America in the King Years, 1954–1963* (New York: Simon and Schuster/Touchstone, 1989), pp. 809–813; see also Nicholas Lemann, *The Promised Land: The Great Migration and How It Changed America* (New York: Alfred A. Knopf, 1991), pp. 126–127.

10. Clark interview with Jean Stein Vanden Heuvel, January 30, 1970, pp. 1–3 (Box 28, Clark Papers).

11. Kenneth B. Clark, narrator, *The Negro and the Promise of American Life,* television program produced by the National Education Television Program, 1963; transcript in Transfile 114, Clark Papers; for this citation see the "Baldwin Bridge" section of the transcript (some portions of the transcript are paginated while others are not).

12. Transcript of interview of Robert F. Kennedy, Robert F. Kennedy Oral History, p. 288 (John F. Kennedy Presidential Library); Clark interview with Vanden Heuvel, p. 5.

13. Lemann, *The Promised Land,* p. 127.

14. This was not Clark's only television appearance in 1963. In July, Clark also moderated another program, entitled "WGBH Symposium on Civil Rights," an edited transcript of which is reprinted in Westin, *Freedom Now!,* under the title "The Management of the Civil Rights Struggle" (pp. 31–40). That fall, Clark also collaborated with the playwright and documentary filmmaker William Branch on "Legacy of a Prophet," a documentary for public television marking the death of W. E. B. Du Bois. Clark and Branch also proposed another program to NET, "The Negro Experience," to be produced by the New York affiliate, WNET, which was approved for broadcast on July 22. According to the proposal approved by WNET, the thirty-minute program was to consist of " 'grassroots' interviews with ordinary Negro Americans of varying economic circumstances: 'An average, lower-income housewife and mother from Bedford Stuyvesant . . . An unskilled or semi-skilled worker . . . from Philadelphia . . . An unemployed youth . . . from the streets of central Harlem . . . A middle-class white-collar worker or professional man . . . from Washington, D. C.' " (proposal by Branch, attached to a letter from Branch announcing approval of the project, Transfile 114, Clark Papers). According to Branch, this program was never produced (letter from William Branch to the author, March 21, 1992).

15. Kenneth B. Clark, *King, Malcolm, Baldwin: Three Interviews with Kenneth B. Clark* (Middletown, CT: Wesleyan University Press, 1988), p. 13.

16. Clark Oral History, pp. 158, 159–160.

17. Transcript, *The Negro and the Promise*, p. 1.

18. Kenneth B. Clark, *King, Malcolm, Baldwin*, p. 64.

19. Transcript, *The Negro and the Promise*, p. 1.

20. Ibid., pp. 1–2.

21. Ibid., p. 2 (on King); "Malcolm X Bridge" (on Malcolm and Baldwin).

22. Ibid., "Clark Summary," p. 1.

23. Ibid., pp. 1–2.

24. "No Place Like Home," *Time*, July 31, 1964, p. 17.

25. Ibid., p. 18.

26. "Harlem: Hatred in the Streets," *Newsweek*, August 3, 1964, p. 20.

27. Ernest Dunbar, "Harlem's Violent Mood," *Look*, July 28, 1964, p. 29.

28. "Liberalism and the Negro," *Commentary*, March 1964, p. 39.

29. *Dark Ghetto* sold 39,735 copies in its 1965 hardcover edition, and 136,384 copies in its 1967 Harper Torchbooks paperback edition (letter from Tracy Silverman of HarperCollins to the author, August 24, 1992).

30. Frank Cardasco, "Wanted: A World Fit to Live In," *Saturday Review*, June 5, 1965, p. 21; Robert Coles, "A Compelling Summons," *The Reporter*, October 21, 1965, p. 62.

31. "The Civil Rights Mystique," *Saturday Review*, October 16, 1965, p. 60.

32. The first edition of *Prejudice and Your Child* had sold only 1,428 copies by April 1963. By October of that year, the new expanded paperback edition had already sold 1,821 copies. For most of the remainder of the 1960s, annual sales fluctuated between 2,000 and 4,000, reaching a temporary peak of 7,500 annually in 1968 and 1969 (letter from Miriam Levinson of Beacon Press to the author, October 23, 1991).

33. Talcott Parsons, "Why 'Freedom Now,' Not Yesterday," in Kenneth B. Clark and Talcott Parsons, eds., *The Negro American* (Boston: Houghton Mifflin, 1966), p. 8. Clark and Myrdal considered collaborating on a sequel to *An American Dilemma* but, according to Walter Jackson in *Gunnar Myrdal and America's Conscience: Social Engineering and Racial Liberalism, 1938–1987* (Chapel Hill: University of North Carolina Press, 1990), Myrdal's frail heath and a fundamental difference in temperament between the two men made such an effort impossible (p. 354).

34. Kenneth B. Clark, "The Dilemma of Power," in Clark and Parsons, *The Negro American*, p. xi.

35. Kenneth B. Clark, "The Civil Rights Movement: Momentum and Organization," in Clark and Parsons, *The Negro American*, p. 614.

36. U.S. Department of Labor, Office of Policy Planning and Research, *The Negro Family: The Case for National Action*, March 1965 (Ann Arbor: University Microfilms, 1982), p. 19.

37. Kenneth B. Clark, *Prejudice and Your Child* (Middletown, CT: Wesleyan University Press, 1988), p. 4.
38. "Kenneth Clark's Statement on Educational Excellence in Harlem's Schools," January 10, 1964, p. 4 (Box 350B, Clark Papers).
39. "Notes from KBC on New York City School Situation," January 30, 1964, p. 2 (Box 350B, Clark Papers).
40. Clark, "A Challenge to Desegregation," pp. 5–6.
41. Ibid.
42. See "Dedication Held at Harlem Center," *New York Times,* March 3, 1946, p. 9. In her inaugural comments, Mamie Phipps Clark said that the fixation on racial difference among children was as rational as refusing to eat spinach.
43. For a highly favorable portrait of Northside, marking the recognition of Northside as an important force in the city, see Gertrude Samuels, "Where a Troubled Child is Reborn," *New York Times Magazine,* June 13, 1954, p. 13ff.
44. Oral History of Mamie Phipps Clark, pp. 39–50 (Columbia University Oral History Research Office) (hereafter Mamie Clark Oral History).
45. See Mamie Phipps Clark, "Evaluation of an Inter-racial Guidance Clinic: Inter-cultural Factors," March 1957 (Northside Papers, New York Public Library) (hereafter Northside Papers). In 1957 the client base of Northside was reported to be 54 percent Negro, 26 percent Spanish, and 20 percent white (p. 1). Phipps Clark's review of Northside's caseload disclosed that neither the race of the therapist nor the patient affected the length or success of treatment. Far more important to the success of treatment than race were such factors as the continuity of treatment with one therapist, the regularity of casework contact, the waiting period after diagnosis, the age of the child, the degree of parental involvement, and parental marital status (pp. 4–9). Among those children seen by "clinic teams" Phipps Clark found "a strong trend for more children to improve when the clinic team is of mixed ethnic background or when the ethnic background of the clinic team is *entirely* different from that of the child. This is most clearly so for Negro children" (pp. 7–8). Phipps Clark speculated that "the mixed ethnic teams afford a greater inter-cultural stimulation and a higher motivation on the part of team members" (p. 8).
46. Kenneth Clark Oral History, pp. 146–147.
47. According to the minutes of a March 9, 1961, meeting of the Northside board of directors, the Committee to Consider the Inter-Cultural Aspects of Northside found that retaining the interracial character of the clinic could not be accomplished with "less than 10 to 15 per cent of any of the three major groups (White, Negro and Puerto Rican)." The committee opposed either redrawing Northside's service boundaries to "obtain the desired proportion of white children," or implementing a formalized quota system, and advocated instead

allowing the "medical director" to "select patients as he sees fit, keeping in mind this percentage when selecting patients" (pp. 1–3); see also the minutes for November 14, 1963, p. 3 (Northside Papers).

48. "Memorandum Concerning the Northside Center for Child Development, Inc.," January 1948, p. 1 (Northside Papers).

49. "Why Northside?" pamphlet (Box 117, Clark Papers). An important contribution to this change was the arrival of sociologist Richard Cloward to the Northside board. Cloward, an influential community activist, had helped establish Mobilization for Youth, the city's first federally funded community action program aimed at combating juvenile delinquency. On Cloward's role, and for discussions concerning changing Northside's mission, see the minutes for October 14 and December 17, 1965 (Northside Papers).

50. Board meeting, October 15, 1965, p. 4 (Northside Papers).

51. According to Phipps Clark, Ascoli's departure cost Northside $100,000. Despite the departure of Ascoli, the center retained a connection to the family through the membership of Ascoli's brother-in-law and daughter, who remained on the board of directors (Kenneth Clark Oral History, pp. 134–136; Mamie Clark Oral History, pp. 54–55).

52. Nat Hentoff, "The Integrationist," *New Yorker,* August 23, 1982, p. 47.

53. Kenneth Clark Oral History, pp. 147–148, 150. Despite a steady base of local foundation support and some municipal grants, deficits were an annual fact of life throughout Northside's history. The situation in 1964, a comparatively good year for Northside, was typical of the center's financial situation in this period: expenses through June 30, 1964 amounted to $133,000, while income, including funds from the Rockefeller Brothers Fund, the Ford Foundation, the Vincent Astor Foundation, and the Taconic Foundation, totaled $121,000; see the minutes for April 2, 1964, p. 3 (Northside Papers). Clark's comments about the grant to the Jewish Board of Guardians are from pp. 147–148 of his oral history.

54. Harlem Youth Opportunities Unlimited, *Youth in the Ghetto: A Study of the Consequences of Powerlessness and a Blueprint for Change* (New York: HARYOU, 1964), pp. 22–24.

55. Kenneth B. Clark, "HARYOU: An Experiment," *Freedomways,* Summer 1963, p. 440; memo dated August 1965, records of the President's Commission on Juvenile Delinquency (Box 22, Record Group 220, National Archives); Kenneth Clark Oral History, pp. 152–153.

56. Clark, "HARYOU: An Experiment," pp. 442, 443.

57. Ibid., pp. 412–425.

58. HARYOU, *Youth in the Ghetto,* pp. xi, 10, 11.

59. An unsigned summary of a September 18, 1963, staff meeting conveys the

difficulty of the President's Committee on Juvenile Delinquency's position vis-à-vis the established political leadership: "Conflicts within the various factions will have to be resolved within the next few weeks. Our strategy will be to work through the city and base our decisions on the merits of the programs. Thus, first assessment of the program content should be made quickly. Ellinger points out . . . the difficulty of an early solution, should ACT 'lose.' " If Powell's program lost, it was likely that the President's Commission would lose its appropriation, for Powell would then act to hold up the Juvenile Delinquency Extension bill, which he could do as head of the relevant committee with oversight of these funds. See "Notes on Staff Meeting, September 18, 1963," p. 2, Papers of the President's Commission on Juvenile Delinquency (Box 22, Record Group 220, National Archives).

60. Memo to David Hackett from Pat Anderson, February 6, 1963. The minutes of a HARYOU board meeting of March 17, 1964, suggest that HARYOU still perceived itself as an independent entity, with only the loosest connection to ACT. The final political relationship between the two groups remained in dispute. Livingston Wingate, the chair of ACT, complained that ACT had been slighted in the presentation of the blueprint to Mayor Wagner and at other key meetings. Wingate also insisted on a joint application for funds to implement the recommendations of *Youth in the Ghetto,* a proposal that continued to meet with strong opposition within HARYOU because ACT had played virtually no role in its authorship. There was also strong feeling that the publication of *Youth in the Ghetto* had strengthened HARYOU against Powell ("HARYOU had played ball with ACT because it was in the seat of power. Now that HARYOU has the document, it should switch and assume that it has the power, that is, to arouse the power of the community.") Thus empowered, the consensus seemed to be that HARYOU could once again approach Powell; see minutes of the meeting of the board of directors, Harlem Youth Unlimited, March 17, 1964 (Box 114, Clark Papers).

61. Kenneth Clark Oral History, pp. 173, 171–172, 174.

62. Charles V. Hamilton, *Adam Clayton Powell, Jr.: The Political Biography of an American Dilemma* (New York: Atheneum, 1991), pp. 425–427; see also Kenneth Clark Oral History, p. 171.

63. The most trenchant obituary for the War on Poverty in the press of the period is Robert Lekachman's essay "Death of a Slogan—Great Society 1967," which appeared in the January 1967 issue of *Commentary.* On the President's Committee on Juvenile Delinquency, see Daniel Knapp and Kenneth Polk, *Scouting the War on Poverty: Social Reform in the Kennedy Administration* (Toronto: Heath Lexington Books, 1971). The most thoughtful analysis of the community action concept remains Peter Marris and Martin Rein, *Dilemmas*

of Social Reform: Poverty and Community Action in the United States (New York: Atherton Press, 1967); the best discussion of the intellectual and political atmosphere that informed the Great Society is Lemann, *The Promised Land,* especially pp. 111–221; and the most acid portrait of the community activists within the Kennedy and Johnson administrations is Daniel P. Moynihan's highly readable *Maximum Feasible Misunderstanding: Community Action in the War on Poverty* (New York: Free Press, 1969). At the other extreme from Moynihan and Lemann are Frances Fox Piven and Richard Cloward, who locate the motivation behind community action and the broader War on Poverty, as well as the fundamental civil rights laws that were enacted in this period, in the Democratic Party's need to capture the black vote so as to counter its loss of the formerly "solid South." See both their *Regulating the Poor: The Functions of Public Welfare* (New York: Pantheon Books, 1971) and *Poor People's Movements: How They Succeed, Why They Fail* (New York: Pantheon Books, 1977).

64. Clark, "Some Problems of Community Action . . . Statement of Kenneth Clark before the Senate Subcommittee on Employment, Manpower and Poverty, March 17, 1967," p. 4 (Box 54, Clark Papers). Clark's study of community action in practice, written with Jeannette Hopkins, was published as *A Relevant War on Poverty: A Study of Community Action Programs and Observable Social Change* (New York: Harper and Row, 1969). Clark's conclusion that many of those involved in "community action" actually discouraged the active participation of the poor and engaged in strategies that precluded fundamental change provoked a rebuke from America's best-known community organizer, Saul Alinsky: "I am writing you for two reasons: first, there is so much of this crap floating around that it really hurts me to see you as part of it (you know my personal opinion of you); and secondly, that I hope you avoid making the same error in any future writing as this kind of stuff ceases to be research and just degenerates into gossip, and that is not your bag"; letter from Alinsky to Clark, October 29, 1969 (Box 54, Clark Papers).

65. Kenneth B. Clark, *Dark Ghetto: Dilemmas of Social Power* (New York: Harper and Row, 1965), p. xv.

66. Ibid., p. xvii.

67. "Light on the Ghetto," p. 81. It is interesting to note that neither Clark nor *Newsweek* cited Stanley Elkins' *Slavery: A Problem in American Institutional and Intellectual Life,* which also drew a parallel between the concentration camp and the African-American experience. This omission may reflect their disagreement with Elkins's belief that a "Sambo" personality of childlike passivity and contentment had been displayed by American slaves and that this personality, rather than being a mask behind which effective resistance might

be pursued, was actually a state of mind enforced by the crushing oppressive-ness of the American slave system.

68. Clark, *Dark Ghetto,* p. 11.
69. Ibid., pp. 14, 12.
70. Ibid., p. 14.
71. Ibid., p. 15.
72. Ibid., p. 16.
73. Ibid., pp. 157–158, 27.
74. Ibid., pp. 71, 81.
75. Ibid., p. 131.
76. Nat Hentoff, "Urban Blight," *New Yorker,* July 31, 1965, p. 74.
77. Clark, *Dark Ghetto,* p. 222.
78. Kenneth B. Clark, "The Wonder Is There Have Been So Few Riots," *New York Times Magazine,* September 5, 1965, p. 38.
79. *Dark Ghetto,* pp. 223, 240.
80. Clark, "Riots," p. 48.
81. Ibid., pp. 10, 38.
82. Ibid., p. 48.
83. Lee Rainwater and William L. Yancy, *The Moynihan Report and the Politics of Controversy* (Cambridge: MIT Press, 1967), pp. 136–154; Lemann, *The Promised Land,* p. 175.
84. "Visceral Reaction," *Newsweek,* December 6, 1965, pp. 38–39.
85. *The Negro Family,* p. i.
86. Ibid, pp. i, 4.
87. "Johnson Address to Howard University Graduates," *New York Times,* June 5, 1965, p. 14.
88. "A Very Stern Discipline: An Interview with Ralph Ellison," *Harper's,* March 1967, p. 85.
89. "New Crisis: The Negro Family," *Newsweek,* August 9, 1965, p. 35.
90. "A Mother Can't Do a Man's Job," *Newsweek,* August 22, 1966, p. 41.
91. Ralph Ellison, "An American Dilemma: A Review," in his *Shadow and Act* (New York: Random House, 1964), pp. 315–316.
92. "Stern Discipline," p. 76.
93. Ibid., p. 83.
94. Ibid., p. 90.
95. Ibid.
96. I am indebted to T. V. Reed, "Unimagined Existence and the Fiction of the Real: Postmodernist Realism in 'Let Us Now Praise Famous Men,' " *Representations* 24 (1988): 156–176, for raising this issue. I quote directly here from p. 157.

97. William L. Leuchtenburg, "The New Deal and the Analogue of War," in John Braeman, Robert H. Bremner, and David Brody, eds., *Change and Continuity in Twentieth Century America: The 1920's* (Columbus: Ohio University Press, 1964).

98. For the extent of this influence, especially on LBJ, see William L. Leuchtenburg, *In the Shadow of FDR* (Ithaca: Cornell University Press, 1983).

99. Herbert G. Gutman, *The Black Family in Slavery and Freedom, 1750–1925* (New York: Random House / Vintage Books, 1976), pp. xvii, 462–464.

100. Lemann, *The Promised Land,* p. 175. Even Rainwater and Yancey, who are considerably more sympathetic to Moynihan than Lemann, concede that the report had a fundamentally polemical flavor and intention, although they blame the use of highly selective quotations of the report by a press ignorant of social science techniques for most of the distortion; see Rainwater and Yancey, *The Moynihan Report,* pp. 297, 153–154. Anthony M. Platt convincingly argues that the process of distortion through the citation of passages emphasizing pathology and disorganization began with Moynihan's *own* selective and highly symbolic manipulation of Frazier as a legitimating voice for his conclusion. While Moynihan did not distort *The Negro Family in the United States,* he did conveniently ignore related work by Frazier, particularly his analyses explicitly repudiating the pathology model for interpreting the Negro family; see Anthony M. Platt, *E. Franklin Frazier Reconsidered* (New Brunswick: Rutgers University Press, 1991), pp. 116–120.

101. *The Negro Family,* p. 2.

102. William Ryan, "Savage Discovery: The Moynihan Report," *The Nation,* November 22, 1965, p. 383. On Moynihan's misuse of "weak and inexact data," see pp. 380–382.

103. Moynihan himself saw the same result occurring from the rejection of his report. Referring to this as well as to the results of the 1966 congressional elections, Moynihan wrote the following in "The President and the Negro: The Moment Lost," *Commentary,* February 1967: "For the second time in [the] history [of Negro Americans], the great task of liberation has been left only half-accomplished. It appears that the nation may be in the process of reproducing the tragic events of the Reconstruction: giving to Negroes the forms of legal equality, but withholding the economic and political resources which are the bases of social equality" (p. 31).

104. Daniel P. Moynihan, "The Moynihan Report," *Harper's,* August 1967, p. 6.

105. Letter from Clark to Moynihan, February 22, 1966 (Box 55, Clark Papers). Dr. Clark had only a slight recollection of this letter and of the manuscript to which it refers when I showed it to him during our interviews in March 1989. It is clear, however, from Clark's public statements of unqualified

support for Moynihan at the height of the controversy that Clark's failure to complete the essay for *Commentary* was not rooted in any reservations he had about the report. His papers suggest that the years 1965 and 1966 were made especially hectic by all the obligations thrust upon him as a result of *Dark Ghetto;* the *Commentary* essay may have been a casualty of this demanding schedule. By the 1970s, however, Clark opposed both the report and its author. He has said very little directly, either in public or in his oral histories, about why his opinion changed so completely; I offer my own speculation from the available evidence later in this chapter. For Moynihan's analysis of the controversy, see his 1967 *Commentary* piece, "The President and the Negro: The Moment Lost."

106. "Visceral Reaction," *Newsweek,* p. 40.
107. Lemann, *The Promised Land,* pp. 209–210. On Moynihan's influence within the administration, see pp. 202–219. In his excellent revisionist study of Richard Nixon, Tom Wicker suggests that Moynihan, the "house Democrat" and "inside gadfly," had relatively little influence on Nixon policy, as his views were more than countered by those of John Mitchell and Arthur Burns. Wicker argues that, to a degree, the strategy of "benign neglect," coupled as it was with an equally quiet offer of federal assistance to Southern districts engaged in desegregation, was successful in achieving progress in the South. Between the fall of 1968 and the fall of 1970, the percentage of southern blacks attending schools that were at least 50 percent white rose from 18.4 percent to 38.1 percent, while the percentage of blacks attending schools that were 80 percent black fell from 78.8 percent to 41.7 percent. Wicker attributes these developments to a Supreme Court still generally supportive of desegregation and to a president—like Eisenhower at Little Rock—whose opposition to federal intervention in local affairs was surpassed only by his determination to enforce federal decrees; see Wicker, *One of Us: Richard Nixon and the American Dream* (New York: Random House, 1991), pp. 406, 408, 415, 484–490, 493–494, 500–502.
108. Clark's comments are included in *Newsweek's* coverage of the Moynihan controversy; see "Case of 'Benign Neglect,' " *Newsweek,* March 16, 1970, p. 27. Clark also discussed Moynihan in a 1985 addendum to his oral history at Columbia University; see p. 64 of that transcript.
109. Wicker, *One of Us,* p. 503.
110. Quoted in ibid., p. 484.
111. Ibid., pp. 489, 488.
112. Transcript of Clark interview conducted by Larry Nyman, May 28, 1975 (Clark and Associates).
113. Ronald Smothers, "Kenneth B. Clark Endorses Buckley," *New York Times,*

October 3, 1976, p. 17. Some prominent black officials were reported to have encouraged Clark to make the endorsement, "in the hope that it might move Mr. Moynihan to show greater concern for the issues affecting black voters." Clark's decision was attacked in the *Times* by the political scientist Charles V. Hamilton of Columbia University, who encouraged Clark to "spend more time educating himself: 'benign neglect' spoke to ending 'racial rhetoric while Negro progress continues' . . . I am certainly not suggesting that Moynihan is the paragon of perfection and Buckley the epitome of evil. But in comparison, Mr. Moynihan is far and away the most attractive of the candidates . . . The outcome is too important to permit the emotion and misinformation of Mr. Clark to confuse the issues. Frankly, there is a point where political naivete becomes political ignorance, and in this case, Dr. Clark has unfortunately crossed that line." Professor L. D. Reddick of Temple University defended Clark's refusal to support Moynihan with the comment that "black people all over the nation realize that with a Moynihan again in Washington there might well be once more a constant flow of scholarly half-truths about the poor and nonwhites from this poisoned fountainhead" (see "Letters to the Editor" under the heading "Kenneth Clark's Move," *New York Times,* October 21, 1976, p. 38). It is interesting to note that the Moynihan report was leaked during its author's first campaign for office, an unsuccessful run for the presidency of the New York City Council, an at-large position. Ralph Ellison, in his rejoinder to Norman Podhoretz on the report, charged that the document had been "leaked and conjured with in an effort to elect Mr. Moynihan to the New York City Council"; see Ellison, "No More Apologies," *Harper's,* July 1967, p. 12. In November 1976, Moynihan beat Buckley, 55 percent to 45 percent.

114. Charles A. Valentine, *Culture and Poverty: Critique and Counter-Proposals* (Chicago: University of Chicago Press, 1968), pp. 80, 78; quote on p. 82.

115. A quote from *Dark Ghetto* accompanies one from an essay by I. F. Stone as a frame to "White Power: The Colonial Situation," the first chapter of Carmichael and Hamilton's *Black Power: The Politics of Liberation* (New York: Random House / Vintage, 1967), p. 3. Extensive quotes from *Dark Ghetto* elaborating the colonial metaphor also appear on pp. 18, 22, 29.

116. Clark, "Black Power, White Backlash and American Racial Cynicism," column written for the North American Newspaper Alliance and the *Boston Globe,* October 12, 1966, pp. 3–4, 5 (Box 54, Clark Papers).

117. Kenneth B. Clark, "Quality Education and Race: The Present American Dilemma," undated speech for delivery sometime in 1966, p. 6 (Box 54, Clark Papers).

118. Ibid., pp. 10–11.

119. Clark, "American Education Today: The Case for Reorganization," pp. 8–9; speech delivered at the planning session for the White House Conference entitled "To Fulfill These Rights" (Box 52, Clark Papers). On the educational park concept see Thomas F. Pettigrew, *Racially Separate or Together?* (New York: McGraw-Hill, 1971), pp. 69–80.

120. Clark, "The Inseparable Destiny," speech delivered to the Fifteenth Annual Westchester Conference of Community Services, White Plains, New York, November 21, 1968, p. 4 (Box 52, Clark Papers).

121. Ibid.

122. Nyman interview, p. 25.

123. Mary Harrington Hall, "A Conversation with Kenneth B. Clark," *Psychology Today,* June 1968, p. 20.

124. Ibid., p. 21.

125. "The L. A. Riots and a View of History," *Nightline,* ABC television program, May 7, 1992 (transcript), p. 7.

126. Interview for Voice of America, January 30, 1980, p. 3 (Clark and Associates).

6. The Political Education of Lorraine Hansberry

The epigraphs are from an FBI memo dated February 5, 1959 (an ideological review of a performance of *Raisin* the previous evening at the Walnut Theater in Philadelphia, Pennsylvania), pp. 1–4 (Lorraine Hansberry FBI file); and John A. Davis, "Introduction," in The First Conference of Negro Writers, *The Negro Writer and His Roots* (New York: The American Society of African Culture, 1960), p. iv.

1. Doris Abramson, *Negro Playwrights in the American Theater, 1925–1959* (New York: Columbia University Press, 1969), p. 241.

2. Gerald Weales, "Thoughts on 'A Raisin in the Sun,' " *Commentary,* June 1959, p. 527.

3. Lorraine Hansberry, "The Negro Writer and His Roots: Toward a New Romanticism," *Black Scholar,* March–April 1981, p. 9.

4. Lorraine Hansberry, "Strange Flower," *Liberation,* May 1959, p. 15.

5. For an excellent discussion of the radical and revolutionary quality of the universalist and integrationist literature of the 1950s and of Lorraine Hansberry's place within it, see Robert Henry Grant, "Lorraine Hansberry: The Playwright as Warrior-Intellectual," (Ph.D. diss., Harvard University, 1982), especially pp. 2–78.

6. "Miss Hansberry on Backlash," *The Village Voice,* July 23, 1964, p. 16.

7. I do not consider the second of Hansberry's plays to reach Broadway in her

lifetime, *The Sign in Sidney Brustein's Window* (New York: Random House, 1965). This play is an examination of the American bohemian left and a meditation on the moral necessity of choosing commitment over a self-conscious pose of alienation and disengagement; because it does not directly engage with the topic of this study—changing cultural representations in racial discourse—I do not discuss this particular drama. An intriguing document in its own right, however, this play deserves further examination.

8. Margaret B. Wilkerson, "TOUSSAINT: Excerpt from ACT I of a Work in Progress," in Margaret B. Wilkerson, ed., *Nine Plays by Black Women* (New York: New American Library, 1986), p. 45. Although a glimpse of Hansberry's personal life is afforded by Robert Nemiroff's adaptation of Hansberry's writing, *To Be Young, Gifted, and Black: An Informal Autobiography of Lorraine Hansberry* (New York: New American Library, 1970)—a text that he describes as "a small representative sampling, a cross-section" (p. xxii)—the full papers have not, as of this writing, been publicly archived for consultation by scholars. The challenges posed by the absence of this resource, and its implications for the treatment of Hansberry's completed body of work versus the work left uncompleted at the time of her death, are sensitively addressed in Adrienne Rich, "The Problem with Lorraine Hansberry," *Freedomways,* 19(1979):247–255. Some of Hansberry's unpublished, unfinished work is anthologized in Robert Nemiroff, ed., *Lorraine Hansberry: The Collected Last Plays* (New York: New American Library, 1972); for a survey of Hansberry's entire body of work, including the material published after her death, see Steven R. Carter, *Hansberry's Drama: Commitment amid Complexity* (Urbana: University of Illinois Press, 1991).

9. Helene Keyssar, *The Curtain and the Veil* (New York: Burt Franklin and Co., 1981), p. 11.

10. Richard G. Sharine, *From Caste to Class in American Drama: Political and Social Themes since the 1930s* (New York: Greenwood Press, 1991), p. 229.

11. Weales, "Thoughts on 'A Raisin in the Sun,' " pp. 528–529.

12. Lorraine Hansberry, "An Author's Reflections: Willy Loman, Walter Lee and He Who Must Live," in Karen Malpede, ed., *Women in Theater: Compassion and Hope* (New York: Drama Book Publishers, 1985), p. 167; Ossie Davis, "The Significance of Lorraine Hansberry," *Freedomways,* 5 (1965): 402. Lorraine Hansberry was certainly not the only African-American woman to achieve public acclaim and then have her work misrepresented and trivialized, although the fact that Hansberry was not a housewife seems to have spared her some of the dismissive rhetoric others received; for a general discussion of this circumstance, see Mary Helen Washington, "The Darkened Eye Restored: Notes toward a Literary History of Black Women," in Henry Louis

Gates, Jr., *Reading Black, Reading Feminist: A Critical Anthology* (New York: Meridian, 1990), pp. 31–43.

13. Davis, "The Significance of Lorraine Hansberry," p. 402.

14. *Hartford Times,* January 22, 1959 (clipping courtesy of Robert Nemiroff).

15. Jerry Gaghan, "*Raisin in the Sun* Warms Walnut," *Philadelphia Daily News,* January 29, 1959, p. 43.

16. Ernie Schier, "*Raisin in the Sun* Opens at the Walnut," *The Philadelphia Daily Bulletin,* January 27, 1959, p. 44.

17. On *Anna Lucasta* and the American Negro Theater, see Loften Mitchell, *Black Drama: The Story of the American Negro in the Theater* (New York: Hawthorn Books, 1967), pp. 113, 122–123; Abramson, *Negro Playwrights in the American Theater,* p. 94; Loften Mitchell, *Voices of the Black Theater* (Clifton, NJ: James T. White and Co., 1975), pp. 117–118, 126–127, 131–145, 147–148; Ethel Louise Pitts, "The American Negro Theater," (Ph.D. diss., University of Missouri, 1975).

18. Kenneth Tynan, *Curtains: Selections from the Drama Criticism and Related Writings* (New York: Atheneum, 1961), p. 309.

19. Walter Kerr, "No Clear Path, No Retreat," *New York Herald Tribune* (courtesy of Robert Nemiroff, undated).

20. Frank Ashton, "*Raisin in the Sun* Is a Moving Tale," *New York World-Telegram,* March 12, 1959, p. 10.

21. Kerr, "No Clear Path, No Clear Retreat."

22. David Elmblidge, ed., *Eleanor Roosevelt's "My Day,"* vol. 3, *First Lady of the World, Her Acclaimed Columns 1953–1962* (New York: Pharos Books, 1991), p. 207.

23. "Negro Talent in a Prize-winning Play," *Life,* April 27, 1959, p. 137.

24. Harold R. Isaacs, "Five Writers and Their Ancestors," *The New World of Negro Americans* (New York: John Day Co., 1963), p. 282.

25. Tynan, *Curtains,* pp. 307–308.

26. In June 1959 the city of Chicago pressed for improvements on thirteen apartments owned by Hansberry Enterprises. The city erroneously listed Lorraine Hansberry as the owner of one of the properties in question. In response to the charges, Hansberry told Helen Dudar of the *New York Post:* "When I first heard the story, I didn't know what they were talking about. I called Chicago and learned that my name had been placed on a piece of property when it was purchased some years ago. I wasn't told about it and I have no legal or equitable title to that building . . . It is not something to be dismissed as 'my business' . . . I'm not a slum landlord. I've never derived a cent from that building—whoever owns it. Parenthetically, I might say I haven't drawn a

cent from the family since I came east nine years ago" (quoted in Helen Dudar, "Counterpoint to *Raisin,*" *New York Post,* July 1, 1959, p. 3).

27. Mitchell, *Black Drama,* p. 182.

28. Gerald T. Goodman, "The Black Theater Movement," (Ph.D. diss., University of Pennsylvania, 1974), p. 133; C. W. E. Bigsby, *The Second Black Renaissance: Essays in Black Literature* (Westport: Greenwood Press, 1980), p. 214.

29. Werner Sollors, *Amiri Baraka / LeRoi Jones: The Quest for a "Populist Modernism"* (New York: Columbia University Press, 1978), p. 14.

30. Allan Lewis, *American Plays and Playwrights of the Contemporary Theater* (New York: Crown Publishers, 1965), pp. 112, 252.

31. Harold Cruse, *The Crisis of the Negro Intellectual: A Historical Analysis of the Failure of Black Leadership* (New York: Quill, 1984), pp. 280–281.

32. Ibid., p. 280; see also Abramson, *Negro Playwrights in the American Theater,* pp. 263–264.

33. Morris Freedman, *American Drama in Social Context* (Carbondale: Southern Illinois University Press, 1971), p. 86. On *Raisin* as a quintessential family drama, see Tom Scanlan, *Family Drama, American Dreams* (New York: Greenwood Press, 1978), pp. 196–201. Another index of the decline of *Raisin*'s reputation over the sixties and seventies was the controversy that attended the Free Southern Theater's decision in 1972 to present this play, which had been a staple of its first season; see Clarissa Myrick Harris, "Mirror of the Movement: The History of the Free Southern Theater as a Microcosm of the Civil Rights and Black Power Movement, 1963–1976," (Ph.D. diss., Emory University, 1988), pp. 24, 207.

34. John Rodden, *The Politics of Literary Reputation: The Making and Claiming of "St. George" Orwell* (New York: Oxford University Press, 1989), p. 69.

35. Although many scholars writing in the 1960s refer to *Raisin*'s use in schools, the only quantitative index of this relates to the 1980s. Hansberry's *A Raisin in the Sun* and Richard Wright's *Black Boy* were the only texts by minority authors to be listed among the most frequently assigned texts in a survey of five hundred public and private schools. Overall, *Raisin* (in the Signet 1966 edition) is the forty-second most taught text in public high schools overall; it is twenty-fifth in cities with a population of over 100,000, and fourteenth in schools with minority enrollments of 50 percent or more; see Robert Nemiroff, "Some Important New Facts and Developments," a memo to researchers dated October 27, 1989 (courtesy of Robert Nemiroff). See also "School Reading Lists Shun Women and Black Authors," *New York Times,* June 21, 1989, p. B6, and Arthur N. Applebee's report, "A Study of Book-Length Works Taught in High School English Courses" (Albany State University of New York at Albany, Center for the Learning and Teaching of Literature, 1989).

36. George C. Wolfe, *The Colored Museum: A Play* (New York: Grove Press, 1988), p. i. Among Wolfe's exhibits is a skit titled "The Last Mama-on-the-Couch Play," in which he satirizes *Raisin,* its critical reception, and the iconization of Hansberry in the stage play *To Be Young, Gifted and Black.*

37. A series of essays by Hansberry scholars and colleagues in the late 1970s challenging the terms of repute surrounding Hansberry is collected in Jean Carey Bond, ed., *Lorraine Hansberry: Art of Thunder, Vision of Light* (special 1979 issue of *Freedomways*).

38. Quoted in Mitchell, *Voices of the Black Theater,* p. 170. See also the essay by Ruby Dee, which trenchantly captures the atmosphere of the early fifties and discusses the consequences of the double blacklist. Especially interesting are Dee's recollections of the pressures placed upon Jackie Robinson to disassociate himself from Paul Robeson's political views. At the time of that flashpoint in the political Cold War at home, Dee and Robinson were in the middle of shooting *The Jackie Robinson Story.*

39. Carl Hansberry died while making preparations for his family to settle in Mexico.

40. "Welcome to the *Freedom* Family," *Freedom,* September 1951, p. 2.

41. "What Are You Doing Out There," *Freedom,* August 1951, p. 3.

42. Among Hansberry's closest friends at *Freedom* was the playwright-actor Alice Childress, whose play *Trouble in Mind* explores an actress's refusal to turn in a racially stereotyped portrayal, which Childress sets brilliantly against the backdrop of the blacklist. The play won Childress an Obie in 1955, but it would receive its largest audience in Great Britain, where it was produced and broadcast nationally by the BBC. On Childress, see Elizabeth Brown-Guillory, *Their Place on the Stage: Black Women Playwrights in America* (New York: Greenwood Press, 1988), pp. 28–30; and Mitchell, *Black Drama,* pp. 125–127, 168–169. Childress discusses her career and her friendship with Hansberry in her oral history at the Hatch-Billops Theater Archives, New York City; she reflects on her life and the pressures for ideological conformity put upon American artists in her essay "A Candle in a Gale Wind," in Mari Evans, ed., *Black Women Writers (1950–1980): A Critical Evaluation* (New York: Anchor/Doubleday, 1984). *Trouble in Mind* is anthologized in Lindsay Patterson, ed., *Black Theater: A Twentieth-Century Collection of the Work of Its Best Playwrights* (New York: Dodd, Mead and Company, 1971). On the black female playwrights who preceded Hansberry and Childress, see Kathy A. Perkins, *Black Female Playwrights: An Anthology of Plays before 1950* (Bloomington: Indiana University Press, 1989). In addition to Childress, another of Hansberry's friends from the *Freedom* years was William Branch, the author of *A Medal for Willie,* a 1951 off-Broadway production that

Hansberry warmly reviewed. The play dramatized the persistence of Jim Crow at home while African-American soldiers fought for freedom abroad. Another important script by Branch, produced off-Broadway in the early 1950s, is the brilliant historical drama *In Splendid Error,* which explored the relationship between Frederick Douglass and John Brown. *A Medal for Willie* is published in Woodie King and Ron Milner, eds., *Black Drama Anthology* (New York: New American Library, 1972), pp. 439–473; *In Splendid Error* can be found in *Black Theater, USA: Forty-Five Plays by Black Americans 1847–1974* (New York: Free Press, 1974), pp. 588–617. For Hansberry's review of *A Medal for Willie,* see Lorraine Hansberry, "*A Medal for Willie* Deserves a Medal," *Freedom,* November 1951, p. 7.

43. Lorraine Hansberry, "Life Challenges Negro Youth," *Freedom,* March 1955, p. 7.
44. Lorraine Hansberry, " 'Gold Coast's' Rulers Go, Ghana Moves to Freedom," *Freedom,* December 1951, p. 2.
45. Hansberry, "Egyptian People Fight for Freedom," *Freedom,* March 1952, p. 3.
46. Taped oral history of Robert Nemiroff (Hatch-Billops Theater Archives, New York City) (hereafter Nemiroff Oral History).
47. Carter, *Hansberry's Drama,* p. 10.
48. Henderson Cleaves, " 'People Get Messed Up,' Says Author of *Raisin,*" *New York World-Telegram and Sun,* March 13, 1959, p. 28; Nemiroff Oral History.
49. Ted Poston, "We Have So Much to Say" (interview with Hansberry), *New York Post,* March 22, 1959, p. M2.
50. *Freedom,* July 1952, p. 7.
51. "Make New Sounds: Studs Terkel Interviews Lorraine Hansberry," *American Theater,* November 1984, pp. 7–8 (originally conducted in 1959).
52. Lorraine Hansberry, *A Raisin in the Sun* (New York: Samuel French, 1959), pp. 5–6. Unless otherwise noted, subsequent page references refer to this edition.
53. Lorraine Hansberry, *To Be Young, Gifted, and Black: An Informal Autobiography of Lorraine Hansberry,* adapted by Robert Nemiroff (New York: New American Library, 1970), pp. 63–64.
54. Lorraine Hansberry, in Robert Nemiroff, ed., *"A Raisin in the Sun": The Unfilmed Original Screenplay* (New York: New American Library, 1992); Hansberry, *Raisin in the Sun* (French ed.), p. 26.
55. Bigsby, *Black Renaissance,* pp. 214–215.
56. "Make New Sounds," p. 8.
57. Beneatha Younger has traditionally been treated as Hansberry's alter ego, the vehicle for the expression of her creator's Pan-Africanism, and little else. However, Beneath also expresses Hansberry's feminism—her frank ques-

tioning of traditional male-female sex roles and of the assumption, prevalent in the fifties, that a young woman's first job was to "catch" a "good" husband and make a "good" marriage (see especially pp. 19, 29, 40). One of the few scholars to discuss this dimension of *Raisin* is Jewelle L. Gomez, in her essay "Lorraine Hansberry: Uncommon Warrior," in Gates, *Reading Black, Reading Feminist*, pp. 313–314.

58. Walter Lee's reverence for American capitalism and its monuments was shared by Hansberry's father, Carl. The rhetoric that Hansberry gives to Walter Lee to describe the man whom he aspires to become is strikingly like that used by Hansberry to describe her own father. In some autobiographical reflections, Hansberry wrote: "My father's enduring image in my mind is that of a man whom kings might have imitated and properly created their own flattering descriptions of. A man who always seemed to be doing something brilliant and/or unusual to such an extent that to be doing something brilliant and/or unusual was the way I assumed fathers behaved. He could talk at length on American history and private enterprise (to which he utterly subscribed). And he carried his head in such a way that I was quite certain that there was nothing that he was afraid of" (Hansberry, *To Be Young, Gifted, and Black,* p. 50).

59. Grant, "Lorraine Hansberry: The Playwright as Warrior-Intellectual," p. 64.

60. In act 2, scene 1, Hansberry has Walter Lee—who has been drinking heavily—join his sister in an African dance. With the emotional release provided by the liquor, Walter becomes Flaming Spear, an African warrior ready to prepare "my black brothers" for "the coming of the mighty war" (pp. 52–53). The liquor and, more important, the sound of African drums has for the moment released Walter from the prison of his false consciousness—the illusion that he can and should aspire to be a titan of American capitalism—and immerses him instead in the African past and the consciousness that lies deep within him and, Hansberry believed, all other American Negroes.

61. Hansberry, *A Raisin in the Sun* (New American Library ed.), pp. 114, 92–93.

7. The Dialectical Imagination of Lorraine Hansberry

The epigraph is from Lorraine Hansberry, "Quo Vadis" (statements by William S. Burroughs, Allen Ginsberg, Lorraine Hansberry, Norman Podhoretz, and others on their hopes for the 1960s), *Mademoiselle,* January 17, 1960, pp. 34, 17.

1. Lorraine Hansberry, "Scars of the Ghetto," *Monthly Review,* February 1965, p. 591.

2. Quoted in Lorraine Hansberry, *The Movement: Documentary of a Struggle for Equality* (New York: Simon and Schuster, 1964), p. 68.
3. Hansberry quoted in Faye Hammel, "A Playwright, A Promise," *Cue,* February 28, 1959, p. 42.
4. "Make New Sounds: Studs Terkel Interviews Lorraine Hansberry," *American Theater,* November 1984, p. 8.
5. Lorraine Hansberry, "The Negro Writer and His Roots: Toward a New Romanticism," *Black Scholar,* March–April 1981, pp. 4–5.
6. Ibid., p. 5.
7. Ibid., p. 6.
8. Ibid., p. 10.
9. Loften Mitchell, *Black Drama: The Story of the American Negro in the Theater* (New York: Hawthorn Books, 1967), p. 182.
10. For the figure of 147 investors, see Jim O'Connor, " 'Raisin' Makes a Capital Mark," *New York Journal-American,* April 22, 1959, p. 17; Lloyd Richards, "An Unlikely History," *American Theater,* November 1984, p. 8.
11. Robert Nemiroff, Foreword to the new edition, *"A Raisin in the Sun": Expanded 25th Anniversary Edition and "The Sign in Sidney Brustein's Window"* (New York: New American Library, 1987), p. xiv.
12. Lorraine Hansberry, "An Author's Reflections: Willy Loman, Walter Lee and He Who Must Live," in Karen Malpede, ed., *Women in Theater: Compassion and Hope* (New York: Drama Book Publishers, 1985), pp. 167–168. (This essay first appeared in *The Village Voice,* August 12, 1959.
13. Ibid., p. 169.
14. Ibid., p. 170.
15. Ibid. Here, Hansberry is explicitly stating an idea expressed in act 2, scene 1 of *Raisin;* see Chapter 6, n. 60.
16. Ibid.
17. "Lorraine Hansberry" (transcript of Hansberry's remarks), *Annals of Psychotherapy,* 5(1964), monograph no. 8, "The Creative Use of the Unconscious by the Artist and by the Psychotherapist," p. 14.
18. See the Random House reprint of Hansberry's revised script included in Bennett Cerf, ed., *Four Contemporary American Plays* (New York: Random House / Vintage, 1961), p. 128.
19. Margaret B. Wilkerson, "Introduction," in Robert Nemiroff, ed., *"A Raisin in the Sun": The Unfilmed Original Screenplay* (New York: New American Library, 1992), p. xxxv.
20. In addition to consulting the published version of the screenplay cited above and a videotape of the film itself, I also examined the still-unpublished shooting script on file at the western branch of the Writers' Guild of America

in Los Angeles. That draft, though trimmed from the original, follows *The Unfilmed Original Screenplay* fairly closely.

21. Nemiroff, ed., *"A Raisin in the Sun": The Unfilmed Original Screenplay*, p. 5.

22. Ibid., p. 43. These lines, as spoken to Ruth Younger in the film, appear in the unpublished script on file at the Writers Guild on a page marked "revised pages 26–34, June 16, 1960."

23. Ibid., p. 141.

24. Nemiroff, Foreword to the new edition, pp. xiv–xv. Additional restorations were also made by Nemiroff in two later editions: *"A Raisin in the Sun": Expanded Twenty-Fifth Anniversary Edition and "The Sign in Sidney Brustein's Window"* and the American Playhouse edition of *Raisin,* published by New American Library in 1988.

25. Lorraine Hansberry, *A Raisin in the Sun* (New York: New American Library, 1966), pp. 113–114.

26. Ibid., pp. 88–89.

27. Julian Mayfield, "Into the Mainstream and Oblivion," in The First Conference of Negro Writers, *The American Negro Writer and His Roots* (New York: The American Society of African Culture, 1960), p. 31.

28. Ibid., pp. 30, 31, 33.

29. Lorraine Hansberry, "The Negro in the American Theater," in Horst Frenz, ed., *American Playwrights on Drama* (New York: Hill and Wang, 1965), pp. 166–167 (first published in *Theater Arts,* October 1960, under the title "Me Tink Me Hear Sounds in de Night"). This essay reached its largest and most general audience in the June 1961 issue of *Negro Digest,* where a slightly abridged version appeared under the title "The American Theater Needs Desegregating, Too."

30. Quoted in Margaret B. Wilkerson, "TOUSSAINT: Excerpt from ACT I of a Work in Progress," in Margaret B. Wilkerson, ed., *Nine Plays by Black Women* (New York: New American Library, 1986), p. 41.

31. Essay dated December 1958 and published under the title "A Note to Readers" in Wilkerson, *Nine Plays by Black Women,* p. 51.

32. Wilkerson, "TOUSSAINT," pp. 41–42.

33. On the genesis of *Les Blancs,* see Robert Nemiroff, ed., *Lorraine Hansberry: The Collected Last Plays* (New York: New American Library, 1983), pp. 27, 31–32. On the symbolic and substantive importance of Africa in the late 1950s and early 1960s, see Richard D. Mahoney, *JFK: Ordeal in Africa* (New York: Oxford University Press, 1983); Dean Rusk discusses the centrality of Africa as a symbol set against segregation in Washington, DC, and as a policy focus in his memoir *As I Saw It* (New York: W. W. Norton and Co., 1990), pp. 570–592. For a sense of Africa as an emerging focus of Cold War liberalism, see

Chester Bowles, *Africa's Challenge to America* (Berkeley: University of California Press, 1956), and Louis E. Lomax, *The Reluctant African* (New York: Harper Brothers, 1960).

34. Lorraine Hansberry, "Genet, Mailer and the New Paternalists," *Village Voice,* June 1, 1961, pp. 10, 14–15.

35. See Robert Nemiroff, "The One Hundred and One 'Final' Performances of *Sidney Brustein,*" pp. xiii–lxi in Lorraine Hansberry, *The Sign in Sidney Brustein's Window* (New York: Random House, 1966). A revised edition of *Brustein,* incorporating material neither performed on Broadway nor published in the Random House edition, is included in Hansberry, *"A Raisin in the Sun": Expanded 25th Anniversary Edition and "The Sign in Sidney Brustein's Window."*

36. Nemiroff completed a "preliminary draft" of *Les Blancs* in 1966. The play debuted at the Longacre Theater on November 15, 1970, with James Earl Jones in the role of Tshembe Matoseh Nemiroff, ed., *The Collected Last Plays,* pp. 31–34).

37. "The Negro in American Culture" (transcript of a radio symposium broadcast over WBAI in 1961); C. W. E. Bigsby, *The Black American Writer,* vol. 1 (Deland, FL: Everett / Edwards, 1969), p. 107.

38. "The Negro in American Culture," p. 107; Lorraine Hansberry, "Strange Flower," *Liberation,* May 1959, p. 14.

39. Hansberry, "Strange Flower," p. 14.

40. Nemiroff, ed., *The Collected Last Plays,* pp. 146–147.

41. The only modern precedent for anything like *The Drinking Gourd* is Theodore Ward's *Our Lan',* a dramatization of the newly freed African-Americans' struggle after the Civil War to obtain forty acres and their full political equality (Ward's script leaves no doubt that obtaining the former is the key to obtaining the latter). Among the inspirations Ward credits in his 1941 script are the works of W. E. B. Du Bois; and the play indeed faithfully reflects the spirit of *Black Reconstruction;* see the credit page of Ward's typescript of the play, dated September 16, 1941 (The Schomburg Center for Research in Black Culture, New York City). After a critically acclaimed run off-Broadway at the Henry Street Playhouse in 1946, *Our Lan'* was taken to Broadway by the Theater Guild, where it closed after only five weeks. Loften Mitchell contends that the director of *Our Lan'* on Broadway, Eddie Dowling, had insisted upon portraying the newly freed blacks "just like children." Ward, like Hansberry, had also tried to convey the political importance of spirituals. In the Dowling production, however, the spirituals "were far from revolutionary in presentation." The author, Mitchell reports, was "justifiably upset and angered over what had been done to his play." According to Mitchell, the unsuccessful run

of *Our Lan'* was "pointed to again and again as evidence that Negro drama does fail—but no one added that it fails when polluted and misinterpreted"; see Mitchell, *Black Drama,* pp. 133–134; see also Abramson, *Negro Playwrights in the American Theater* (New York: Columbia University Press, 1969), pp. 117–135, and especially C. W. E. Bigsby, *The Second Black Renaissance* (New York: Greenwood Press, 1980), pp. 211–212. According to Robert Nemiroff, Hansberry conducted extensive research at the Schomburg and, although *Our Lan'* is not mentioned by Nemiroff, it is possible that Hansberry came across it during her work there.

42. Lorraine Hansberry, "The Drinking Gourd," in Nemiroff, ed., *The Collected Last Plays,* p. 167. Unless otherwise specified, subsequent page numbers are to this edition.

43. James V. Hatch, "The Drinking Gourd," in James V. Hatch, ed., *Black Theater, U.S.A.* (New York: Free Press, 1974), p. 713; the script is reprinted on pp. 714–735. On the black drama of the nineteenth century, see also Leo Hamalian and James V. Hatch, eds., *The Roots of African-American Drama* (Detroit: Wayne State University Press, 1991).

44. Gloria T. Hull and Patricia Bell Scott, "Introduction: The Politics of Black Women's Studies," in Gloria T. Hull, Patricia Bell Scott, and Barbara Smith, eds., *All the Women Are White, All the Blacks are Men, but Some of Us Are Brave: Black Women's Studies* (Westbury, NY: The Feminist Press, 1992), p. xxiii. In addition to Hansberry's published plays, the most widely accessible statement of her views on the social role of women published in her lifetime was "This Complex of Womanhood," *Ebony,* September 1963, p. 88. For the fullest understanding of Hansberry's thinking on these and many other issues, based on both her published and unpublished writings, we must await the opening of the Hansberry papers as well as the planned biography of Hansberry by Margaret Wilkerson, which is based on them.

45. Jewelle L. Gomez, "Lorraine Hansberry: Uncommon Warrior," in Henry Louis Gates, ed., *Reading Black, Reading Feminist: A Critical Anthology* (New York: Meridian, 1990), pp. 313–314; quote on p. 316.

46. Hansberry, "The Negro Writer and His Roots," p. 3.

47. Ibid., p. 6.

Conclusion

The epigraph is from an interview of Ossie Davis by Linda Laney, January 12, 1972 (Oral Tape Recording, Hatch-Billops Theater Archives, New York City).

1. John Rodden, *The Politics of Literary Reputation: The Making and Claiming of "St. George" Orwell* (New York: Oxford University Press, 1989), p. 4.

2. Philip Fisher, Introduction, in Philip Fisher, ed., *The New American Studies: Essays from Representations* (Berkeley: University of California Press, 1991), p. 4.

3. See Raymond Williams's 1958 essay, "Culture Is Ordinary," in his *Resources of Hope: Culture, Democracy, Socialism* (New York: Verso, 1989), pp. 3–18.

4. Warren I. Susman, *Culture as History: The Transformation of American Society in the Twentieth Century* (New York: Pantheon Books, 1984), pp. 288–289.

5. Ralph Ellison, *Invisible Man* (New York: Random House/Vintage, 1952), p. 3.

Acknowledgments

From the very beginning of my public school education in the watershed year of 1968, I have been drawn to the study of American history in this century. However, I would not have chosen history as my undergraduate major had it not been for David Shibley of Santa Monica College, who introduced me to the study of history as a way of thinking and of writing that is important and useful no matter how one actually earns a living. I owe a special debt to David Brody, Wilson Smith, Richard Schwab, Morgan Sherwood, and Joe Trotter, all then of the history department at the University of California, Davis, and to Marvin Zetterbaum of the political science department, whose enthusiastic encouragement led me to press on to graduate school and become a historian. I was especially fortunate to have the benefit of Joe Trotter's counsel again some years later, during my graduate work at UCLA. He took time from a very crowded visit to read an early formulation of my project and to encourage me to strengthen my treatment of several important issues.

This work would never have been completed without the support I received as a graduate student in the Department of History at the University of California, Los Angeles. My chair, Richard Weiss, reintroduced me to the 1930s as a period of unappreciated importance to the ongoing struggle to perfect American democracy. Most important of all, he joined me in a leap of faith, reading drafts of each chapter, and seeing the final shape of this project long before I could. Robert Dallek's questions on the interconnections between American domestic politics and foreign policy provided me with my first point of entry into this topic. His research seminar in the spring of 1987 gave me the opportunity to begin thinking and writing about Ralph Bunche. Jeffrey Prager's long-standing engagement with the way in which beliefs about race become powerfully crystallized as "collective representations" provided me with some indispensable tools for digging more deeply into the cultural politics of race. His thoughtful reading of early drafts also helped me uncover new themes and ways of thinking about the project. Barbara Bernstein, graduate counselor in the Department of History at UCLA, gave me much sound advice and friendship from the beginning.

Robert A. Hill, the editor of the Garvey papers, listened patiently and offered sound advice at a formative point in my thinking. I also benefited from the insights of Gerald Gill, who visited UCLA from Boston University in the fall of 1986. Our long discussions of the key texts in the historiography of the civil rights movement provided me with a foundation upon which to build my own contribution. Barbara Bair, of the Garvey papers, encouraged me to gather together some of my ideas on Kenneth B. Clark for presentation to the annual meeting of the California American Studies Association. She also read an early draft of Chapter 1 with care, and offered excellent advice. Jonathan and Nantwan McCloud, of Mesa Community College in San Diego, California, were enthusiastic about my project at an important juncture. Jonathan McCloud contributed to my progress by making it possible for me to present, on two separate occasions, some early thoughts on Ralph Bunche and Lorraine Hansberry as part of the Occasional Lecture Series sponsored by the Social Science Division of Mesa College. The discussion that followed each talk strengthened this project in many ways.

The Department of History at UCLA supported me with a two-year teaching assistantship (1986–1988) and the Carey McWilliams Fellowship (1988–1989). The graduate division of UCLA also consistently supported my work through the Charles F. Scott and Will Rogers Fellowships. In 1990, the Manuscript Society honored my work in the Bunche papers with an award that helped me continue my progress. I thank David Zeidberg, director of the UCLA Department of Special Collections, for nominating me for this recognition.

The Franklin and Eleanor Roosevelt Institute supported my work in the Eleanor Roosevelt papers at the Franklin D. Roosevelt Library in Hyde Park, New York, with a Beeke-Levy Research Fellowship. I am grateful to William R. Emerson and his colleagues at the Institute for their early vote of confidence. The Center for Afro-American Studies supported much of the writing of this manuscript with a predoctoral fellowship during the 1990–1991 academic year. Sandra Sealey, Cherie Francis, and the rest of the Center staff made me feel welcome and gave me the opportunity to present an early draft of Chapter 2 to an attentive audience of students and faculty.

Ann Cager, Jeff Rankin, and Simon Elliott ably assisted me during my long tenure in the Ralph Bunche papers. Jane Taylor shared her understanding of the Bunche family history and prevented me from making several factual errors. The late Barbara Nelson of the Ford Foundation took an early interest in my project and shared her copies of important documents from the Bunche papers.

During my stay at the Roosevelt Library, my search for documents benefited from the help and advice of Susan Elder, John Ferris, Alita Black and Robert Parks. I am especially indebted to John Ferris for his willingness to field my further inquiries from California. Ronald Grele and Andor Skotnes, of the justly renowned Oral History Program at Columbia University, helped make my visits there productive.

Without the unconditional cooperation of Kenneth B. Clark and his extremely competent and generous administrative aide, Russia Hughes, this study would have been impossible to complete. In addition to permitting me unrestricted access to his unprocessed manuscript collection at the Library of Congress and his oral history at Columbia University, he also filed the necessary documents so that I could request his FBI file. Dr. Clark also graciously devoted the substantial portion of two days in the spring of 1989 to answering my many questions.

My work in the Clark papers at the Library of Congress was made easier and more productive by the assistance of Debra Newman Ham, Specialist in Afro-American History and Culture at the Library of Congress, who gave me the benefit of her wide knowledge of African-American manuscript sources. She and her colleagues also labored long and hard to bring me each and every bulky and very weathered box of the unprocessed Clark collection. Aaron and Jackie Epstein generously opened their home to me during my second research trip to Washington, DC, in the spring of 1990.

My understanding of African-American theater was significantly advanced by the oral histories of the Hatch-Billops Archives in New York City. James V. Hatch and Camille Billops, in whose home the archive is located, made me feel welcome. Esme E. Bahn, a research associate at the

Moreland-Spingarn Center at Howard University, and Clifford L. Muse, the university archivist, helped me make the most of my time in their collections. I also thank Howard Dotson, Director of the Schomburg Center for Research in Black Culture, for discussing this project with me at some length. Diana Lachatanere, head of the Manuscripts, Archives, and Rare Books Division, facilitated my work in several of the Center's collections.

Michael Desmond and William Johnson of the John F. Kennedy Presidential Library forwarded relevant materials from the Robert F. Kennedy papers. The Amistad Research Center at Tulane University made it possible for me to receive the microfilm of the Julius Rosenwald Papers on interlibrary loan.

As a citizen and as a scholar, I have come to have a profound appreciation for the Freedom of Information Act. I thank Special Agent Emil P. Moschella and his staff for their assistance in obtaining the files of Ralph Bunche, Kenneth B. Clark, and Lorraine Hansberry. The reference staffs of the University Research Library at the University of California, Los Angeles, and of the Central Library at the University of California, San Diego, handled innumerable interlibrary loan requests.

The most personally rewarding chapter of my research experience was the time spent interviewing individuals who have worked to improve American democracy. Jack Greenberg, James A. Jones, Hylan Lewis, and Henry Morgenthau III shared their recollections of Kenneth Clark. John A. Davis and Robert C. Weaver discussed Ralph Bunche and helped me to better understand the intellectual atmosphere of Depression-era Washington, DC. The late Robert Nemiroff, former husband of Lorraine Hansberry, and the playwright William Branch, a friend and contemporary of Hansberry's, shared their recollections of her with me.

I thank Eric J. Sundquist and Robert L. Harris, Jr., whose suggestions helped me to clarify my ideas and consider issues that I might otherwise have missed. I am grateful to Aida Donald, whose early enthusiasm brought this book into print. Elizabeth Suttell was an exceptionally able guide through the daunting process of obtaining copyright permissions. I owe a special debt to Donna Bouvier for her deft copyediting of the manuscript. Of course, I accept all responsibility for whatever errors of fact or infelicities of style remain.

My wife, Katherine Pandora, shared her encyclopedic knowledge of the early years of academic psychology, listened to every draft of this manuscript, and helped me with the many technical details involved in preparing this book for publication. Her wisdom and rigor were indispensable as this project and its author weathered some very difficult years. Without her confidence in me, this book might never have been completed.

The following have granted permission to reprint copyrighted material:

Excerpts from *The Correspondence of W. E. B. Du Bois,* Vol. I Selections, 1877–1934 by W. E. B. Du Bois, ed. by Herbert Aptheker (Amherst: University of Massachusetts Press, 1973), copyright © 1973 by The University of Massachusetts Press; and Vol. II Selections 1934–1944 by W. E. B. Du Bois, ed. by Herbert Aptheker (Amherst: University of Massachusetts Press, 1976), copyright © 1976 by The University of Massachusetts Press.

"Let America Be America Again" by Langston Hughes reprinted by permission of Harold Ober Associates Incorporated. Copyright 1938 by Langston Hughes. Copyright renewed 1965 by Langston Hughes.

Excerpts from Bruno Bettelheim, "Discrimination and Science," *Commentary,* March 1956, reprinted by permission; all rights reserved.

Excerpts from *Dark Ghetto: Dilemmas of Social Power* by Kenneth B. Clark copyright © 1965 by Kenneth B. Clark. Reprinted by permission of HarperCollins Publishers, Inc.

Excerpts from Ralph Ellison, "A Very Stern Discipline," *Harper's,* March 1967, reprinted by permission of the William Morris Agency, Inc., on behalf of the author. Copyright © 1967 by Ralph Ellison.

Excerpts from Gerald Weales, "Thoughts on 'A Raisin in the Sun,' " *Commentary,* June 1959, reprinted by permission; all rights reserved.

Excerpts from *A Raisin in the Sun* by Lorraine Hansberry (New York: Samuel French, 1959) reprinted by permission of Jewell Gresham Nemiroff for the Estate of Robert Nemiroff. All rights reserved.

Excerpts from "An Author's Reflections" by Lorraine Hansberry © 1959 by The Village Voice and © 1990 by Robert Nemiroff; reprinted by per-

Index